STRIFE ON THE

WATERFRONT

Books by Vernon H. Jensen

Strife on the Waterfront: The Port of New York since 1945.

Decasualization and Modernization of Dock Work in London.

Hiring of Dock Workers and Employment Practices in the Ports of New York, Liverpool, London, Rotterdam, and Marseilles.

Collective Bargaining in the Nonferrous Metals Industry.

Nonferrous Metals Industry Unionism, 1932–1954.

Heritage of Conflict: Labor Relations in the Nonferrous Metals Industry up to 1930.

Lumber and Labor.

STRIFE ON THE WATERFRONT

The Port of New York since 1945

VERNON H. JENSEN

Cornell University Press

ITHACA AND LONDON

First published 1974 by Cornell University Press.
Published in the United Kingdom by Cornell University Press, Ltd., 2-4 Brook Street, London W1Y 1AA.

International Standard Book Number 0-8014-0789-3
Library of Congress Catalog Card Number 73-14137

Printed in the United States of America by York Composition Co., Inc.

To Esther

Preface

The year 1945 is a convenient starting point for a study of labor relations in the longshore industry of the Port of New York because the strike that occurred then—the first associated with negotiations in over twenty-five years—was a significant after-the-war event and marks, in some ways, the beginning of a new period. No sharp break with the past was made—or could have been made in an industry so ruled by custom—yet the strike was a portent of things to come and a revelation of unsatisfactory conditions. It was the first in a series of major work stoppages that have punctuated the scene ever since and seem likely to continue. The year 1945 is remote enough to provide perspective, yet recent enough that reliable firsthand information is available.

It seems remarkable that for a quarter of a century collective agreements were negotiated in the Port of New York without strikes, especially when during these years unionism in general passed through two intensive organizing periods—World War I and the immediate postwar years, and the middle and late thirties —both accompanied by a good deal of strife. It was not that the New York City area was less a scene of struggle for collective bargaining rights than many others in the nation. Nor was the longshoring industry itself immune to strife: on the West Coast, where longshoring unions had been ruthlessly abolished during the nationwide open-shop drive of 1919–1922, unionism was re-established in 1934 accompanied by much violence and a general strike. During all this time, however, the International Long-shoremen's Association (ILA) maintained continuous negotiating relationships with the New York Shipping Association (NYSA). Generally speaking, from the mid-thirties to the mid-forties, West Coast labor relations were turbulent while East Coast labor relations were peaceful. Afterward, when the East Coast became turbulent, the West Coast settled into a period of peacefulness. The West Coast relationships since 1945 have been praised, until most recently, while those in the Port of New York have been widely criticized.

The purpose of this book is to describe and explain the strife on the New York waterfront in the context of the institutional practices of collective bargaining. The story is a product of many years of research, although not continuous research, and relies on the assistance of many people. Not everyone who helped me will like all of the story. I can only say that I have tried to be judicious and to present the account without favor. Some of my sources are not revealed because I agreed not to reveal them. In other cases, I have chosen not to reveal them in order to protect their privileged status. For these reasons, although I am deeply indebted to many people, the story that follows will have to be accepted, in large part, on my own integrity.

VERNON H. JENSEN

Ithaca, New York

Contents

Contents

STRIFE ON THE

WATERFRONT

1 | Introduction

A Model for a Yardstick

An account of labor relations in any industry should not be solely descriptive; it should also explain phenomena which make up the substance of the relationship. Yet, careful description of the facts, properly assessed, can do much to explain satisfactorily what has happened. Analysis should precede description, with the consequence that explanations, even conclusions, will flow naturally from such telling. Accordingly, a well-told story will not need many special iterative explanations, for interpretation will inhere in the account. Nevertheless, whenever it seems desirable, for the sake of emphasis, special analytical statements will be made.

Description is most effective when conceived within an explicit frame of reference. This account of labor relations in the longshore industry in the Port of New York is told within the context of the process of collective bargaining as defined below.

Collective bargaining is a private rule-making process, emerging in a free society as an alternative to rule-making by unilateral decision of employers or by government. It is integral to an enterprise society but, as a practical matter, it functions within a legal context, that is, laws—whether common or statute. Hence, it can be denied existence or it can be emasculated by government. The traditional ideal in the United States (all too often respected in the breach, particularly in recent years) has been noninterference by government, except when it intervenes to administer the rule of law. But the enactment of laws by the legislature—reflecting, as they do, political pressures—has set

13

some of the rules, and of course the rules have been modified from time to time.

For the years within which this account falls the rule of law has been favorable generally to collective bargaining as an institution. Furthermore, unlike bargaining in some other industries, in the longshore industry in the Port of New York collective bargaining early received institutional accommodation, dating back at least to 1916. In the 1930's, a strike to gain recognition was not needed, as it was in other industries and in the longshore industry on the West Coast. In the early and mid-1930's, when unionism developed massively throughout the nation, the International Longshoremen's Association (ILA) had long since achieved recognition, so that it did not need the guarantees under the National Industrial Recovery Act (NIRA) and the National Labor Relations Act (NLRA) of the right to bargain collectively, although the latter law has been a factor in labor and management relationships in the industry.

Some basic postulates of the process of collective bargaining help to explain it as a frame of reference. The first of these is that collective bargaining presupposes some degree of *mutuality of interest* between labor and management, both pecuniary and ideological. Each party accepts the other as a constituent part of the enterprise system—that is, ideologically each accepts the system as well as the other; each recognizes the other institutionally, while each mutually and broadly respects and defends the society. Also, each has a self-centered interest in keeping the industry or the enterprise going—the pecuniary mutuality. The parties will not consciously destroy the industry, for their welfare is tied to its continuity and profitability. They may inadvertently jeopardize it, however, or their leaders may subvert the process to personal ends.

There is also a concurrent *conflict of pecuniary interest*, the second postulate. If the mutuality of interest were not present there could be a fight to the death, yet both parties have diverse interests about division of the proceeds from industry and about the way certain activities are conducted. It is these areas of controversy—the disputation about the rules which govern the inputs of labor and the rewards which flow from the productive process—that comprise the grist for the process of collective bargaining.

The parties to collective bargaining are governed by *internal restraints* and *external restraints,* additional postulates of which the parties are aware. If they can manipulate these restraints they will, but they cannot escape them. By external restraints is meant, in addition to the laws of the land which are applicable to them, the whole range of economic, political, and social conditions which limit the parties. The state of development of the economy and the condition of its health, and particularly that of their own industry, are always factors which cannot be ignored by the parties, except at their peril. Likewise, they must consider the political climate and the objectives of the political and governmental bodies—municipal, state, and federal. Also, the social restraints created by the larger society or its units—the other institutions with their institutional needs—stand to limit conduct and programs of labor and management negotiators.

Internal restraints are those conditions existing within the organizations of labor and management—within the unions and companies and their associations—arising from their purposes, their structures and functions, their formal and informal rules, their internal politics resulting from their plurality of interests, and the like. Management and labor organizations are hardly ever internally homogeneous; they have regulations and requirements—both formal and informal—which emanate from the various groups and functions within each. Within unions, in particular, there is usually a presumption of democracy and of representation of interests, but there is often much infighting among disparate interests. Corporations also have their internal interest groups, which are "represented" even if democracy may be less featured than it is in unions. But in employer associations, as with labor unions, there is also a formal representation function.

Collective bargaining, when carried out by sophisticated practitioners, entails interaction and understanding between the principals on each side, but in basic bargaining situations *the parties do not know the settlement positions of each other* or, at any rate, not all of the principals on each side know the settlement positions.

Not least of the postulates, collective bargaining is a process entailing the *use of power*. As an operating reality there must be a sort of power balance, but either side must be prepared, and must be able, to use power to bring, or keep, the other in line. The power to strike and the power to take a strike are absolutely necessary, although strikes do not necessarily occur. The knowledge that hurt can be inflicted by the other in the absence of agreement is the reality which produces ultimate agreement.

Collective bargaining is engaged in for the purpose of *finding out the settlement position of the other*. It becomes a fine art of simultaneously hiding and revealing positions, or portions of them, until real understandings are eventually produced. "Exorbitant" demands, random actions, cajoling, argumentations, and the like, running through numerous meetings leading to a deadline with its concomitant threat of work stoppage, are all utilized to find out settlement positions. It ought to be obvious, but unfortunately it is not, that collective bargaining is a process of power, not of rational persuasion by the logical presentation of facts.

But this power process, as well as it can be made to work among experienced negotiators, works concurrently with another process involving communication to constituents in the respective organizations, sometimes a process of internal bargaining. This half of the bargaining process is directed to the task, and the very fine art, of gaining the *consent of the respective constituents*, and is not less important than the half devoted to finding the settlement positions. Because it produces consent to the terms of settlement, it is the part of collective bargaining that makes this rule-making process so valuable in a free-enterprise society. The constituents on each side *accept* the results and will, therefore, live by them. Good agreements are those accepted by the constituents.

We will evaluate practices in the longshore industry in the light of the characteristics, conditions, and requirements of collective bargaining. When performance is at variance with the ideal model, it will be interesting to find out why. Factors which interfere with the process in either of its basic purposes will be analyzed. Also, we will be concerned with the performance of the parties in humanistic and institutional terms as well as in economic and political terms.

An Overview, or Prejudgment, of Collective Bargaining in the Industry

A brief overview of collective bargaining in the longshore industry in the Port of New York may alert the reader to particulars in the account which follows.

Bargaining in this industry is infinitely more complex than in industries where one employer, operating a single plant, deals directly with representatives of his workers. Nor is the industry just another in which there is a multiplicity of employers or a complex union structure, although in some ways it appears to be. The industry encompasses a variety of employers with diverse interests, whose appearance of unity through the New York Shipping Association (NYSA) has been misleading. A crunch has always revealed great differences and lack of single-mindedness, even divisiveness. The International Longshoremen's Association (ILA), originally affiliated with the American Federation of Labor (AFL), but expelled from it in 1953, yet admitted into the merged American Federation of Labor–Congress of Industrial Organizations (AFL-CIO) in 1959, also has always seemed to be highly centralized—even authoritarian—but this appearance has been delusive, obscuring the power of autonomous groups (or bosses) which could always press independently for objectives of self-interest over those of the International. It has even obscured near-anarchy at times. Also, both employers and leaders of the ILA have had their special friends in the other's ranks. The situation has been shot through with deals or understandings.

The great deterrent to normal collective bargaining has been the lack of spokesmen, particularly on the union side, with sufficient acceptability and authority to make clear-cut agreements with force behind them. The multiple voices, even though not always audible in public, have made it difficult for the negotiators to ascertain the basic terms needed for viable settlements. For quite some time the top negotiator in the union has hardly been able to lead to a concession, let alone to a settlement, so that the employers have been unable to know when a concession offered would become a firm commitment. Who could be held to it? As a matter of fact, would employers stand firmly for it?

Ironically, the employers, recognizing that a program has been needed, have usually tried to work one out in advance, sometimes even agreeing among themselves, only to succumb to wearing and protracted haggling. This difficult, sometimes comical, situation has been troublesome because of conflicting reports about what was transpiring among the groups on the other side. The employers could hardly please one part of the union without running the risk of offending others. Thus, a program got shot to pieces quickly or often turned out to be no program at all. Negotiating has certainly been more than the common facing across the bargaining table or the common internal facing apparent in most other collective bargaining situations.

Usually when positions have become ossified so that outside pressures proved to be the final catalyst in achieving the agreement, the employers have failed to realize their *quid pro quo* for the concessions they have given. The ILA has often made promises it knew would not be kept, partly because it knew that the employers would not collect. Failure to administer agreements forcefully has been the usual experience. Time and again the employers have found themselves victims of their own default, partly from being preoccupied with their private affairs, but often from fear of causing local retaliation, for concerted

defense of the ageement was often weakened by haphazard administration and policing, willful disregard, intentional under-
cutting, or side concessions.

The government, too, has contributed to the quality of collective bargaining in the industry. All negotiations have been carried
out in the brooding presence of government, be it mediators or
the Waterfront Commission, both of whom were presumed to
be neutral or merely helpful. The Waterfront Commission, while
required under law to accept the results of collective bargaining,
nevertheless has had to make sure that settlements did not con-
travene the law. With the ILA constantly at war with it, the
Waterfront Commission, in warding off direct and indirect
attacks on its province, at times has seemed officious; it has
seemed to interfere with collective bargaining, but, then, it has
had to make sure that the ILA did not influence the hiring of
longshoremen. Governmental mediation agencies, particularly
the federal and sometimes the city—hardly ever the state, which
was not welcome—seemed always at the door of, if not inside,
the bargaining chambers. One party or the other—usually the
ILA—has sought the aid of governmental mediators; often the
employers felt that the mediators in their desire to achieve a
settlement had led them down the primrose path. The role of the
mediators, of course, has been symptomatic of the governmental
concern that work stoppages on the docks be avoided, and the
government has hardly ever been prepared to let negotiations go
to the strike stage, certainly not to let a strike run its own course.
The federal government has invoked the emergency provisions
of the Taft-Hartley Act at the slightest provocation and in every
bargaining occasion from 1948 on. Top-level governmental intervention has been due mostly to the fact that the parties, by
their own devices, seemed unable to produce the final settlement, although it has been due in part to the pressures from those
who would suffer from a stoppage.

Some of the unusual features of collective bargaining in the
longshore industry are structural. Others are procedural, emanating from both management and union. Still others are functional,

or inherent in the nature of the industry, and some are human or personal. These unusual elements do not alone make collective bargaining in the longshore industry unsatisfactory, for other unusual collective bargaining relationships produce an agreement-making apparatus which enables the parties to accept each other in a more or less businesslike way under jointly determined rules.

Collective bargaining in the longshore industry in New York has been unpredictable, except in the negative sense. It is too turbulent, too unstable, lacking responsibility. Its processes are often drawn out to lengths far beyond the needs of the typical bargaining process and to the point of almost complete enervation of the many bargainers. It lacks almost completely the art of communicativeness. There has been either a lack of meaningful communication or too much irresponsible talk, which has blurred communication. To be sure, even at best in bargaining elsewhere, subtleties exist, but they do not cripple the process of communication. An outsider can quickly observe that too little has been known by the rank and file and, surprisingly, by principal parties on both sides about what has been going on, yet, it is amazing that the industry is often characterized as one with "no secrets." A lack of trust and confidence has prevailed inside the ranks of management as well as of labor, particularly in the latter. There has commonly been a failure to appreciate the need to secure acceptance of others whose daily operations and working lives have been affected by the terms of settlement.

The Industry—Its Functions and Some Interrelationships

The chief functions of longshoring have been discharging cargoes brought to the port in ships and stowing cargoes carried away by them. Related to discharging have been assemblage and storage of cargoes on the pier or in adjacent warehouses or the physical transference of them to the consignee. Related to stowing have been receiving and arranging of cargoes for hoisting into the ship. The functions have not included the hauling of cargoes to the piers or away from them, although there has been a close and sometimes crucial interrelationship with such activities.

Longshoring is not an industry, except by common usage. It encompasses a group of activities in the movement of waterborne freight. It may be thought of as a part of the maritime industry, although the distinction between offshore and onshore activities is important. These complement each other and, in some instances, are incorporated into the affairs of single companies; that is, some steamship companies engage in both. Numerous companies specialize in specific functions. Some steamship companies control their own piers and do their own work. Others who control their own piers contract to have the work done. Still others contract with stevedores who operate piers and offer services. Also, there have been different types of stevedores: house stevedores—either subsidiaries or contractors—who provide all, or part, of the services; stevedores who perform on anybody's pier; and stevedores who operate piers and offer services to all comers. Also, besides stowing and discharging of cargoes there have been ancillary activities, concerned with checking, ships' carpentry, pier security, and pier maintenance, and these have also been handled in a variety of ways.

The Port of New York handles transoceanic, intercoastal, and coastwise shipping. While one would find almost every type of heavy and bulk cargo being handled, the port has been conspicuously a general cargo port, the largest in the world. Its work has differed substantially from that in other ports like Philadelphia and Baltimore, which are smaller and relatively more specialized to heavy and bulk cargoes.

The industry has not been comprised of a homogeneous collection of operators. There are American-flag steamship companies, some of which have been subsidized and others not; and foreign-flag companies, governmentally operated or private, but with the latter having been subsidized in one way or another. There are large and small shipping companies, engaged in various types of shipping. The employers never have been a unified group. Below any surface appearance of unity, it has been easy to discern aloofness, suspicion, narrow self-interest, and real conflicts of interest.

In labor relations, onshore and offshore affairs have been under separate labor and management structures, although some employers—some of the steamship companies operating in both spheres—have been members of the onshore group as well as of one of the offshore groups. The unions in the offshore industry have been separate from those on the shore, but the offshore unions—not always in harmony with each other—often have given support to the longshore unions; and the reverse has been true. Certainly the onshore and offshore unions have been affected by each other's activities. The quarrels among the offshore unions, partly ideological and partly political and personal, have spilled over into or impinged upon the relations with the ILA. Alignments with factions within the ILA have been significant, too, at times. Interunion relations between onshore and offshore unions have not always been good. Seamen and longshoremen have not always gotten along well with each other, particularly when longshoremen thought seamen were after their work. Similarly, longshoremen and teamsters have sometimes come into conflict at the pier head over the loading and unloading of trucks and the work at the warehousing stage.[1]

The Port of New York and Its Changing Character

The most important physical characteristic of the port is its size. The next is its configuration. In a sense there are several ports which operate somewhat as a unit and somewhat as separate entities. Some of the areas are large themselves, as ports go, and the various areas add up to a huge port.

The port straddles the North River and Upper Bay and thus lies in two states. It encompasses several-odd hundred square miles of water and land area, the size and complexity of which

---

[1] Warehouse work has not been an issue in New York, certainly not as in the issue on the West Coast. See Philip Ross, "Waterfront Labor Response to Technological Change: A Tale of Two Unions," *Labor Law Journal*, July 1970, pp. 397ff.

are dramatized when one takes a view from the top of any New York City skyscraper and scans its parts, stretching away in many directions within the richest and most populous area of the nation. It is estimated that the port and its interrelated activities provide a livelihood for at least a half million people, that the handling of waterborne commerce generates more than one-fourth of the total wages earned in the port district. Such estimates do not include those people supported by industries which are not directly or indirectly integrated with the shipping industry but which locate in the area in order to have access to the shipping facilities. The dependence of many people upon the business of the port is important for the labor relations story, because it underscores the public concern about work stoppages on the docks. The port's uninterrupted operation is necessary for the economic welfare of many people, as well as for the countless consumers whose lives are touched, sometimes quickly and sharply, whenever port operations cease. For this reason government has become intimately involved in many ways.

The extensiveness of the shoreline facilities is impressive. Starting with the concept of a New York–New Jersey port, but looking to the parts, we find (1) the great sweep of Manhattan's North River waterfront, which runs from the Battery to midtown and includes the well-known areas of Greenwich, Chelsea, and the luxury liner piers north of Forty-second Street; (2) the East River and the area around the horn in Manhattan with about two miles of piers, which are in a badly deteriorating condition; (3) the extensive Brooklyn area, across the East River on Long Island, running for eleven miles commencing at Greenpoint north of Brooklyn Bridge and running southward through the old New York Docks area—modernized by the Port of New York Authority (PNYA) in the early sixties—the Atlantic and Erie Basins, and the Bush Docks; (4) Staten Island, westward from Brooklyn across the Upper Bay, the piers lying along the north rim of the island; (5) the sprawling Jersey area running from Bayonne northward to Jersey City, and including several railroad terminals; (6) the Hoboken area north of Jersey City;

and (7) Port Newark, and the more recently developed Port
Elizabeth, on Newark Bay to the west and south of Jersey City.

Historically, the port developed around the tip of Manhattan
and inched its way up the East and North rivers as the city grew.
With the development of railroads, the Jersey shore of the North
River developed. In part, the Jersey port has been supplementary
to Manhattan's. Railroad terminals developed in Jersey City and
Hoboken, and car floats and barges have been utilized to get
cargoes to the piers in Manhattan and to carry incoming cargoes
out of Manhattan to the rail lines for shipment throughout the
country. Similar services developed in Brooklyn.

As the years passed, relentless economic and technological
forces affected the distribution of activity at these ports. As late
as 1925 Manhattan still claimed slightly over 50 per cent of the
shipping activity of the port, Brooklyn about 30 per cent, Hoboken and Jersey City together about 12 per cent, Staten Island
about 4 per cent, and Port Newark about 2 per cent. But Manhattan became congested, particularly in the second quarter of
this century, and the increasing use of motor trucks contributed
to major shifts which have continually been working themselves
out. By 1960 two-thirds of all cargoes came to the piers by truck,
and congestion in Manhattan was choking longshoring out. Manhattan's percentage had dropped to 23, Staten Island's to 2, Hoboken and Jersey City remained at 12, while Brooklyn's had increased to 46 and Port Newark to 17. The latter area has
continued to increase its share. A projection for 1980 places Manhattan at less than 10 per cent, Brooklyn at less than 40 per cent,
but Port Newark at more than 40 per cent.[2] But this projection
was made before the container revolution, the widespread conversion to shipping by means of huge boxlike containers which
became pronounced after the mid-sixties. The container revolution has speeded the decline in Manhattan and the growth in

---

[2] New York, City Planning Commission, *The Port of New York:
Proposals for Development* (New York, 1964); Port of New York
Authority, *Metropolitan Transportation—1980* (New York, 1963), chs.
10 and 11.

Port Newark, although container berths and facilities have been built recently in Jersey City and Staten Island and should revive business in both places. Also, Brooklyn, which smugly ignored the container business for a short while, is fighting to get it, too. Manhattan will have to be content primarily with cruise business, particularly in view of the rapid decline, if not elimination, of trans-Atlantic passenger service.

Economic Realities Affecting Labor Relations

The nature of the shipping business has affected the supply and behavior of labor. The business, historically, developed patterns of activity related to the movement of ships; it still must conform. An individual company with more or less regular runs could control arrivals and departures to some extent, but the industry as a whole could not. The irregular coming and going of ships created erratic and casual employment conditions, the hallmark of the longshore labor market. The large size of the port did not produce a leveling out of work, because each pier and section looked only to its own interests. The result has been that the work on one pier, or in one section, has not dovetailed with that at others. Like other ports, the Port of New York has been a prime example of uncoordinated activities. The men—to some degree but not extensively because they were really not very mobile—congregated at places where they thought opportunities to work would be greatest. Those who did not enjoy priorities in hiring had to compete vigorously for jobs, and hiring agents callously exploited them.

Competition for business by the companies has also been very keen. Hence, both employers and workers have added to the legacy of competitive groveling. For the shipowner it was important, in defraying the costs of the ship and its operation, that the ship sail with a full cargo. The pressures to achieve this created a dog-eat-dog struggle for cargoes, which were easily transferable from one steamship company to another, even at the last moment. Getting the business while it was available has been the essence of the competition, and this was affected greatly by the movements of ships, which in turn have been affected by such uncontrollable things as "wind and wave."

Capital investment in ships has been an important economic factor in labor relations. Even when the industry over all has been labor intensive, with upward of half the costs of longshoring going to loading and discharging of cargoes, nevertheless, investment in the ship has been large enough to be important, too. A ship exists only to carry cargo and it is contributing to a return on investment only while it is moving at sea. When a day at the pier has represented a cost on capital investment of from three to five thousand dollars, it is easy to understand the pressure to turn the ship around quickly and to minimize pier-time. Astute longshoremen have realized this and have utilized the work stoppage to get concessions, because individual companies have been vulnerable to such tactics in the absence of effective portwide employer control. The easiest way for a company to get out of a difficulty has been to buy out with a concession that would not cost more than having the ship idle. Proliferation of pier-by-pier customs and practices has been a consequence.

It is interesting to note—for its importance toward the end of the story—that the container revolution of recent years has been turning the industry around from a labor-intensive one to a capital-intensive one. The containers are expensive, but the labor cost of handling the same volume of cargo in containers at shipside as compared to conventional handling is very small. The difference, of course, would not be anywhere near so great if the containers were stuffed or unstuffed at the pier by ILA labor, who, to protect their volume of work, have exerted pressure to have the work done at the piers. Then, too, the turnaround of the ship is as a day to three, and this makes for a tremendous saving. The advantage heavily favors the companies which have converted to containers over those who carry on in the conventional way.

At first the labor force lived near the piers, partly because in earlier times transportation facilities precluded travel over any distance and local acquaintanceship helped in getting jobs. The

result was that the men came to have pier priorities to employment, that is, claims to jobs in preference to strangers or men
from other piers or sections. These have accentuated provincialism. Even with the improvement of urban transportation and
the comon use of the automobile, which has made it possible
for the men to live in the larger community, the men still cherish
their employment rights on the pier. These rights have been of
singular importance with respect to many problems. Critics of
the shape-up—that method of hiring where selection of individuals was made by the hiring agent from the men assembled in
the open at the head of the pier—seldom understood the extent
of these pier priorities. Aware of the extensive abuses of hiring
through the shape-up, like "kick backs" or payment for jobs and
favoritism, critics have not seen the total picture, including the
importance of the stance often taken by the men but otherwise
unexplainable. In the early fifties, when the Waterfront Commission came to the industry, it secured the cooperation of stevedores to help devise its hiring regulations; they knew the
importance of the priorities and made sure that they were
recognized.

Another feature of the labor force has been the existence of
ethnic groupings, largely a product of mass immigration at the
times when particular areas of the port were developing. The
Irish have predominated among Manhattan longshoremen while
Italians have predominated in Brooklyn. Negroes were accepted
in some places but had great difficulty in getting employment in
others because of the established priorities, although one would
be naive not to recognize racial discrimination, too. But racial
discrimination ran beyond color. Italians were hardly welcome
in Irish areas and the reverse was likewise true. Racial accommodations were sometimes worked out, with the arrangement in
Port Newark being a special example of arbitrary division of
the work between Negroes and whites, the latter being mostly
Spaniards and Italians.

Whatever unity the workers have had has been produced by
a common feeling of insecurity and abuse, both from market

forces and agents of employers. Dock workers everywhere in the world seem to be imbued with a general solidarity, sometimes characterized as "blind solidarity" or "strike proneness." In many ports they have been notorious for quickness of action when aroused. This has been explained by the casualness of the work and the insecurity which has kept many of the men in necessitous circumstances. The Port of New York has not been different in this respect from most others. Strikes at the pier have been commonplace. They were not uncommon even when there were no industry-wide strikes at times of negotiations.

In any port there have been those who have lived off the industry, either by providing needed services or, trailing off into the illicit, preying upon those who found themselves in need. From the earliest sailing days, areas adjacent to piers have been notorious for rough and shady characters. New York has been no exception, and may have been as bad as the worst, or at least worse than most. The reputation of the port as a place of corruption has a long history. If it has been exaggerated by some, it is not to be denied. The corruption of underworld characters spilled over into union and employer affairs and has had an impact upon labor relations. The precise measure of this impact has been impossible to determine, nor has the subject been pursued in this study.

Government Organizations in the Industry

Because the union and management organizations were beholden to and made use of government, it should be noted that the Marine Department of the city—for some time, now, the Department of Marine and Aviation—was a prominent owner, developer, and lessor of port facilities. This particular role diminished in importance with the rise of the Port of New York Authority (PNYA), a quasigovernmental corporation set up on a bistate basis, which has become the dominant agency in port development. The interesting point here is that the latter was not subject to political manipulation or favor and, in essence, has been looked upon antagonistically by the ILA and by many employers.

Even if the city had not been directly involved in building and leasing piers, its role would probably have been important. The business of the port could not have escaped surveillance, or some manipulation, by city politicians. The protective role toward business and the community would have required involvement. Hence the intermeshing of political and private undertakings, some reaching to the illicit, has been an important factor in port life. It would have been strange indeed had not the unions, and the ILA in particular, become involved in the politics of city government and made use of political power. But employers, too, found City Hall worth cultivating; it could not be ignored.

The ILA—Its Organization

For preliminary understanding of the ILA, it will be useful to lay out its structure. The headquarters of the International has been in Manhattan for many years, as were the headquarters of the Atlantic Coast District Council—actually the two were in the same office—and the New York District Council. Without a doubt these three hierarchical bodies were the dominant part, and, for many purposes, the whole union. However, the Executive Board of the ILA was comprised of the president, executive vice-president, secretary-treasurer, and twenty-two vice-presidents from the whole organization, including those from New York. The Atlantic Coast District, covering ports from Norfolk, Virginia, into Canada, has been the most important of four geographical districts. The others, in order of importance, were the South Atlantic and Gulf Coast District (later this one would become three, the South Atlantic, the Gulf, and the West Gulf), the Great Lakes District, and the West Coast District. The latter, since 1937, when the West Coast longshoremen forsook the ILA and called themselves the International Longshoremen and Warehousemens' Union (ILWU) and affiliated with the Congress of Industrial Organizations (CIO), has been comprised only of the few longshoremen in Tacoma, Washington. The

Great Lakes District has not been very important, either, although it played a role in early longshoremen's history.

Within the Atlantic Coast District there have been district councils, one for each port: one for Boston, another for Baltimore, and a third for Philadelphia, to name the most important ones outside of New York. The largest and the most important, naturally, has been the New York District Council, comprised, at the outset of this story, of some sixty-odd locals organized by job functions, for example, longshoremen, checkers and clerks, cargo repairmen, grain handlers, general maintenance men, and port watchmen. Locals in each functional grouping have had their own geographical bases.

The longshoremen have been the most numerous, divided into locals by pier, or piers, or other geographical area: for example, the major ones in Manhattan, Local 856, holding jurisdiction over piers on both the East and lower North rivers, Local 791 in Chelsea, and Local 824 in the luxury-liner area above Forty-second Street, both on the North River. The Manhattan locals have been predominantly Irish. There have been many longshoremen locals in Brooklyn, predominantly Italian, extending through the area from Greenpoint to the Bush Docks. In the decade after World War II, the many locals—several of which before the war were known as "Camarda locals" under the control of the Camarda family, in which the notorious Albert Anastasia was involved—were consolidated by Anthony Anastasia, brother to Albert, into Local 1814, becoming the largest in the port. Staten Island also has locals, although they have not been very important; New Jersey has four areas—Jersey City, Hoboken, Port Newark, and Bayonne—each distinct from the others with its own structure of local unions.

The checkers and clerks, at the beginning of our story, were found in four locals, one each for Manhattan, Brooklyn, Staten Island, and New Jersey. They were soon to be consolidated into one portwide local through the efforts of Thomas (Teddy) Gleason. The other so-called craft groups usually had one or more locals in each port area.

The control of locals in the ILA was mixed. Many local leaders have used their positions for personal purposes, having used control over jobs to enrich themselves through kickbacks and the like. But some have pursued their own ends while simultaneously supporting the men. Many have come up from the ranks, having worked as longshoremen, and have known the problems firsthand, although some have come from the fringes of the industry with less experience working on the docks. While from a union viewpoint their performance has been shoddy at times, it has not been without some deference to union objectives. To stand up for the workers has not necessarily interfered with personal objectives—although there undoubtedly have been collusive, or cozy, relationships between some of the local leaders and some of the employers—on the contrary, to have a loyal or beholden group of men as a core of power on the pier was helpful. This is not to deny the presence of conscientious local leaders imbued with honest, trade union objectives, but leadership generally has often left much to be desired.

The ILA had a certain security in the Port of New York because of its close association with the local labor movement and with the AFL. This was a conservative, business-type unionism, often having ties with local politicians. The ILA leaders found association here; in fact, ILA headquarters was located in the same building with many of these unions. Like the craft unions, the ILA was recognized and accepted, as we have already noted.

In the bargaining realm, within the Atlantic Coast District, dominated from New York, has been a Wage Scale Conference Committee (hereafter referred to as Wage Scale Committee), composed, at the opening of our story, of some 130 representatives from the various local unions and district councils. The Wage Scale Conference Committee, in turn, has had subcommittees representing the various functional groups in the organization. This structure is not altogether unified, because of the great autonomy of the district councils and local unions, particularly those in the Port of New York, and the uneven importance of the various locals and district councils. Representatives of one group have hardly presumed to speak for, or to impose upon, the others.

The NYSA—Organization of Employers

While the ILA has been organized for bargaining on a coast-wide basis and has aspired to establish uniform collective agreements throughout the North Atlantic area, the employers have not been organized on an interport basis, except very recently. The New York Shipping Association (NYSA) has claimed no jurisdiction beyond the Port of New York, in fact, has always denied having any jurisdiction over employers in other ports; although some steamship companies engage in operations in some other ports. The structure of NYSA is of interest, too, alongside that of the ILA. At the outset of our story it was composed of some sixty-odd steamship lines and agents engaged in domestic—coastwide or intercoastal—and foreign shipping, variously engaged in handling passenger traffic or freight or both and, with respect to freight, either on scheduled runs or on a "tramp" basis. At that time there were almost sixty stevedores, ranging from large to small, who contracted to discharge and load cargoes, some working under fairly stable and continuous contracts, others as they could gain work.[3] In addition, there was a mis-

[3] The following is a listing of the most important companies, by functional types, as of the early 1950's (names abbreviated):

American flag, subsidized lines: United States, American Export, American President, Isthmian, Moore-McCormick, and Farrell.

American flag, unsubsidized lines: Grace (subsidized on some runs), States Marine, Isbrandston, Luchenbach (intercoastal only), Pan Atlantic, and Bull.

Foreign flag, government operated: Grancolumbiana, Venezuelan, Chilean, Vacuba, and Argentine State.

Foreign flag, private but subsidized: Cunard, French, Italian, Belgian, Swedish-American, Mersk, and Furniss-Withy.

House stevedores: T. Hogan (U.S. Lines), Atlantic (Barber), and Bay Ridge (Furniss-Withy).

Companies doing own stevedoring: Grace, American Export, and Moore-McCormick.

Contracting stevedores: Maher, American Stevedores, International

cellaneous group of about forty cargo repair, checking and clerking, maintenance, and marine carpenter companies. Altogether, the NYSA had about 160 members, and in the association voting was one company, one vote. For collective bargaining activities there was a Conference Committee of sixteen members, practically all representing major steamship lines. The stevedores, in fact, were excluded for a long time from voting on policy matters.

From the mid-fifties and throughout the period of this study generally, management in this industry has failed to develop the quality of relationships with employees and their unions such as those commonly found in many other industries. Personnel departments have been almost unknown. Perhaps the casual nature of much of the employment accounts for the lack of concern with employment relationships, which elsewhere had come to be a major concern of many managements. Notwithstanding major exceptions, the reputation of management has been poor, generally. From the time of the investigations of the New York State Crime Commission in 1952, the public view has been that management was either weak or corrupt. This has hardly been a fair characterization, applicable across the board, because there have been great differences. Most important, the nature of the industry has been at the root of some of the difficulty and one might conclude that management has been a victim more than a culprit; yet it must be said that management collectively has not been forward-looking and has lost much by default. No doubt too much dependence has been placed upon the NYSA to administer labor relations when individual employers could have done a great deal to improve relationships with their regular employees, at least. But it has been customary to live as they did and to effectuate local deals if necessary. What is somewhat curious is that things have often been done without reporting them to the NYSA in its centralizing role. Little effective leader-

Terminal Operating Company, Turner and Blanchard, John T. Clark, McGrath, Universal, and Sottneck.

ship could be, or has been, given, partly, maybe largely, because responsibilities within management hierarchies were divided and scattered with little provision for real accountability. While working conditions contributed much to worker dissatisfaction, most managements have remained unconcerned about them. Strangely, to some people, management, neither individually or collectively, has a program designed to defend managerial functions and long-run interests; managements have been mostly opportunistic meeting problems as they arose.

The attitudes of the men toward management varied considerably from place to place. In some areas of the port the relationships between the men and the first levels of management, particularly at pier level, have been very good, with mutual respect prevailing. In other areas management representatives at the pier level have been considered overbearing. Supervisors have often been poorly selected and largely untrained. Often workers have felt that supervisors lacked knowledge and effectiveness. Looking upward through the hierarchies of management one can also see a varied picture, with many very able people in some situations, but all too often the relationships and lines of authority have been blurred or indefinite. Ties have often been of the loosest sort. Expediency has been the usual hallmark. Top management could be seen as unable or unwilling to exercise control. The NYSA could not do the job that the companies have been unwilling to perform. It has made the job of standing up to the union doubly difficult. Yet, if management had control, had been responsible to needs of leadership, and had been concerned about work conditions, it still would have faced a quandary because of the character of the leadership of the ILA.

In spite of the appearance of good organization through the NYSA, management was fundamentally split on most major issues according to the operating interests and the requirements of its differing competitive companies. Thinking has been dominated (as already noted) by the compelling importance of ship turnaround time, and has been focused on ship operations rather than cargo handling. In consequence, it is not strange that management failed to deal with labor relations on the piers with a constructive long-term approach. The day-to-day problems of the men easily got lost in the shuffle. It has been commonly believed that the big steamship companies had too much power in the port, while being the most vulnerable to union pressure. Some people might have argued that the NYSA was not an association in the true sense, but simply a group of different kinds of companies with conflicting interests who have been competing against each other. Inconsistencies have been bound to exist in management approaches. Wage rates and working rules governing employment have been negotiated by the NYSA, but the application of those rates and rules has been largely in the hands of independent or subsidiary stevedores, with varying degrees of control by the individual shipping companies.

2 | The Strike in 1945:
The First Revolt

The strike in 1945 began in Chelsea when members of Local 791 walked off six piers on the afternoon of October 1 in protest against the failure, or neglect, of Joseph P. Ryan, president of the ILA, and the Wage Scale Committee to negotiate a limitation on the size of sling load. Although there was some disagreement about whether there was a strike or a lockout (the men claimed that when they refused to handle sling loads of more than 2,240 pounds the companies covered the hatches and locked them out) there was a work stoppage.

The collective agreement had an expiration date of September 30. Negotiations had been under way for some time prior to this, yet had moved along with little publicity. Toward the deadline, a strike of elevator operators delayed some meetings, but it was not the delay that sparked the men's action—it was leakage of the fact that limitation on the size of sling loads was not included in the settlement. If there had been no delay, the leakage might have occurred sooner and Ryan might have got the message from the rumblings, for the first dissenters were from his home area of the port. As it was, the leakage came at the last moment, just before the newly negotiated agreement was scheduled to be referred to the New York District Council, the voting having been set for the evening of October 2.[1]

[1] The terms of the prospective agreement provided for an increase of 10 cents per hour in the day rate (from $1.25 to $1.35 per hour) and an increase in the overtime rate of 15 cents (from $1.875 to $2.025), and a reduction of the work week from 44 hours to 40 hours, of significance only for the payment of overtime.

The Insurgents from Local 791

The strike, at the outset, was limited to the Chelsea area and was under way when the District Council met to vote on the agreement. The vote was unanimous to recommend acceptance, with the explanation that size of sling loads could be discussed subsequently with the employers. Ryan described the action of the men in Local 791 as "hasty" and said they should have stayed on the job pending action of the District Council. With the favorable vote—from a body sympathetic with him—Ryan announced that the strike was over. The men in Local 791 would not have it. They were further incensed because they now felt they were being forced to agree to something they had already rejected.

The next day men from Local 791 called upon other longshoremen to walk out. The strike spread rapidly and by midday had reached the whole port. ILA officials admitted that it was complete. The action the rank and file assumed took on the face of a serious revolt against the leadership, not just a protest against failure to reduce the size of sling load. Local union officials conceded that the men had a right to refuse the recommendation of the District Council; nonetheless, they echoed Ryan's contention that the strike was illegal and contrary to union regulations, because the men had not voted on the agreement.

The men in Manhattan added to the demands. Although they seemed to accept the negotiated increase in wages and the reduction in weekly hours, they wanted an agreement with a duration of only one year, a minimum of four hours' pay per day, two shape-ups (or times of hiring) instead of the current three, and time and one-half pay for work done through the lunch period. At a rank-and-file meeting of men from eight Brooklyn locals, which took place in a vacant lot at President and Hicks streets, the men discussed how to get each local involved in working out a contract suitable to all. As yet, however, no overall leadership of the insurgents had emerged.

From the outset, the National Maritime Union (NMU) supported the insurgents. It distributed 25,000 leaflets along the waterfront containing the text of a telegram sent to Ryan (and to officials of the shipping lines, the War Shipping Administration, the NYSA, and the American Merchant Institute) condemning failure to meet "the just and modest demands" of rank-and-file longshoremen.[2] The leaders of the ILA saw in this a Communist influence.

The officials of the NYSA expressed surprise, saying, "At no time in the history of collective bargaining between representatives of the employers and of the employees in this port has there been a stoppage of work once their respective committees had orally agreed on the terms of renewal."[3] They were not prepared to give in to direct action and grant what they had not given in negotiations. They insisted upon the terms agreed to.

Under the rules of the ILA the recommendation of the District Council was put to a vote of the membership by the local unions on Saturday, October 6. The vote was favorable but the balloting was light. For example, in Local 791, with 1,500 members, only 276 cast ballots. Of these only 150 voted "yes." Overall, the turnout in the port was hardly better, only 17 per cent. Although the majority of those voting favored acceptance, the lightness of the vote made it inconclusive. Federal mediators met with the leaders of the ILA. Afterward Ryan announced that he would recommend strongly that the men return to work, even asserting that they would comply. Responding to his lead, local union officials recommended acceptance and urged a return to work.

Still another demand was added by the insurgents. They insisted that all gangs have a fourth deckman. The background for this demand was the fact that on many piers during the war a fourth deckman had been added to gangs to spell off winchmen, who often virtually worked around-the-clock, because it was deemed more efficient to use gangs continuously until the

[2] *New York Times*, Oct. 4, 1945, p. 13.
[3] *Ibid.*

ship was finished, rather than bring in new men unfamiliar with the work. The demand now was to make the practice universal.

Twice in five days ILA leaders announced that the strike would be terminated, but it continued. Hence, in spite of the new pronouncement from Ryan after the balloting, it was doubted that the walkout would end. Besides the indefinite meaning of the "yes" vote, there were continued rank-and-file pronouncements against returning to work. Of interest, too, was a report of a stormy mass meeting of members of Local 791.

Federal mediators, although active, felt they could do little, but Edward C. Maguire, expert on labor relations for New York City, announced that he had received assurances—perhaps only from the ILA leaders—that the negotiations would continue until he had an opportunity to resolve the dispute. The fact is that when Ryan and his committee met with the employers and presented new demands, they faced "a hell of an argument" regarding the propriety of presenting new demands after an agreement was once reached.[4]

Ryan reiterated that the strike was over and predicted that 75 per cent of the men would be at the shape-up the next morning. This optimism was not shared by Eugene Sampson, business agent of Local 791. Even while Ryan was making his prediction, a report circulated that a mass meeting would be convened in Brooklyn the next morning to consider whether or not to return, but it was announced that the men intended to name a committee to participate in the new negotiations.[5]

Although the employers modified their stance somewhat by notifying Ryan that they would resume negotiations once the men were back at work, the dock workers continued their defiance. A real showdown was brewing between the insurgents and the hierarchy.[6] The situation was frustrating for the mediators because as long as the men were in rebellion they could

[4] New York Times, Oct. 6, 1945, pp. 1, 3.
[5] New York Times, Oct. 8, 1945, p. 21.
[6] New York Times, Oct. 9, 1945, pp. 1, 14.

achieve little through Ryan and had little prospect of meeting with rank-and-file leaders whose identity was not known.

Mayor Fiorello La Guardia, with community pressures upon him to do something about the stoppage, became actively involved. He tried to determine the identity of the rank-and-file committee so he could have a conference. At the same time three maritime unions—the Marine Fireman, Watertenders and Wipers Association (independent), the Marine Cooks and Stewards Association, and the National Maritime Union (the latter two, both CIO)—distributed thousands of copies of a statement supporting the longshoremen. Ryan, sure that outside influences were fostering the strike, declared emphatically that Communists were behind it.[7] Sampson agreed.

When Ryan appeared at a somewhat disorderly mass meeting at Prospect Hall in Brooklyn on October 10, he was booed, hissed, and shouted off the stage. The rank-and-file speakers, declaring that Ryan was trying to ram the settlement down their throats, said that they were sick and tired of the dictatorial attitudes of ILA leaders.

When Harry Bridges' West Coast longshoremen, the ILWU, in convention in Washington, voted to support the strike, Ryan got another opportunity to charge that "outside influences" were responsible. To leaders of the ILA the action of the ILWU was designed to oust the ILA from the New York waterfront, even though the leaflets distributed by the three maritime unions said, "Stay in the AFL and fight for your rights."

On the night of October 10, an unidentified rank-and-file committee sent a message to the *New York Times*, obviously intended for Mayor La Guardia. It said: "In response to your statement in the press this morning, be advised that the rank-and-file committee is ready to meet with you to settle the issues of the strike as soon as you give us a guarantee of protection from the goons employed by Ryan to terrorize the rank-and-file."[8]

[7] *New York Times*, Oct. 10, 1945, pp. 1, 14.
[8] *New York Times*, Oct. 11, 1945, pp. 1, 14.

Federal mediators toured the waterfront and talked to members of the various locals. The mayor met with Ryan and officers of the ILA, also with the NYSA. At this same time it was revealed that William E. Warren, a member of one of the insurgent locals in Brooklyn, was named temporary chairman of the rank-and-file committee. He announced that a mass meeting would be convened in Manhattan on the next Sunday afternoon for the purpose of creating a portwide negotiating committee to settle the strike.

Mayor La Guardia, freshly supplied with commendations from the War Department concerning the longshoremen and their work, "the best of any port in the country during the hardest days of the war," met with the full committee of the ILA, the federal mediators, and a group of state labor leaders headed by Thomas A. Murray, president of the New York Federation of Labor. Following this conference he made a broadcast in order to appeal directly to longshoremen and their wives. He described a proposal he had made, accepted by the NYSA and the ILA committee, which provided for immediate resumption of negotiations; return to work the next morning; new terms won in negotiations to be retroactive to October 1; new terms to be submitted to the entire membership for approval; new terms to be agreed to within one week of the resumption of negotiations; and submission of unsettled issues to "the proper agency of government in the event no solution is reached." In concluding his broadcast, the mayor strongly urged, "In the name of common sense go back to work."[9]

Warren, however, notified the mayor in a telegram that they would not return to work, and this stance was confirmed at a mass meeting that night in Brooklyn. Concurrently, when Warren held a press conference in the office of attorneys Nathan Witt and Harold Cammer, sophisticated persons concluded that Communistic influences were present in the insurgency movement.

[9] *New York Times,* Oct. 12, 1945, p. 15.

The ILA was quick to assert that Warren had been a member of the ILA for less than a year (he insisted he had three-and-a-half years of membership) and that he was not in good standing for failure to pay dues. Warren retorted that he and his committee, not the ILA Wage Scale Committee, represented the striking longshoremen and that Ryan and his lieutenants, "the so-called committee of 100 which has been picked by Joe Ryan and his stooges," were not in a position to take the men back to work. He denied that communistic influences were present and affirmed the intention of going ahead with the mass meeting scheduled for Manhattan the next Sunday.[10] Again, the three maritime unions, joined by the American Communications Association, affirmed their support of the insurgents and said that ships would not be allowed to move. Bridges arrived from Washington, D.C., and participated in a press conference held at the NMU hall, where it was proposed that the mayor meet with the insurgent committee; even called upon him to appear at the mass meeting. Although the mayor did not appear, he met with Warren and another member of the rank-and-file committee, accompanied by Witt.

It was reported at this time that men in Local 856, at the lower tip of Manhattan, and Local 920, Staten Island, returned to work and that shipping officials were pleased with the evidence of a back-to-work movement. The Seafarers International Union (SIU) issued a statement criticizing the CIO unions and pledged support to the ILA. The action of the CIO unions was called "a brazen attempt by Communist-run and Communist-dominated organizations to make political capital of the ILA differences." It was added that it was "extremely important to the SIU that Bridges and his cohorts be kept off the East Coast." Concurrently, the president and secretary of the Central Trades and Labor Council of Greater New York City, the president of the State Federation of Labor, and the eastern representative of the AFL, issued a formal statement supporting the ILA.[11]

On Sunday, October 14, the mayor made a new proposal and

[10] *New York Times*, Oct. 13, 1945, pp. 1, 2.
[11] *New York Times*, Oct. 14, 1945, p. 36.

dispatched motorcycle police with a lengthy, detailed letter addressed to three parties (the ILA, the NYSA, and the rank-and-file committee). He also read it over radio station WNYC. He stated that the factional dispute had become serious for the community but noted that each party—employers, ILA officials, and rank-and-file leaders—had expressed willingness to get back to work pending negotiations. Acknowledging that neither he nor the employers could settle the internal differences in the ILA, he offered a plan to give the members an opportunity to settle their differences among themselves through election—under supervision of prominent outsiders—of a negotiating committee. Matters not settled in negotiations would be arbitrated.[12] The mayor found only the insurgents willing to accept his new proposition, but strict instructions were given by their leaders not to go back to work until the attitude of the employers was known.

The NYSA judiciously issued no immediate comments. The maritime unions which had been supporting the insurgents, joined by Bridges, informed the mayor that they endorsed the plan. Ryan, however, was quick to reject it and was supported, emphatically, by the four officials of the AFL who had earlier taken a position in the affair. Ryan characterized the mayor's proposal as "the silliest I have ever heard." Emphasizing that the ILA committee was composed of elected members, he said that the ILA could not relinquish its recognition and jurisdiction. He asserted that four thousand men were then working and "tomorrow most of the men will be back at work, so that the owners and the ILA wage negotiating committee" could resume negotiations and conclude them within a week.[13]

On Monday morning five thousand longshoremen were back to work, but the NMU ordered its men to shut down the steam and walk off their ships if longshoremen appeared. The employers, meanwhile, also rejected the mayor's proposal. J. V. Lyon, chairman of the NYSA, said that the NYSA would continue to deal with the ILA's "accredited representatives" until

[12] *New York Times*, Oct. 13, 1945, p. 1.
[13] *New York Times*, Oct. 15, 1945, p. 2.

legal procedures [meaning those of the National Labor Relations Board] demonstrated that the ILA no longer represented the longshoremen. He said, "We cannot agree to negotiate with any committee not so determined."[14]

The Central Trades and Labor Council described the mayor's proposal as "outrageous," also saying, "The American Federation of Labor will take care of its own members and unions," and served notice on Bridges to get out of town. Criticizing the mayor for "playing into the hands of the CIO," it asserted that his usefulness in the strike "is at an end." On the other hand, officials of the NMU went to City Hall. They failed to see the mayor, but one spoke from the steps, saying to the assembled men that the NMU would not stand by to see them become victims of Ryan's "goons." "Don't go back on no ship 'til we get a position from the mayor," he warned. The upshot was that the ILA formed a special committee "to combat subversive propaganda now being put out by the NMU and other organizations."[15]

At this time another group of ILA members, who wanted no part of the insurgent faction led by Warren, expressed interest in having an election under NLRB auspices to choose new leaders. A member of Local 808, in Brooklyn, said, "The men have lost confidence in Ryan and think the ILA is corrupt because of its close-knit control. But even within the machine there are healthy elements. We just need an election for new officers."[16] But nothing came of this, for the NLRB could not entertain an election for officers within the ILA, but only an election, upon proper petition, to determine the choice between contending unions.

The Return to Work

Each day an increasing number of men were found at work, but the insurgents continued their agitation. Manhattan was de-

14 *New York Times*, Oct. 16, 1945, p. 1.
15 *Ibid.*
16 *Ibid.*

scribed practically solidly at work, yet a demonstration took place in Chelsea on October 16, just before the 12:55 P.M. shape-up, when two hundred men carrying American flags and placards marched to the piers shouting to the longshoremen to "strike and beat Ryan." But mounted policemen kept them on the sidewalk opposite the piers. A little later, a much larger group, reported to be three thousand insurgent rank and filers, plus supporting maritime union men, marched from their meeting hall at Manhattan Center and Thirty-fourth Street to have a demonstration in Chelsea. As they marched, the men shouted, "Down with Ryan" and "Down with finks." As they passed the piers, they called to the dock gangs to walk out. The police denied entry to the piers and the marchers finally ended up at NMU headquarters. Meanwhile, in Brooklyn, fifty army veterans, wearing army jackets and shirts with ILA buttons alongside their discharge buttons, appeared for work for the Barber Line at Pioneer Street. When touring antiwork squads appeared, the veterans defied them to keep them from work.[17]

The employers considered the strike sufficiently broken to resume negotiations, and a preliminary meeting was held with the ILA committee on the eighteenth, where it was decided to start bargaining the next day. During the preliminary meeting, a group of 150 "Warren insurgents" gathered on Broad Street in front of the building, then moved one block down the street to be addressed by Warren. At this juncture a group of seamen from the SIU, about the same number, appeared, wearing white caps and accompanied by a sound truck. They attempted to break through the police line but without success, although there was considerable scuffling. Later the SIU issued a statement saying, "If the police are going to protect the Communists with their clubs and the law, we are going to have to take more drastic measures." An "Army Veterans' Committee" was formed within the ILA "to take up the Communist challenge," but the NMU sent a telegram to the secretaries of the Army and Navy

17 *New York Times*, Oct. 17, 1945, p. 1.

and to Mayor La Guardia, saying that gangsters were planning to provoke violence on the waterfront "in Army and Navy uniforms."[18]

It was obvious, however, even to the rank-and-file leaders that the strike was broken. On October 18 they advised their remaining followers to go back to work. Nevertheless, speaking from the offices of Witt and Cammer, Warren claimed victory because the rank and file had demonstrated their unity. The recommendation to return to work was made, he said, "to preserve the unity of longshoremen that has developed during this strike, and to continue that unity to achieve our just economic demands and a clean democratic union. . . . We make this recommendation because the continuance of the strike at this time in the face of Ryan's gangsterism, the strike breaking of [Harry] Lundeberg [president of the Sailors International Union of which the SIU was an affiliate], the lies in the anti-labor press, and the active collusion of the shipowners with Ryan and Lundeberg, convinces us that the unity of the ILA rank and file may suffer." The NMU acquiesced in this decision, saying, "It was their strike and we supported them; we can do nothing but concur." But on the West Coast all CIO maritime unions had been notified to stand ready for a twenty-four-hour-work stoppage in support of the strikers in the East. Although this was canceled in view of the decision in New York to return to work, the ILWU said that it would continue to support the longshoremen in New York who wanted to be freed from the current leadership.[19]

Although Warren was given a physical beating the next day by a gang of men in Brooklyn and was formally expelled from the ILA for not paying his dues, he made a startling revelation shortly afterward. He said that he had been misled and "wrongly steered . . . into the Communist camp," and he resigned, along with Sal Barone, from leadership of the rank-and-file committee. Warren said they were "just a couple of plain ordinary long-

[18] *New York Times,* Oct. 18, 1945, p. 1.
[19] *New York Times,* Oct. 19, 1945, pp. 1, 19.

shoremen who only want[ed] a good, strong, honest union."
Declaring that as soon as they found out that one of their lawyers, Witt, and others who were supposedly helping them were
"Communist controlled," they decided to quit. They said their
purpose in making a statement was to "clear ourselves with the
rank and file." They confessed, "We were just being used as
dupes." Witt retaliated, however, by charging that "the beat-
ings administered to Warren and Barone . . . have apparently
convinced them to work with Joe Ryan. . . . The surrender
. . . will not keep the rank and file from continuing the fight
they began for their just economic demands and for an honest
democratic union."[20]

New leaders for the rank-and-file committee were found. A
statement from the office of Witt and Cammer identified John
Berg as one of three temporary cochairmen, along with Charles
Anderson and James Glasgow, as temporary secretary and treasurer, respectively. But Ryan was quick to say that they had
been "waiting for Berg and Anderson to appear in the picture"
and asserted that they were part of a small group that had been
"boring from within for the Communists" during the previous
five years.[21]

No settlement was reached in negotiations but it was agreed
to let the members of the union vote on employer proposals.
These were rejected by an "overwhelming vote." The employers announced that they would make "no further concessions" but agreed to meet to consider the next steps. In the
meantime, the fight between the officialdom of the ILA and the
so-called rank-and-file committee turned to the courts, when the
attorneys for the latter moved to get an injunction to prevent
the ILA leaders from signing any agreement with the employers.
Witt held that his clients were "seeking to prevent another
strike such as occurred on October 1 when the men protested
Ryan's original contract by walking out." Louis Waldman, attorney for the ILA, labeled the action as "a smear" and said,

[20] *New York Times*, Oct. 21, 1945, p. 35.
[21] *New York Times*, Oct. 22, 1945, p. 9.

"No injunction is necessary because the vote that has come in so far [on the employers' offer of settlement] shows . . . the members . . . have voted against the agreement." He asserted that "the so-called rank-and-file committee is actually a tool of certain Communist forces in this city aligned with the National Maritime Union to undermine Ryan, and the ILA and install Harry Bridges in control of the East Coast."[22]

The rank-and-file committee issued a statement hailing the vote on the employers' proposal as "a great victory for the men" but warned against any "phony" arbitration proceeding.[23] After filing a brief and arguing the matter, it won the temporary restraining order which it sought. The effect was to prevent the signing of a contract until duly advertised meetings were conducted at which the longshoremen would be given an opportunity to vote. The judge ruled that "an injunction will not harm the defendant [Ryan] and . . . equity and justice in the public interest are best served by granting the injunction rather than subjecting the union members to the possibility that the defendant may change his mind after securing a denial of a motion." The latter part of the statement was made because the rank-and-file committee's statement did not show whether the constitution of the ILA authorized Ryan to sign a contract without referring it to the membership. In this connection, the judge observed that many longshoremen had returned to work under Ryan's assurance to the mayor that no contract would be signed until it was approved by the membership.

The insurgents contended, but incorrectly, that the order would prevent Ryan from proceeding with further negotiations with the shipowners or with any plans he had to submit the controversy to Secretary of Labor Lewis B. Schwellenbach, or to another governmental agency. They interpreted the decision of the judge as "a great victory" and said, "King Joe can't sign any phony contract behind our back. The decision is proof that the

[22] *New York Times*, Oct. 24, 1945, p. 13.
[23] *New York Times*, Oct. 25, 1945, p. 3.

rank-and-file committee is fighting for the longshoremen under the ILA constitution and within the ILA."[24] Ryan went ahead, nevertheless, as he said he had a right to do, and met with the shippers as scheduled. After a long session they agreed to submit the issues to arbitration. The ILA and NYSA committees joined in sending a telegram to Secretary Schwellenbach asking him to inform them which governmental agency was the proper one to designate an arbitrator; the ILA said it was the secretary whereas the NYSA said it was the National War Labor Board. The rank-and-file committee, however, asserted that "the joint request for arbitration by King Joe and the shipowners is another deliberate attempt to sell out the longshoremen by violating our right to be consulted. This deal comes as no surprise. All week we have been warning the longshoremen in our Waterfront Bulletin that a phony arbitration request was being cooked up. We do not oppose arbitration as such. We do oppose any attempt to settle the longshore situation without giving the longshoremen an opportunity to decide democratically and free from coercion what steps shall be taken in our behalf."[25]

The agreement to arbitrate was obviously not a "phony" one, as the arbitration itself attests, but it is true that the decision to arbitrate and to be bound by the terms of the award—both the NYSA and the ILA agreed to abide by the decision of the arbitrator—was never submitted to the rank and file. But settlement by arbitration, in the event of failure to come to a settlement privately, had been previously suggested by the mayor. When Secretary Schwellenbach made the suggestion that he and the NWLB jointly designate the arbitrator, the parties accepted it. Accordingly, William H. Davis, who had distinguished himself successively as chairman of the New York State Board of Mediation, chairman of the NWLB, and economic adviser to the President, was named. This appointment was enough, alone, to quiet any but frivolous opposition, and the port settled down to the more quiet proceedings of arbitration.

[24] *New York Times*, Oct. 26, 1945, p. 1.
[25] *New York Times*, Oct. 27, 1945, p. 16.

The Arbitration Award

The award made by Davis is interesting.[26] Whereas the original agreement provided for a wage increase of 10 cents per hour, the ILA had come back with a demand for a 20-per-cent increase and this is what Davis awarded, that is, twenty-five cents per hour. He justified it under the national wartime wage stabilization policy to avoid impairment of the peacetime wage standards of longshoremen. He, therefore, directed the straight-time rate of $1.50 per hour. He recognized that the hourly wage rates were relatively high but said, "This is a reflection of the casual nature of employment."

With regard to hours, Davis took special note of the reasons for the special arrangement for payment of overtime and affirmed it as sensible, writing into his award what the employers had granted, that is, a forty-hour week instead of a forty-four-hour week. This eliminated straight-time pay on Saturday forenoons, leaving straight-time hours for work performed on week days between 8:00 A.M. and 12:00 noon and from 1:00 P.M. to 5:00 P.M. All other hours worked were still considered overtime hours.

One of the three daily shape-ups was eliminated. The employers, in fact, conceded to Davis that it was undesirable to call men out three times a day if one shape-up could be dropped without leading to payment for work not done. Davis eliminated the 6:55 P.M. shape-up, but he permitted men who worked the previous night to be ordered back for the next night, if wanted, before they left the dock in the morning. The employer, between 4 and 5 P.M., was also free to order for night work "through established channels." Also, new or additional gangs for night work could be hired at the 12:55 P.M. shape-up, or might be chosen from the men who worked in the afternoon. But it was made explicit that both the NYSA and the longshoremen were in basic agreement that the shape-up system of hiring

[26] Bureau of National Affairs, *Labor Arbitration Reports*, vol. 1, pp. 80–87.

—that system, as noted, where selection and employment of longshoremen was made by the hiring agent from among the men standing at the head of the pier—should be maintained in preference to a system of rotation through hiring halls—wherein men would be allocated for employment as their names rotated to the top of a hiring roster. Both the ILA and the NYSA were sure that the inconveniences of the shape-up system were more than offset by its advantages.

The union's request for rigid assignment of men in the gang, including deckmen, was denied. Davis felt that efficiency required the retention of flexibility of job assignment, "so that the men [might] be assigned to work where they [were] most needed and particularly so that dockmen [might] be assigned to work in the hold when, because of the nature of the cargo or for other reasons, the required minimum of eight men in the hold [was] insufficient to handle the work smoothly and efficiently." Also denied, for the needs of efficiency, was the request for a maximum weight of sling load for general cargo, the issue that had led to the work stoppage in the first instance. Davis insisted that efficiency was as important for the long-term welfare of the workers as it was for the long-term welfare of the employers. He said that rigid rules forcibly applied do not produce efficiency. Considering the interests of the men, he directed that the contract be amended to provide for reasonable adjustment of the sling load and of the gang to the nature and requirements of the work at hand, that is, with special consideration given to safety.

Davis also awarded the first guarantee of pay for reporting for work, that is, when men were hired and reported for work only to find there was no work, because the ship had not arrived or the weather was too severe, they were to receive two hours' pay. Also included was a requirement that management provide "suitable shelter" for men working on deck in bad weather. Travel time and cost of transportation were provided under very specific situations. In addition, one week's vacation with pay was granted with the provision that the parties would set up a committee to negotiate the details. Davis also directed the parties to amend the grievance sections of the contract to improve grievance procedures, commending for their consideration the recommendations of the Committee on Existing Collective Agreements approved by the Labor-Management Conference at Washington, D.C., in 1945.[27]

Conclusions

The strike in 1945 revealed much about labor relations in the Port of New York. ILA leadership was not in touch with the men. Bargaining was too limited in scope and many men had no sense of involvement or feeling of being represented. The leaders, particularly Ryan, were smug in their belief that they were doing what labor leaders customarily do and gaining what the men wanted, but they did not know, or ignored, what had happened in the labor movement. Ryan no doubt thought that he had negotiated a good agreement. An increase of ten cents an hour, from his perspective, was a substantial increase. It never occurred to him, or to the shippers for that matter, that not only were the men entitled to know something of what was going on but that their consent to an agreement needed to be achieved by some form of communication. Longshoremen could be militant, but were easily led. The rank and file expected improvement in their job situation and were willing to demonstrate for things they thought important. Yet they were susceptible to mass movements, but perhaps not to class movements. It is clear that the rebellion in Local 791, which started the strike, had no Communistic impetus at all, although it was easy for Communist sympathizers to move in, as widely alleged, as long as they remained under cover. But this is a mixed picture. The ability of the Communists to make themselves felt effectively was due, in part, to their presence in unions otherwise acceptable to the longshoremen, such as the NMU,[28] and because they easily

[27] *Ibid.*; U.S. Department of Labor, Division of Labor Standards, *The President's National Labor-Management Conference, November 5–30, 1945,* pp. 44–47.

[28] It was to be a few years yet before Joseph Curran, president of the

identified themselves with the issues that were important to the rank and file. The cries of the ILA leaders, while appearing unfounded, were nonetheless based on knowledge of the roles played by the dissenters, whether or not some of them were duped.

The settlement of the dispute in voluntary arbitration was an obvious solution under the circumstances, and the parties were fortunate in obtaining the services of Davis. The award might have provided a base from which to improve the quality of relationships, but it did not. Practices could not change quickly in this custom-encrusted industry, particularly when principals were satisfied with their own performance.

NMU, successfully ousted the Communists from leadership roles and cleared himself from their clutches. But in 1945, they were present and active.

3 | Overtime-on-Overtime

Just before the two-year contract was to expire on August 21, 1947, Congress enacted the Labor-Management Relations Act (Taft-Hartley Act). Its restrictions upon union security had the effect of hurrying the pending longshore negotiations, because it provided that agreements in effect on August 22, 1947, would be permitted to run for one year. Partly because of the awakening caused by the insurgency in 1945 and because of the improvements gained in the Davis Arbitration, both of which elevated rank-and-file expectations, the Wage Scale Committee of the ILA had made demands greater than in previous negotiations: another twenty-five-cents-an-hour increase, a more liberal vacation payment, a welfare fund paid for by employers, and a guarantee of eight hours of pay whenever a man was hired. Negotiations proceeded quietly. But the employers, being in a good position to wait, refused to make any concessions other than an increase in wages of ten cents an hour. To get an agreement before August 22, the ILA negotiating committee finally accepted this without pressing the other issues.

Before the formal voting, the members of Local 791 held a meeting; echoing 1945, they rejected the settlement. Sampson, the business agent, expressed surprise but stood with the men. On August 20 they walked out, as they had in the insurgency two years before, but this time only two other locals followed suit. A group of seamen in the NMU supported the insurgents and delayed the sailing of the steamship *America* on the ground that it would be "unsafe." They would not sail unless the longshoremen were working. The officials of the company blamed

Sampson for not controlling the longshoremen and "left-wing agitators." A former official of the NMU who had been active in support of the insurgent longshoremen in 1945, and who had subsequently lost his union post, was working as a member of the crew. As one of the local spokesmen, he said that if the longshoremen had the right kind of leadership and a democratic union the strike could have been avoided. Although there is little doubt that the refusal to sail the ship had been engineered by left-wing elements, Local 791 was certainly not acting because of Communist influence. Also, the NMU did not support the insurgent longshoremen as in 1945; Joseph Curran had won out over the Communistic faction. On August 22 a half-dozen locals in Brooklyn started to walk out but were deterred by one of the ILA vice-presidents. He said, "The men know they have been fooled. It was Communistic all the way."

Over the weekend Sampson urged the men of Local 791 to return to work, and they voted 428 to 177 to do so. The real difficulty among the men in Local 791 had not been their reluctance to accept the ten-cent wage increase, or the failure to get the other new things demanded, but dissatisfaction with a provision of the 1945 settlement which gave the employer the right to split a gang and put dockmen into the hold.[1] But the issue was not important, because only Brooklyn employers had exercised that option, and never in the area of Local 791.

The Background of the Dispute in 1948

A legal question of "overtime-on-overtime" proved to be a strange obstacle in the negotiations in 1948. The matter arose as a major factor just prior to the first negotiating meeting, although it had been in the offing for some time.

For many years, going back to 1916, the parties had a unique arrangement covering overtime; the hours between 8:00 A.M.

---

[1] *New York Times*, Aug. 20, p. 3, Aug. 21, p. 1, Aug. 22, p. 1, Aug. 23, p. 1, Aug. 24, p. 3, Aug. 26, p. 1; *Agreement negotiated by the New York Shipping Association with the International Longshoremen's Association for the Port of Greater New York and Vicinity*, 1947, p. 11.

and 12:00 noon and 1:00 P.M. and 5:00 P.M. were defined as straight-time hours and all other times as overtime hours.

When the Fair Labor Standards Act (FLSA, or the Wage-Hour Law) was passed in 1938, requiring time-and-a-half rates for all hours worked in excess of forty in a week, the ILA and the NYSA decided that their contractual arrangement satisfied the overtime requirements of the law. The intention behind the arrangement in the longshore industry was to deter work at night and concentrate it during daytime hours. Yet, with respect to the controversy in 1948, it is clear that the contractual language had not been negotiated to meet the overtime requirements of the law, for it antedated the law. It is also of significance that the arrangement gave longshoremen a better deal than the FLSA alone would have given them. The ILA had preferred to keep what it had. Furthermore, the arrangement was certainly not intended as a shift differential, that is, a payment for working at night. Shift differentials in industry generally were running to penalties, or premiums, of five cents and ten cents, and only occasionally to as much as fifteen cents, per hour. More to the point, the longshore industry was not a shift-working industry. Employers customarily kept their gangs intact and worked into the night with the same men who worked during the day, rather than bring in new workers unfamiliar with the ship or the cargo.

But portents of trouble under the FLSA had arisen. The administrator of the FLSA had informed the War Shipping Administration in October 1943 that he felt the industry was not in compliance with the law. He based his opinion on the phrase "regular rate" found in the law. A man who worked more than forty hours in one work week was entitled to a premium of 50 per cent over his regular rate. If an employee worked at two or more different rates during a work week, his "regular rate" for the week was the weighted average rate, and hours worked in excess of forty were to be paid at a 50-per-cent premium over this rate. Furthermore, if an employee worked in a situation where his hours fell within two shifts and one of the shifts

carried a differential, his "regular rate" for purposes of computing overtime was the weighted average of his hourly earning
rates during the first forty hours and his rate for overtime work
was time-and-a-half this rate.[2] Assurances from various sources
had been given to NYSA employers, however, that they need
not worry. Nevertheless, there had been enough uncertainty at
the time of the Davis Arbitration award in 1945 that the employers had sought to tidy up the situation by limiting straight-
time hours to forty hours. One reason for the concern of the employers at the time was the fact that many longshoremen were
filing suits for overtime under the FLSA, claiming they had been
deprived of overtime compensation due them.[3]

Early in 1948, Judge Simon Rifkind, of the U.S. District
Court, denied the claims. He rejected the contention that the
contractual overtime rate was a shift differential, because the
overtime rate provided for more pay than required by the statute. He cited Ryan's testimony, as a witness for the defendant,
that the ILA had wanted the work done in daytime and on
weekdays, as much as possible, and intended to make work during all other hours expensive in order to achieve this end and to
cause the spreading of work, a purpose of the statute. He
pointed out that the controversy required a delicate adjustment
of three national policies: the NLRA, designed to encourage the
practice of collective bargaining; the FLSA, designed to correct
or eliminate certain labor conditions; and Executive Order 9301,
designed to establish the forty-eight-hour week for the duration
of the war. He could see nothing in the FLSA which precluded
negotiations for a shorter work week than forty hours, and noted
that some unions and employers had done it, but that employees
did not receive an overtime rate on top of the overtime earned
within forty. He noted, also, that unions and employers nego-

[2] Senate, Committee on Labor and Public Welfare, *To Clarify the
Overtime Compensation Provisions of the Fair Labor Standards Act of
1938, as Amended; Hearings before a Subcommittee*, 81st Cong., 1st.
Sess,. 1939, p. 655.
[3] *New York Times*, Oct. 5, 1945, p. 14, Aug. 27, 1947, p. 16.

tiated overtime for hours worked in excess of eight in a day and that payment of overtime on a daily basis had not led to a higher average rate of payment for hours worked in excess of forty. He saw no reason to convert true overtime premiums into shift differentials.[4]

The employers breathed more easily, but unhappily for them the matter did not rest there. Much money was at stake and Judge Rifkind's decision was appealed. He was reversed when the U.S. Circuit Court held that the overtime rate was the regular rate for unpleasant hours and was like a shift differential. The issue was then appealed to the Supreme Court, with the Department of Justice being the chief petitioner because it was the United States under its cost-plus contract that would bear the burden of the claims for the war years. The shipper-petitioners, however, would bear the burden of the claims in the postwar years, and a disruption of past practice under their collective bargaining contracts would cause trouble for them. It might seem strange, therefore, that the leaders of the ILA supported the employers. Yet, they were not acting differently from other union leaders who were interested in preserving the integrity of collective bargaining. An amicus brief was filed by the ILA. Similarly, such briefs were filed by the Waterfront Employers' Association of the Pacific Coast (later to be the Pacific Maritime Association) and by the National Association of Manufacturers. All urged the Supreme Court to reverse the Circuit Court. It did not do so. It saw the contractual overtime payment as not different from a differential for dangerous, hard, or disagreeable work. Furthermore, it saw that the contract was directed to an entire group of longshoremen whereas the FLSA was written to protect individual workers. It held that the straight-time hours could be the regular working hours only to those who worked in those hours.[5] Justice Felix Frankfurter thought that the majority had disregarded "industrial realities," saying, "No time is a good time needlessly to sap the principle

---

[4] Bureau of National Affairs, *Wage Hour Cases*, vol. 6, 1947, pp. 527ff.
[5] *Ibid.*, vol. 8, 1949, pp. 20–39.

of collective bargaining," but he pointed to the long-run way out for the industry, that is, to appeal to Congress.

Long before such redress could be obtained from Congress, the problems of negotiating a new agreement faced the industry. The Supreme Court decision was handed down on June 7, while negotiations commenced on June 22, with the current contract expiring on August 21. The major obstacle to reaching an agreement was the inability to devise a mutually acceptable plan that would solve the "overtime-on-overtime" issue. Other issues could hardly be considered until this major one was disposed of. While the ILA had supported the employers before the courts, the negotiating committee was unwilling to give up conditions which the union had won for longshoremen through collective bargaining. They looked upon their agreements as far more beneficial to the men than the standards prescribed in the FLSA. They were adamant in refusing to modify their traditional work and pay pattern. The employers, who considered that they were already paying high straight-time rates, plus 50-per-cent contract premiums, would not agree to renew an agreement that would saddle them with pyramided overtime liabilities.[6]

Taft-Hartley

Numerous meetings were held, particularly after mid-July, when formal demands were exchanged. In mid-August, with the deadline fast approaching and with every prospect of a strike, Cyrus Ching, director of the Federal Mediation and Conciliation Service (FMCS), reported failure to resolve the dispute.[7] A threatened strike of seagoing workers had been averted in June, by invoking the "emergency procedures" of the Taft-Hartley Act. An eighty-day injunction was then in effect in the offshore industry and was set to run until September 2. It was hardly likely that President Harry S. Truman, having already invoked the procedures under the Taft-Hartley Act in the dispute of seagoing workers, would have refrained from the use of them in

[6] New York Times, Aug. 17, 1948, p. 43.
[7] New York Times, July 13, 1948, p. 47, Aug. 18, p. 51.

the longshore situation. Consequently, he promptly named a Taft-Hartley Board of Inquiry.

The Board of Inquiry in the longshore dispute was inadequate, if not an outright mistake. The board itself realized its general impotence to do anything about the basic problem.[8] The parties also realized the inadequacy of the so-called "emergency" machinery. They sent a joint request to President Truman in October, asking for the establishment of a reconstituted fact-finding board with powers of recommendation, a power denied to a Taft-Hartley board. They desperately wanted to find a way out of the impasse. Ryan went so far as to say that Congress should be called back into a special session to enact legislation to take care of it, and he called upon Mayor William O'Dwyer to intervene with the President.[9]

The procedures under the Taft-Hartley Act provided for a rank-and-file vote on the employers' last offer if a settlement was not reached in sixty days. The Board of Inquiry convened on October 19 to receive the employers' "last offer." At this time the NYSA gave a new wage offer of ten cents an hour and a specific overtime clause, contingent on its legality under the FLSA. The ILA offered to accept the NYSA proposal on wages and overtime, provided that the NYSA was willing to accept an ILA program providing for a four-hour daily guarantee, a welfare fund, retroactivity of wages to August 1, a one-year instead of a two-year contract, and various improvements in working conditions. The NYSA rejected the ILA proposition and resubmitted a "last offer" to the Board of Inquiry.[10]

The Strike

The employers' "last offer" was rejected by a vote of 12,436 to 2,502. Cyrus Ching recommended an armistice of three weeks

[8] U.S. Board of Inquiry, *Final Report to the President in the Labor Dispute in the Maritime Industry*, June 3, 1948; see 11 *Labor Arbitration Reports* 388ff, 1948.

[9] *New York Times*, Oct. 2, 1948, p. 31, Oct. 6, p. 59, Oct. 12, p. 51.

[10] *New York Times*, Oct. 19, 1948, p. 55, Oct. 20, p. 59, Oct. 22, p. 51, Oct. 27, p. 55.

to get additional time to work up some new approach. It appeared, however, that a strike was going to be averted after all when the parties, following a long session, came to an agreement which Ryan recommended to the men. It provided for a one-year contract, a revised work week, a four-hour guarantee with two exceptions, plus the employers' "final offer." But the men voted this down and a walkout followed, again as a wildcat strike on the part of the men in Local 791. But this time, because Sampson had not approved the terms of the settlement, a bitter feud between Ryan and Sampson was apparent. The strike, however, soon got the blessing of other union officials and Ryan did a complete about-face and stood with the men. The employers were quick to say the new crisis was solely attributable to the feud between Ryan and Sampson, which they saw as a struggle for power in a disorganized union. Ryan, on his part, attributed the strike to a double-barreled protest of the men against the FLSA and to a series of articles which had just run in the *New York Sun* dealing with crime on the waterfront, which, he said, angered the dockworkers because they were put in such a bad light.[11]

The strike spread to other cities as the men in Philadelphia, Boston, and Baltimore went out. On November 12, the officers of the ILA made the strike official, the first official one in twenty-eight years. The employers insisted that they would make no more concessions. Cyrus Ching suggested a "cooling-off" period and a presidential fact-finding board with power to make recommendations. Ryan said, "Well, the President will surely have to get into it. This is a national calamity. This harbor will clam up tight, even without picket lines."[12]

While Ching, the mayor, and others were trying to find the best approach, and Paul G. Hoffman, Economic Cooperation Administrator, was appealing to the ILA to allow Marshall Plan grain and coal to move to Europe, a mass meeting at Manhattan

[11] *New York Times*, Nov. 7, 1948, p. 53, Nov. 9, p. 55, Nov. 11, pp. 1, 31; cf. Malcolm Johnson, *Crime on the Labor Front* (New York: McGraw-Hill, 1950), which is based on the articles.

[12] *New York Times*, Nov. 13, 1948, p. 1.

Center was scheduled by dissidents in the ILA to press for payment of the overtime claims. Ryan and scores of leaders of the ILA and of other AFL unions formed a picket line at the Manhattan Center and distributed leaflets asserting the meeting had been called by the Communist party to seek control of the ILA and to sabotage the Marshall Plan. Nevertheless, some eight hundred men attended the meeting and Ryan's name was booed lustily.[13]

Negotiations resumed shortly and the parties had a joint session with Harry Weiss, of the Wage and Hour Office, to discuss the "overtime-on-overtime" problem. He was formally asked to postpone enforcement of the overtime claims until January, when Congress would be in session. The employers, seeking an end to the walkout, made an additional concession, appealing to the men to go back to work and promising a pension plan. The employers afterward offered a welfare plan instead. One employer felt this offer should settle the strike, but he said, "The only question is whether the Union can untangle its own internal conflict long enough to put this proposition before the men for their vote." The ILA leaders thought the employers' settlement formula was "too vague" for submission to the men.[14]

The employers became impatient at long delays, which they attributed to the 125-man Wage Scale Committee of the ILA, whose members strolled in and out of the bargaining sessions, injecting local and sectional issues into the discussions.[15] The employers felt that even when the Wage Scale Committee accepted something it was never clear whether they could get the approval of the rank and file.

The turning point in the strike was the receipt of a telegram from the secretary of labor, advising that he would support legislation in the Eighty-first Congress to validate in principle the traditional form of contract in the longshoring industry. With

[13] New York Times, Nov. 16, 1948, p. 35.
[14] New York Times, Nov. 20, 1948, p. 1, Nov. 21, pp. 1, 48, Nov. 22, p. 1, Nov. 23, p. 1.
[15] New York Times, Nov. 24, 1948, p. 10.

this assurance, other issues were soon resolved with the aid of federal mediators, who "nudged" the parties a little and met with them separately. Terms were agreed upon on November 24: an improved vacation, providing for one week of vacation pay after 800 hours of employment and two weeks after 1,350 hours of employment; a 13-cent-an-hour increase in wages, retroactive to August 21; and a welfare plan. Although Ryan submitted the terms of settlement without recommendation, the men approved the terms and the strike ended on November 28.[16]

While the operators felt that they had suffered from "an old-fashioned shellacking" and were gloomy about the increased costs that the new terms would impose upon them, ILA officials were pleased; but some insurgents in Brooklyn called a meeting to keep the strike going. This later move was characterized by Ryan as "the usual Communist attempt" and it amounted to nothing.[17]

The Legislative Battle

Following the settlement, the Department of Labor and its administrator of the Wage and Hour Division approved the language of a bill introduced into the House at the request of the AFL to outlaw overtime-on-overtime in the future. Many testified at the hearings because the issue had implications across the nation. Most companies in the longshoring industry claimed they faced bankruptcy, and government agencies involved in extensive shipping activities during the war also faced tremendous liabilities. Hence, considerable pressure developed to make the legislation retroactive to wipe out liabilities and nullify pending claims. The Wage and Hour administrator delayed prosecution of suits until Congress had an opportunity to act.

The draft of the bill prepared by the Department of Labor applied to all industries, but upon recommendation of the Committee on Education and Labor, the bill was limited to the longshore and building and construction industries. It provided that

[16] *New York Times,* Nov. 25, 1948, p. 1, Nov. 26, p. 1.
[17] *New York Times,* Nov. 27, 1948, p. 1, Nov. 28, pp. 1, 66.

premium rates, not less than one and one-half times the rate established in good faith for like work, could be credited toward overtime payments required under the FLSA.

Testimony on the bills during seven full days was voluminous and revealing, indeed, of many opposing and discordant voices in the longshore industry. Louis Waldman, counsel for the ILA, read a statement for Ryan, laying blame for most of the "over-time-on-overtime" suits to the machinations of Communists and their followers and, in his own statement, stressed the same point. Both criticized the efforts of opponents or enemies to discredit the ILA by charges that it did not represent the men and lacked internal democracy. Both thought it strange that "the natural foes of democracy—are ironically the champions of democracy in unions where they have failed to get a foothold." Each charged that the suits by individuals against the employers were promoted "by the Communists to further their ends . . . to undermine the ILA."[18] No doubt they exaggerated this aspect of the situation for there were others who were differently motivated, simply pushing an opportunity to gain a windfall.

Congress was impressed by the arguments favorable to the pending bills limiting the liabilities and giving retroactive effect so as to "wash out" the liabilities. Legislation accepted the nego-tiated arrangement as being in compliance with the FLSA, and the lawsuits were nullified.

The issues raised about the ILA and its leadership, the rebel-liousness witnessed in the ranks of the longshoremen—although it would turn out to be much less ideological than some of the past incidents would imply—and the generally poor character of the labor-management relationship were simply a foretaste of much more complex problems.

[18] Senate, Committee on Labor and Public Welfare, *To Clarify the Overtime Compensation Provisions of the Fair Labor Standards Act of 1938, as Amended; Hearings before the Subcommittee*, 81st Cong., 1st Sess., 1949, pp. 636–637.

4 | The Strike in 1951:
Challenge of the Rank and File

Although the strike in 1951 echoed earlier ones, the reverberations were louder. It was more complex and revealed the problems besetting the industry. Many of the actors—including many of the same persons—played roles similar to previous ones. The lessons of 1945 and the echoes in the intervening episodes—particularly in the "overtime-on-overtime" dispute—had little, if any, effect; difficulty in learning was to be symptomatic of the industry for years.

The meetings of the ILA in July and August, the convention of the Atlantic Coast District, and the meetings of the Wage Scale Committee and of the district councils produced an accumulation of demands with little winnowing. At the convention Local 791 presented an elaborate set of demands and—of more interest because of what was to follow and in light of the rebellious opposition to Ryan in 1945, 1947, and 1948—introduced a motion, unanimously adopted, reaffirming Ryan as "life president." He had been given life tenure in 1943, but Local 791's resolution, affirmed that the life office was a fitting tribute to Ryan's "successful campaign against the Communists who sought to invade the East Coast waterfront." The motion also condemned those who called him a dictator.[1]

The ILA constitution was revised to give the national office more control over recalcitrant locals and to provide for an executive vice-president. Patrick ("Packy") J. Connolly was unani-

[1] *New York Times*, July 21, 1951, p. 23.

mously elected without contest. He had previously been serving as a vice-president and as the president of the Atlantic Coast District. His election over the organization's seventeen other area vice-presidents, most of whom outranked him in seniority, was an indication that he was "heir apparent" to the leadership.[2]

After the convention, the various district councils scheduled meetings. The New York District Council met on August 25 to review the bargaining demands and prepare for a meeting on September 4 of the Wage Scale Committee, which would finally set the demands to be presented to the NYSA on September 10, leaving three weeks to achieve a settlement prior to the termination of the current agreement on September 30.[3]

The Opening of Negotiations

When negotiations began on September 10, Ryan presented the ILA demands to the NYSA.[4] In the traditional manner, each member reviewed them separately, and on September 18 the NYSA produced an offer of an eleven-cents-an-hour increase in a "package proposal," saying their offer was within the Wage Stabilization Board's formula (the Korean War was on and a wage stabilization program was in effect) but also that the offer was conditioned on the union's acceptance of certain changes in the agreement and on the inclusion of a provision calling upon the ILA to cooperate in preventing sporadic work stoppages, which had caused serious loss to companies and injured the reputation of the port. The ILA spokesmen were quick to reject the offer as "absolutely inadequate." Nevertheless, following some long bargaining sessions, progress was made as each side made concessions, with the employers agreeing to a slightly higher wage and welfare rate and one shape-up a day and with the ILA giving up its demand for an eight-hour guarantee, except that

[2] *New York Times*, July 29, 1951, p. 80. Although he did not overshadow Ryan, he was soon to come into his own as a real leader of the ILA. When Ryan resigned in 1953, he became the chief negotiator for the ILA as well as General Organizer, see below, p. 254.

[3] *New York Times*, Aug. 25, 1951, p. 23.

[4] *New York Times*, Sept. 11, 1951, p. 49.

men continued on the job after lunch would get at least eight hours' pay.[5]

Even so, with about a week to the deadline, negotiations hit a snag, and the FMCS intervened, asking the parties to intensify their efforts. The ILA then presented a new hiring proposal to the employers. But ILA officials, not unmindful of the possibility of rank-and-file dissenters, and fearing that negotiations might not be concluded by October 1, sent a telegram in the name of the Wage Scale Conference Committee to every local union asking that a special meeting be arranged (1) to receive a report from their delegates concerning the progress of negotiations and, if negotiations were not concluded before October 1, (2) to grant an extension.[6] An extension was granted and negotiations continued through October 3, when all issues were resolved.

The Wage Scale Committee met the next day to decide whether to submit the settlement with or without a recommendation. A disparity between the vacation and welfare eligibility clauses was brought to light. Eligibility under the welfare clause had been reduced from 800 hours to 700 hours of employment during a year but eligibility for a week's vacation stood at 800 hours and at 1,350 hours for a two-week vacation.

As the parties met on October 8 to begin negotiations of the so-called craft agreements—it had always been the practice to negotiate the longshore agreement first and then turn to the other agreements—the ILA proposed to reopen the longshore negotiations for the purpose of equalizing the disparate eligibility clauses. The employers were prepared to reopen the contract and equalize vacation and welfare eligibility if the committee would recommend the contract to the membership. All except two or three on the Wage Scale Committee agreed. Those who said they could not—not that they would not—were

[5] *New York Times,* Sept. 19, 1951, p. 53, Sept. 21, p. 53, Sept. 26, p. 53.
[6] *New York Times,* Sept. 27, 1951, p. 55; Sept. 28, p. 47; Sept. 29, p. 29; N.Y. State, Department of Labor, "Board of Inquiry on Longshore Industry Work Stoppage, Report of Proceedings," 3 vols., cited hereafter as "Board of Inquiry, Proceedings." See vol. 1, no. 5, take 1, p. 18.

still willing to report and make it clear to the membership that in their judgment that it was the best contract to be obtained. The employers then granted a week's vacation for 700 hours of work and two weeks for 1,200 hours of work a year.[7] Both sides thought approval was "virtually assured."

A special edition of the *Longshore News* was distributed to the members summarizing the terms of settlement. The ballot read, "Do you favor the employers' proposition—"yes" or "no"? The voting was conducted by the respective locals and the results telephoned to headquarters. In the Port of New York two-thirds favored approval, 6,552 for and 3,031 against; but it was a modest-sized vote. Outside the Port of New York in the Atlantic Coast District (none of the employers in the other ports had been involved) 4,531 voted for and 1,335 against, making for a total of 11,083 for and 4,366 against. However, in several locals in Manhattan—numbers 791, 895, 1124, and 1258—and one local in Brooklyn—number 808—the majority voted "no"; and the majority in all four locals in Boston voted "no."

On completion of the tabulation on the night of October 11, a telegram was sent to the NYSA, notifying the employers of the results, confirmed by letter next day. In turn, the NYSA notified its members and instructed them to comply with the new agreement.[8] On October 12 the parties began living under the new contract, and the members of ILA who worked accepted the pay and other terms.

The Wildcat Strike

Dissidents in Local 791 were not satisfied with the wage settlement. On October 15 they walked out. The unofficial work stoppage quickly spread to the other locals that had voted

[7] "Board of Inquiry, Proceedings," vol. 1, no. 5, take 2, p. 8; *New York Times*, Oct. 9, 1951, p. 51.

[8] "Board of Inquiry, Proceedings," vol. 1, no. 5, take 3, pp. 1–3; New York State, Department of Labor, *Final Report to the Industrial Commissioner from Board of Inquiry on Longshore Industry Work Stoppage, October–November, 1951*, pp. 35–36; hereafter cited as *Board of Inquiry, Final Report*.

against acceptance, and gradually spread beyond. Sampson supported the men from the outset, as he had not in the stoppage in 1945. Subsequently he said, "Our men went out because they felt that the contract negotiated by the wage scale committee did not fit into what they thought they were entitled to." He claimed that during negotiations he had said, "[If] you can't give this money which we are asking—give it [the issue] to the Wage Stabilization Board and let them decide." Sampson apparently held this to be futile because the WSB had cut down shipping industry rates to the formula, and it was not believed longshoremen could get more.[9]

John Dwyer, one of the dissidents in Local 791 who assumed leadership and who was later to become even more active, visited Ryan and voiced his complaints about the settlement. It is reported that Ryan said, "Johnny, you get a majority and I'll lead you." Later, Dwyer said, "When Mr. Ryan told me 'get a majority' I went out and told all the men that and . . . came back to Ryan's office, only to have Ryan say, 'I don't listen to no minority group.'" Regarding reopening of negotiations, Ryan said, "I wouldn't lower the dignity of the International to open up negotiations."[10]

As the wildcat strike spread, ILA leaders denied implication but admitted their inability to stop it. Ryan described the Manhattan strikers as "honest dock workers with sincere grievances," but at the mention of the Brooklyn dissidents he flared up, accusing Bridges' men as the instigators in that borough. He said, "We will meet Bridges' strong-arm squads with our own squads —we're not looking for trouble but if that's what they want they'll get it." An official of Local 808, in Brooklyn, thought that some of the boys who were out would soon shape up because they "are beginning to realize that they fell for Communist propaganda."[11] But the strike continued to gain momentum and,

[9] "Board of Inquiry, Proceedings," vol. 1, no. 5, take 4, p. 9, take 6, p. 11.
[10] "Board of Inquiry, Proceedings," vol. 1, no. 5, take 4, pp. 8–9, and take 5, p. 12.
[11] *New York Times*, Oct. 17, 1951, p. 1.

to some observers, appeared to be out of control. In Brooklyn possible Communist influence was another force of great portent for the future. Anthony (Tony) Anastasia, later to rise to prominence in the ILA, tried unsuccessfully to stop the strike. Climbing atop a sound truck, he exhorted strikers to return to work. "I am Anastasia, one of the head foremen on the water-front," he shouted. "This is one place you gotta work. If you don't, I supply the men. This is Army Base controlled by United States Army. I was here yesterday and I'm back as a good American citizen." When the men ignored him, he sent seventy-five of his men into the base. As they arrived, one of the strikers, Salvatore Brocco, a hatch boss, climbed atop a truck and shouted, "Anyone who calls us Commies is a damn' liar. We are patriotic. We have worked this base since before the war. Gene Sampson is our man and a better leader than Joe Ryan." Turning toward Anastasia, who stood glaring at him, he yelled, "Get those stooges out of there and we'll go in." Anastasia ordered his men out and three hundred others went in, but at noon they walked out again and the situation steadily deteriorated.

Paul Hall, leader of the SIU (Seafarers), sought unsuccessfully to induce strikers in Brooklyn to return. After a couple of days, Ryan said that he could do no more; the insurgents, he declared, "must decide for themselves whether or not they want to work . . . the next move is up to them." After three days three thousand were out on thirty-three piers, but many piers were still unaffected, East River, half of Brooklyn, Staten Island, and New Jersey.[12]

Sampson, on the eighteenth, announced that he would take over leadership of the strike, saying, "I'm sick and tired of these references to Communism that emanate from Ryan's head-quarters and elsewhere. . . . These men who refuse to work are more patriotic than any of their critics." Acting Mayor Joseph T. Sharkey told the city labor relations director to take steps to settle the unauthorized walkout, making reference to "our fighting men on the Korean front."[13]

[12] New York Times, Oct. 18, 1951, p. 1.
[13] New York Times, Oct. 19, 1951, p. 1.

On the fifth day, the strike spread. Things began to happen in staccato fashion. A "pull-them-out" motorcade of two hundred cars roamed the waterfront in Brooklyn. Ryan met with insurgent leaders in a stormy session, insisting that the union had a contract and saying, "You are a minority group." When one of the strikers retorted that they would soon represent the majority, Ryan said, "If the majority go out then that is a problem for the International . . . and we'll meet it if it comes. But it is now an outlaw strike. We wouldn't have any kind of an organization if we failed to carry out our agreement." Nevertheless, the insurgents went right out to try to spread the strike further, insisting that negotiations had to be reopened.[14]

The insurgents held a mass meeting at Manhattan Center on Saturday afternoon, October 20. Several resolutions were passed, including one to call in Anastasia's membership book because he was considered to be working as a strikebreaker.[15]

The port is usually quiet on the weekend, but Monday seemed just as quiet. By sundown the whole port seemed at a standstill. Furthermore, the strike spread to Boston and Baltimore. The harbor in New York was congested enough to require an embargo on incoming cargo by rail.[16]

The feud between Sampson and Ryan was paradoxical inasmuch as both were out of Local 791, but the Chelsea local was beset by perennial factionalism under the surface. Where did the local leaders stand, with Ryan or with Sampson, or really with neither? Newspapers reported that they were with Sampson. Yet, was Sampson the undisputed boss?

The Executive Committee of the Atlantic Coast District Council, in order to "put an end to irresponsible talk," directed Ryan to call upon Cyrus Ching, director of the FMCS, to name

[14] *New York Times,* Oct. 20, 1951, pp. 1, 8.

[15] *New York Times,* Oct. 21, 1951, p. 1.

[16] *New York Times,* Oct. 23, 1951, p. 1. Daniel J. Donovan, vice-president of the ILA in Boston, said that the work stoppage was a "rebellion against New York mobsters who have a stronghold on the ILA and against a group who sold us out by accepting an entirely unsatisfactory contract."

a three-man commission to conduct hearings on all phases of the dispute. The federal mediators at work, meeting with the ILA leaders and the dissenters, were accomplishing little. Ryan would not reopen negotiations, saying, "We cannot allow a minority to nullify a majority decision. We have both a legal and moral responsibility in this situation." AFL leaders, particularly those in the Maritime Trades' Department, including Hall, supported this view. But, as in 1945, the NMU, in opposition to its rival, the Seafarers, pledged support to "the striking dockers."[17]

Some of the dissidents called for a reballoting, claiming a lack of responsible supervision over the polls and in counting the votes. They wanted to vote under the supervision of a disinterested third-party like the Honest Ballot Association.[18] Sampson offered to return to work if such a new ballot was promised. This was rejected by the Executive Committee.

The appearance of leaflets enunciating various demands made it clear that the dissidents were not in agreement about what they wanted. Some wanted 15 cents more on the basic wage. Some wanted a guarantee of eight hours of work. Others wanted to stop the splitting of gangs.[19]

Clyde Mills, assistant national director of the FMCS, joined the team of three federal mediators. He met with Ryan and, in different rooms, with Sampson and other rebel leaders. Up to this point no meetings with representatives of the NYSA had been called, because the dispute was considered strictly a union squabble in which the employers were bystanders. Meanwhile, the Chamber of Commerce sent a message to Governor Thomas E. Dewey saying it was "shocked and bewildered" and asked him to pick a special deputy attorney general to conduct "a complete investigation of New York's waterfront situation."[20]

After three days of intensive effort the federal mediators withdrew, saying that the situation was intolerable because of the

[17] *New York Times*, Oct. 24, 1951, pp. 1, 21.
[18] *New York Times*, Oct. 25, 1951, p. 24.
[19] *Ibid.*
[20] *Ibid.*, pp. 1, 24.

outbursts of shouting and name-calling between the rival groups and that the dispute had to be resolved within the union. In bowing out, the federal mediators could only recommend that the work stoppage be ended and the employees return to work. President Truman also called on the strikers to return to work. Sampson angrily accused Mills of bias.[21]

Loyal ILA supporters began to assert themselves concertedly. Two hundred dock workers entered Pier 92 in Manhattan, pressing through a group of pickets of equal size. The police, having been alerted to the move, had expected them to enter by making a flanking move, but the men went straight in amid jostling, swinging fists, and unfriendly words. The police quickly broke up the fighting, but bruised knuckles and black eyes led ILA officials to protest to Mayor Vincent Impellitteri about inadequacy of police protection.[22]

Roving pickets and violence became marks of the strike. Ryan sent a telegram to President Truman, saying that longshoremen had to fight their way through long picket lines, augmented by "several thousand strangers . . . evidently [being paid with funds] . . . contributed by various subversive organizations." He said, nevertheless (lacking some internal consistency in his statement), that "the Port of New York is open" and dock workers the next morning would "go through and over" picket lines if necessary, adding, "The minority who feel they have any grievance to adjust can do so before any tribunal that you may suggest." Simultaneously, Sampson sent a telegram to the President saying, "We maintain, and are prepared to prove, that Ryan's proposed agreement was never submitted to, considered by, or decided on, by all the locals affected or their members and definitely was never ratified by a majority of the membership affected. We urge you, Mr. President, to set up an emergency impartial body to review this issue and our needs for honest balloting machinery. If we are thus assured of justice we will immediately urge the men to return to work and await and

---

[21] *New York Times*, Oct. 26, 1951, pp. 1, 15.
[22] *New York Times*, Oct. 28, 1951, p. 1.

accept the decision of that body." When Ryan was told of Sampson's telegram, he said, "We offered to do the very same thing before the federal mediators [and] Sampson rejected the proposal."[23]

Concurrently with the withdrawal of the federal mediators, Merlyn S. Pitzele, chairman of the New York State Board of Mediation, announced that the board would enter the strike if it could "go in without doing any harm . . . we will continue to analyze it . . . if we feel that we can do even the slightest good, we will act."[24]

Workers continued to enter piers 90 and 92 on the North River but had to brave massed pickets and threats "to get you scabbies when you leave tonight." Alex Di Brizzi, the leader on Staten Island, advised the men to resume work. Yet a new assurance from Ryan that there would be a massive return to all piers failed to materialize. Governor Dewey, no doubt to give some force to the move, announced publicly on October 29 that the State Board of Mediation would intervene, but said, with political overtones, "The State of New York has stood aside while city and federal agencies attempted to find a solution. . . . Now the Board will offer its services and its chairman will continue to keep me informed of all developments." Pitzele, after a meeting with Sampson and a large group of his aides, said, with characteristic aplomb, the situation was "far from hopeless."[25]

But the situation continued to be highly complex. Insurgents tightened their control at certain piers as pickets in some areas blocked back-to-work movements. Meanwhile, the NYSA filed charges with the NLRB against five insurgent locals for breach of contract. Employers hoped that the NLRB would move to have the locals enjoined. Sampson wired Governor Dewey to get the negotiations opened and they would return to work. At the same time he participated in setting up a formal Strike Committee of twenty-three insurgents and announced that this

[23] *New York Times*, Oct. 29, 1951, pp. 1, 37.
[24] *Ibid.*, p. 1.
[25] *New York Times*, Oct. 30, 1951, pp. 1, 49.

committee would speak and make any "final or binding commitments." Peter Johnson, who was to play an important role from this point on, became their attorney.[26]

Pitzele worked vigorously but could not gain sufficient acceptance to make progress. While it was hoped that the State Board of Mediation could succeed where the federal mediators had failed, the fact was that state mediators had never been effective on the docks before, and they were no more successful this time. Pitzele found that neither Ryan nor Sampson would yield. The insurgents insisted that a contract did not exist, since it was not signed. Ryan, of course, held that it had been put into effect on October 12, three days before the walkout started, after ratification and official notification to the employers. When Pitzele could made no headway he recommended, under a state law passed in 1941, that the Industrial Commissioner establish a board of inquiry. Concurrently, twenty-four steamship companies in New Jersey obtained a restraining order to prevent roving pickets from New York from appearing on New Jersey piers.[27]

The Board of Inquiry and Its Recommendations

Commissioner Edward Corsi, on November 2, appointed a board of inquiry.[28] Sampson, at the outset, served notice that the insurgents would not recognize the board; but the board held subpoena powers and Sampson and his group had little choice. When the board convened they were present. Concurrently a group in Local 791 asked Sampson to hold a local meeting to vote on a return to work; they also appealed to the president of the New York District Council to call a meeting—which he

[26] *New York Times*, Oct. 31, 1951, pp. 1, 25. Johnson's father had been a longshoreman and Johnson was raised around the piers.

[27] *New York Times*, Nov. 1, 1951, pp. 1, 18.

[28] Professor Martin P. Catherwood, Dean of the New York State School of Industrial and Labor Relations, chairman; Msgr. John P. Boland, a member of the State Board of Mediation; and Dean Alfange. George J. Mintzer was named as counsel and Arthur Stark, executive secretary of the State Board of Mediation, was chosen as executive secretary.

could do under the ILA rules if petitioned to do so, provided local leaders refused. These anti-Sampson men complained that they had been "railroaded" into the strike and wanted an opportunity to vote on the question.[29]

As the fact-finders went quickly to work, the split in Local 791 seemed to widen. Ryan said that the men were clamoring for "an unintimidated meeting" and a chance to vote on returning to work. A petition was presented to local leaders, as well as to Sampson. The latter denounced it as illegal, saying six of the ten signatories had not paid their monthly dues. The petition was also presented to the president of the District Council and to Packy Connolly. The latter said a meeting would be called for Monday morning, November 5, at St. Bernard's Parish School. Accusing Ryan and his supporters of trying to "supersede Local 791's autonomy," Sampson promptly said that his men would picket the school. Ryan rejoined that to picket the school would make "as much sense as the rest of the stoppage." The meeting was effectively blocked, however, by eight hundred insurgents. Sampson was there to tell the crowd that the twenty-three-member-strike committee had voted to "stand pat" on their original demands.[30]

The Board of Inquiry opened its hearings as scheduled, on the afternoon of November 5. Sampson now said he welcomed the hearing, yet, when invited to open with a presentation, he declined, saying, "We are here as defendants to defend what we think is right. The complainants are here to force on us something we don't think is right. We feel they should present their case first." Attorney Waldman accepted the opportunity to speak—but, he was careful to say, not as a complainant. Also, while he was quite willing to give the ILA's version of the facts, he stressed that the ILA was not conceding that there was a strike, lockout, or other labor dispute within the meaning of the state's labor law, because it might interfere with processes in-

[29] *New York Times*, Nov. 3, 1951, pp. 1, 28.
[30] *New York Times*, Nov. 4, 1951, pp. 1, 36, Nov. 5, p. 1, Nov. 6, p. 1.

ternal to the ILA and might deprive thousands of idle members from entitlement to unemployment compensation. Thereafter, he covered in detail the background of the controversy.[31]

The Board of Inquiry, together with Commissioner Corsi, met in an all-night session with the insurgent strike committee on the evening of November 8, finally effectuating a return to work at 1:00 P.M. on Friday, November 9, to permit a full inquiry into the controversy under circumstances more propitious for it than if the stoppage continued.

Aside from the assurances that the Board of Inquiry gave that a full investigation would be made and that no strikers would be discriminated against, there were a number of reasons why the stoppage came to an end: the injunction in New Jersey and an expectation, in spite of the New York antiinjunction statute, that a similar one in Manhattan and Brooklyn might issue on the ground that the stoppage was not a labor dispute; the fact that a number of longshoremen, approximately five thousand, were at work and there were signs that the drift back was increasing; and the approaching holidays and increasing pressure from families to reestablish the income stream. But the Board of Inquiry could not give assurance that there would be another vote on the agreement or that negotiations would be reopened—the things the Strike Committee had continuously demanded.

The work stoppage could not end without some difficulties, because the waterfront is not like a factory which can open up operations more or less simultaneously. Men are hired for the ships that are in the harbor or as they arrive and, at best, work requirements are not regular. There were charges of discrimination, both ways—that is, by insurgents that Ryan's men prevented them from returning and by Ryan's men that the insurgents were preventing them from returning. But after the long stoppage the port did return to normal operations and the Board of Inquiry went about its task of interrogating and investigating to

[31] "Board of Inquiry, Proceedings," vol. 1, no. 5, take 1, p. 6ff; *New York Times*, Nov. 6, 1951, pp. 1, 25.

ascertain the facts about the controversy and to make recommendations.

The Board of Inquiry took its job seriously, persistently carrying on through fifteen days of private and public hearings, during which more than thirty witnesses were heard under direct, and cross, examination by respective counsel—the testimony comprises over two thousand pages and over eighty exhibits were received.[32] Numerous conferences and discussions with individuals and groups were held, too.

Some said the board exceeded its authority. It certainly did not limit itself simply to the question of ratification and validity of the collective agreement but took evidence and gathered information on a broad range of subjects. It interpreted its assignment as extending to the prevention of work stoppages in the industry through improvement of conditions as well as to the settlement of the existing controversy.

It gave considerable attention to collective bargaining, of course, but this led to consideration of conditions within the ILA and its constituent bodies, and to employment conditions and hiring practices. Recommendations were made on a number of subjects: the status of the agreements; voting procedures for ratification; election of delegates to the Wage Scale Committee; grievance procedures; a fact-finding board composed of public representatives to resolve problems internal to the ILA; nondiscrimination for participation in the strike; and implementation of the board's recommendations. It also discussed, but without making recommendations, public loading, communism, criminal activities, and the problem of Local 968 and its complaint of discrimination against Negro longshoremen.[33]

The full report deserves review because it provides an understanding of the problems which then existed in the industry, but it cautioned that "problems and relationships on the waterfront

[32] "Board of Inquiry, Proceedings."
[33] *Board of Inquiry, Final Report*, p. 5, *passim*.

are so varied, complex, and of such long standing" that a simple solution would be impossible.[34]

The board invited the ILA, the Strike Committee, and the NYSA to present recommendations, but it also invited persons or other groups to appear or give information. The Port of New York Authority, for one, registered detailed complaints. The board reviewed recommendations from the parties[35] before formulating its own. The arguments and differences between the ILA and the insurgents, and the position of the NYSA, become clearer in juxtaposition to the board's recommendations; the reactions of the three parties to the board's findings and recommendations also clarify their positions.

Shortly after the hearings got under way, Governor Dewey announced that the New York State Crime Commission would undertake a full-scale investigation of crime on the waterfront. Consequently, the Board of Inquiry did not examine the subject. The board devoted much time to the question of ratification of the agreement. The insurgent Strike Committee contended that delegates to the Wage Scale Committee had not been properly chosen and that most were subservient to Ryan and a small group of top officials, that delegates had not been given sufficient opportunity to have their views presented and discussed, that the ILA had failed to give sufficient notice before balloting and failed to inform the membership of the new proposals, that balloting in the locals had been unsupervised and irregular, and that there had been fraud in some locals in tabulating and reporting the vote, as well as ballot-box stuffing. The Strike Committee, therefore, urged the board to find that the agreement was not duly ratified and to order that negotiations between the ILA and the NYSA be reopened with new terms to be submitted to the membership for ratification.

The ILA challenged most of these allegations and contended that delegates had been properly chosen, that balloting procedures

[34] *Ibid.*, p. 3.
[35] They are included as appendixes to the final report.

had been supervised, and that there had been no consequential irregularities. It contended that balloting, tabulation, and reporting had been free from fraud and had been conducted in accordance with established ILA custom and practices. The ILA conceded that it had failed to give adequate notice of the proposals to the membership but explained this on the fact that, the agreement having expired on October 1, it had been urgent that balloting be done quickly. Waldman pointed out that the contract had not only been approved, it had been in effect for three days when the men walked out. He insisted that it was valid and that the actions of the dissidents should be recognized as unlawful.

The NYSA simply contended that it was duly notified that the agreement had been ratified and was in full force and binding; it urged the board so to find. The association said, "We certainly are not going to renegotiate something that we have negotiated and . . . [which was] accepted by a majority of the members . . . just because a . . . certain group or minority did not get everything . . . asked for . . . there'd be anarchy in the industrial relations between the employers and employees." Also, "We have done business on the basis of mutual understanding and confidence in each other's integrity once understandings are reached. We do not intend to reopen it even at the request of Mr. Ryan," let alone of the insurgents.[36]

Many critics charged that the basic cause of the stoppage was lack of democracy in the ILA, the prevalence of strong-arm control, the failure of employers—and union leaders as well—to assume the responsibilities their roles required, and the casual labor market, which bred evil practices associated with employment.

The ILA challenged the board's authority to delve into its internal affairs, but the board insisted that to fulfill its assignment it had to investigate all the claimed causes of the work stoppage. Waldman advised union officials not to answer questions on internal administration, "only those questions dealing with the

[36] "Board of Inquiry, Proceedings," no. 5, take 6, p. 12, take 7, p. 1.

issue before the Board," namely, the making of the contract and the balloting. When the board threatened to issue subpoenas to all local officers, Waldman took the position that, deplorable as it might be, the ILA would be compelled to resist, make an open and public fight, and take the board through every court of the state, if necessary, until the power and jurisdiction of boards of inquiry could be authoritatively determined. The issue was never pushed to such a resolution, although the ILA thought that it had won because the board did not take testimony on the matter. The board, however, called for suggestions on the subject by the three parties and the ILA itself set out an explicit list of requirements for internal governance.

Investigation of collective bargaining in the industry led into the matter of bargaining structure.[37] Who represented whom, and who had a right to participate in negotiations, and who had a right to vote on ratification of agreements? The board found that the employers had resisted pressure from the ILA to bargain for the whole Atlantic Coast District, insisting that bargaining covered only the Port of New York. Nevertheless, the board found that the employers in New York willingly met with the Wage Scale Committee. It recognized an anomaly in that the ILA talked only to the employers in the NYSA. This situation, however, had given little trouble over ratification before because the employees in the outports usually had voted the same as in New York.

The board's investigation also reached into employment conditions and hiring practices. Here, it did not simply rely on evidence from the hearings but sought out information. It called on Professor Leonard Adams of the New York State School of Industrial and Labor Relations to ferret out information on the demand for longshoremen, hiring practices, supply of longshoremen, and a review of plans for regularization of employment, and it included these in its report.

On December 6 the ILA and the NYSA presented their programs, but the insurgents did not, saying, "Our program is a

[37] "Board of Inquiry, Proceedings," vol. 1, no. 5, take 1, pp. 11–14.

reopening of the contract." Belatedly, on December 20, they submitted a statement.

The ILA's response was prefaced with the statement that its program was "to improve and further stabilize labor and industrial conditions in the port." It took pains to point out that "many of the projects embodied in this program have to do with matters clearly beyond the jurisdiction of the Board." It specifically stated that it was recommending some things in order to present "a complete, integrated program" but did not waive its charge that the board had overstepped its bounds. Although not so intended, the ILA statement and recommendations can be read as something of a confession, for if the union situation was as healthy as it would have people believe, why the need to set out so extensive a program? Naturally, it was defending itself, but in so doing it helped establish that an unwholesome situation existed.

It condemned wildcat strikes vigorously and urged the enforcement of contracts. It noted that the NYSA and the ILA, in their recent negotiations, had agreed to establish a joint committee to work out an effective solution to the problem of wildcat strikes. It now proposed its own plan for a portwide "Court of Industrial Justice," a high-sounding name for a more elaborate grievance system along the lines found in other industries. To improve balloting, it would begin negotiations earlier to allow more time for the early submission of results to the district organizations and to the membership, with careful control of voting and reporting of the results. Improvement of the internal administration within "some of the subdivisions" would be done "within the framework of the ILA constitution," but preserving the existing "large degree of autonomy" which the ILA held to be a virtue as long as it did not perpetuate conditions in any local which would "prevent it from living up to the normal standards of a democratic organization." The ILA insisted that the majority of its locals maintained democratic standards but it would conduct a survey to ascertain if any did not come up to them. All locals were to keep accurate records of finances, maintain bank accounts, and bond officers, and the financial affairs would be audited periodically. Kickbacks, it stated, were largely a thing of the past, but the ILA would do its utmost to cooperate with the police and the district attorneys "as we have in the past . . . to eliminate this vicious practice." Loan sharks were condemned as an evil preying on longshoremen, "a crime and should be wiped out by law." The ILA suggested, also, that employers should be prepared to make loans without interest up to approximately 75 per cent of wages in order to eliminate the men's need to resort to loan sharks. Pilferage, "unquestionably a problem facing our industry," would be reduced because the ILA would not defend anyone found guilty of it; but the ILA claimed that pilferage was largely a result of bad packing for which the shippers and exporters should assume responsibility. In conclusion, "progress would come through the process of collective bargaining and mutual understanding," and the ILA took credit for achieving "a high level of wages, reasonable hours, and excellent conditions of employment." It emphasized that the ILA was not a "johnny-come-lately" union "in fighting Communist saboteurs. . . . If our country today, as in the last war, feels safe and secure in the loyalty of the union men who work on our nation's piers, it is, we are proud to say, because we in the ILA have done our job well."[38]

In its response the NYSA avoided comment on the ILA's charges that the internal administration of the union was outside its province. In defending the practice of collective bargaining, it said that it had to "accept without question all persons designated by the responsible officials of the Union as the duly authorized members of the Union's negotiating committee." It wanted assurance that once negotiated terms had been accepted they would be observed, and it wanted effective discipline of violators. Regarding hiring practices it could say only that the existing shape-up "has been found by the employers and the Union best fitted to meet the needs of the industry." It rejected the notion of a hiring hall, insisting that it would have an adverse

[38] *Board of Inquiry, Final Report*, pp. 66–75.

impact on the industry. It explicitly rejected the Pacific Coast system of hiring by rotation but said that it would welcome, from competent sources, any other constructive suggestions for hiring. It did complain, however, that while the negotiated agreements gave employers the right to select hiring foremen, the ILA had insisted that such persons be approved by it, although the NYSA was willing to concede that hiring foremen should "give preference in hiring to men who have regularly worked on the pier."[39]

The Strike Committee's recommendations came in belatedly, after the board had reviewed both the ILA and NYSA statements. The tone is revealed in the following quotation:

There is a crying need for democratization. The rank and file member is not a voice crying in the wilderness. He is not even a voice. As a result of corruption, inefficiency and bland indifference aided and abetted by an undemocratic constitution, which has been rammed down the mouths of the rank and file, the ILA has become a feudal estate dedicated to the enrichment of a chosen few. The vast minority is exploited socially, financially and physically.

The Strike Committee wanted the Wage Scale Committee to be composed of at least 75 per cent nonofficeholding members, with the unit of contract negotiation being limited to the Port of New York and with parliamentary procedure to prevail in all meetings. It wanted central balloting locations, voting machines, voting on Sundays, checking names against particular ILA ledgers and stamping of members' books, and it wanted every local to have a meeting to acquaint the rank and file with the proposals. Existing grievance machinery was a farce—members feared to use it and officials gave half-hearted representation. It wanted an impartial arbitrator to adjust all complaints, with any member having the right to appeal directly to the arbitrator. As for internal grievances in the ILA, it wanted all officers of the Atlantic Coast District to resign because they had forfeited their stewardship through misfeasance; and it wanted all incumbent officers of locals who had held office for five years or more without an

[39] *Board of Inquiry, Final Report,* pp. 75–79.

intervening election to submit to election. "Steady gangs," associated with given piers, should be recognized, and extra labor should be hired from paid-up membership; no labor from outside the area should be hired until all members of the local were hired. All individuals who had been employed more than 30 per cent of their time in the previous year in other industries should be eliminated from union roles. Each pier was to select a steward from members working on the pier. Finally, it recommended that the board find that negotiations in 1951 were never closed because there was no ratification and, hence, no contract. Therefore, negotiation of a new contract should be ordered.[40]

The board found no single factor that accounted for the work stoppage. It found many longshoremen dissatisfied with the terms of the settlement, with the balloting, and with the conduct of the internal affairs of the ILA. It found that the basic causes were of long standing. "The stoppage was an outbreak of a long-festering accumulation of complaints and dissatisfaction."

The finding of most immediate importance was that the agreement was validly ratified. It found, however, that many delegates to the Wage Scale Committee were not properly chosen, that the committee was dominated by Ryan and a small group of top officials, but it added that "such domination was not necessarily sinister . . . [because] delegates had reasonable opportunity to present their views and have them discussed." Although it found that balloting in several locals had not been properly supervised and that some locals had resorted to ballot-box stuffing and other acts of fraud, it found that these were not sufficient to set aside the election. Although much was to be desired in the conduct of the negotiations and in the procedures of ratification, it recommended that the agreement be recognized as in full force and effect.

It then set down its other recommendations seriatim and discussed the basis on which it arrived at them. Individual union members were unable to assert their rights under the contract and have their grievances taken up in a proper manner; that is,

[40] *Board of Inquiry, Final Report,* pp. 79–85.

grievance machinery was inadequate. Shop stewards did not exist on many piers, the responsibility of handling complaints resting with the delegate who normally was not on the pier, certainly not at work on the pier. Even where shop stewards existed, they functioned haphazardly. The board therefore recommended that the grievance machinery be improved by establishment of a permanent full-time arbitrator to serve for the duration of the agreement, to be selected by the ILA and the NYSA from a list supplied by the Industrial Commissioner. The arbitrator was to be given power to adjudicate all disputes under the contract, including claims of violations by employers, union, or employees, and to award financial damages if justified in any breach. Any member of the NYSA or the ILA was to be given the right to appeal directly to the arbitrator, who was to "use his best efforts and the influence of his office to maintain peaceful labor relations" and to "prevent labor disturbances, work stoppages, and strikes, irrespective of the causes from which they arise." He was also to serve as chairman and public member of the pension and welfare funds.

To complement machinery in the ILA constitution for filing of complaints against the International, the board recommended establishment of a body to be known as the "Fact-Finding Board for the Port of New York," consisting of three public members to be selected by the ILA from the list of arbitrators maintained by the New York State Board of Mediation. Any grievance not adjusted within the ILA within thirty days after the filing of a written complaint could be referred to this fact-finding board. It was to have the power to find the facts and make advisory recommendations to the executive board of the ILA, which would make final decisions. The ILA was to meet with the Industrial Commissioner for the purpose of implementing the recommendation.

With regard to practices internal to the ILA, the board found a failure to maintain democratic standards and procedures, to hold periodic elections in many locals, to have bank accounts in many locals, to hold regular meetings, to elect delegates to the Wage Scale Committee, to keep adequate records, to bond officers handling funds, to have financial affairs of each local audited by a certified public accountant, and to correct the practice of officers employing ILA members, that is, engaging in public loading. As a corrective the board endorsed the recommendations submitted by the ILA itself. Specifically, the ILA would make a survey of all its locals with respect to the observance of minimum standards of record keeping, bonding, auditing, meetings, elections, and admission of new members. The board only added that the Industrial Commissioner should consult with appropriate officials of the ILA not later than ninety days from the date of its report to ascertain what steps had been taken. The board recommended that all delegates to the Wage Scale Committee be elected at announced membership meetings, that all members should be allowed to nominate candidates, and that each local should keep a full record of its proceedings. All delegates were to be certified in writing by the president and secretary of the local, and no delegate could serve without credentials.

Regarding ratification of collective agreements, the board recommended that voting should continue to be by all members in the Atlantic Coast District, at least with respect to wages, and in the event that the vote in the Port of New York was against the agreement, it should constitute a veto. With respect to bargaining procedure the board recommended completion of negotiations two weeks before the termination of the contract, that in the interim special meetings be called in each local for explanation of the terms and conditions negotiated, that the actual vote be taken not less than ten days after the final proposition was circulated to the locals, that the balloting be at central polling places and preferably on Sunday afternoon, that voting machines be used, that voting be uniform and clearly specified in advance of the voting, that balloting be supervised by a committee of not less than six with at least half to be nonofficeholding members, that a record be made of all members who voted by checking their names against the ledger of the local and by stamping their union dues books, and that the committee members examine the final results in the presence of each other.

In approaching the subject of improving employment conditions and hiring practices, the board noted chronic excess supply of workers, unequal distribution of work, abuses in hiring such as "kickbacks" and "loan sharking," speedup of work and excessively long hours, and a general lack of regular attachment of workers to particular employers. It concluded that these were causes of unrest, intraunion difficulties, and unsettled labor-management relations. It doubted that "the present form of the 'shape-up' as it now operates is consistent with the employment conditions required to achieve good labor-management relations." Modification of the hiring system or an alternative was required, but it specifically declined to recommend or endorse any particular system. It noted that it was unfortunate that employers generally had lost control of selection of hiring foremen. It found, however, that "the system of employment, including hiring practices, wage-payment practices, the distribution of work, determination of the size of the work force, and related problems" were in need of a more thorough and extensive investigation than the board had been able to make.

Although the board did not go into the matter of crime on the waterfront, it easily found testimony and evidence of notorious practices such as pilferage, extortion, "kickbacks," and "loan sharking." It found that some organizers, public loaders, and hiring bosses had substantial criminal records. It said that it could understand why such men might find a haven in employment on the waterfront, but it was deeply concerned that men with serious criminal records could occupy key positions.

It was pointed out that public loaders were not employees of the steamship companies or trucking companies, but independent contractors. It made no extensive investigation but on testimony found that they acquired their operating rights by reason of force and intimidation, fixing charges at what the traffic would bear; that loading services were compulsory, whether needed or wanted, with cash payments on the side as a condition of getting cargo handled. But it left the question to the New York State Crime Commission.

Because charges of Communist involvement in the stoppage,

if not perpetration of it, had been bandied about so often, the board naturally had to look into this issue. Previously there had been some Communist involvement in waterfront disputes, but the board found both the ILA and the Strike Committee "singularly free from Communistic influence" and commended the ILA for its "diligent anti-Communist Policy—an important achievement in a critical industry." Yet it also said that to the extent that "communists vociferously supported the strike, it [was] clear that such support was wholly unsolicited by the Strike Committee."[41]

Peter Johnson, for the Strike Committee, said that the report of the board "violated the principles of logic" and "ignominiously arrived at an invalid conclusion," for the board found fraud at the polls but accepted the agreement as valid. He said, "We are appalled, . . . the report is despairing" and is "sophomoric with platitudes."[42] The ILA was even more critical and prepared a full bill of particulars. It warrants a detailed review, not because the ILA was able to absolve itself, but because it further reveals the state of affairs.

The ILA felt that the board's recommendations were such a flagrant offense to the labor movement that it called upon the AFL to make an investigation of the board and the report, asserting that governmental bodies should act within the laws which create them and not be usurpers and meddlers. It was angry because the board made recommendations on its internal affairs wholly unrelated to evidence adduced at the hearings. It charged that the board was making a farce out of collective bargaining and held that when it found there was a valid contract it should have found that no dispute existed with the employers, and it should have terminated its inquiry.

One by one the ILA analyzed the board's recommendations. It had no quarrel with the recommendation for the establishment of a permanent arbitrator—a very minor matter, it said, in light of the existing grievance machinery. It did not mind a single

[41] *Board of Inquiry, Final Report,* pp. 27–28.
[42] *New York Times,* Jan. 23, 1952, p. 18.

arbitrator, rather than a board of arbitration, but it felt that there was real vice in the recommendation to permit each individual, independent of the union, to appeal to the arbitrator. Such would be ridiculous and dangerous, particularly in the longshore industry, where dissidents and insurgents could use the privilege to harass and disrupt the union and good labor relations. Minorities, it was said, could "bypass majority rule, bypass the Local and Local representatives, bypass the International, and create for the ILA the maximum possible trouble." Little imagination was required "to foresee what would happen if the Board's recommendation were accepted. . . . The sworn enemies of our country and the ILA would have a field day. . . . The Communists [would have] an opportunity not only to create false grievances, . . . but to carry forward their fictitious charges." It charged that the board practically gave "a blank check to dissident, irresponsible groups and individuals." Similarly the ILA took exception to the recommendation regarding the establishment of a fact-finding board to hear internal organizational complaints. It insisted that the board acted "on no evidence of any kind in the record," whereas the ILA constitution provided for machinery dealing with charges, trials, and discipline involving officers of the union or individual members. The ILA resented the implications and rejected the recommendation flatly as a gratuitous insult, asserting that it was another example of the board meddling in the internal affairs of the ILA contrary to the power conferred by the law.

With regard to the recommendation concerning election of delegates to the Wage Scale Committee, the ILA said that nowhere did it appear that the method of election of the delegates was an issue in the wildcat strike. It noted that Sampson had admitted that he had been a regular delegate to the Atlantic Coast District Convention for over thirty years. The ILA pointed out that Sampson had testified that neither he nor any other delegates to the Wage Scale Committee objected to any member of that committee as having been improperly selected. Also, Local 791, of which Sampson was business agent, did not elect its five delegates, including Sampson. They had been appointed by the president of the local. Yet the ILA stated that the board, going out of its way, devoted a whole section of the report to this question and somehow related it to the wildcat strike. "Incidentally," it went on, this gave "the Board an opportunity to take another kick at the ILA."

The ILA held that the findings and recommendations concerning employment conditions and hiring practices were an invasion of the union's right to do its own collective bargaining. With regard to the right of employers to select their foremen, the ILA said that for the board to throw to the employers its weight in the scale of such bargaining was beyond comprehension. "Certainly," it said, "this question has no relevancy to the wildcat strike. There is no evidence whatever that this matter was the cause of the wildcat strike."

The ILA was very critical of the board for making recommendations on public loading about which no evidence was adduced in the record, while failing to investigate the matter of communist influence on the waterfront as a cause of the strike. While the ILA was careful to say that it did not consider Communist influence as *the* cause of the strike, it insisted that the Communists were *a* cause. The ILA felt that the board let slip a real opportunity to render a service to the community. It twitted the board for its "naive view of Communist activities on the waterfront . . . to expect that they would have a Communist . . . on the Strike Committee. That is not the way the Communists act." It specified failures of the board to meet its opportunity by not investigating who published the *Dockers News*, how the recruits were obtained to distribute it, who were the rank-and-file committees and how they functioned, and who their leaders were and how they were chosen. It insisted that the section of the report dealing with the communist question was so superficial that it was in fact a liability to the public.[43]

William Green, president of the AFL, upon complaint of the

43 ILA, Waldman and Waldman, "Statement of the International Long-

ILA appointed a committee of five to evaluate the report. Without delving into the merits of the dispute, the committee cited the implications for the labor movement, generally supporting many of the same points made by the ILA. It concluded that the law had been stretched, that the board had been officious and unwise. Noting that the board found the collective agreement valid, it was surprised that the board proceeded further and made recommendations which were in conflict with the agreement entered into. It found it ludicrous that having found the agreement valid it would recommend reopening. It was particularly critical of the recommendation giving the right to each individual member of the union in the first instance, and without regard to the union itself, to institute charges under the collective agreement. It felt the board was completely disregarding the authority of the union and depriving it of enforcement of the contract for which the union was responsible. Similarly, the committee was critical of the recommendation for the creation of a "Fact-Finding Board to hear internal organizational complaints of Union members, again evading the authority of the ILA in the management of its own internal affairs."[44]

Because of the allegations made concerning practices in various local unions, Ryan asked Waldman to make a study, giving him authority to make a broad inquiry. The various locals were ordered to produce their books and cooperate, and a rather extensive report was issued, based upon the responses of some sixty-odd locals. Although these responses may not have been completely accurate, the report contains interesting material about internal affairs in the ILA. It appears candid and fair and reveals a wide range of practice. Financial records varied considerably from local to local, reflecting some fair practice—as

shoremen's Association, AFL, on the Report, dated Jan. 22, 1952 of the Industrial Commissioner Corsi's Board of Inquiry" (mimeographed, 1952).

[44] AFL, Executive Council, "Report by the Committee of Five to Inquire into and Evaluate the Report of the New York State Board of Inquiry in Connection with the Claimed Difficulties Involving the Longshoremen in New York" (mimeographed; New York: AFL, 1952), p. 32.

judged against union practice generally—and very poor practice. Bank accounts were maintained by most of the locals, but nine had none. The state of the accounts was not revealed, nor was the relationship of bank accounts and other records considered, because this was held to be a task for certified public accountants. Election practice varied greatly with regard to tenure of office and notice and manner of elections. Likewise, the holding of membership meetings varied considerably regarding frequency, notice, and minutes. Salaries of officers were hardly ascertainable, and about one-third of the locals had no bonding of officers. Less than half the locals had their books audited by independent accountants; about one-third had their records audited by the trustees of the local. Nine locals, which had no accounting or auditing report, had periodic financial reports to the membership by the financial secretary or treasurer. Nine other locals had no audits or examination of financial reports at all. Admission to membership was variable, too, from place to place.

The report recommended a broad educational program: a seminar for local officers on parliamentary procedure, one for secretary-treasurers on proper bookkeeping and maintenance of financial records, and one for recording secretaries on the proper keeping of minutes. Also, it recommended that the ILA secure an educational director to develop programs for members concerning collective bargaining, safety, history and practice of unionism, and principles of government and citizenship.

Minimum standards to be observed by all local unions was recommended, including membership by written application only on a standard form provided to all locals; minimum standards of financial accounts with all income recorded and deposited in a bank account and with all payments recorded. These books would be audited at least annually by certified public accountants. All locals were directed to have regular membership meetings not less than once every three months on a fixed date and fixed place. Minutes of all such meetings should be kept. Elections should be held at least each four years, with salaries for all officials determined by the membership.[45] But little that was constructive ever followed from this report.

The strike of 1951, the investigation by the Board of Inquiry and its report, and the reactions of the ILA are a revealing episode, but the intransigence of the union leaders seems to be the factor most deserving of criticism. They could not see, or would not admit, that there was a genuine revolt by a large segment of the rank and file. They could only see that they were under attack. Their only reaction was to fight back, defend themselves, and try to prove that nothing really was amiss. Yet before the dust of this struggle had a chance to settle, they would be involved in a much deeper attack on their bastion. Both the government and the labor movement would become antagonists against the ILA.

[45] ILA, Waldman and Waldman, *op. cit.*; cf. *New York Times*, Feb. 7, 1952, p. 47, Aug. 5, p. 41.

5 | Challenge of Government:
The Crime Commission Investigation

If the dreadnought that was the New York State Crime Commission, with its carefully chosen crew, its deftly selected and ample supply of ammunition, and its well-aimed volleys, publicly exposed the ILA as the enemy of port stability, it hardly could have avoided creating considerable disturbance, and this was its intention. Several groups cheered the assault, hoping it would clear the port for a more wholesome future. It brought new forces into being, or aroused submerged ones, which added complications to the longshore industry.

The Crime Commission investigation of 1952–1953 had three important and interrelated consequences. Each must be treated somewhat separately, albeit they had overlapping and interrelated movements. These consequences were, first, the events related to the expulsion of the ILA from the AFL—with the creation by the AFL of the International Brotherhood of Longshoremen (IBL)—and the resulting bitter struggle over union representation before the NLRB; second, the collective bargaining negotiations between the ILA and the NYSA, with the confusion in these arising from the creation of the Waterfront Commission as well as the appearance of the IBL, plus the invocation of the emergency dispute settlement provisions of the Taft-Hartley Act; and, third, enactment of the New York–New Jersey Waterfront Commission Compact (Bi-State Compact) and establishment of the Waterfront Commission, following directly from the legislation recommended by the Crime Commission.

These three developments were observable simultaneously, but expulsion of the ILA from the AFL and the interunion struggle, for a time, substantially obliterated collective bargaining negotiations, while regulation of the industry under the Waterfront Commission, although never out of sight and appearing at first somewhat uncertain, shortly came on importantly and with great force. But once the interunion struggle quieted, the collective bargaining negotiations reemerged and ran their course, too, but now in the context of the Waterfront Commission's actions. Its regulations and program became and remained an important ongoing factor in the industry.

The Investigation

The timing of the investigation of crime on the New York waterfront was, in part, politically inspired, yet the subject was ripe for investigation.[1] The commission was composed of distinguished citizens above political opportunism and genuinely interested in the welfare of the port. Its objective was to expose evil practices, not to "balance" the good against the bad, an important consideration in view of the criticism made by the ILA that it was treated unfairly.

---

[1] The date of Governor Dewey's directive was Nov. 20, 1951, during the strike then under way. The governor's announcement had been preceded by about three weeks by a request from Spruille Braden, chairman of the New York City Anti-Crime Committee, that action be taken against "inefficiency, crime, and political corruption" along the docks (New York Times, Nov. 20, 1951, p. 53, Nov. 21, p. 51). Mayor O'Dwyer had established a Mayor's Joint Committee on Port Industry in the spring of 1950. A subcommittee issued a report about this time on "labor conditions as they affect waterfront commerce" (New York Times, Nov. 29, 1951, p. 59). There had been a succession of earlier reports, too, a rather extensive one in 1946 by the Citizens' Waterfront Committee, chaired by William J. Schieffin (A Report to the Public of New York City—the New York Waterfront). In the background, of course, were three major studies (C. B. Barnes, The Longshoreman [New York: Survey Associates, 1915]; U.S. Department of Labor, Bureau of Labor Statistics, Cargo Handling and Longshore Labor Conditions, Bulletin No. 550, 1932; E. E. Swanstrom, The Waterfront Labor Problems (New York: Fordham University Press, 1938).

The need for investigation was recognized in labor's own house, although this acknowledgement may have been only a tactical move as a counter to what was in the offing. Regardless, it is significant that all unions affiliated with the Maritime Trades' Department of the AFL created an organization on January 13, 1952, called "The Greater New York Harbor Port Council." The organizational meeting was attended by two hundred, representing every local of the ILA, Seafarers, Master Mates and Pilots, Radio Officers, and Teamsters. The program adopted is worth attention, for it recognized procedures needing correction and set standards to be achieved. The new organization said that its interest was in stabilizing waterfront conditions and protecting members of the unions from their enemies; although it was primarily the ILA that the Crime Commission was publicly putting on the spot.

The program adopted included fourteen points,[2] designed (1) to guarantee internal union democracy by providing for local union membership meetings at least once a month, written financial reports, secret balloting, and membership participation; (2) to guarantee support for affiliated unions; (3) to provide for expulsion of any union official or union member "found guilty of either forcing or receiving kickbacks or of participating in shakedowns" or for taking or inducing bribes; (4) to permit discharge for pilferage; (5) to provide for expulsion for "shylocking," or usury; (6) to provide that no man would be barred from working on the waterfront because of a prison record; (7) to assure hiring systems preferred by the workers; (8) to investigate and establish, if possible, machinery for making loans to needy waterfront workers in order to soften the impact of the "feast or famine" nature of employment; (9) to designate representatives from the respective organizations and give them power to implement the program; (10) to take action against individuals responsible for illegal work stoppages; (11) to study public loading; (12) to oppose development of licensing systems

[2] AFL, Maritime Trades Department, *Program for the Greater New York Harbor Port Council*, 1951, p. 5.

smacking of totalitarian control; (13) to regulate new membership; and (14) to inform the AFL and seek its support. In conclusion it was stated, "The trade unions of the A F of L are fully capable of straightening out that part of the situation which is the union's responsibility. . . . This program is a must, the time for talk appears to have passed. The time is now for action."

The Crime Commission, however, would not wait upon the house of labor for action. Led by Joseph M. Proskauer, it created a special waterfront section and assembled a capable staff to carry out the work. Cooperation of officials in New Jersey was sought and obtained. It held many private hearings and public ones, the latter running for twenty full days in the period from December 1952 to January 1953.[3] Once the commission began its public hearings in December 1952, the newspapers gave extensive coverage.[4]

Some ILA leaders sought to present a united defense but many balked at this group approach, revealing some dissension and distrust within the ranks. The commission examined all basic pier operations, docking and sailing of vessels, unloading and loading of cargo and handling between the hold of the vessel and the floor of the pier, checking of the cargo, protection of the cargo, handling and loading and unloading of cargo between the floor of the pier and trucks, and maintenance of the piers. It concerned itself with the supervisory forces, from top officials of steamship and stevedoring companies to pier superintendents, hiring foremen, and dock bosses. It gave particular attention to the quasiunion, quasicompany institution of public loading, the practice of independent companies—some operated by ILA members—controlling the loading and unloading of trucks at the piers. Being independent of other pier operations,

[3] *Fourth Report of the New York State Crime Commission* (*Port of New York Waterfront*), Leg. Doc. No. 70 (1953), pp. 75–76, pp. 5–8.
[4] *New York Times*, Dec. 1, 1952, and daily through Dec. 5, p. 1, Dec. 19, p. 1, Dec. 20, p. 8.

and at a point in place and time in the handling of cargo, it was where malpractices could easily flourish.

The Commission's Report

The commission issued its final report in May 1953. While it made findings on the economic status and physical condition of the port, it found "the most important factor threatening the welfare of the Port[was] the entrenched existence of deplorable conditions involving unscrupulous practices and undisciplined procedures, many of which [were] criminal or quasi-criminal in nature." Pointing out that ship turnaround was the most important consideration in steamship operations, it found the origin of malpractices in the fact that the "high cost of delay is an open invitation to blackmail." It also found that the nature of the labor market had made exploitation and abuse of workingmen easy.

The commission found collusion between employers and union officials which operated to the detriment of the dock workers and the public. Some companies improperly gave large amounts of cash to union officials for "services rendered." Payments made to "phantoms"—that is, money passed to union officials and persons influential in union affairs by adding fictitious names on payrolls—was seen as a form of extortion. Various holidays were revealed as occasions when employers made illicit payments to leaders of the union. But not just the ILA was put in the spotlight. The commission found contracting stevedores who bought "goodwill" from steamship company officials in order to gain business, a cost the public had to pay for. The books of many stevedores did not show how some large amounts of cash were disbursed; in some instances petty cash vouchers had been destroyed and financial records altered.

The commission revealed that the ILA and its component local unions had flagrantly disregarded the welfare of dockworkers. It found considerable exploitation and betrayal of the rank and file. It charged that the ILA did not effectively supervise its local unions nor concern itself with leaders who abused their powers and defaulted in their responsibilities. It stated categorically that "Ryan and many ILA organizers [were] demonstrably unfit for their posts." It showed that Ryan had accepted Christmas gifts and other payments from stevedoring and steamship companies. Sometimes these were crudely characterized as donations to an "anti-Communist" fund. The ILA was charged with allowing known criminals to control local unions; these men were found to extort money from local union treasuries. In addition, the financial affairs of local unions were loosely and irresponsibly conducted and records destroyed, altered, or never kept. "No attempt has been made," it was said, "to insure democratic procedures or financial responsibilities." The commission charged that the ILA, aware of the abuses, did nothing to rectify conditions.[5] After citing evidence and charging grand larceny, embezzlement, forgery, and destruction of union books and noting lip service to reform by the ILA hierarchy, the commission charged, "Even today these locals continue under the domination of the same officers who have controlled them for many years." It was established that at least 30 per cent of the officials of ILA locals had police records: "Waterfront criminals know that the control of the local is a prerequisite to conducting racket operations on the piers. Through their powers as union officials, they place their confidants in high positions on the docks, shake down steamship and stevedoring companies by threats of work stoppages, operate the lucrative public loading business, and carry on such activities as pilferage, loansharking and gambling." Many examples of criminal control in places around the port were cited.

More than half of the forty-five ILA locals whose financial records were subpoenaed failed to produce a complete set of books and records for the previous five years.[6] The explanation

---

[5] As an example, it said, "Thus, six Brooklyn locals known as the 'Camarda Locals' were for at least ten years under the control of a group of notorious criminals headed by Albert Anastasia, Vincent Mangano and their two lieutenants, Giocchino (Dandy Jack) Parisi and Anthony (Tony Spring) Romero."

[6] The ILA in New York was then comprised of about 64 active locals

given was usually that they had been lost or stolen. The financial records of only thirty-four locals were examined. Of these only eleven were found to have had reasonably good accounting form. The commission strongly condemned hiring practices, particularly the shape-up and the use of hiring foremen forced upon the employer. It cited many examples. The practice was clearly stated by W. L. Swain, superintendent of terminal operations for a company operating on Pier 92 on the North River. Testifying about a meeting with the ILA president regarding selection of hiring foremen, Swain said, "The position of the Union, as stated very clearly on more than one occasion by Mr. Ryan, was this . . . 'Under the contract, you have the right [to select hiring foremen] but our men like to select their own hiring boss, and I doubt if the union could force the men to work unless you let them choose the hiring boss.'" It was demonstrated how unscrupulous hiring foremen exacted tribute from the dock workers while dispensing patronage to relatives, friends, and associates.

The commission condemned depredations of the public loaders and pointed out that they kept practically no books or records even though they were collecting millions of dollars annually, the money going largely to union leaders and known criminals. Also condemned was the watchman system, the private protective system, for being administered loosely and carelessly. It found that the watchmen were ineffective and that thefts in the port cost consumers millions of dollars, that watchmen were not only discouraged from reporting thefts but were reprimanded for doing so. The ILA was found to have opposed efforts by steamship companies to improve the system.

The commission concluded that the time had come for drastic action. The City of New York should actively address itself to the physical improvement of the piers. Steamship and stevedoring companies were admonished to have their officials act in accordance with fundamental standards of business morality and

—27 in Manhattan, 22 in Brooklyn, 4 in Staten Island, and 11 in New Jersey.

resist extortion and blackmail. Having learned that the AFL was prepared to take action within its own house to see that the ILA conformed to legitimate union standards, the commission exhorted the federation to stamp out the abuses in the ILA. But beyond voluntary efforts, the commission urged the legislature to enact a program to eliminate the evils.

It proposed two statutes, one to create a "Division of Port Administration," with power to abolish the shape-up and to remove all other abuses from the docks, to establish employment information centers in which dock workers would be registered and through which all hiring would be done, to license all supervisors and stevedoring companies, to abolish public loading and to license all who would be engaged in loading and unloading of trucks, and to license all port watchmen. Violations of the statute would be subject to appropriate criminal sanctions. The second proposed statute was designed to provide that labor organizations meet certain minimum standards, "to give legal sanction to certain fundamental requirements now voluntarily observed by most labor unions."[7]

Reactions of the ILA

Waldman tried strenuously to counter the report of the commission, submitting to the governor and members of the legislature the answer of the ILA.[8] He attacked the procedures and methods used, contending that the investigation was not impartial nor designed to ascertain the facts, that it was nothing less than an inquisition, a violation of civil rights, and an undisguised attack on the labor movement through castigating the ILA. He asserted that the commission's recommendations would not only

[7] *Fourth Report of the New York State Crime Commission,* pp. 67ff.

[8] "Answer of the International Longshoremen's Association, AFL, to the Report of the New York State Crime Commission Dealing with the Waterfront of the Port of New York," U.S. Congress, House, Committee on Judiciary, *New York–New Jersey Waterfront Commission Compact; Hearing on H.R. 6286,* 83d Cong., 1st Sess., July 1953, Appendix, pp. 205–236; hereafter referred to as *New York–New Jersey Waterfront Commission Compact Hearings.*

be crippling and destructive to collective bargaining but would create regimentation through a supergovernment having the power of economic life or death over workers in the port.[9]

The ILA complained bitterly that it had not been allowed to present its position publicly through the commission. Its own witnesses were marshaled. Although the commission had heard eulogies to the longshoremen for their work in the war effort, most of these had been directed to the men, not to the leaders. Similarly, statements of praise for opposition to communism were cited, including two from George Meany, president of the AFL,[10] and one from Governor Dewey given in response to an invitation to attend a dinner given in honor of Ryan. Furthermore, Waldman pointed out that Dewey, as special prosecutor and as district attorney of New York County for several years, had prosecuted and convicted labor racketeers but "during this entire period, however, he prosecuted no officials of the ILA."[11]

Charges of the ILA's failure as bargaining agent were denied. High wages—including exceptional overtime and premium pay guarantees—vacation payments, and welfare and pension benefits were cited. Waldman charged that the commission's findings of high wage rates but low average earnings was "sheer nonsense and simply untrue," stating that some fifteen thousand longshoremen earned good wages and only 10 per cent of the work was done by casuals.[12] It must be noted, however, that it was

[9] *Ibid.*, p. 207.

[10] This, in retrospect, was a little ludicrous because at the very time the ILA was publishing its public defense, Meany was preparing to oust the ILA from the AFL because of the revelations of misconduct. See below, p. 121ff.

[11] *New York–New Jersey Waterfront Commission Compact Hearings*, Appendix, pp. 214–216.

[12] *Ibid.*, pp. 217–218. In 1953 the hourly wage rate of longshoremen in the Port of New York was $2.35 and modal annual earnings were $4,500. Average weekly earnings were $86.00. In comparison, the average hourly rate in manufacturing in New York City was $1.78 with weekly earnings of $67.49 (lower than the longshore rate), and in construction the average hourly rate was $2.73 with average weekly earnings of $101.83 (higher than the longshore rate).

only fifteen thousand who earned good wages, if the number was that large, out of the forty-five thousand dock workers. Also, although only 10 per cent of the work on any one day was done by casuals, the casual group was much larger than 10 per cent of the work force.

The ILA response attempted to show that the ILA president was not derelict and that he had not received contributions in secret. It strongly emphasized the statement that the ILA had already taken steps to institute its own internal reform. What was not said was that any steps taken were a result of the revelations of the Board of Inquiry or that practically no changes had been, in fact, effectuated.

The ILA—particularly in view of the AFL attitude—could not check the course of events. The governor, on June 8 and 9, held public hearings on the recommendations of the Crime Commission. All interested parties were represented.[13] Following this a bill conforming to the recommendations for the first statute was prepared,[14] and legislation was enacted in the New York State legislature on June 25, and in the New Jersey legislature on June 30, entitled the New York–New Jersey Waterfront Commission Compact. Because of the bistate nature of the program it was presented to the United States Congress for approval. Hearings were conducted by a subcommittee of the Committee on the Judiciary of the House of Representatives on July 22, and the compact was approved by Congress on July 30 and signed by President Dwight D. Eisenhower on August 12. The Bi-State Compact became effective on December 1,[15] although the commissioners were appointed in August and busily set out to build a staff and set up the program.

[13] N.Y. State, *Record of the Public Hearings Held by Governor Thomas E. Dewey on the Recommendations of the New York State Crime Commission for Remedying Conditions on the Waterfront of the Port of New York;* hereafter cited as *Dewey Hearings.*

[14] The second proposal was dropped because the implications for the whole labor movement were too great.

[15] *New York–New Jersey Waterfront Commission Compact Hearings,* p. 120.

Expulsion of the ILA from the AFL

Immediately following the public hearings but before the final report of the commission came out, the Executive Council of the AFL took unprecedented action. It told the ILA that it deplored "the reign of lawlessness and crime . . . disclosed on the New York City waterfront." It pointed out that it had "given thorough consideration" to the findings of irregular and objectionable practices, saying "one of the most serious . . . is the clear and definite indication that workers of the Port of New York are being exploited in every possible way and that they are not receiving the protection which they have every right to expect as trade unionists and members of your organization." The ILA was told that it had to restore clean and wholesome trade unionism and immediately oust officers at the national and local levels who had accepted gifts and bribes from employers or who had criminal records. It was directed to eliminate the shape-up and to substitute a system of regular employment and legitimate hiring methods. The ILA was also told emphatically to place itself above suspicion and completely free itself from all "racketeering, crime, corruption and other irregular activities" as a condition of continuing affiliation with the AFL.[16]

The letter from the AFL, received early in February, had set an April 30 deadline for response. The ILA, never geared to move swiftly, did not make a formal reply until after meeting with officials of the AFL in Washington, D.C., at the end of March. Meany was told verbally that progress was being made on the job of cleaning up. Apparently the meeting was a lively one, at least Meany said it was. The ILA said it needed a little

[16] Letter, Executive Council, AFL, to officers and members of the ILA, Feb. 3, 1952. See AFL, *Proceedings of the Seventy-Second Annual Convention, St. Louis, September 21–25, 1953*, pp. 54–56; cf. U.S. Congress, House, Committee on the Judiciary, *New York–New Jersey Waterfront Commission Compact Hearings*, pp. 122–124, and *Dewey Hearings*, pp. 229–231.

more time and was given a new deadline, to respond before the AFL Executive Council meeting on May 19.[17]

On the day following the meeting the Executive Council of the ILA unanimously adopted a resolution calling upon the New York District Council to supplant the shape-up with "another method of hiring suitable to the needs of the workers in the port." While the council subsequently voted, on April 7, to eliminate the shape-up, it conducted a referendum of the membership in New York on the single question, "Are you satisfied with the present method of hiring?" The Honest Ballot Association was asked to supervise the balloting. The result was 7,020 "yes" and 3,920 "no." The officials said that this was an answer to the "false charge that the ILA leadership in New York had forced and foisted a hiring system on a reluctant membership." No mention was made, however, of the fact that on a typical midweek workday, sixteen thousand to eighteen thousand men worked and that forty-odd thousand men comprised the longshore work force. The ILA leaders were careful to add that the referendum did not mean that they would "not work out a system of hiring which might retain the constructive seniority and priority features inherent in the present system of hiring through steady and regular gangs," thus eliminating the shape-up, which it said "has largely disappeared already."[18]

Although we will be looking at developments in the matter of hiring in more detail later,[19] some observations should be made here. Because the Crime Commission was recommending the elimination of the shape-up and the establishment of some sort of employment centers, and because the AFL had directed the ILA to get rid of the shape-up, the notion of hiring halls was given serious consideration. It is of some interest that the New York District Council expressed itself in favor of the estab-

[17] *New York Times,* March 31, 1953, p. 45.

[18] *New York Times,* April 1, 1953, p. 1, May 10, 1953, pp. 1, 35; cf. *Dewey Hearings,* p. 23.

[19] See pp. 140ff.

lishment of twelve geographically located hiring halls, under union supervision, of course. Still other plans were suggested within the ILA. Anthony Anastasia, who was emerging as the leader in Brooklyn but not yet fully ensconced, proposed a single hiring hall for Brooklyn under union control. Those familiar with the situation believed that new opposition to the shape-up in Brooklyn came, primarily, from the seven locals in which the Crime Commission had charged gangster control.[20] The employers did not talk about hiring halls, for they feared that these would fall under union domination—even if established through negotiations and jointly administered as on the West Coast, where for all practical purposes the ILWU did control them. But government-operated hiring halls might have been more acceptable to the employers.[21]

In its mid-May letter to the Executive Council of the AFL, the ILA, trying hard to retain affiliation, stated that it intended to eliminate the shape-up. It would insist "at its next negotiations," those beginning in the summer, upon the abolition of the shape-up and see that it was supplanted by "a system of hiring which meets the members' needs, conserving the desirable seniority and priority features of the present steady gang system."[22] The ILA said that it, too, condemned the taking of bribes; however, it insisted that monetary gifts given during "the Christmas season" and occasionally at other holidays were merely gifts and nothing more. But it added that the ILA Executive Council had recently adopted a resolution forbidding any officer from receiving a gift or gratuity from an employer with whom the ILA did business. The ILA also said, "We agree unequivocally with the principle that criminals should not be allowed to obtain positions of influence and power within labor unions," but

[20] *New York Times*, May 10, 1953, pp. 1, 35.

[21] *Dewey Hearings*, pp. 218–222.

[22] Letter, Executive Council, ILA, to Executive Council, AFL, May 15, 1953. See AFL, *Proceedings*, 1953, pp. 56–66; cf. *Dewey Hearings*, pp. 232ff; *New York Times*, May 16, 1953, p. 1.

urged the AFL not to victimize the ILA or its International President.[23]

As for democratic administration of locals, the ILA conceded that "internal democracy is a prime duty and minimum prerequisite . . . [for] a labor union." It agreed that "democratic procedures in our local unions should be observed and preserved." It added, "To that end various concrete and effective steps have been and are being taken." It argued, however, that condemnation based on disclosures of the Crime Commission was a travesty on justice. The ILA claimed that it had taken steps before the advent of the waterfront investigation "to institute its own internal reform" and recited a long list of requirements that had been drawn for internal control; it asserted that "the ILA Executive Council will continue to assume a direct and active role in seeing to it that the above minimum standards of democratic local administration are observed and maintained." Finally, a concluding reminder:

This report is being submitted to you in the spirit of fraternal cooperation. For over a half-century the ILA . . . has been a loyal component part of the AFL . . . when internal dual unionism was started 18 years ago, which . . . threatened the very life and existence of the AFL, the ILA stood firm, steadfast and unwavering. And when our own industry and union were threatened . . . from organized Communism and the CIO, the ILA, at first almost alone, bore the fight to preserve the AFL position in the maritime and transportation industry.[24]

The AFL Executive Council promptly responded by saying that while the ILA recognized the existence of evils and indicated a desire to cooperate, the report could not be accepted as constituting compliance with its directive. The overall defect was its failure to disclose what, if any, remedial action had been taken. It stated, "It is clear from your report that further steps

[23] AFL, *Proceedings*, 1953, p. 61; *Dewey Hearings*, p. 238.
[24] AFL, *Proceedings*, 1953, pp. 64–66; *Dewey Hearings*, pp. 242–243; *New York Times*, May 16, 1953, p. 1, May 17, p. 1.

must be taken forthwith. This fact cannot be emphasized too strongly." In the matter of the abolition of the shape-up, commendation was given for the actions taken, but the council added:

However, we are not satisfied that the abolition of the present shape-up system, which you agree has been productive of great evil, cannot be effected before October 1 . . . and we are left in the dark as to the manner and means of effectively enforcing full compliance . . . [The ILA was] directed to attempt to make immediate changes in contracts . . . with the employers, rather than await the termination date of the contract.

The Executive Council again stressed the evil in bribes and gifts, slapping the ILA for trying to make a legitimate distinction. It strongly criticized the ILA for having done nothing to remove criminals or those having close association with them; it sharply added, "None of these individuals have to date been removed nor has any action been taken to suspend them pending removal trials." The council also asserted that, while progress had been reported on achievement of democratic administration in ILA local unions, "your report, however, fails to disclose what has been done by the international to see to it that such standards are actually adopted and fully enforced by all ILA locals." Nevertheless, inasmuch as the ILA had requested a hearing, one was set for the next meeting of the council in Chicago on August 10, but another written report was demanded on the "state of compliance" before the hearing, with copies addressed to each member of the council.[25]

Rumors began to circulate that a new union to displace the ILA from the piers was being contemplated.[26] Toward the end of July, the ILA submitted a supplemental report. Again, it was a very long letter, largely the response the ILA had made at the Dewey Hearings in answer to charges made by the Crime Com-

[25] Letter, Executive Council, AFL, to Joseph P. Ryan, President, ILA, May 26, 1953. See AFL, *Proceedings*, 1953, pp. 66–69; cf. *Dewey Hearings*, p. 131; *New York Times*, May 22, 1953, p. 17, May 27, p. 1.

[26] *New York Times*, June 10, 1953, p. 1.

mission.[27] It showed no more than the earlier report, and the Executive Council of the AFL, when it met in August, decided to suspend the ILA. It decided for suspension and against expulsion in order to give the "clean" elements a chance to set the house in order and to pressure the ILA to reform. Said Meany, "We decided to take the intermediate step to drive home to the decent people that the AFL was not taking an arbitrary or adamant position—that we're hopeful something can be done." When Ryan was asked if he considered the suspension order a reprieve, he said, "No," and added that the ILA was intending to comply prior to the AFL convention in September. But Meany was almost beyond patience, for he said, "This is a very rotten situation, the worst in my experience—we want action, not promises of action."[28]

Within the ILA the "clean-union group" was routed when it attempted to file charges against union officers with criminal records and gangland associations. The "clean-union group" went so far as to make overtures for a new charter, but AFL leaders informed them that no such action could be taken before the convention acted.[29]

On the eve of the convention, the Executive Council of the AFL unanimously decided to expel the ILA and to set up a new union, thinking to call it the "American Federation of Longshoremen," and it set up a five-man committee to direct affairs at the outset. The members of the committee were Dave Beck, Teamsters; Paul Hall, Seafarers; William Doherty, Letter Carriers; Al Hayes, Machinists; and Meany. Eight vice-presidents of the ILA, mostly in the Great Lakes and South, had notified the AFL that their locals wanted to stay in the AFL.[30] Ryan appealed in vain to check formation of a union dual to the ILA. Meany said, "This is not something that we looked forward to with any great feeling of joy. . . . It is a serious step to ask for

[27] AFL, *Proceedings*, 1953, pp. 70–77.
[28] *New York Times*, Aug. 13, 1953, p. 1.
[29] *New York Times*, Sept. 10, 1953, p. 1.
[30] *New York Times*, Sept. 19, 1953, p. 1.

the revocation of a charter," but added that there was too much to overlook. He put the matter in a nutshell when he said, "Yes, we got some promises, but no performances." The vote to expel, the first in AFL history, was 79,079 in favor and only 736 opposed.[31] In a final desperate effort to stay in the AFL, the ILA offered to submit to receivership. Ryan said, "Instead of chartering a new union, with all the chaos that will create, we hope the AFL will give us a chance to clean our own house under its supervision." But the AFL leaders had set their course. The reasons that dictated expulsion also seemed to dictate "no receivership." The AFL had to remove itself from the stigma of the organization. In retrospect, however, one wonders, if the AFL had moved in and really cleaned house itself, could it have done the job? Its efforts to establish a dual union, as will be seen, did not succeed.

Before we examine the struggle over representation between the ILA and the new union, eventually to be called the International Brotherhood of Longshoremen, we will turn to the two other developments influenced by the Crime Commission report, ILA's collective bargaining with the NYSA and the establishment and activities of the Waterfront Commission.

Confused Collective Bargaining

With the intent of complying with the order of the AFL to eliminate the shape-up immediately, but also to get a jump on the soon-to-be-created Waterfront Commission, the ILA, on July 15, 1953, had submitted a proposal to the NYSA for abolition of the shape-up and establishment of a new hiring system. The employers submitted a counterproposal within a few days, but the parties could not resolve their differences and decide upon a program. Too many uncertainties were ahead for the employers. The Bi-State Compact and the evolving program of the Waterfront Commission forced them to delay and see what was ahead in the matter of hiring. Even if they did not relish the whole

[31] AFL, *Proceedings*, 1953, pp. 486–493; cf. *New York Times*, Sept. 21, 1953, p. 15, Sept. 22, p. 36, Sept. 23, p. 1.

range of regulations being imposed upon the industry, some employers welcomed the prospect of governmental regulation of hiring, although some did not. The most that the parties could agree to in these early meetings were eight principles looking to the abolition of the shape-up, but retention of established practices pertaining to gangs and other regularly attached workers.[32] This marked the end of the effort to achieve a new hiring system in early negotiations. The ILA was thereafter more or less completely preoccupied with its efforts to stay in the AFL.

The regular negotiations were formally opened on August 23, however, with the ILA in customary manner presenting a long list of demands to the NYSA. It would have liked to get an agreement in a hurry, as the best defense for a challenge from a rival, but it also made strong demands because with the rival in mind it could not afford to be criticized for not being aggressive in representing longshoremen. Strong demands and a quick settlement were inconsistent. Furthermore, the employers had to be cautious. They were already smarting from public criticism for being too cozy with the ILA. Also, they were not only fully aware that the Waterfront Commission was formulating hiring regulations, but were even conferring with the commission on the matter. They had no intention of joining the ILA in a race to outguess, or outrun, the commission. They were aware that the AFL was creating a new union of longshoremen and expected a struggle over representation. Although the ILA unquestionably was the bargaining agent at the time, and the NYSA could hardly refuse to deal with it, yet, would a negotiated agreement stand up under the circumstances? What would a challenge over representation do if the new union won?

As negotiations continued it was clear that some in the ILA wanted an agreement without a strike. Consequently, Ryan sharply reduced the demand for a wage increase, coming quite close to the offer of the NYSA. The employers got a telegram

[32] AFL, *Proceedings*, 1953, p. 78.

sent by Peter Johnson, who had been counsel to the insurgents in 1951, and John Dwyer, who had been an insurgent in 1951 and who was to play a prominent role in the new AFL union, warning that many locals would repudiate a contract between them and Ryan. Men in Ryan's own ranks, in Brooklyn as well as Manhattan, denounced the reduction in contract demands, calling it an unwise sell-out that would not help in the fight with the new union.[33]

Governor Dewey, keeping in close touch with developments, said publicly that he would be shocked if the employers signed a contract with the ILA. To this, Connolly retorted, "The Governor is talking . . . through both sides of his face . . . he had a man from the State Mediation Board sitting in our negotiations trying to get us to settle; now he tells the employers never to settle with us." Concurrently Meany accused the NYSA of carrying on collusive negotiations with the ILA in an effort to obtain a cheap contract. Denying this, the NYSA defended itself by saying that it had no alternative but to negotiate with the duly recognized representatives of the ILA.[34] When the employers on September 29 rejected the ILA demands, Ryan, perhaps because of the internal pressures upon him, returned to the earlier demands and threatened to call a strike.

While these developments were taking place, the Waterfront Commission mailed applications for registration to twenty-seven thousand longshoremen and warned that no one could work on the piers after December 1 without being registered. The AFL soon filed a petition with the NLRB seeking certification as bargaining agent. Thereupon federal mediators, who had kept in touch with the negotiations, were called off, for it was the policy not to become embroiled in interunion disputes. It was also true that the FMCS was under pressure from the AFL, as well as from some government officials, not to get itself into a position that would enable the ILA or the employers to contend

[33] *New York Times*, Sept. 9, 1953, p. 1, Sept. 24, p. 1, Sept. 25, p. 1.
[34] *New York Times*, Sept, 29, 1953, p. 1, Oct. 2, p. 1.

that they had signed a new contract at urging of federal mediators.[35]

Governor Dewey, responding to an appeal from the NYSA, supported the request for a Taft-Hartley injunction; but President Eisenhower seemed reluctant to act because he would appear to be following the pattern of intervention of the recent Democratic administrations, which the Republicans had criticized. The NYSA complained that it had been thrown into the middle of a situation over which it had no control. A prepared statement to the governors of New York and New Jersey said, "Because of statements made characterizing these negotiations as 'collusive' and an 'attempt at cheap settlement,' we serve notice here and now that our final contract offer made to the ILA will apply to any union and regardless of who the authorized representative may be in the future." It also gave assurance that it was seeking to negotiate a contract whose provisions would comply in every respect with the new Bi-State Compact.[36]

When, under the ILA rule of "no contract, no work," a strike began on October 1, President Eisenhower promptly invoked the emergency provisions of the Taft-Hartley Act and appointed a fact-finding board. The board quickly ran into issues which raised fine legal and policy questions. The work stoppage clearly was not basically a labor-management dispute, but a representation dispute for the NLRB to resolve. The Taft-Hartley Act provided that once a board was appointed and an injunction issued, federal mediators should assist the parties in reaching a settlement; yet it was not their province to settle rival union disputes.

The issue became confused, indeed. The interunion battle would only be settled with certification by the NLRB. Negotiations would necessarily be at an impasse in spite of the appointment of the Taft-Hartley Board. Implementation of the Bi-State Compact had to run its course. The ILA challenged the consti-

[35] *New York Times*, Sept. 30, 1953, p. 1.
[36] *New York Times*, Oct. 1, 1953, pp. 1, 20, and 24.

tutionality of the Bi-State Compact—in what proved to be the first in a long sequence of suits—and this added to the uncertainty. Simultaneously, the ILA, in an act of defiance, called upon its members to refuse to register with the Waterfront Commission.[37]

The Taft-Hartley Board had little difficulty in laying out the straightforward bargaining issues, although it was quite obvious that two of them intermeshed with other current controversies. Wage increases, greater welfare contributions, guarantee of call-in pay, and the matter of a permanent arbitrator were all controversial. But the latter became mixed with the program of the Waterfront Commission when the ILA insisted that all existing customs and practices on the piers be reduced to writing and agreed upon for guidance of the arbitrator, notwithstanding the fact that new hiring methods and procedures complying with the law would nullify some of them. Another issue brought the interunion controversy to the table. Because of the AFL challenge of the ILA, the employers had withdrawn an offer to grant a union shop and were saying that any agreement negotiated with the ILA would cover only its members and no others. This, of course, the ILA would not accept.[38] The board faced a very difficult problem. Although it was not dealing with a straight-out labor-management dispute, the board had to approach it as such. The Taft-Hartley injunction was set to run to Christmas Eve. The law said that if the board could not bring the parties to a settlement within sixty days it was to make a final report and there should be a secret ballot conducted by the NLRB on the employers' "last offer." But, as already noted, the parties were forbidden by another section of the law, as interpreted by NLRB, from making an agreement when there was a question of representation. Accordingly, the NYSA was barred from making an agreement. Nevertheless, a vote on the em-

[37] *Ibid.*, Oct. 1, pp. 1, 4.
[38] Board of Inquiry, *Interim Report*, p. 4; Bureau of National Affairs, *Daily Labor Report*, no. 194, Oct. 5, 1953, pp. D-3, AA-1, no. 195, Oct. 6, p. A-3.

ployers' "last offer" was required. If the workers voted for the
last offer, would that settle the dispute? Could the NLRB hold a
representation election before the vote on the employers' "last
offer"? It had never been able to work that fast in a case of any
complexity. Before holding an election, decisions had to be made
on who would vote. The parties had different views. Also, in
this situation, the Waterfront Commission was in the process of
determining who were going to be legitimate longshoremen.
Could the NLRB hold an election that was truly representative
of the workers? How would it decide who would be allowed to
vote? Should the NLRB hold the election promptly and distribute ballots on the basis of past payrolls, as was usual, even
though some of the longshoremen might be ruled off the piers
by the Waterfront Commission after December 1, when the
employment register went into effect? Or should the NLRB
delay until the Waterfront Commission had sifted out the legitimate longshoremen under the terms of the Bi-State Compact?
A representation election while the employees were working
under a Taft-Hartley injunction was a novelty, but that was the
prospect. The tasks before the NLRB and the Taft-Hartley
Board was unusual, indeed, and the diverse requirements
created much awkwardness. Time kept rolling on, and many
pressures and incidents punctuated developments. The next
chapter will pick up the story; meanwhile, a closer look at the
Waterfront Commission is necessary.

The Waterfront Commission

Immediately after passage of the Bi-State Compact, General
George P. Hays and General Edward C. Rose had been appointed as commissioners by the State of New York and the State
of New Jersey, respectively, and offices had been opened in
downtown Manhattan. With Lawrence E. Walsh as general
counsel and executive director, a staff had been quickly re-
cruited.[39] The two chief operating units were "Licensing and
Information Centers" and "Investigation and Enforcement."

[39] *New York Times*, Sept. 9, 1953, p. 1.

Percy A. Miller, Jr., became the director of the former and Joseph Kaitz the director of the latter. It is to be noted that the NYSA was required to finance the Waterfront Commission—eventually it cost about $2 million a year.

Rules and regulations had to be developed and the licensing activities gotten under way. Physical properties to house the employment and information centers had to be obtained. This was not easy because landlords in several waterfront areas were reluctant to lease properties to the controversial, and challenged, Waterfront Commission. A "Preliminary Draft of Proposed Regulations," six in number, was issued on October 28, and additional ones were released soon after. The NYSA, the ILA, and public agencies were given an opportunity to respond. The regulations conformed to the requirements of the Bi-State Compact and explicitly covered such matters as pier superintendents and hiring agents, stevedores, longshoremen, employment information centers, port watchmen, and appeals procedures. By mid-November a set of some dozen regulations had been issued, spelling out in detail the procedures, requirements, and responsibilities under each.[40] While licensing of pier superintendents, hiring agents, and stevedores was an important part of the work of the Waterfront Commission, the central task was the registration of longshoremen and the setting up of procedures and rules governing the hiring process through the new employment and information centers.

Regulations on hiring were worked out in conferences with experts from the Port Authority and a committee from the NYSA. They recognized the widespread use of regular gangs—those of long standing on each pier—and conformed substantially to the needs of the employers and to practices which prevailed widely throughout the port. The system adopted permitted each employer to prevalidate, that is, file with the Waterfront Commission, the gangs—his own and others he customarily used—and names of men who would constitute his dock list. On a given

[40] Waterfront Commission, "Regulations," 1953 (mimeographed),

day, each employer would hire gangs and men from among those prevalidated. If men, among those prevalidated, were not hired on a given day, they could go to one of the information and employment centers and stand for hiring as casuals to some other employer. If not employed there, he received a "show-up" card, because it was intended that men who did not achieve satisfactory employment or attendance were to be decasualized following a year's experience. Neither the prevalidation nor the hiring of casuals at the centers eliminated favoritism, but the Bi-State Compact left the choice of men with the employers, whose licensed hiring agents did the selecting; but all men were considered employed *through* the centers, because the agents of the Waterfront Commission maintained close control and surveillance. The old shape-up at the pier was gone, but *a* shape-up had been moved indoors, inside the employment centers, for daily hiring of casuals in excess of the men prevalidated. The prevalidation system, however, permitted a small "private shape-up" at the pier among the prevalidated men. This is not to be confused with the fact that men employed shaped at the pier head at the beginning of the shift for checking in. But in addition, the employer selected from among his prevalidated men those he desired to employ. As will be seen, the prevalidation program was later eliminated because the Waterfront Commission came to the conclusion that it was perpetuating some of the old evils.[41]

As the Waterfront Commission developed its program, it was not effectively deterred by the ILA, although it had to defend the Bi-State Compact in the courts. The ILA's challenge of the constitutionality of the law was ruled upon in mid-November. A three-judge federal court held unanimously that it was within the police power of the two states to require all longshoremen to register. Shortly the ban on public loaders was upheld, too.[42] The latter decision raised the immediate possibility of a jurisdictional clash between the ILA and the Teamsters. The latter had char-

[41] See below, pp. 136, 143ff.
[42] *New York Times*, Nov. 10, 1953, p. 1.

tered a new local to enroll the 2,500 men who had been employed in public loading.[43]

With the upholding of compulsory registration, the ILA bowed to the requirement, advising its members to register to avoid exclusion from their jobs after December 1. As a matter of fact, thousands had already registered. Of course the ILA was not giving up on its opposition to the law or in its determination to fight it in courts and in the legislatures of the two states. The AFL had also issued a strong statement against the Bi-State Compact, denouncing it as "regimentation" and pledging to seek the law's repeal once its new union had become firmly established; it blamed the ILA for passage of the law. Yet the AFL cautioned the longshoremen not to defy the statute while it remained on the books.[44]

Few longshoremen refused to register. As a matter of fact, there was a flood of registration, including many Seafarers who did not intend to work as longshoremen but who thought they might be able to influence the result of the pending election on representation. Others registered, too, who wanted to be eligible to work as longshoremen if they desired.

The register was open to any man who wanted to seek employment—as a matter of fact the question of an open or a closed register was to be a continuous bone of contention between the Waterfront Commission and the ILA, and the NYSA, too—and men were screened only with respect to criminal records. Even so, only 120 of the initial applicants were denied registration on these grounds. All men were at first given temporary registration pending further investigation.[45]

By mid-December the Waterfront Commission announced that it had gone a long way in operating its substitute for the outlawed shape-up. It claimed that the scrapping was accomplished with almost incredible smoothness. One reason for this

[43] *New York Times*, Dec. 10, 1953, p. 1.
[44] *New York Times*, Nov. 12, 1953, p. 1.
[45] Waterfront Commission, *Annual Report, 1953–54*, pp. 28–29.

was that the NYSA cooperated. But with the sudden elimination of public loading, the loading of trucks passed through a period of confusion and delay, although the NYSA recommended to its members that they employ only properly registered longshoremen to load and unload trucks. Joseph M. Adelizzi, managing director of the Empire State Highway Transportation Association, asserted that the loading situation on the docks after the court decision in mid-December was "a mess." There was insufficient manpower, and many trucks experienced much delay. The sudden ban on public loading had given the truckers little opportunity to adjust to the new situation. It did not take long, however, to get the new system to work, and rivalry between the Teamsters and the ILA did not become pronounced. The men were ILA and they stayed that way, but the question of their loyalty meshed in with the interunion controversy, which is covered in the next chapter.

6 | Challenge of the Labor Movement: Interunion Conflict

The drive by the AFL to displace the ILA came center stage late in 1953. Its contribution to the chaos that beset the industry has already been noted. Many from outside the industry actively supported the AFL. None was to play a more significant and colorful role than Father John Corridan, the "waterfront priest" who had befriended many longshoremen and served as their confidant and adviser. His message was that the ILA was corrupt and was due to fall if decent hard-working longshoremen got a real opportunity to choose. He encouraged the men to switch unions to be free from "totalitarian leaders" and to give themselves a democratic organization that would recognize "morality of conduct." So that they would not jeopardize their jobs, however, he advised all to sign the loyalty pledges issued by the ILA, but also to sign AFL membership forms being sent to their homes.[1]

Union rivalry became more intense, and both the Seafarers and the Teamsters played important roles. A particularly revealing episode took place in Brooklyn. Tony Anastasia had pushed through his program of consolidation of locals. Although his rise had not been without opposition in the hierarchy of the ILA, he now staunchly supported the hierarchy to protect his own domain. He, like the others, would have no future if the AFL won. Just before checking-in time on October 7, he appeared with a squad of seventy-five men outside the Bull Line

[1] *New York Times*, Oct. 3, 1953, p. 1; A. Raymond, *Waterfront Priest* (New York, 1960).

121

pier and proceeded to check the men's credentials to enforce an ILA policy against employment of AFL men alongside of ILA men. Many on the pier were reported to be supporting the AFL, and Anastasia confiscated union books of twenty-one AFL men. Although these were returned when the police intervened, he would not let the AFL men work. Then, at 8:30 A.M., with Anastasia still at the gate, the AFL decided to make a test. Seafarers walked off the freighter *Kathryn,* cutting off the steam for the winches. This made it impossible for longshoremen to work. Also, truck drivers in Tom Hickey's Teamster local were told not to make deliveries. The AFL strategists then decided to follow up this action with a sortie into Erie Basin, heart of Anastasia's empire. Shortly after noon, Seafarer crew members of an Isthmian Line freighter quit work. Without steam, five gangs of Anastasia's longshoremen had to quit.

The ILA struck back. Packy Connolly warned that the ILA might retaliate, saying, "Our men are incensed . . . and . . . feel that the only way to protect themselves is by refusing to handle anything brought in by truck." But he emphasized that the ILA was issuing no instructions to boycott goods, because, he said, "We are living up to the terms of the Taft-Hartley injunction and we are telling our people to work, but many of them are insisting on getting back at the AFL for their tactics."[2]

Conflicts occurred in many parts of the port, with varying degrees of physical encounter. Some involved theatrics with motorcades and blarring loudspeakers. Pamphlets flooded the docks. Police intervened in some situations and some arrests were made. Disruptions of work led employers to seek injunctive relief under the secondary boycott and jurisdictional provisions of the Taft-Hartley Act. Work stoppages, even though brief, led to the issuance to Anastasia and the ILA of show cause orders why they should not be cited for civil and criminal contempt of the no-strike injunction. At the same time the NYSA asked the

[2] *New York Times,* Oct. 8, 1953, p. 1.

courts to broaden the injunction to include the AFL unionists.[3]

The AFL appropriated $200,000 as a starter to organize its new union and said that it expected cooperation, not injunctions, from federal authorities. Meany said that the AFL would consider broadening the injunction "an unfriendly act," contending that it would only "lend aid and comfort to the gangsters in control of the New York Waterfront." He did not think it would be legal because the AFL was not on strike, had no collective bargaining relationship with the employers and, therefore, no dispute.[4]

The AFL filed charges against the ILA of interference with organizing, and Charles T. Douds, director of the NLRB in New York, issued a complaint alleging repeated violation of the NLRA, accusing the whole ILA, as well as the Anastasia brothers, of threats, coercion, and violence on the piers. He set a hearing for November 9, listing numerous violations: checking membership books of employees reporting for work; segregating AFL adherents from ILA adherents and detaining AFL supporters; threatening to inflict bodily injury and harm upon AFL longshoremen and actually doing just that; threatening to shut down the various shipping lines and stevedoring companies; promising benefits and rewards to dockworkers if they stayed loyal to the ILA, and threatening them with loss of benefits and rewards if they changed allegiance; and causing or attempting to cause shipping companies and stevedoring concerns to discriminate against the AFL dock group. Douds sought and obtained an injunction against the ILA and the brothers Anastasia, restraining them from committing acts of violence, intimidation, and coercion.

A couple of interesting developments took place within the ILA. Sampson quit his job as business agent of Local 791, agreeing to serve as an organizer for the AFL; but he failed to carry Local 791 with him. At a turbulent meeting in St. Bernard's Hall

[3] *New York Times*, Oct. 14, 1953, p. 1.
[4] *New York Times*, Oct. 15, 1953, p. 36.

only twenty-one men lined up with him; the others at the session, variously estimated at four hundred to nine hundred, voted to stay with the ILA.[5]

But an open call for the ouster of Ryan and other officers came from Michael Clemente, union overlord of the East River piers. He publicly said that their retirement was "the only way to clean up the dirt on the waterfront." Clemente, not without blemish himself, said that he had told Ryan to get out, but that Ryan had said, "Why do you say that to me now that I've got an indictment hanging over my head?" Shortly thereafter, at a meeting in Philadelphia, the ILA retired Ryan, giving him a pension of $10,000 a year for life. The successor had to be free from taint, and Captain William V. Bradley, from the Tugboatmen's local, was named president.[6]

On October 23 the Taft-Hartley injunction was extended to the AFL. The judge said that he was acting because the AFL was party to the dispute inasmuch as its activities contributed to the calling of the strike.[7]

The NYSA called upon the NLRB to determine the bargaining representative "without delay" because it feared a quick resumption of the strike at the expiration of the eighty-day injunction. Ace M. Keeney, a newly appointed chief of the AFL organizing drive, announced that the AFL would attempt to keep the ILA from being included on the NLRB ballot, saying that acceptance of employer gifts had proved that the old pier union was company-dominated and not a legitimate union. In rebuttal Packy Connolly said that this was simply a confession of weakness and that the AFL was afraid to let the longshoremen make their own decision. When the NYSA sent a telegram to President Eisenhower appealing for a prompt election, Keeney said that the President should do nothing "until we can . . . have a fair election and not one that is gang controlled." Also,

[5] *New York Times*, Oct. 20, 1953, p. 51.
[6] *New York Times*, Oct. 9, 1953, p. 1, Nov. 17, p. 1, Nov. 19, p. 1.
[7] *New York Times*, Oct. 24, 1953, p. 1.

"We feel the employers should be concerned with a clean water-front and not with backing up the mob."[8]

The NLRB

In mid-November the NLRB held hearings on the question of representation. The NYSA was still pushing for early resolution, but the AFL sought for a delay. The NYSA sought to limit the scope of the bargaining unit to the Port of New York; in this the AFL concurred. The ILA, on the other hand, wanted a bargaining unit that included all ports in the Atlantic Coast District. It also contended that the bargaining unit should consist of craft groups as well as longshoremen. The NYSA agreed with the ILA that six classifications named by the ILA were appropriate in a single unit, but the AFL sought to separate them.

The NLRB limited the bargaining unit to the Port of New York for the reason that the NYSA had no authority to bargain for employers in the other ports. As for separating longshoremen from the craft groups, the NLRB found an interchange of work and a mutuality of interest among the men in the six classifications, that none of the classifications could be described as a craft of the type the NLRB had recognized in other cases as separable. Hence, notwithstanding that separate agreements were negotiated with each group, it found that there was essentially one bargaining activity. Bargaining history and mutuality of interests dictated one bargaining unit for the whole port, comprised of the men in six classifications.[9]

The NLRB rejected the ILA contention, opposed by both the NYSA and the AFL, that public loaders and chenangoes—the latter were men who worked exclusively on cargoes transported on barges—should be included. Men in these two categories were not employed by members of the NYSA nor did NYSA bargain with the ILA with respect to them.

In deciding a man's eligibility to vote in an election, the NLRB looked to past employment but this industry had a large number

[8] *New York Times*, Oct. 23, 1953, p. 28, Nov. 4, p. 1, Nov. 19, p. 45.
[9] NLRB, *Decisions and Orders*, 1953, vol. 107, pp. 368ff.

of casuals. Because the NYSA and the ILA had for a number of years determined eligibility for vacation pay and welfare and pension benefits on the basis of seven hundred or more hours of work during the year, the NLRB limited eligibility to those men who had worked seven hundred or more hours. A second test was whether they had registered in the manner required by the Waterfront Commission.[10]

Another problem was the timing of the election. Normally the NLRB did not hold an election while charges of unfair labor practices were pending, and the AFL had filed such charges. But the expiration of the Taft-Hartley injunction was due shortly. Could an election be held prior to December 24? Then there was the requirement to conduct a ballot under the Taft-Hartley Act on the employers' "last offer." Could it be done?

Before these questions were answered, the Waterfront Commission opened its Information and Employment Centers.[11] A short, widespread walkout occurred. It was said that 75 per cent of the piers were idle. Those striking had placed themselves in double jeopardy as being violators of the eighty-day injunction as well as of the Bi-State Compact. It was a misdemeanor for anyone to interfere with the registration of longshoremen or with their employment on the docks, and a strike against the commission was probably not legal. The employers quickly protested and Captain Bradley soon instructed the men to go back to work after he and Teddy Gleason, newly appointed general organizer, were haled into court.[12]

The Taft-Hartley Board soon made its final report to the President.[13] It reported that a December 24 strike should be ex-

[10] NLRB, *Nineteenth Annual Report*, 1954, p. 56.

[11] These centers were strategically located throughout the port to be available to both men and employers—five in Manhattan, four in Brooklyn, and one each in Staten Island, Port Newark, Jersey City, and Hoboken.

[12] *New York Times*, Dec. 2, 1953, p. 1; Waterfront Commission, *Annual Report, 1953–54*, p. 36.

[13] U.S. Board of Inquiry, *Report to the President on the Labor Dis-*

pected, "a strike that will defy solution by the most expert of mediators." The employers, of course, had filed their "last offer," but after due consideration it was decided by the NLRB not to conduct a ballot inasmuch as it would be meaningless. In spite of pressures to delay, the board decided to hold the representation election on December 22–23, just before the expiration of the Taft-Hartley injunction. Various notable governmental officials[14] had urged the NLRB to move slowly. The NYSA, however, complimented the NLRB for expediting the vote and said, "We feel sure that we will be able to negotiate an agreement very quickly with whoever wins." Opponents of the ILA felt that the NLRB had made a serious mistake. The AFL bitterly protested. Meany criticized the timing and said that it was a "moral disgrace" to let the ILA appear on the ballot, adding that the NLRB deserved "public castigation for succumbing to pressure from the New York Shipping Association."[15]

The rival unions stepped up their organizational drives. The ILA cry was, "Vote ILA all the way." The AFL themes were, "The ILA will rob your pay"; "Vote AFL and get rid of the mob"; and "Get rid of those five and dime raises." At this juncture John L. Lewis, president of United Mineworkers, threw his protective mantle around the orphaned ILA, making a much-needed loan of $50,000. As a result of it, Captain Bradley announced that thirty-three special organizers would be employed, saying, "Our financial worries are over," and expressed his personal view that the ILA should affiliate with Lewis' union after the balloting. The ILA tried to capitalize on its newly established ties by distributing leaflets along the waterfront which said, "We cannot be wrong. John L. Lewis is with us. The only man in

---

pute Involving Longshoremen and Associated Occupations in the Maritime Industry on the Atlantic Coast, Dec. 4, 1953.

[14] Among them were James B. Mitchell, secretary of labor; Bernard Shanley, special counsel to the President; Governor Dewey; Joseph M. Proskauer, chairman of the State Crime Commision; and Lawrence E. Walsh, executive director of the Waterfront Commission.

[15] New York Times, Dec. 12, 1953, p. 1, Dec. 17, p. 1, Dec. 18, p. 1; NLRB, Nineteenth Annual Report, 1954, p. 58.

the history of labor to successfully defy the AFL. This man whose name is a byword throughout the world has proven he is for the working man, knows we are right and is with us all the way." Also, on the eve of the election Captain Bradley met with Lewis in Washington, D.C., and posed for pictures. On the other hand, Meany appeared on television to reach the longshoremen and said, "We want you in the AFL. [But] we won't take you . . . with the corrupt leaders that are now at the head of the old ILA. We don't want the gangsters; we don't want the underworld characters who are exploiting you day in and day out. We want you to run your own union."[16]

The voting was heavy on the first day as a result of the machinelike organization set up by the ILA to get workers to the polls. Workers finishing the night shift on the West Side found ILA automobiles or buses ready to transport them to the polls. Buses were used through the day on both sides of the Hudson, and all the transportation was provided by the ILA. The AFL had considered setting up a parallel commutation service but decided against it on the ground that many dock workers might fear to enter AFL buses thereby risking future disfavor of pier bosses allied with the ILA.

Despite the bitterness of the preelection campaign, the voting on the first day was peaceful. Electioneering was barred around the polls, and agents representing the rival unions were kept at a distance while the men voted. The men, many still clutching their hooks, stood in line patiently, impassively. They voted quietly. On the second day, however, violence broke out at several spots in Brooklyn. A number of men were stabbed and there were many fist fights.[17]

The election was inconclusive. The ILA received 9,060 votes and the AFL 7,568, with 95 votes for neither union, 116 void, and 4,405 challenged. The challenged ballots might have determined the outcome, but the AFL charged that the balloting had

[16] *New York Times*, Dec. 18, 1953, p. 1, Dec. 23, p. 1, Dec. 22, p. 1.
[17] *New York Times*, Dec. 23, 1953, p. 17, Dec. 24, p. 1; see NLRB, *Nineteenth Annual Report*, 1954, pp. 61–62.

been conducted under circumstances of intimidation and violence by known criminals. Meany said, "We do not accept the tally as indicating the true and free choice of the longshoremen, many of whom were forced to vote under threats and actual physical assault," and the AFL promptly petitioned the NLRB to set aside the election. The ILA put off strike action for ten days—the Taft-Hartley injunction had expired—ostensibly to give the NLRB time to act on the challenged ballots. Nevertheless, a couple of days later Captain Bradley issued a public warning to the NYSA to begin negotiations at once or face a strike any time after the ten-day extension.[18]

Governor Dewey was spurred to action. He requested immediate reports on the events and atmosphere surrounding the election. Plainly the governor wanted to delay a decision and intimated that he would call upon Senator Irving M. Ives to press for a Senate investigation of the NLRB if it proceeded to certification of the ILA. The ILA expressed defiance of the Dewey-ordered investigation, yet withdrew its threat to strike.[19]

In a move without parallel in the history of the NLRB, Governor Dewey, putting the full prestige of the state behind the AFL petition, announced that he would send a special representative to show that coercion and intimidation surrounded the election. In turn, the ILA called on President Eisenhower to appoint a special coordinator to iron out the waterfront labor muddle; Captain Bradley made it plain that the intention was to outflank Governor Dewey. Connolly joined Bradley, describing the governor as "a little man with too much power, who is trying to intimidate the labor board and take over its functions." But President Eisenhower simply said the matter was up to the NLRB.[20]

The AFL insisted that the NLRB rule on its objections to the election before taking up the question of the challenged ballots. Douds, regional director, reported to the NLRB that men wear-

[18] *New York Times*, Dec. 25, 1953, p. 1, Dec. 27, p. 1, Dec. 30, p. 1.
[19] *New York Times*, Dec. 28, 1953, p. 1, Dec. 29, p. 1.
[20] *New York Times*, Dec. 31, 1953, p. 1, Jan. 1, 1954, pp. 1, 14.

ing ILA campaign buttons had threatened dock workers with bodily harm and loss of their jobs if they did not vote for the ILA. He called for a hearing on the question of a new election. The NYSA thereupon ruled out negotiations pending a decision.[21] While the NLRB was working out the steps to be taken, the port was far from peaceful.

Between Election Events and the Second Election

Under criticism for having conducted the representation election so quickly and under multiple pressures to set it aside, the NLRB trod carefully. Time was needed to sort things out. John L. Lewis warned the ILA that it would get no more financial aid unless it cleaned its house. It is said that the president of the Teamsters, Dave Beck, had a meeting with Lewis, his old associate, and this was responsible for Lewis' apparent change of view. Concurrently, the ILA said that there were too many local unions and it planned to merge fifteen into four. This may have been a response to Lewis or simply a move to strengthen the ILA against the AFL, or it could have been aimed at Tony Anastasia, who was getting too strong; the plans included some consolidations in Manhattan but not of the key locals.[22] But nothing came of this.

All was not well in the ILA. In mid-February the executive committees of the Atlantic Coast, South Atlantic, and Gulf Coast districts met in Washington. It appeared that some locals in southern ports were drifting toward the AFL.[23] The ILA, therefore, had to work hard to prevent defections.

The ILA also had a major problem with the Teamsters, who thought the time opportune to claim the work of loading and unloading of trucks at the piers. The drivers, of course, were Teamsters, and Dave Beck thought that his program would be easier if the trucking companies took over the work. He offered

[21] *New York Times,* Jan. 3, 1954, p. 1, Jan. 12, 1954, p. 1, Jan. 13, p. 1.
[22] *New York Times,* Jan. 14, 1954, p. 1, Jan. 17, p. 68, Jan. 19, p. 45, Feb. 6, p. 14.
[23] *New York Times,* Feb. 17, 1954, p. 49.

New York truck operators a two-million-dollar loan to set up an equipment pool so that they might do the work instead of the steamship companies and stevedores who had the work thrust upon them. When clashes between Teamsters and ILA members occurred at a number of places, Beck obtained an injunction against interference with truck loading. The NYSA let it be known that it was considering legal action for damages caused by work stoppages resulting from the fight between the ILA and the Teamsters.[24] When some local ILA leaders refused to handle cargoes unloaded by Teamsters, top ILA officers quickly instructed members not to violate the injunction, fearing fines or jail sentences; but it is interesting that Local 807 of the Teamsters, the one involved in the fight to claim the work, voluntarily withdrew pickets. ILA men did not shift membership, and the dispute over loading became submerged by a different, and larger, dispute.

The AFL set up a picket line outside Pier 32 of the Moore-McCormack Line, on the North River, to protest the discharge of an AFL steward resulting from ILA pressure on the company. The next day disgruntled ILA supporters shut down a large part of the port, estimated at more than half of the piers. An observer on the waterfront described the tie-up as "one of those well organized unauthorized strikes." NLRB investigators were on the piers to determine whether the stoppage was spontaneous or planned. The NLRB quickly got a contempt citation against the ILA for violating the injunction against harassment of AFL men, and a fine of $50,000 was levied on the ILA.[25]

A rank-and-file committee of ILA members then bobbed up as sponsors of the strike, although members of the committee refused to identify themselves for fear they would be blacklisted by the Waterfront Commission. They asserted that they had won the election in December and that the strike proved that they had the overwhelming support of the men; and they added, with cynicism, "If the AF of L is so strong why can't it

24 *New York Times*, Jan. 26, 1954, p. 1, Feb. 5, p. 20.
25 *New York Times*, March 6, 1954, p. 1, March 9, p. 1.

work the port. . . . [If it] had won an election, it would have been certified the next day. We are not going to work the piers until we get certified or get a contract."[26]

On March 10, when half of the longshoremen in Brooklyn, the only section of the port that had been operating normally, joined the week-old walkout, Mayor Robert Wagner intervened, conferred with several governmental officials, and held two emergency sessions with top labor and commerce advisers. His efforts ran abruptly into a dead end when his proposal, to name an individual or a committee to decide waterfront grievances and disputes as they arose on a day-to-day basis, received a quick, negative answer from the AFL. It would not "carry forward any conferences that involve[d] negotiations or agreements direct or individually—even though through the high office of the Mayor of New York—with the racket-infested and mob-controlled ILA." Meany was "incensed" at employers who he believed were backing the strike by refusing to have their hiring agents perform hiring duties. The AFL's formula for waterfront peace was an immediate second election. To this the ILA was opposed, saying there was no reason for a new vote when all that was needed was for the NLRB to certify its victory.[27]

Government agencies adopted a "get tough" policy toward the wildcat pier strikers. The army announced that it would hire dock workers under civil service regulations. Striking members of the ILA were pulled out of picket lines and interrogated before a federal grand jury on who started the strike. The Waterfront Commission called four hiring bosses in for questioning after the AFL complained that they were refusing to blow the work whistle when men were available to load and unload ships. Mayor Wagner phoned Guy Farmer, chairman of the NLRB in Washington, and urged the board to hold day and night hearings to speed up its decision on the validity of the

[26] *New York Times*, March 10, 1954, p. 1.
[27] *New York Times*, March 11, 1954, p. 1, March 12, p. 1, March 13, p. 1.

election. Farmer promised to do everything to expedite a ruling.[28]

On April 1, the NLRB decided that there was misconduct on the part of the ILA,[29] and it invalidated the December election and ordered a new one. To ensure that the new election would be held under proper conditions, it stated that any union which before the election engaged in conduct designed to thwart or abuse the process of the NLRB would be denied a place on the ballot. It also informed the ILA that it could not appear on the ballot unless the dock strike was ended "forthwith." The ILA promptly called off the strike. The NLRB then ordered the new election to be held on or before May 26; May 26 became the fixed date by agreement of the two unions.[30]

Before the election the Waterfront Commission released information that two associates of Anastasia had gone to the West Coast to confer with Bridges, seeking funds for the ILA. Packy Connolly thereupon accused the Waterfront Commission of seeking to win the election for the AFL and said that the top leaders of the ILA knew nothing of Anastasia's effort to raise money from Bridges. But the ILA was in trouble with the federal government because of the $50,000 fine imposed for criminal contempt, and its bank assets were impounded to assure payment. And two days before the election the ILA was thrown into federal receivership.[31]

This time the voting was peaceful. The ILA received 9,110 of the ballots and the AFL 8,791, while 1,797 were challenged. Again, the results were indecisive, but the ILA this time led by only 319 votes. Early in June the NLRB announced a formula for counting the challenged ballots, recommending that only 655 ballots, the technical challenges based on improper identification in spelling of names, be opened and counted, although 472 other technical challenges, based on lack of registration with the

[28] *New York Times*, March 14, 1954, p. 1, March 15, p. 18.

[29] NLRB, *Nineteenth Annual Report*, p. 62.

[30] *New York Times*, April 3, 1954, p. 1, April 28, p. 1.

[31] *New York Times*, May 1, 1954, p. 1, May 22, p. 1, May 23, p. 1, May 25, p. 1.

Waterfront Commission or less than 700 hours of work, would be sustained. A block of 666 other ballots, challenged on the ground that the men were supervisors, would be held for a hearing provided the 655 ballots to be opened did not determine a winner. The formula was followed. In July a revised tally was released, showing 9,407 for the ILA, and 9,144 for the AFL, 55 for neither, and 12 void. The ILA lead was cut to 263. Without counting or disposing of the 666 other challenged ballots the matter was still undecided. A hearing had to be held. The NLRB accepted the AFL contention that 491 hatch bosses were supervisors, and their ballots were thrown out—the AFL would have lost most of them and it knew it. The ILA condescended because this left only 175 ballots, not enough to change the result, even if the AFL got all of them, and they were not opened. The ILA, was the victor, but by a very narrow margin, and was certified as the bargaining agent.[32]

The temper of many longshoremen may account for the failure to oust the ILA. Many longshoremen believed that their jobs were in danger if the ILA were defeated. They knew full well that the Seafarers and the Teamsters were active on the waterfront. They knew that many Seafarers had registered with the Waterfront Commission as longshoremen and that the Teamsters were trying to control the work of loading and unloading trucks. Some public officials, aware of fears in the minds of many longshoremen that the Seafarers and the Teamsters intended to take waterfront jobs, sought out Paul Hall and Dave Beck to ask them to make a public pronouncement that no Seafarer or Teamster would take longshore jobs. They were not successful in their request. The truth is that many longshoremen voted for their jobs first, and only secondarily for the ILA. Failure within the AFL to recognize the longshoreman's fear of losing his job, and the need to extend assurances that none would lose jobs, no

[32] NLRB, *Decisions and Orders*, vol. 108, pp. 137–158, vol. 109, pp. 310–312, 791–793, 1075–1079; cf. *New York Times*, June 4, 1954, p. 1, June 19, p. 1, July 28, p. 37.

doubt contributed heavily to the failure of the IBL to win, even when the AFL lavishly financed the organizing effort.

The ILA, not without suffering many scars of battle, had now weathered attacks by some rank-and-file groups—although it must be conceded that it had much support from other rank-and-file groups—by the government, and by the labor movement. It still had a lease on life. But it had lost the territory of hiring control and had to accept a permanent governmental agency with the power to regulate some of its activities. It had been expelled from the AFL. Life under these conditions would not be so easy, but the need to do a better job in collective bargaining seemed to have been carried home. The public eye was upon it and, even though it had won the right to continue with its union affairs, it knew that it was subject to further attack.

The employers, too, had not come through these years unscathed. Many chafed about their image, feeling that they did not deserve it. They would strive to conform to the new controls—although some were reluctant to do so—and they would strive to be more progressive at the bargaining table.

7 | Intercurrence: Bargaining, the Waterfront Commission, and Hiring

Because the parties had come close to a settlement in 1953 before the interunion fight blocked consummation of negotiations and they had lived under the old agreement without change, it might have been expected that a quick settlement would have been made. For a number of reasons, this was not to be. The closeness of the vote and IBL criticisms pressured the ILA to seek a good agreement. But questions of retroactive pay and union shop created real difficulties. Because the NYSA had offered an increase in wages and welfare payments in 1953, the ILA argued that the men were entitled to these increases for all hours worked in the interim. But the employers argued that there was no way to pick up such costs because they could not levy shipping charges retroactively. The employers also, or at least some of them, were not sure they could, or should, continue the union shop clause in view of the great numbers of men who had joined or supported the AFL. But the ILA was adamant, and called a one-day strike, primarily to stress the demand for retroactive pay, but also to demonstrate resentment against the Waterfront Commission for its allegations in its first annual report that gangsters controlled the ILA and for its hiring regulations, and to show support for the union shop.[1]

Proposed Changes in Hiring Regulations

The Waterfront Commission, having concluded that current mechanics of hiring under the prevalidation program did not

[1] *New York Times,* Oct. 5, 1954, p. 1, Oct. 6, p. 1; Waterfront Commission, *Annual Report, 1953–55.*

conform to the Bi-State Compact, abruptly announced a public hearing on a proposed change in hiring regulations. It was believed that the ILA was illegally playing a role in selection of gangs and men, even that a limited, private shape-up at the piers was being continued. Samuel M. Lane, executive director, accused the employers of cooperating—willingly or reluctantly—to allow it. The hearing caught both the NYSA and the ILA by surprise. Both were angry. The employers had sat with the commission at the outset and helped devise the existing system; this time they had not been consulted. They were upset, too, because they thought the proposed hiring system and method of getting men to the docks would be too time-consuming, and they were opposed to several other features of the proposal. The ILA, of course, did not want to lose its remaining influence over hiring.[2] The anger over shortness of notice, coming while negotiations were under way, is understandable. The negotiators on each side were the very persons who possessed the practical knowledge about the needs in a hiring system, and negotiations and the hearing could not go on simultaneously. The commission was charged with deliberate disruption of collective bargaining. But this anger was only a flurry compared to the basic opposition. However, when the employers better understood what the commission had in mind much, but not all, of their opposition was dissipated. Not so with the ILA. Besides, the matter of hiring was a major issue in negotiations.

The hearing reflects the basic struggle between the ILA and the commission as well as the role of the employers. Both parties were strongly critical of the commission for not seeking advice from practical men in the industry. Both thought the only sensible way to proceed was through small committees sitting down and hammering out needed changes. The NYSA had prepared a memorandum in which it emphasized that the existing regulations had been the product of many months of study by a committee of employers sitting with the commission and that it was

[2] Waterfront Commission, "Public Hearing, IV, Oct. 15, 1954" (mimeographed); *New York Times*, Oct. 3, p. 1.

agreed that they were in conformity with the Bi-State Compact; and if there were abuses the commission had punitive powers and could eliminate them. Furthermore, the proposal was seen as placing an unnecessary economic burden on the industry by requiring hiring at a center.[3] The NYSA also stressed the protection the law gave to collective bargaining, explicitly the right to "agree upon any method of selection . . . by way of seniority, experience, regular gangs or otherwise," although it was conceded that methods agreed upon had to conform with the law.[4] The employers were opposed to creation of voluntary gangs because they thought this would lead to lack of control and possibly to rotation in hiring, to which they were unalterably opposed, citing what they considered to be the unfortunate experience on the West Coast.[5] They also feared that the commission was giving hatch bosses too much authority to commit employers to unrevocable hiring; this issue—that is, the elimination of the so-called 'weather clause' which permitted cancellation of orders to report without incurring an obligation to pay the men—was an important one in the current negotiations.

The commission was most concerned by the fact that employers were allowed to prevalidate gangs and lists of dock workers for five days but from among those prevalidated they

[3] Lyon said that when the law was being enacted at Albany he had asked, relative to hiring, "Do you mean through or at?" and that he got the answer "We do not mean at." Lane responded, "We are thinking about the regulation which will be practicable and workable. It can be 'through' rather than 'at' but if it can't be worked out that way, then we think it will have to be 'at' " (ibid., pp. 31, 33).

[4] Ibid., pp. 24–26.

[5] Andrew Warwick, well-known stevedore who had a major responsibility in shipping war material on both the Atlantic and Pacific coasts, speaking of the dislike of rotational hiring, said, "The best example is the West Coast . . . and I want to tell you the three and a half years I spent in the Army when the West Coast was doing 11 tons an hour, we were doing 18 here" (Waterfront Commission, op. cit., p. 66). The difference in productivity may be surprising to some who have idealized the West Coast in comparison to the Port of New York. In a private negotiating caucus in New York in 1968 a prominent West Coast employer warned against moving to rotational hiring, saying, "Tonnage is much better here than on the West Coast."

were selecting each day at the pier those they wanted to work; this was interpreted as a shape-up. Andrew Warwick, a prominent stevedore, disputed this: "I don't think we are asking the men to shape, if I understand what a shape is." Told that the commission's records showed that he had averaged using only 45 per cent of the men prevalidated, he said defensively, "We sat down with the members of your Commission at the inception of this program . . . to try and devise a scheme that was workable. Your Commission bent over backward to give us the very thing we needed, our regular employees . . . and we came up with this plan of validation . . . and we have followed it meticulously right to the letter. Now, you tell me . . . we have a shape. I don't agree with it at all." But, a commission spokesman rejoined, "What the Commission has required you to do and what you have, in good faith, tried to do, does not carry out the mandate of the law. . . . It is the fault of the procedure which we are trying to correct . . . the regulation will not prevent you from having your regular employees. . . . It will not prevent you from hiring the same gangs you have hired. The only difference . . . you will hire them through the center rather than post a notice at your pierhead."[6]

An example of the commission's concern is revealed in the testimony of Edward Carroll, another prominent stevedore. He said, "If I need an extra gang, . . . I can contact other employers to find out if they have gangs . . . then I have called the [ILA] and asked them if they know of gangs. . . . If they . . . gave me the names of . . . foremen, then I would contact the foremen, and ask them to come to my office, bringing with them the list of the men in their gangs, with their bi-state numbers. . . . If they showed . . . I would make a [Waterfront Commission] sheet . . . and I send my hiring agent with it to your center and have the gang prevalidated and order the gang to work at the same time." He was a little taken aback to hear "that system that you have described is not hiring either at or through the center." He protested, "If you say it's not hiring

[6] *Ibid.,* pp. 54–57.

through the center, then I'll disagree with you . . . we're hiring through the center." He was challenged further, "You have explained . . . that you hire the gang in your office and then you tell the center about it afterwards." Rejoined Carroll, "On the contrary. We have made arrangements for the hire. We don't hire the men until they appear at our pier, then we check them in and put them on the payroll. Prior to that they are not hired."[7] The commission doubted that this practice was hiring through the center, for the center was merely advised after the fact of hiring, arranged either through connection with other employers or the union.

The Waterfront Commission would not concede that it was interferring with collective bargaining. With a positive duty to establish a hiring system, it was certainly unwilling to sit back and wait on collective bargaining to produce an acceptable one. It would not postpone the hearing but decided to take the matter under advisement. But the conclusion it had reached before the hearing was not effectively challenged and the parties were clearly warned:

One thing should be made clear, that the regulation is not carrying out the mandate of the statute as long as it permits the hiring to be arranged through the union or through anyone else and merely recorded at the information center. And that . . . is what is possible and, in many cases, being done under the present regulation.[8]

No one should have been in doubt that some change was ahead. But the commission delayed implementation of the new regulations, allowing a lapse of time and a second hearing in March 1955, after the parties had completed their collective bargaining negotiations but before issuance and effectuation.

Collective Bargaining—Hiring Practices

While the Waterfront Commission was marking time, the ILA and the NYSA continued with their negotiations, but

[7] *Ibid.*, pp. 79–80, 84, 85.
[8] *Ibid.*, p. 168.

slowly. In early December, with the assistance of federal mediator Andrew Burke and a city official, Vincent O'Connor, they
reached an agreement on a seventeen-cent package with eight
cents retroactive to October 1, 1953. The ILA submitted it to a
vote by longshoremen, who rejected it by a vote of 6,199 to
4,590, something of a surprise to ILA leaders as well as to employers.[9] It could be explained partly, perhaps substantially, by
AFL obstruction, perhaps in pure spite. But it could be explained also by failure of ILA leaders to "sell" it. Captain Bradley admitted publicly that not enough effort was made to explain
the new agreement. Also, the men had become accustomed to
rejection of agreements, first, because they did not always like
them and, second, because they had learned that they could get
more without cost. Even some ILA leaders criticized failure to
consider local priorities. Important, perhaps, were the "untied
ends" to be endorsed in principle, with details to be worked out,
such as the arbitration machinery and port customs and practices.
The fact that only the longshoremen, exclusive of the crafts,
voted may have made a difference. The craft groups were more
loyal to the hierarchy. When the ILA brought back twelve
special demands, the NYSA turned them down, saying that the
seventeen cents had been given on condition that these items
would be dropped. In a second vote with some 4,000 checkers,
clerks, coopers, and carpenters also voting, the result was 11,572
for acceptance to 4,222 for rejection. It may be of some interest
that the balloting was conducted by locals individually, not by
the Honest Ballot Association, which had conducted the first
one.[10]

On February 24, 1955 the agreement was signed.[11] The notable points, besides the wage increases, were the union shop, but

[9] Edward P. Tastrom, "Shipping Outlook," *Journal of Commerce,*
Dec. 17, 1954; *Waterfront News,* Jan. 7, 1955, p. 1.

[10] *Waterfront News,* Jan. 7, 1955, p. 1.

[11] NYSA and ILA, *Agreements negotiated by the New York Shipping
Association with the International Longshoremen's Association for the
Port of Greater New York and Vicinity,* Effective Oct. 1, 1951.

this had been a feature of the old agreement; a clause requiring hiring foremen "to be selected solely by the employer [to conform with the requirement of the Bi-State Compact] from men familiar with the men in the area who . . . had Port of New York Waterfront work for at least two years," who would give preference in hiring to men who had worked regularly on the pier for which they were being hired; deletion of the "weather clause"; and provision for shop stewards on all piers and a new grievance system with a permanent arbitrator. Of special note, a section on "Shaping Time" was deleted—but details about hours of work, starting times, special conditions, knocking off, suitable shelter, minimum number of men in the general cargo gang, and specialized gangs, transfers, size or weight of the sling load, working rules, travel time, were all carried over from the former agreement. A new clause, "customs and practices, in effect on December 28, 1954 shall remain in effect," was demanded by the union because of the new grievance and arbitration system, where the rules of the pier or section might be involved but which were too varied to be written down. These, supposedly, were understood but hardly documentable; certain practices varied from place to place and were known only locally. They were to be the source of some contention; certainly employers who would sit on the Labor Relations Committee (LRC), the third step in the new grievance system, would have to be educated about practices as cases were considered. They would not be able to tell easily whether a practice claimed was established or a new contrivance.

Most important was a section on hiring practices and procedures which took the place of the deleted clause on "Shaping Time." It was set forth in what was called "Annex A." It gave definitions and the rights of both regular and extra gangs and men and the ordering procedures, most noteworthy of which was "Paragraph 7," which read: "In the event that the employer desires extra gangs organized in units in addition to the regular gangs he shall notify the union of number of extra gangs needed.

The employer shall at the same time take such action as may be required under existing law to validate such extra gangs."

The Waterfront Commission accepted the ordering procedures, but saw illegality in this clause. The commission considered the word "notify" to be just another way of saying "order," and the union, therefore, would have an active role in designating gangs, something that was explicitly illegal under the Bi-State Compact. It ordered the employers not to notify the union at all.

New Hiring Regulations of the Waterfront Commission

As will be seen, revision of the regulations regarding hiring was intertwined to a degree with collective bargaining. The Waterfront Commission mulled over the criticism and suggestions made at the hearings in October and March. It prepared to go ahead on April 1, but the ILA tried to block it. Packy Connolly, under date of March 29, prepared a statement and sent it to the NYSA, intending to present it to the LRC meeting for adoption. In it Connolly held that the contract was legal and valid, providing proper safeguards and recognizing customs and practices, and that any departure from its terms would be a breach. Alexander Chopin, a newspaperman originally hired for public relations, had just succeeded J. V. Lyon as chairman of the NYSA, and he immediately made it clear that any action by the ILA to disrupt port activities would be in violation of the agreement and would not be condoned. The employers did not want to get into a battle with the Waterfront Commission.

The new hiring regulations went into effect on April 1 and the practice of prevalidation was abandoned. Each employer filed the names of the men in his regular gangs, designating the hatch boss or gang foreman, while the commission assigned numbers to the gangs by pier and section of the port within the area covered by each of the employment and information centers. At each center a wall-sized "availability board" was constructed and all gangs in the section were listed with their numbers. To engage his regular gangs for the next day, the hiring agent simply informed the center by 4:00 P.M. and posted the information at the pier. The manager of the center showed on the "availability board" that the gang was engaged. The members of the gang reported directly to the pier.

Any gang not engaged for work on its own pier might be ordered for work on another pier. In addition, there were some new "voluntary" gangs which had no pier and others whose regular pier had been shut down. These, too, were available. Some gangs were listed as "regular extras," and there were customs and practices pertaining to hiring them. Regardless, when an employer needed gangs beyond his regulars, his hiring agent appeared at the center and, where gangs were shown on the board to be available, he was put in touch with the hatch boss of the gang he selected, perhaps by telephone although the hatch boss could be present, too, and an engagement was worked out for the next day. The manager of the center then entered this information on the availability board. The gang foreman informed his gang members of the engagement and they reported to the pier the next morning as ordered. As it turned out, men often called the center, or their wives did, to find out if a gang had been ordered and where it would be working. Gangs once hired could be continued at work on successive days by informing the manager of the center.

Each employer also was allowed to establish and maintain rosters at each pier or terminal of regular employees by classifications. No initial restraint was imposed on the size of the lists, but to remain on a list an employee had to work twelve days during the month, or 80 per cent of the days that workers in the classification were employed during the month, whichever was less. The commission supplied forms for the lists and the men were identified as one, two, three, and so on. Copies were filed with the employment and information centers. Hiring was consummated by the use of another form consisting of a series of numbers, and the hiring agent simply circled the number of each man wanted and sent a copy to the center by 4:00 P.M. the day before and posted one on the bulletin board at the pier.

The men reported directly to the pier in the morning. If a man did not report for work his failure to do so had to be reported to the center within twenty-four hours; no discipline was intended by this, only a check on the use of the roster.

A third—not new—aspect of the hiring concerned the selecting of men as casuals at the center. Any man on a list who had not been engaged by his regular employer, or any man in a gang which had not been ordered, or any man unattached, could appear at the center in the morning for work that day. The hiring agents selected men in this shape-up in the center, making their choices as they saw fit for fill-ins for gangs, for additions to them, or for additional dock labor by whatever classifications. Men so hired could be continued in employment on succeeding days if the hiring agent informed the manager of the center and the men.

This hiring system was a decided improvement. It built in the gang and pier priorities in a simple and reasonable way. The ILA, of course, chafed under the new regulations. Other critics derided the arrangement for hiring of casuals as the "steam-heated shape." Some men liked the old shape-up at the pier, but others realized that with the centralization of the casual shape-up they had more than one chance for a job, because several companies were hiring at the same center.

Customs and Practices Agreements

Following the hearings on the new hiring regulations, and growing out of them, were a number of meetings between representatives of the commission, employers, and local union leaders by sections of the port, for the purpose of spelling out existing customs and practices pertaining to the hiring of gangs. Some agreements already existed in writing, others were generally known, whereas some were "negotiated" or formulated. North of Forty-second Street in Manhattan, where the luxury liners docked, and where Local 824 held sway, an agreement was written which conformed generally to the hiring customs and practices then in effect. It pertained to hiring of baggage porters carried on areawide labor lists as well as gangs. Local 856, in the lower Manhattan area, had a system of "equalization" which had been established about 1941 for the assignment of gangs beyond the regulars from the pier. All gangs in the area, some forty-nine in all, were carried on a roster which had been maintained in the local's headquarters. If an employer wanted more gangs than his regular ones, they were assigned on the basis of least cumulated earnings. This system was placed under the control of the manager at the center, although the union meticulously ran the system, too, as a check on the manager. No other agreements were worked out for Manhattan, but pier or terminal practices on some of the piers were clearly understood. No written agreements existed in Brooklyn, although there were many understandings related to individual piers, terminals, or companies. Some companies transferred their gangs from certain piers to other piers in a customary way. Surprising to some, a written agreement was worked out with Anastasia, but was promptly abandoned because it interfered too much with earnings that gangs had enjoyed previously. Anastasia, under pressure from the gangs, rescinded the agreement, but put blame on the Waterfront Commission. Staten Island had a system similar to that of Local 856, but a formal written statement of it had to be produced. On the Jersey side, Jersey City, Hoboken, and Port Newark operated separately. In Jersey City an agreement was worked out but never signed. Hoboken gave up on an agreement when it learned that one was not required. Port Newark, a unique area, developed without finger piers common everywhere else, had a system of equalization between gangs of two locals, one Negro and one white, with some preferences within each group of gangs; but no written agreement was accepted.[12]

Even while customs and practices agreements were being worked out, the ILA continued its attacks on the Waterfront

[12] For a more detailed description of these agreements see Vernon H. Jensen, *Hiring of Dock Workers and Employment Practices in the Ports of New York, Liverpool, London, Rotterdam and Marseilles* (Cambridge, 1964), pp. 74–82.

Commission. At its convention in July pent-up animosities were given free reign. Captain Bradley set the tone, criticizing the press for "highlighting articles handed down by the Bi-State," as he usually referred to the commission, and printing "stories that nobody—God, himself, couldn't straighten out." Vincent O'Connor, head of the Department of Marine and Aviation in the city government, always friendly to the ILA, commended their collective agreement for producing "the most effective basis for decent labor relations this port has ever had," but he startled some ILA leaders by saying that "the Waterfront Commission deserves its just share of credit for the continuance of labor stability . . . keeping troublemakers on both sides of the industry-labor fence in line," and adding that he was "not in sympathy" with resolutions "condemning the Waterfront Commission and calling for its abolition. . . . I consider them short-sighted, ill-advised . . . inflammatory . . . [and convincing to] . . . most government officials that the Waterfront Commission's controls certainly are still required today." He could not forgo criticizing "rigid gang practices" which he said were handicapping city-owned piers and were "a stumbling block for the City in its efforts to rent good piers in certain areas." What he was referring to was the fixed distribution of men in the gang as between, dock, deck, and hold, regardless of whether work was being required of some men. He said, "Men on the dock frequently render no service for substantial periods of the day. The gang load is therefore distributed among 15 to 16 men rather than 20. Gang productivity proportionately drops . . . [and] for every special dock man whom it favors, it helps keep from employment hundreds of longshoremen who would find jobs if shipping lines . . . would be encouraged to lease piers in certain areas now plagued by the union-imposed custom."[13]

But Captain Bradley and others answered that "the Bi-State . . . discriminates against our union." Teddy Gleason vitriolically expressed the ILA's justification for its battle against the

[13] ILA, *Proceedings of the Thirty-seventh Convention, July 1955*, pp. 11–16.

commission. He said that behind it was "a drive against our organization unprecedented in a democratic country." He saw a veritable vendetta against the ILA by the newspapers, the state legislatures, the United States Congress, Chamber of Commerce, the Port Authority, the shipping industry, all "to destroy our union . . . supposedly in the interest of ridding the waterfront of 'racketeering' gangsters. Every fundamental tenet of American fairplay and democracy was violated." Then he challenged the principal enemy, the Waterfront Commission.[14] The convention thereupon resolved to petition the two governors "to exercise all possible means to effectuate the removal of Samuel M. Lane"; "resolved to summarily dismiss, disqualify, and forever deny membership in any local of the ILA to any person holding membership in the IBL"; and demanded that the register be closed and when reopened to make sure the ILA was "a part of that registration," asserting, "We are running our union with dignity."

A little later, the ILA got Governor Averell Harriman's ear, or, more precisely, that of his counsel, Daniel Gutman. A proposal to create a buffer committee to settle differences between the Waterfront Commission and the ILA was explained by Gutman. The buffer committee would be unsalaried and have no power to enforce decisions but would try to settle grievances. Further, it would be comprised of one representative each from the ILA and the NYSA and two or three members appointed by the governor. Strong public reaction quickly knocked the notion down and the NYSA clearly refused to participate.[15]

The IBL continued to needle the ILA. It repeated demands to stop speed-up, to limit sling loads, and to establish a seniority system. Partly, these attacks were designed to point to failures of the ILA to take care of the interests of the men. While the IBL itself was critical of the Waterfront Commission, it lost no opportunity to blame the ILA for existence of the Bi-State Compact. The IBL lost no opportunity to embarrass the ILA publicly.

[14] *Ibid.*, pp. 57–61.
[15] New York *Herald Tribune*, Aug. 26, 1955, p. 1, Sept. 2, p. 16.

For example, when a news story broke identifying Charles Velson, frequently seen with Gleason, as an ILWU representative from Bridges' West Coast longshore union and the *Dispatcher* contained a story that the ILA might accept financial and organizational assistance, the *Waterfront News* challenged Captain Bradley to carry out his pledge to dismiss any union official found to be dealing with Bridges: "If Bradley does not fire Gleason it proves he is no president but just a stooge for the real powers who control the ILA." Bradley remained silent. One longshoreman is reported to have said, "We've been sold out lots of times before. The mob owns us, the shippers got a piece, and so everybody else is making a buck off us. Now we've even been peddled to Bridges."[16]

Concurrently the ILA, in September, demanded that the NYSA return to the bargaining table to renegotiate the hiring clause which the Waterfront Commission said was unlawful. Gleason had just described the "notify" clause as "the heart of our agreements," adding, "The Waterfront Commission has promulgated a set of hiring rules and regulations which *strips* our Union and its membership of its rights. [It] . . . has brazenly notified [the employers] to disregard the contract provisions providing for the hiring of extra gangs."[17] The ILA considered these rules an interference with collective bargaining. The ILA intended that the Wage Scale Committee meet with the Conference Committee of the NYSA, because it claimed the matter was beyond the authority and province of the LRC; but the NYSA did not consider any part of the agreement null and void and argued that interpretations could be worked out in the grievance machinery.[18] Oddly, a copy of the ILA letter to the NYSA was sent to the Waterfront Commission.

Having received a copy of Bradley's letter, Lane felt impelled

[16] *New York Times*, Sept. 26, 1955, p. 42; *Waterfront News*, Aug. 26, 1955, p. 1, Sept. 2, p. 1, Sept. 23, pp. 1, 2, Sept. 30, p. 1.

[17] ILA, *Proceedings of the Thirty-seventh Convention, July 1955*, p. 62 (my italics).

[18] NYSA, Report No. 1200, Sept. 1, 1955.

"to set the record straight." He explained how the paragraph originally contained the word "order," which "was clearly . . . in violation of the Compact" and that upon the advice of counsel for the NYSA, the word was changed to "notify," a subterfuge because the union interpreted "notify" as synonymous with "order." He then reproduced a colloquy that took place at a meeting in the commission's office on May 26, 1955, when they were discussing Brooklyn hiring practices:

Gleason: We have a proviso in there and your people [the employers] agreed to it, that the local union hall would be notified of the need of extra gangs and we were supposed to supply them. I mean we laid the cards on the table; we thought we were going to order the gangs, Mr. Lane, and that was my belief. Now we come down here and the Commission tells us we are in defiance of the law. . . .

Mr. Chopin: Teddy, I don't want to get into this, but the contract says [interruptions]

Mr. Gleason: Wait a minute. We know what is meant, Mr. Chopin. We knew. Listen, Mr. Lane, you might not like what I am going to say, but I say what I think is in my mind and I think we agreed upon. We tried to circumvent the law. There is no question about it. We thought we had it circumvented and we thought by the notification that we would tell our gangs that you are going to be the gangs. No question about that.

Lane pointed out that mere notification would not have been illegal but they obviously intended more. The commission had to make sure that an agreement was not used to circumvent the law.[19]

The NYSA refused to renegotiate, interpreting the ILA move as simply an effort to challenge the Waterfront Commission. Whether directed at this refusal or against the Waterfront Commission, a wildcat strike broke out on September 7 among long-

[19] Letter, Samuel Lane to Vincent G. Barnett, copy to Bradley, dated Aug. 29, 1955, see NYSA, Report No. 1200, Sept. 1, 1955; cf. Supreme Court of the State of New York, *Referee's Interlocutory Report,* Index No. 11232/1955, pp. 29–30.

shoremen in Manhattan. Concurrently, dock worker meetings in each of the boroughs reflected much opposition to hiring regulations. ILA officials appeared to bless the stoppage but carefully stated that it was not a strike, just a rank-and-file rebellion. The employers quickly sought and obtained a restraining order based on violation of the collective agreement and also filed a suit for $10 million damages. The Waterfront Commission also obtained an injunction on the grounds that there was no labor dispute and that it was illegal to strike against administration of the Bi-State Compact.

The ILA meetings were well attended, the one in Brooklyn being the largest, and Captain Bradley was cheered wildly when he said that all that was wanted was for the men to be "treated like human beings" and for the governors of the two states to listen to their grievances. The ILA distributed mimeographed copies of a bill of particulars asking cooperation in "freezing" the register to stop the flow of men to the waterfront, cessation of favoritism by the commission to the IBL, a more humane approach to the men, elimination of subpoena abuses, and recognition that local unions control hiring, not the commission.[20]

The ILA openly defied the injunctions. Bradley said that he would do nothing to get the men back, he had not called them out, it was a spontaneous demonstration of bitterness. This charge was not without some foundation in view of the large number of men who attended ILA meetings, which seemed to belie the contention of the Waterfront Commission that the rank-and-file longshoreman was opposed to the strike. Commissioner Joseph Weintraub said, "If free to choose, the men would go back," but he explained that this would be difficult because of the "long history of slugging and goonism." A blatant example of such intimidation was reported about an ILA meeting in Newark. Gleason was presiding. When a longshoreman stood up and asked, "What are the principles for which we are going out?" a burly man walked up from the back of the room and

[20] *New York Times*, Sept. 8, 1955, pp. 1, 62; *New York Herald Tribune*, Sept. 8, p. 1.

punched him in the nose. Then Gleason continued, "Now, I'll answer the question. The principles are these: you go home and you don't work. We don't want you guys asking questions."[21]

The two waterfront commissioners, General Hays and Weintraub, charged that ILA leaders had planned the stoppage. To an offer of outside mediation Lane stated points on which the Waterfront Commission would insist: the longshoremen go back to work; the ILA formulate its grievances in writing and present them to the commission; the ILA accept the commission as the lawful authority on the piers and stop its obstructionist tactics; the ILA sit directly with the commission in any dispute or discussion and do so without any intermediary.[22]

The men returned to work after voting on September 10 to accept a citizens' committee to hear their grievances against the Waterfront Commission. State Senator James F. Murray, Jr., of Hudson County in New Jersey, suggested and created the committee with Godfrey Schmidt, attorney, as chairman. But Governor Robert Meyner promptly announced that he had nothing to do with it.[23]

Two days later ILA leaders rescinded the back-to-work order after the chairman of the joint committee on labor and industry in the New York legislature repudiated an offer to hold a committee hearing later in the month. Only Anastasia refused to order his men off the docks again. Bradley, issuing a general strike call, said, "It has become necessary to call a general strike . . . to preserve the ILA. You are hereby ordered to stop work immediately. . . . To be specific, this is a general strike order." Anastasia's opponents in the ILA charged that his refusal to call his men back on strike was due to his fear of a prison sentence for contempt. Half the men in Brooklyn left the docks, anyway. Captain Bradley, when asked if he did not fear a prison sentence

[21] *New York Herald Tribune*, Sept. 12, 1955, p. 6.
[22] *New York Herald Tribune*, Sept. 9, 1955, p. 1, Sept. 11, pp. 1, 46; *New York Times*, Sept. 9, 1955, p. 1; *Voice of 856* (ILA), Sept. 12, 1955, pp. 1–2.
[23] *New York Herald Tribune*, Sept. 11, 1955, pp. 1, 6, Sept. 18, sec. 2, p. 12.

simply said, "There comes a time in every man's life to stand up and be counted."[24] It was not bravery he lacked but, perhaps, good judgment, and the port was back to normal in a couple of days.

In October the ILA was still exerting considerable pressure upon the NYSA to join in an attack on the Waterfront Commission. Hearings on the contempt charges were under way, and the ILA was defending itself by charging that the Waterfront Commission was illegally interfering with collective bargaining. Meetings of the LRC could not be held because ILA representatives failed to appear in sufficient numbers to transact business. The employers, upset, appealed to the ILA. Gleason balked because of the proceedings in court—including the NYSA suit for $10 million damages. When Chopin said that court cases ought not to interfere with the work of the LRC, Gleason retorted, "How can you sit around a table with people who are going to court and swearing out charges against you?" But Chopin insisted that whatever the employers did to protect their rights in an illegal strike had nothing to do with cases before the LRC. In turn the ILA complained about company representatives testifying to Waterfront Commission agents who were investigating the strike. It was even claimed that information in LRC minutes had been given to the commission, but the employers denied it. Holding that the commission was the cause of all the trouble, by setting aside the agreement on hiring practices, the ILA wanted the employers to insist on their right to manage by taking a stand that they were not going to let the commission interfere. The employers, for their part, were simply not going to engage in battle with the Waterfront Commission.[25]

Refusal to Work Short Gangs

Early in December the ILA put a different pressure on the employers by causing a slowdown, particularly in Manhattan,

[24] *New York Herald Tribune*, Sept. 13, 1955, pp. 1, 8, Sept. 16, pp. 1, 10; cf. *Referee's Interlocutory Report*, pp. 19ff.

[25] *New York Herald Tribune*, Sept. 24, 1955, sec. 2, p. 5.

by having gangs refuse to work at the beginning of a shift until all needed replacements were present.[26] The NYSA, facing a desperate situation, met with the Waterfront Commission to seek a change in the rules, asking it to permit hiring agents to recognize any substitute presented by the gang boss, if the substitute were acceptable, and postvalidate him at an employment and information center. The Waterfront Commission would not agree. Getting no help, the NYSA informed the ILA that it would pay only for time actually worked. The upshot was the calling of a special meeting of the LRC, with an invitation to Judge Jacob Grumet, the port arbitrator recently named, to sit in.[27]

An agreement was reached on a new procedure calling for a detailed exchange of information between employers and ILA locals before extra gangs were hired *through*, as they said, the employment and information centers. Designed to resolve the question of interpretation of the word "notify," the new agreement provided three steps in hiring extra gangs, which were as follows:

(1) the employer will notify union locals of the number of extra gangs he will require. (2) the union will notify the employer which gangs are unemployed and available. (3) the employer will have the right freely to select such gangs as he desires from among all unemployed available gangs in the area, subject only to any existing equalization agreement covering the selection of gangs in an area, and will notify the union what gangs, if any, he is prepared to validate in accordance with the requirements of existing law.

The Waterfront Commission, however, would have none of it,

[26] A notice to all ILA members was issued by Harold Bowers:

"To all members of the ILA. I, as vice president of the Manhattan District, direct you not to work short in any gang."

"If at any time anyone attempts to work without a full gang, call the ILA headquarters and ask for me" (*Voice of 856*, Dec. 2, 1955, p. 1).

[27] *New York Times*, Dec. 9, 1955, p. 54; *New York Herald Tribune*, Dec. 8, sec. 3, p. 7, Dec. 9, sec. 2, p. 8.

contending that the employers could get all the information necessary at the employment and information centers. It insisted that this procedure of "notifying" was really one of "hiring" through the union rather than through the centers as required by law.[28]

Seeing the agreement as an open attempt to circumvent the law, the commission subpoenaed officials of both groups to explain the meaning of the procedure and how the agreement was reached. The NYSA thereupon suspended application of the new agreements. After a three-hour session, the commission still maintained that the agreement was illegal. Captain Bradley, nevertheless, said he expected the employers to live up to the agreement or "we will be right back where we began." A second meeting with the Waterfront Commission, at which Waldman, counsel for the ILA, and Alfred A. Giardino, counsel for the NYSA, were present, produced no different results, but the ILA said it was going to court against the commission for interference with collective bargaining.[29]

Ominously, a couple of days later, about three hundred hatch bosses and shop stewards assembled at union headquarters in Brooklyn, seeking instructions because rumors were circulating that the commission would not accept the clarification agreement and Anastasia had told them to come in "for a report." But Bradley persuaded them to go to work, promising that the ILA would take the matter to court if the commission continued to reject the agreement.[30] But the commission stood firm and the Brooklyn gangs resumed work.

The next episode was before Judge Simon Rifkind, who had been designated to act as referee to determine whether the ILA and its top leaders were guilty of contempt in connection with the eight-day strike. The ILA took the position that it was a

[28] New York Herald Tribune, Dec. 10, 1955, sec. 2, p. 6, Dec. 13, sec. 3, p. 6; New York Times, Dec. 9, 1955, p. 54, Dec. 13, 1955, p. 78.
[29] New York Herald Tribune, Dec. 14, 1955, sec. 3, p. 6, Dec. 15, sec. 2, p. 8, Dec. 17, sec. 2, p. 7.
[30] New York Times, Dec. 20, 1955, p. 62.

labor dispute with the NYSA and not a stoppage directed against the Waterfront Commission and, therefore, the judge had had no authority to issue the injunctions. Waldman, attorney for Captain Bradley, introducing a series of articles written by Lane and just published in the *New York Herald Tribune*, charged that the Waterfront Commission was simply determined to undermine the ILA.[31]

Judge Rifkind, on the evidence and the statements of the defendants, found that the wildcat strike was "caused not by the conduct of the employers, but by resentment against the Waterfront Commission." Explicitly noting that an early draft of the agreement contained the word "order" instead of "notify," he found also that it was obvious that the ILA officials knew, from the moment they negotiated, that it was a violation of the Bi-State Compact. He found that they were aware of the commission's consistent rulings outlawing the agreement and that it was anger against this, not against the employers, that led to the strike. On the evidence, Judge Rifkind recommended that the ILA, Captain Bradley, and Gleason be adjudged guilty of civil and criminal contempt, saying,

It is difficult to conceive any act more contumacious of the restraining order than Bradley's official strike call of September 12 . . . he deliberately defied the order—with full knowledge of the fact that the act he was committing was expressly forbidden, [and] with awareness of the possible punitive consequences to himself and to the union.[32]

A strange calm in the port followed; one union spokesman declared, however, that "our men have been unjustly convicted." When asked about the apparent lack of concern in the union, Captain Bradley said, "I can tell you one who is upset, and that's myself. You try to do a job and then you get stopped in your tracks like this—it's upsetting." The *Times* editorialized that

[31] *New York Herald Tribune*, Nov. 25, 1955, sec. 2, p. 10, Nov. 29, sec. 2, p. 6; cf. *ibid.*, Oct. 9, 10, 11, 1955.

[32] *New York Times*, Jan. 11, 1956, p. 1; *New York Herald Tribune*, Jan. 11, 1956, pp. 1, 8; *Referee's Interlocutory Report*, pp. 10, 21.

Bradley and Gleason had "sowed the wind . . . when they called the longshoremen out on strike. They, and all the members of their union . . . have now begun to reap what promises to be a whirlwind—of penalties—for that stupid and illegal act." In May, Bradley was sentenced to fifteen days in jail and fined $1,250. To check the possibility of direct action by longshoremen, he advised, "A walkout will get you nowhere."[33]

Citizens' Waterfront Committee

The Citizens' Waterfront Committee, which had come into existence as the strike was called off, invited various persons and organizations to appear before it; it held several hearings. The Waterfront Commission would not recognize the extralegal committee. Schmidt retorted that he thought any citizens' group was entitled to a little cooperation. Meany, with hostility, also rejected his invitation, saying, "I won't fall for that." Nevertheless, Schmidt was not to be deterred. The ILA, of course, was interested in appearing, designating Waldman to represent it.[34]

The report which Waldman prepared is a revealing document.[35] It lamented the "negative criticism alone" spread before the public, the "constant needling of many thousands of longshoremen," the "incessant name-calling," the "gloating publicly over claims that [ILA] strikes were defeated," and the assumption that "the ILA and its members are guilty of virtually every crime in the book unless they prove themselves innocent." He said that the ILA constantly had to resist "exaggerated and caricatured evils," and he laid out its "bill of abuses" numbering eight: violation of civil rights of longshoremen, failing to enforce the Bi-State Compact with respect to Communists, usurpation of

[33] *New York Times*, Jan. 12, 1956, pp. 30, 54; *New York Herald Tribune*, May 26, 1956, sec. 2, p. 1.

[34] *New York Herald Tribune*, Nov. 17, 1955, sec. 3, p. 6, Nov. 22, p. 6, Nov. 29, sec. 3, p. 6.

[35] ILA, "Petition of Grievances of the International Longshoremen's Association and the Longshoremen of the Port of New York and Their Program for Relief and Improvements for a Better Port" (mimeographed, 1955).

power by the commission in areas where it had no jurisdiction, use of subpoena power in violation of rights of longshoremen, denial of the right to bargain collectively without coercion or interference from the commission, interference with the long-shoremen's right to strike, using decasualization to destroy the ILA and to deprive veteran longshoremen of the opportunity to work at the same time that the industry was being flooded with inexperienced nonunion men, and unwarranted denials of the right to rehabilitation by barring men from registration on the basis of crimes previously committed which had no relation to the waterfront.

Late in December, Schmidt issued a draft of his committee's proposed "Code of Fair Dealing," comprised of sixty-one items for the ILA to follow in its dealings with its members, the employers, and the Waterfront Commission. In some respects it was stricter than the Bi-State Compact. The ILA took exception to many of the points in the prepared code. In its final form the code was reduced to twenty-eight points, of which the ILA subsequently accepted ten.[36]

Meanwhile, the ILA's attack on the Waterfront Commission continued, partly in the courts and partly through appeals to political friends. Captain Bradley was pleased when Governor Harriman requested the resignation of General Hays, under the pretext that he wanted a commissioner of his own choosing. The request stirred up a controversy with friends of the Waterfront Commission contending that the governor was thoroughly misguided. John P. McGrath, former New York City Corporation Counsel and who had been Harriman's campaign manager, was appointed. But soon after, Governor Harriman and Governor Meyner agreed on a strong policy to defend the basic objectives of the Waterfront Commission. By the end of November a new

[36] *New York Herald Tribune*, Dec. 21, 1955, sec. 4, p. 8, Jan. 31, p. 15; *New York Times*, Dec. 21, 1955, p. 58, Dec. 29, p. 40; Citizens' Waterfront Committee, Godfrey Schmidt, *et al.*, "Code of Fair Dealing Proposed to the International Longshoremen's Association for Its Approval and Implementation" (mimeographed, 1956).

executive director had been found, Michael J. Murphy, head of
the New York Police Academy. He had been suggested by
Austin Tobin, executive director of Port of New York Authority, and this appointment presaged continuation of strict administration of the Bi-State Compact.[37]

Standing lonely on the outskirts of organized labor, the ILA,
after flirting with John L. Lewis, made a startling mutual assistance agreement with James Hoffa, chairman of the Central
Conference of Teamsters. However, Einar Mohn, executive
vice-president of the Teamsters, said that no financial help would
be given and he pointed out that the International had not endorsed the agreement.[38] Later, toward the end of February,
Hoffa announced a $400,000 loan to the ILA, but Meany hinted
suspension if the Teamsters went through with it. Nevertheless,
in February there was talk of a joint ILA-Teamster organizational drive, which raised some questions because the IBL had
already started a new drive to unseat the ILA. The IBL urged
Meany to expel the Teamsters from the AFL-CIO if the pact
were permitted to stand.

Lane sent a letter to Meany appealing to him to "kill that loan"
and to "call off Hoffa." Lane said, "If Meany can't take Hoffa
off the backs of longshoremen, the longshoremen can't be
blamed for thinking no one in labor can do it." In his letter to
Meany, Lane said:

Nothing has changed in the ILA. . . . Some of its leaders like Ryan,
Clemente, Roche, and Ferrone have recently been convicted of one
crime or another. . . . But there has been no voluntary houseclean-
ing and there never will be. . . . Into this picture there now moves
another ruthless labor racketeer. I refer to James R. Hoffa. . . .
This, then, is where you come in, Mr. Meany. The honest working
men and labor leaders in this port want no part of the ILA, no part
of Hoffa. . . . As I see it, it is up to you and Dave Beck to call a

[37] *New York Times*, Nov. 2, 1955, p. 1, Nov. 5, p. 32, Nov. 8, p. 26;
New York Herald Tribune, Nov. 3, 1955, pp. 1, 14, 20, Nov. 4, pp. 1,
10, Nov. 8, pp. 1, 8, Nov. 29, pp. 1, 6, Jan. 28, 1956, pp. 1, 28.
[38] *New York Times*, Dec. 1, 1955, p. 70.

halt. It may be that Beck cannot control Hoffa, . . . but I feel that you have the power and that you will exercise it.

When Meany intervened shortly thereafter, the loan was postponed at the request of Beck.[39]

The ILA had its own internal squabbles, too. Anastasia was busily consolidating additional locals. This upset Bradley and others. There was talk of dumping Fred Field from the presidency of the New York District Council because he was too friendly with Anastasia. Frank Murray of Jersey City was slated to succeed him.[40] At the same time leaders of locals in Manhattan were angry about Anastasia's "medical clinic," a facility he was creating to give medical services to members of his local, and the "deal" he had made with the shippers to achieve it. They wanted to know why Bradley and Gleason had let Anastasia negotiate with the shippers and by-pass the ILA. The ILA had done little to stop him, and Anastasia was allowed to swallow up the last locals. In one local election it is said that the vote was forty-seven to thirty-six, whereas there were 1,200 members; in 1954, it was claimed that the men in the local had voted 514 to 359 for the IBL. But Anastasia stood his ground and carried off his consolidations. Soon after, Harold Bowers and Field were said to be planning to gobble up the locals and divide Manhattan into two. More important was Gleason's plan to consolidate all checkers in the port into one local, which he did even in the face of opposition by Anastasia.[41]

The middle fifties were years following the major challenges and before the time when the parties would settle into a pattern of repetitive but difficult bargaining episodes. They had trouble reaching an acceptable agreement after the long period of turmoil, but finally did so early in 1955. Concurrently and afterward they were deeply preoccupied with adjustment to the

[39] New York Herald Tribune, Feb, 28, 1956, p. 8, Feb. 29, p. 20; March 7, p. 19; Waterfront News, Jan. 20, 1956, p. 1, March 9, p. 1, May 4, p. 1.
[40] Waterfront News, April 13, 1956, p. 1.
[41] Waterfront News, April 17, 1956, p. 4, May 11, p. 1; New York Herald Tribune, May 3, 1956, sec. 2, p. 1, May 4, sec. 2, p. 1.

presence of the Waterfront Commission and to the new hiring regulations which it imposed—which both parties did, although the ILA was not graceful. Because the ILA could not knock the commission out through the courts, it tried to do so through collective bargaining. It found this to be only partially successful, and through indirection, that is, through establishing customs and practices on a more formal basis. There were encouraging developments in the relationship of the parties, notable in the handling of grievances—the subject of the next chapter—and in the calling of more continuous meetings between the NYSA and the ILA about current problems, which gave promise of the emergence of more businesslike relationships.

8 | Grievance Handling

The development in 1955 of a new system for handling and settling disputes arising in day-to-day relationships under the collective agreement was a significant event in the industry and a bright promise for the future; it was conspicuous against the previous failure to achieve wholesome relationships at the pier. Certainly there had been little success portwide. The problem had long needed attention; the absence of a decent approach to grievance handling had been glossed over by employers as well as the union, and it accounted, in part, for the poor reputation the industry had for not creating more constructive labor and management relations.

Desirability of improvement had been recognized in the 1945 arbitration by Will Davis, who saw that quick and effective grievance machinery was necessary. In his arbitration award, Davis had pointed out the inadequacy of existing arrangements and directed the parties to make improvements.[1]

More than an agreement was needed. Nothing less than a fundamental change in attitude would make a difference. The collective agreement had provided only for an Arbitration Committee of four, two from each side, and for the selection by them of a fifth person, on an ad hoc basis, to resolve disputes if the four failed to do so. Such a body, of course, was what in other collective agreements corresponded to the last step in an explicit structure that laid stress on action at earlier steps. In the long-

[1] Part of what follows is based on Vernon H. Jensen, "Dispute Settlement in the New York Longshore Industry," *Industrial and Labor Relations Review*, vol. 10, July 1957, pp. 588–608.

shore industry it was assumed or intended that matters would be handled at pier-level in the traditional way, and, failing settlement, appeal to the Arbitration Committee would be available. The only change made after Davis' admonition was to provide that grievances not settled at the pier were to be submitted to the NYSA in writing.

The Arbitration Committee was activated only occasionally. Its operation was highly informal. The extent of its use is reflected in the fact that about five cases a year reached the Arbitration Committee, and in the ten-year period to the middle of 1953 only twelve cases reached arbitration. This, of itself, would not warrant criticism if the handling of grievances at the piers had been adequate. A work stoppage was the common means for resolution of disputes. Sometimes the men were called off the job by the union delegate, who considered this the most effective way of securing an adjustment. As frequently, it was the men who walked out of their own accord and stayed out until an adjustment satisfactory to them was made. This course was less satisfactory to the companies, but they usually made whatever settlement was needed to get on with the work. The waterfront had an unsatisfactory reputation as a result of work stoppages.

Little wonder that the historic rank-and-file rebellion in 1951 brought forward the lack of a grievance system as a major issue. The Board of Inquiry, as we have noted, gave considerable attention to the Strike Committee's protest that the arbitration machinery had seldom been used. More to the point, the board found that the rank-and-file member was afraid to set forth his grievance to indifferent local officials. Also, in the absence of seniority and in the face of summary actions by hiring bosses, he feared retribution. The board stated that new machinery was needed. Of course, both the ILA and the NYSA had recommended changes. In turn, the board recommended two principal ones: (1) the establishment of a permanent arbitrator for the Port, and (2) the privilege of each worker and each member of the NYSA, on his own initiative, to have adjudicated any claim that his rights under the agreement were being violated.

The ILA bitterly attacked the second recommendation, holding that there was real vice in permitting individuals on their own initiative to carry cases to arbitration because dissidents could create no end of trouble.

In spite of their own recommendations, the parties made no effort to renegotiate grievance handling. In fairness, however, it must be said that the parties were engulfed by other developments, particularly the investigation by the New York State Crime Commission. Yet, the NYSA did propose more specific grievance machinery to this body. It submitted this same plan to the ILA in the negotiations in 1953. A major obstacle to reaching an agreement at this time lay in the employers' insistence that all customs and practices prevailing on the several piers were to be agreed upon and reduced to writing if they were to be accorded weight by an arbitrator. The ILA held that customs and practices could not be reduced to writing but, nevertheless, should be considered contractually binding.

The negotiations in 1953 were never completed. The parties had to wait upon settlement of the question of representation. Meanwhile, employers recognized IBL shop stewards on those piers where AFL sentiment was strong, just as they had recognized ILA delegates. The employers, however, had to be careful in handling grievances to make sure they were not laying themselves open to charges of "unfair labor practices" by one of the contending unions. As a result, almost all grievances were settled at pier level.

After the controversy over certification, many individuals on both sides of the bargaining table appreciated more fully the need for an improved grievance system. The parties quickly came to a preliminary understanding that there should be "an arbitration plan for fair and equitable administration of the contract," a "no-strike clause," and new grievance machinery which would "handle grievances at the closest possible point to the dispute and as fast as possible." Nevertheless, they disagreed over the issue of sanctions in the event of work stoppages. Some ILA representatives who were strongly opposed to a "no-strike clause" and to any form of arbitration railed against sanctions. When they appeared to reach an impasse, and some employer spokesmen were at a loss as to where to turn, one put the issue squarely to ILA leaders and asked if they believed in settlements by work stoppages. When they answered, "No," he sharply said, "Then let us work something out." Under the challenge, they worked out the details of the plan which was incorporated into the agreement, a compromise between the position of some of the employers who wanted a "strong working arbitrator" and those in the ILA who wanted no arbitration at all.

The grievance procedure created was comprised of four steps. The first provided for consideration of grievances or disputes at the pier by a management representative and the shop steward. In the second step, also at the pier, a dispute not settled in step one was considered by an ILA local delegate and the pier superintendent (or his designee) plus an NYSA agent. Failing settlement at the pier, the dispute could be referred to the Labor Relations Committee (LRC) by either party. The fourth step was arbitration.[2]

The first step of the procedure was implemented by provision for an elected shop steward on each pier. While shop stewards had long been active in some parts of the port—serving in various ways, depending upon the traditions and practices of the particular pier—none had been utilized on many piers. Both parties now gave them universal and uniform standing. A new functionary of the employers' was the NYSA agent. He was a counterpart of the ILA delegate, who represented the local at the second step, but he, as a representative of the entire association, could help to establish uniformity in settlements as well as guidance.

The Labor Relations Committee

The LRC was the central feature of the new procedure. Because the NYSA had desired a "strong working arbitrator," one who would be available at call and settle disputes, hopefully, at

[2] NYSA and ILA, *Agreement between the International Longshoremen's Association and the New York Shipping Association of the Port of Greater New York and Vicinity, General Cargo*, Effective Oct. 1, 1954.

the pier, and some ILA members did not want any arbitrator, the LRC grew out of compromise, but it was well conceived to meet the peculiarities of the industry and the relationships between the NYSA and the ILA. It provided the nucleus and moving spirit of a simple, easily managed system, and gave leading spokesmen from each side the opportunity to present their grievances before their peers. This had the virtue of contributing to consent, so essential to the successful working of any grievance system. Also, it left the real decisions and responsibilities for settling issues with the group most competent to resolve differences and make interpretations. As skillful as a single "working arbitrator" might have been—and it is doubtful that the parties could have found an acceptable one—he could not have contributed as much as the LRC was in fact able to do. In addition, the LRC made possible some approach to standardization of action in the various parts of the port in so far as the complicated nature of the industry allowed. The promise was the LRC could greatly improve the structure of relationships throughout the port.

The LRC, which met weekly, was composed of five representatives of the NYSA and five representatives of the ILA. Each maintained a panel of eligible persons. The NYSA developed a system of rotation with one change a week to provide for continuity and certainty of appearance. The ILA simply called on five to appear. Frequently more than five representatives of the ILA were present, but the employers did not object, for only five voted, although the others sometimes participated in discussions.

The LRC was "in general charge of the Grievance Machinery and the day-to-day relations between the ILA and the NYSA." It discussed and, on the basis of merit, disposed of all cases referred to it. In the event of final disagreement, upon a motion from either side, any issues under consideration moved to arbitration. The LRC also had authority to review the relations between the parties and to make suggestions and recommendations for improvement; but this was never done in a formal sense, although it must be kept in mind that persons active on the LRC were the ones most active in negotiations, too. To help achieve standardization in grievance handling and contract interpretation, the agreement provided that the LRC be notified, either for information or review, of all settlements at step one or two. The LRC had authority to revise a settlement, but new facts could not be introduced. In practice, few such settlements were reported and none was ever formally reviewed.

Even before the agreement that brought it into being was signed on February 24, 1955, the LRC had begun to function because the parties got to work on grievances that needed attention after the long interunion controversy; indeed, some grievances had grown out of the controversy.

It took some time for the LRC to settle down to a routine, and it almost died in its infancy. Without rules of procedure, the early meetings were more informal than later ones, and some got somewhat out of hand. Many of the employer members were on the verge of giving up. During this time Chopin was named chairman of the NYSA and he, knowing the importance of the work, strove to keep the system alive. Fortunately, too, "Packy" Connolly worked hard to lead the ILA representatives into a new posture. The committee decided to alternate chairmen at the weekly meetings—Chopin serving as chairman at one meeting and Connolly at the next. The records of the early meetings are spotty but reflect a trial-and-error approach to the establishment of the machinery.

In April 1955 an NYSA agent was hired, Captain Samuel S. Mossman; he served also as reporter and secretary to the LRC. He was subject to call upon short notice whenever a dispute could not be settled at step one. If an agreement was not reached, he prepared a written statement of the issue and the facts and reported them at a meeting of the LRC. The ILA acquiesced to his serving in both roles because of the esteem in which Mossman was held and the meticulous, objective way he reported; also there was no single individual who was his counterpart in the ILA—but as many delegates as there were local unions—and perhaps none could have reported as he did.

All cases to be heard were placed on an agenda, and Mossman read his report at the opening of the case. Immediately afterward, the principals in the dispute, who had been notified to be present, took exception, if any, to the report or attempted to clarify the issue or the facts. Essentially their task was to explain the facts, rather than to present additional information. A free discussion was held until all members of the committee were satisfied that they understood the case. Upon the motion of a committee member the disputants were dismissed. If the agenda contained more than one case, the next disputants were brought forward, and the same procedure was followed until all scheduled cases were heard. At this point all but the committee members were asked to leave and the LRC went into executive session, where its members argued the merits of each case separately and voted upon motions made in parliamentary fashion. A majority vote settled the matter. Some cases were returned to the parties; if there was a tie vote either party could refer the case to arbitration.

Shop stewards presented a special problem for the grievance procedures. It has been noted that they were expected to function more universally and effectively than they had in the past. At one pier where the elected shop steward was a member of a regular gang the union contended that he should be regularly employed whenever there was a possibility of work, so that he could be available to function at the first step of the procedure. The ILA believed that the shop steward should work with his gang when the gang was working or, at other times, he should be hired as extra labor whenever any extra labor was employed. The company involved held that the shop steward was a part of the gang only and refused to give him work when his gang was not working, insisting that under the new clause the shop steward was not to be given special treatment.

The case reached the LRC and revealed the situation in the

industry. The ILA insisted that the grievance procedure could not work if the shop steward was not on the job. The ILA pointed out that in some parts of the port shop stewards were the first ones in and the last ones out, even if work on the ship went around the clock for three days, although it was admitted that this practice did not prevail everywhere in the port. Union spokesmen also stated that some employers were glad to keep the shop steward around because he kept a lot of problems from falling on their shoulders. Above all, the ILA stated that "the shop steward is definitely a part of this grievance clause. He is the first step in it, and if you are not going to have the first step in there, you could never get to the second or third step, and if there is ever any trouble, you are out of luck, in plain English." It is only fair to say that the ILA was simultaneously arguing for the machinery and for pay, even sinecures, for shop stewards. However, when asked whether the ILA was urging that a shop steward be engaged whether or not there was work for him the answer was "No." Nevertheless, one union spokesman argued that "by electing a shop steward the men consent and they expect him to be present to hear their 'beefs' at all times. This is not something we are setting up. This is universal the world over. Everybody understands that the shop steward becomes 'top kick' so to speak." By way of clarification, one union spokesman sagaciously said that shop stewards had preferential treatment in hiring but not preferential treatment in working. When employers argued that preferential treatment of any kind was beyond the power of the LRC to grant in view of the new clause, a union spokesman rejoined:

When we made this contract everybody knew what we said about the preferential stuff. We don't like to say it, but years ago we had stewards that maybe were tough guys and they just walked around, but this doesn't exist today. All of our stewards have to be working people, and they have to assume an obligation on the pier in a job, and that is the part that we meant by "preferential treatment" and I think everybody understood it as such.

When the talking was over, the LRC unanimously agreed that the new clause meant that the shop steward was to be given work he was qualified to perform, as long as his services were satisfactory, but there was no requirement to create a job for him nor was he to displace any regular employee.[3]

In spite of this clarification and affirmation of the status of the shop steward, some employers continued to treat shop stewards with special deference, carrying them on the payroll all the while the ship was at the pier. What is more important, the evidence indicates that the shop steward and the first levels of management involved in grievance handling did not become as active as good grievance handling would warrant. The first step in the procedure was often not made explicit in practice. Little attention was ever given to training the people at this level to handle their work satisfactorily under the grievance system. Neither the NYSA nor the ILA came to grips with the problem of training, which has been given so much attention among other unions and managements generally.

Informality marked the meetings of the LRC, but it was agreed early that the meetings should be conducted under rules of parliamentary procedure. In January 1956 the port arbitrator was invited to sit in on a meeting to observe the committee's operations. Someone suggested that he ought to chair the LRC meetings, which he thereafter did. A number of factors influenced this development. Some of the members of the LRC thought that the arbitrator would gain a greater understanding of the problems of the industry by sitting in at the meetings. Some thought that a neutral chairman would add to the general decorum. Still others felt that the arbitrator's presence would save time, in the event of disagreement, for he would not have to go over all the facts of the case a second time within a few days after they were considered by the LRC.

Regular meetings were held on Tuesday mornings. When ILA representatives could not attend because of union affairs,

[3] NYSA, Report No. 1166, June 9, 1955.

such as conventions, or during vacation times, meetings were canceled, but postponements in the early period were infrequent. Later they became more common, and there were times when meetings could not be held because of the lack of a quorum on the union side. Of course, sometimes there were no pressing cases on the agenda, and meetings were canceled.

The LRC usually did not meet during the periods of negotiation. The principals were otherwise engaged and it was probably desirable to shunt the controversy and antagonisms of the bargaining sessions away from the grievance meetings. The second-step activity continued, of course, whenever issues arose at the piers.

Judge Jacob Grumet was named as the first arbitrator under the contract, largely because the ILA approved of his arbitration of a dispute growing out of the controversy with the IBL over employment rights of a group of men, and because the employers were anxious to get the system working. He served until 1957, when, because both parties were mildly dissatisfied with his performance, he was succeeded by Burton Turkus. Both parties wanted a more forceful arbitrator. Turkus fit the bill admirably on this score: he had a tough demeanor, he had been reared in the rough and tumble of the East Side, and he had served as a district attorney and a prosecutor and a member of the State Mediation Board. He remained in the post until negotiations in 1968–1969 provided for a five-man team of arbitrators to work in rotation.

The LRC continued to be important over the years, although not as spectacularly as at the outset and not always effectively. An early, and perhaps prejudiced, criticism was that "the Labor Relations Committee is a farce [and] they don't get any of the real grievances. They just get the things that the delegate can't squeeze out of the company on the pier." The accusation was probably made by a former member of the IBL, who had found the committee's ILA members had failed to pursue some grievances of its rival union with vigor. Nevertheless, it contained some truth, for the members had difficulty in escaping the inertia of the old ways of doing things; and the lack of skill in arbitration on the pier has been noted above.

It was Captain Mossman, later supported by his assistant, Captain T. F. Christopher, who saved the day for the system as well as for the NYSA. He worked effectively as a troubleshooter, going directly to the pier whenever a dispute developed, serving dually as the representative of the NYSA and as an aide to pier-level management.

9 | Negotiations in 1956: Was It Comedy?

The agreements between the NYSA and the ILA were set to terminate at midnight, September 30, 1956, and both parties started early to prepare for negotiations. Both were acutely aware of recent history and speculated on the unsettling possibility of another contest over representation with the IBL. The employers, caught in the crossfire between the rival unions, were resentful that Meany had not declared publicly whether the IBL would again be financed, for without financial help no challenge could be launched.

Two types of maneuver mark efforts within the ILA to escape another struggle over representation. First, it tried to be accepted into the AFL-CIO,[1] and, second, it sought to work out deals with the IBL and some of its supporters. Although Meany had rebuffed Bradley, hope of getting back into the "house of labor" lived on among some ILA leaders. Others did not relish the prospect and maneuvered to block it. Strange alliances emerged. A secret meeting took place in Dallas, Texas, in July, while Bradley was serving his fifteen-day jail sentence for contempt of court. Gleason and Anastasia, an odd and unlikely duo, met with Harry Lundeberg, president of the Sailors' Union of the Pacific, of which the SIU was a part, and Einar Mohn, executive vice-president of the Teamsters, to work out a deal to make sure the ILA would not get into the AFL-CIO in the near future. Reaffiliation would have meant, for Gleason and Anastasia, the possible end of their waterfront-labor careers, because

[1] The AFL and the CIO merged into one federation in 1955.

top officials of the AFL-CIO had said that reaffiliation would not take place as long as either was a leader. For the Seafarers, reentry would have meant the possible loss of a considerable investment that Hall—Lundeberg's lieutenant—had made in the IBL in order to increase his strength in his struggle with Curran and the NMU. For the Teamsters, reentry would have meant the probable end of any hope they had of reallocation of work on the docks which they might gain as a concession from an independent ILA, as "payment" for alliance, but not from an ILA back in the "house of labor." Returning to New York with a draft of a proposal involving the three unions—ILA, Teamsters, and Seafarers, Gleason and Anastasia presented it to Captain Bradley upon his release from jail. He refused to accept it, largely because it called for recognition of the IBL as a parallel union in those areas where it had contracts, that is, in the Great Lakes and Puerto Rico. Bradley was outvoted by New York colleagues, but when he called in the executive board members from the outports, who were distrustful of the Seafarers, Bradley argued the New York board members to a standstill.[2] Bradley called upon Waldman to amend the proposal, which made it unacceptable to the others.

Some of the same persons involved in this maneuver tried still a different tack to keep the IBL, on the eve of negotiations, from filing a petition for an election with the NLRB. At the instigation of Anastasia, a delegation comprised of himself, Gleason, and Harry Hasselgren, secretary-treasurer of the ILA—the latter going at the request of Bradley—went to the SIU headquarters in Brooklyn on the evening of July 30 to hold a meeting with Hall and John Dwyer, vice-president of the IBL. When the meeting resumed the next day, William Lynch, president of Local 791, joined the group because some in Manhattan feared that a deal was afoot that would not be to their liking. These meetings proved fruitless, and the IBL immediately filed with the NLRB a petition for certification on the very eve of com-

[2] *New York Times*, Aug. 12, 1956, p. 51.

mencement of negotiations betwen the ILA and the NYSA.[3] Anastasia still would not give up and agreed with Hall on a proposal to avoid the contest, which was submitted to the ILA. Although the points were acceptable in principle, when they were rewritten by Waldman they became unacceptable to the IBL. Hence, on August 7 the IBL issued a long statement condemning the ILA's failures and stating that it was definitely going ahead with its petition before the NLRB.[4]

Also, during these negotiations, the NYSA devised a program to be followed in bargaining. It is doubtful that the employers, collectively, had ever looked at themselves so closely. Actually the roots of the development reached back to 1954, when some employers had encouraged Fred Rudge Associates to devise a program; but the question of union representation and the adjustment to the presence of the Waterfront Commission had made it impossible for the NYSA to do anything at the time. They let the matter ride, partly as a result of their chronic tendency to respond only to crises. Preoccupied with the struggle to run their businesses in the hectic competition of this disjointed industry, they seemed unable to take time to seriously formulate a program. This, plus the lack of unity, perhaps, had always led to a last-minute "deal approach" to problems. Often they were unhappy with the results, yet they had done little to alter their approach. This time, some thought, they should take a lesson from those in other industries who managed more successfully, particularly from the experience of the General Electric Company under its program colloquially known as "Boulwarism." Those sponsoring Rudge were enamored of the "success" of General Electric in thwarting or dominating its unions through study and communication with its employees to produce the proper package upon which the company then

[3] *Waterfront News*, Aug. 3, 1956, p. 1; *New York Herald Tribune*, Aug. 1, 1956, sec. 3, p. 6.

[4] *New York Herald Tribune*, Aug. 4, 1956, p. 4, Aug. 10, p. 10; *New York Times*, Aug. 4, 1956, p. 26, Aug. 7, p. 40, Aug. 8, p. 42, Aug. 10, p. 30.

stood, taking a strike if necessary, not budging unless it could be demonstrated that the company had erred in composing its proposal.

The NYSA decided that it would have to develop more understanding among the longshoremen, because the ILA always failed to communicate effectively and the men rejected negotiated settlements. The NYSA would contract for a study to reveal basic problems and prevailing attitudes and desires of the men, and in turn would feed information to them as to what would constitute a fair settlement. Constructive negotiations and persuasion might produce what had been problematical, if not impossible, to secure by the old bludgeoning method and distasteful, protracted strike. The upshot of this thinking, new to most of the employers, was a decision in 1956 to enter into a contract with Rudge. The NYSA recognized that there was not time to make a deep study for the current negotiations, and, if a crisis in negotiations developed, Rudge could shift attention to current contract problems. An extensive study was quickly made, and Rudge became intimately involved in the negotiations.

The first bargaining session, on August 1, took place under the cloud of the IBL's filing of its petition with the NLRB, as already noted. But the ILA and the NYSA proceeded as though it had not happened. Connolly distributed mimeographed copies of fifteen demands to the fifteen members of the Conference Committee and to the 130-odd members of his Wage Scale Committee.[5] The demands startled some of his associates, who expected a much longer list—the Wage Scale Committee having drawn up a much longer list late in July[6]—and the employers were amazed at the magnitude of them; they quickly learned from others, however, that there were still more demands. Con-

[5] "Proposal of the ILA to the NYSA and All Steamship Companies and Stevedoring Companies Covering Loading and Unloading of All Cargoes from Portland, Maine to Brownsville, Texas," Aug. 1956 (mimeographed); *New York Herald Tribune*, Aug. 2, 1956, p. 4; *New York Times*, Aug. 2, 1956, p. 40.

[6] "Tentative Draft Proposal: ACD, WSC," July 25, 1956 (mimeographed).

nolly by himself had prepared the partial list because, as a realist, he knew that the total list was absurd. Afterward, he simply said that he did it to get started and that there was no harm in keeping the employers guessing and uncertain.[7]

Chopin attempted to set the tone of the negotiations with a prepared statement, saying the employers wanted to avoid the "pattern of a contest" and follow instead "a mutual approach to a common goal" to improve "the welfare of both labor *and* management." They should "avoid 'deadline' collective bargaining where problems have a tendency of being 'fought' out instead of 'thought' out." Also, he added, "We intend to keep everyone fully informed on the facts and issues involved."[8] High-sounding words, but he might have saved them for all the good they did.

Demands for Coastwide Bargaining

The next day, in their second session, the ILA made coastwide bargaining its chief demand, insisting that it had to be conceded before any talk about the other demands. The NYSA reacted strongly, stating that the employers could not accede to coastwide bargaining for they had no authority to do so; that other associations opposed joint negotiations. In turn, they insisted that they receive all of the ILA proposals so that they could see what was before them.[9] But the ILA stood firmly on coastwide bargaining, Connolly saying, "They have member companies in all the ports. We believe they can speak for the others."[10] Achievement of this demand was necessary to the ILA to protect against assaults by the IBL. Almost every leader in the ILA wanted it. Outport leaders, too, whose locals were not free from raiding by the AFL-CIO, wanted it. Anastasia was a notable exception, because he was so heavily committed to the construction of a

[7] Conversation with Patrick J. Connolly, Aug. 13, 1956.

[8] NYSA, Report No. 1296, Aug. 1, 1956.

[9] NYSA, Release, Aug. 2, 1956.

[10] *New York Times,* Aug. 3, 1956, p. 32; *New York Herald Tribune,* Aug. 3, 1956, p. 4.

clinic in Brooklyn that nothing else could be important to him. Later he would argue that coastwide bargaining was not worth all that the ILA claimed for it.

By taking the stance that it did, the ILA was unwittingly getting itself into a legal predicament. Connolly even sent a telegram to the NYSA, on August 9, saying that the ILA would not present its other demands until the employers agreed to grant coastwide bargaining. It then tried to assemble employers from all the ports in Washington to negotiate a coastwide agreement. All declined, but the ILA met anyway.[11] The men cheered when Bradley said, "Go back and tell your ports that we are going to stick to coastwide bargaining. We don't want strikes. We won't have them if they bargain in good faith. But we will strike if necessary. The responsibility is with the employers." Waldman attended the meeting. He said that the employers had done a "foolish thing" in not coming to the meeting and he advised the ILA to request the government "to ask the employers to sit down—before it is too late, before tempers are frayed, before bad blood sets in—so we can have a contract by September 30." He also said, "You have a right to go to New York and bargain with those companies on a nation-wide basis," but he did not approve of strike action. But Gleason added, "The employers will know we are not kidding," and—perhaps revealingly—he served notice that "the ILA has *become* an international union."[12]

Early in September another bargaining meeting between the ILA and the NYSA produced the same stand-off. Connolly demanded coastwide bargaining and Chopin promptly said the employers were unalterably opposed. The ILA negotiators left within ten minutes saying they would sit it out.[13]

[11] NYSA Report No. 1307, Aug. 28, 1956; *New York Herald Tribune,* Aug. 28, 1956, p. 8; *New York Times,* Aug. 27, 1956, p. 32, Aug. 28, p. 42.

[12] *New York Times,* Aug. 31, 1956, p. 46 (italics mine).

[13] U.S. Board of Inquiry, "Proceedings before the Board of Inquiry on the Labor Dispute Involving Longshoremen and Associated Occupations

By this time the NLRB was convinced that the IBL had made sufficient showing to warrant an election.[14] This precluded further bargaining until the question of representation was determined. Nevertheless, the date for termination of the existing agreement was coming near and the ILA and the NYSA agreed to a one-month extension, with the understanding that any increase in wages or welfare payments would be retroactive to October 1.[15] But the NLRB had to hold a hearing on the question of the scope of the bargaining unit because the ILA, making a different effort to gain coastwide bargaining, asked the NLRB to recognize the whole industry, or at least the North Atlantic District, as an appropriate unit for bargaining. It also insisted that hatch bosses be included within the unit. The hearing began early in September. The arguments were a repetition of those in the earlier case, and the NLRB left the bargaining unit just as it was, holding against the ILA on the coastwide unit but for it on the matter of inclusion of hatch bosses. It set the election for mid-October.[16]

The ILA's Approach to the AFL-CIO

It is of some interest that in mid-September, while the matter of representation was pending before the board, Meany surprised people by announcing a meeting with Bradley to review the fitness of the ILA to enter the AFL-CIO. Meany denied Brad-

in the Maritime Industry on the Atlantic and Gulf Coast," vol. 1, p. 38 (mimeographed).

[14] The IBL had submitted 13,000 pledge cards. The ILA had countered by sending squads to the piers to have the men sign a pledge of loyalty to the ILA by acknowledging that since the previous NLRB election they had authorized only the ILA to represent them. The IBL, in turn, advised everyone to sign the ILA cards to "escape reprisals," saying, also, that "if the ILA were not afraid of the longshore workers, it would not so bitterly oppose a second vote."

[15] NYSA, Report No. 1324, Sept. 28, 1956; New York Times, Sept. 27, 1956, p. 1; New York Herald Tribune, Sept. 26, 1956, sec. 2, p. 1.

[16] NLRB, Decisions and Orders, vol. 116, p. 157; New York Times, Aug. 14, 1956, p. 40, Aug. 17, p. 36; New York Herald Tribune, Aug. 14, 1956, p. 8, Aug. 17, sec. 2, p. 4.

ley's request for a "private and confidential" meeting and invited Larry Long, president of IBL, to sit in. The Citizens' Waterfront Committee publicly urged admission, but Lane, just resigned as executive director of the Waterfront Commission, sent another long letter to Meany stating that the ILA was still full of rascals and characterized the Citizens' Waterfront Committee as only a "face-saving committee" set up to get the ILA off the hook. Lane said, "Let the facts speak, Mr. Meany. Don't listen to Schmidt. Ask Bradley for the facts. He can't give you the truth and still qualify the ILA for membership in the AFL-CIO."[17]

After Meany met with Bradley he said he would not refer the matter to his executive council, saying, "It would be insulting to their intelligence to ask them to consider the ILA application for admission. The matter is closed." Bradley not only was disappointed but he charged that he had been "double crossed," explaining, "I went to Washington at the request of five vice presidents of the AFL-CIO, who told me to go down and see Mr. Meany and straighten things out." He also said that his request to Meany was sent at the suggestion of one of "Mr. Meany's official family."[18]

While Bradley was trying to get the ILA back in the good graces of the AFL-CIO, he was also waging battle with Anastasia. In part, the battle could have been a product of Bradley's efforts to seek entry into the AFL-CIO. Anastasia feared the possibility and he was still working to entrench his power in Brooklyn. He was also deeply involved financially with "his clinic" and was unhappy that the ILA had not placed the matter at the top of the agenda for bargaining. It had hardly been mentioned at this stage. Anastasia had angered Bradley by urging longshoremen, before the extension agreement was negotiated,

[17] *New York Times*, Sept. 18, 1956, p. 1, Sept. 19, p. 1, Sept. 20, p. 1; *New York Herald Tribune*, Sept. 18, sec. 2, p. 9.
[18] *New York Times*, Sept. 22, 1956, p. 1; Sept. 24, p. 1; *New York Herald Tribune*, Sept. 21, 1956, sec. 2, p. 1.

not to go out if a strike took place; "Disregard the propaganda of Captain Bradley and Teddy Gleason" and stay on the job, was his instruction.[19]

The voting on representation was set for October 17. Campaigning ran its course with typical waterfront gusto. Shortly before the election, Meany called the ILA "a disgrace to the good name of organized labor" and called upon the longshoremen "to get the old ILA off your backs and gain the protection of an honest and hard-hitting trade union." But Bradley promptly issued a rejoinder accusing Meany of being a "holier-than-thou hypocrite" and quoted Meany's laudation of the ILA in 1952.[20]

The voting was heavy but there was no disorder; 20,191 voted. This time the ILA won by 11,827 to 7,428, improving its margin considerably over that of the previous election. The only consolation Meany could take was that "as long as this hard core of opposition exists, there is hope that the ILA can be cleaned up from within."[21]

Back to Bargaining

The bargaining was quickly resumed. As before, Chopin read an opening statement declaring that the employers and the ILA could settle their problems with "a new and fresh look" at them.[22] With Rudge as adviser, the NYSA had reviewed carefully demands presented by the union, but they still needed to know all the ILA demands. The employers had anticipated that coastwide bargaining would be pushed at the meeting and they had prepared accordingly, intending to get some "bargaining

[19] *New York Times*, Sept. 20, 1956, p. 1; *New York Herald Tribune*, Sept. 23, 1956, sec. 2, p. 9, Sept. 24, p. 1.

[20] Letter, Meany to ILA members, Oct. 10, 1956; *New York Herald Tribune*, Oct. 12, 1956, sec. 3, p. 6, Sept. 25, p. 1, Oct. 15, sec. 3, p. 4, Oct. 16, sec. 1, p. 22; *New York Times*, Sept. 25, 1956, p. 1, Oct. 12, p. 1, Oct. 15, p. 42.

[21] *New York Herald Tribune*, Oct. 19, 1956, sec. 2, p. 1; *New York Times*, Oct. 19, 1956, p. 25.

[22] NYSA, Report No. 1332, Oct. 22, 1956; see also NYSA, Report No. 1331, Oct. 19, 1956; *New York Herald Tribune*, Oct. 21, 1956, p. 29,

mileage" if the ILA was adamant about it and to set the stage for the new approach to bargaining that Rudge had helped them develop.

Connolly wanted to know at the outset whether the employers had counterproposals, but Chopin said they had to know all the union was asking before preparing management demands. Connolly then said that the ILA had many demands that were portwide, many that were district-wide, and six that were coastwide, as follows: (1) wages, (2) sling load, (3) paid holidays, (4) welfare, (5) eight-hour day, and (6) seniority. He stated that the members of the NYSA controlled 80 to 90 per cent of the shipping industry in the country and, therefore, could bargain coastwide. It was made clear by Bradley, as well as by Connolly, that the employers had to discuss the six coastwide demands first. The upshot was that the employers let the ILA spokesmen trap themselves by taking a categorical position that they had to get coastwide bargaining before they would negotiate on other demands. They even went so far as to say there was no sense in having other meetings until they got other associations to meet on coastwide bargaining.

Anastasia had been at the meeting, but his clinic was not mentioned and he bolted from the room. He sent an urgent telegram to Chopin, warning that the Wage Scale Committee was "not negotiating any contract for the Port of Brooklyn." Newspapermen said that they heard him in anger say to Gleason, "Stay out of Brooklyn—or you don't come back alive." Later Anastasia denied that he had made the last half of the statement. Gleason acknowledged that he had heard the first part of the statement but not the latter part and said, "Nobody is keeping me out of Brooklyn. I'll be over there tomorrow."[23]

Actually Anastasia could not stay away from the negotiations. It was not for him to say who was bargaining for whom. The NLRB had just certified the ILA as the bargaining agent, and he could not keep the ILA from negotiating for Brooklyn as

[23] *New York Herald Tribune*, Oct. 23, 1956, sec. 2, p. 1, Oct. 24, sec. 2, p. 10.

well as the rest of the Port. The ILA leaders knew he would be back.

The employers also had internal troubles. Although they had agreed to file a suit against the ILA for refusal to bargain if it persisted in its effort to require coastwide bargaining as a condition for bargaining on other demands, some employers began to change their minds. Cautious ones wanted to delay and some thought they ought to consult with the outports, while others wanted action immediately and forthrightly. As was often the case, the employers had trouble remaining unified when an issue came to the crunch. Yet, at the next session the NYSA told the ILA that coastwide bargaining would not be granted. Immediately, some union members moved to walk out. Connolly tried to check them, but succeeded only temporarily. Soon Bradley said to the employers that he was sending the men back to their own ports with freedom to strike, if necessary, on October 31. The NYSA subsequently notified its members that an unfair labor practice charge had been filed with the NLRB, because of "the ILA's action in walking out of the bargaining meeting with the ultimatum that they would refuse to participate in any further contract negotiations except on a coastwide basis."[24]

Also at this time, as a part of their set strategy, the NYSA issued the first of a series of letters planned to inform the long-shoremen of the status of negotiations; it explained that they were facing a strike because the ILA had walked out, although the NYSA was "eager to bargain for New York, as we have in the past." It emphasized NYSA's desire for an agreement beneficial to both labor and management and promised to keep the men informed.[25]

Federal Mediators

At this stage, federal mediators, headed by Robert H. Moore, stepped into the dispute,[26] and Waldman was brought in by the

[24] NYSA, Report No. 1333, Oct. 24, 1956.
[25] NYSA, Report No. 1334, Oct. 25, 1956.
[26] *New York Herald Tribune*, Oct. 24, 1956, sec. 2, p. 1.

ILA. The mediators brought the parties back together and, although Connolly opened the discussion by saying that coastwide bargaining on the six points was still before them, Waldman promptly and deftly got into the act, saying, "Let's agree we're deadlocked on the issue of coastwide bargaining, but don't let it preclude discussing all the issues." Then he started a tack of putting the NYSA on the defensive, noting that the employers had not yet furnished the union with a statement of their demands. Pressing the point that the extension agreement would expire in less than a week, he insisted that the union ought to have a statement of employer demands. Chopin sensed what Waldman was doing and said that they were glad to get down to the issues but they were there to bargain for the Port of New York only, and added that they could not offer much until they had discussed the demands of the union. Connolly, probably now advised by Waldman, pressed for counterdemands and Waldman tried to tie the employers down to an obligation to give them. In order to offset the position the ILA had placed itself in by insisting on coastwide bargaining before it would discuss anything else, Waldman intended to build a charge that the employers were not bargaining in good faith.

Agreeing that the employers had an obligation to get their demands out, but in order to let Waldman know that the employers knew what he was up to, NYSA counsel Giardino said that it was unfortunate that Waldman had not participated in the previous discussions, otherwise he would not be so positive about his charges against the employers. He forcefully reminded Waldman that the ILA had been adamant on coastwide bargaining as a precondition for negotiations. Yet, the employers were careful to say that the NYSA would proffer demands promptly but made it clear that before they could make counterproposals they had to know the full extent of the union's demands.

Waldman, pushing his tack, asked for a date when the NYSA would give its demands, wryly saying, "We promise not to file an unfair labor practice charge if you don't give them to us today." But Chopin was quick to query, "You are not proposing that you won't discuss your demands today unless we give you our counterproposals?" Waldman replied, "I won't answer that directly. You're trying to trap me as you did my principals last week when I wasn't present. I am saying, give us what we ask, we'll negotiate." One of the employers took Waldman to task, saying, "You are talking as though we have been in negotiations since last August 1. That's not true. Never once in our previous meetings did we negotiate. We were always held up by the union's insistence on coastwide bargaining."

In caucus the employers discussed their position. Rudge felt that they were being pressured into a reversal of positions and were falling into a trap. Much argument followed. Upon returning to the joint meeting, Chopin said that they would act as quickly as possible and would have their demands by Monday, October 29. Connolly reminded him that the deadline was close and said, "We're ready to work on the weekend and would like your demands tonight or tomorrow." Chopin answered that they were mindful of the deadline and were glad to have got, finally, into proper negotiations, but that they could not be ready before Monday. Immediately someone from the floor demanded negotiations on Saturday and Sunday, saying that the employers were simply playing for a further extension. Chopin responded, "Let's examine it. We know it's doubtful if we can complete negotiations by Thursday. What is your actual intention? To hit the bricks on any excuse?" Connolly answered, "We didn't say that. If we are close to agreement we can go on, but we are not even close or likely to be unless you give in to us." An outspoken rank-and-file representative said, "You are writing letters accusing us of trying to foment a strike and the men are asking what's wrong with you guys." But Chopin insisted that the employers were not looking for a strike and explained the letters—a second one had been issued—by saying, "The last time we reached a contract you couldn't sell it to your men because they were not informed. Also, they are our employees, too. We want them to be informed on all matters."[27] When Moore at-

[27] *New York Herald Tribune*, Oct. 24, 1956, sec. 2, p. 1.

tempted to stop this haranguing, Waldman agreed not to respond to some statements, but he insisted on challenging the propriety of the NYSA's letters to the men. It was not "free speech" he said, because "it was an act of war to tell the men their negotiating committee was not doing its duty," making it difficult to hold back the angry Wage Scale Committee from immediate reprisal.

This angry reaction caused some employers to wonder whether they should continue sending the letters. Opinion was divided. Because the repercussion was more than was expected, some wanted to reconsider, but they were rebuffed by others pleased that union representatives seemed worried. Rudge, masterminding the letter-sending campaign, wanted to know if they were going to be scared off. Some said, "Let's keep it up. We'll see what the reaction is from the men. That'll be our real answer," although several continued to worry over possible reaction in some of the local unions. The decision, finally, was to go ahead.

The differences among the employers about sending the letters caused some to question whether Rudge was playing too much of a role. The Conference Committee, however, settled the air by reaffirming that it was making policy and negotiating the contract, that Chopin was the chairman, and that Rudge was hired to direct communications, although Rudge wondered whether they desired his services even for this.

With the deadline imminent, intensive negotiation and jockeying began. The mediators, still feeling their way, sensed that their primary role would be to pave the way to an extension of the contract beyond the deadline, for a settlement was not possible in the time remaining. Yet, when the employers approached them to get an extension, they felt it was premature to raise the issue. They would bide their time and see what progress could be made.

In a joint session on September 29, the employers submitted their demands,[28] but the parties first resumed discussion of the

[28] NYSA, Report No. 1339, Nov. 1, 1956; *New York Herald Tribune*, Oct. 31, 1956, sec. 3, p. 1.

ILA demands, item by item. During the first recess the employers quickly reviewed their tactics, believing, as one put it, that "the reason Waldman wants to talk as fast as possible is that he wants to get a 'no' from us. Then we will get no extension." Learning from the corridors that some ILA representatives were talking of a day-to-day extension, the employers agreed to avoid this eventuality, because the first flare-up would bring a strike and they could not live with the uncertainty. Chopin again asked the mediators to make a bid for extension but was again told it was not yet the time.

When it was their turn to present demands, the employers carefully explained that they were not counterproposals. This angered Connolly, who threatened the deadline if they did not get counterproposals. Again the employers reemphasized that they had been prepared to bargain as early as August 1, but were held up by the controversy over representation and by the demand for a coastwide contract, and that only in the last few days had they had a chance to question the ILA on its proposals. They appealed for an extension of time, needed, they said, by both parties. When Waldman affirmed the last point, Fred Field said, "If we do not get counterproposals we will only have your demands to give to the men. We ought to give them something —you be the judge." This was something in the nature of a threat. Chopin then suggested that the terms not be retroactive if there were no extension. The mediators now came into the act, saying that it would not be wise to get into a false position and get into a strike that nobody wanted. Bradley responded, "I don't want to light any fires, but these men from Portland, Maine, to Hampton Road, Virginia, have negotiated for twenty years and found by experience that they never got anywhere until the last day," charging, "We find very little good faith here." Noting the charge of unfair labor practice and the letters, "all of which was not doing negotiations any good," he said, "we give our own information. We are not strike-happy. We don't expect to get a contract tomorrow but you are putting us on a spot with our men. You've got to give us an answer to some of our demands tomorrow. If you are not too anxious for a settlement, say so and we will tell that to the men tomorrow. We'll answer your letters in due time. Whoever wrote them will do a real flip, because you've left yourselves wide open." Moore again urged them not to get into false positions which would bring the strike which no one wanted.

In private session, the consensus among employers was that the ILA delegates were in a foul mood and that meeting further that night would be a mistake. Rudge spoke up, "If you are not ready to give them something tomorrow, say so now, and be prepared to face the issue. . . . A strike would put them in a box." One said, "The mood indicates that control has left the table and has passed to the back of the room. Don't let them get away with it. A meeting tonight would be dangerous." Chopin called in the mediators to tell them so; prolonging the session would only steam tempers more. Moore felt that they were putting themselves in a bad position, but he was promptly told, "We've had a lot of experience with this group in night sessions and doubt seriously if we could get as far tonight as we could tomorrow morning. Instead of explaining questions we'd only get recriminations." Nevertheless, they finally agreed to meet again that night, but in caucus debated whether to send another letter to the men in the nature of a progress report. Some employers opposed it violently but still others said that if they did not send one that tonight they were through. Although the spirit of the meeting was to fight the union vigorously, to keep hitting them to make it hurt, the vote to send the letter was carried by only a narrow margin.

No progress was made that night, and once the question of inclusion of a no-strike clause had come up, the session ended with accusations, the union charging that the NYSA was "suit-happy," and the employers suggesting that the ILA might be "strike-happy."

The next day Moore told them separately that the federal government would not move to prevent a strike. To complicate matters the NYSA was served with an unfair labor practice charge based on refusal to bargain on a coastwide basis. The employers believed that this was part of a strategy to get the employers to withdraw their charge against the ILA. When a rumor was reported that if they would stop sending letters they could have an extension of the contract, some employers wanted to stand firm, as had General Electric, and "not be bludgeoned out of a position that is fair to employers and employees alike," arguing that the NYSA should "force the ILA to accept the fact that the men are a force in negotiations," that the employers had a right to appeal to them.

On the last two days before the deadline there was much sparring and some recriminations. When the employers tried to tell Moore why they did not have counterproposals ready, Waldman rejoined, "You filed the unfair labor practice charge. You insisted on bargaining. Now we insist that you bargain." The employers thought that Waldman was trying to force them into a position of saying "no" to the demands of the union, that he was trying to work the situation into something more than a discussion of coastwide bargaining. Of course they did not have their counterproposals prepared and kept trying to avoid saying "no" to anything except coastwide bargaining, while looking for an extension of the agreement.

The ILA also had trouble in maintaining unity. In one of the joint meetings Anastasia tried to interrupt, only to be shouted down from the floor and ruled out of order by Bradley. He had a meeting in Brooklyn scheduled for the evening and wanted badly to be able to say something on clinics.

The ILA "Package"

Late in the afternoon on the thirty-first, when the ILA returned from a caucus, Waldman announced a "package" proposition, saying, "We wish to extend every opportunity to give you time to prepare different answers. You have your work cut out; therefore, some extension of the contract is in order. You asked for a month. We will sign an extension to November 15, with retroactive wages and welfare. Employers will submit written counterproposals in one week, by November 7, and we will name committees on (1) Safety, (2) Grievances, (3) Clinics, (4) Hiring Practices, and (5) Seniority."[29] Chopin thanked Waldman, saying, "You have today made a proposal on the basis of which we can make some headway," but he noted that if they met in one week with counterproposals, there would only be one week to button up a contract. He called attention to the fact that a short extension would hurt movement of freight and asked for a month's extension. Waldman said, "We have considered this. We feel we can work it out in two weeks. Thirty days is not acceptable." The extension agreement to midnight, November 15, was signed,[30] and the five joint subcommittees were immediately set up.

"Three Years of Industrial Peace"

The Conference Committee met to prepare the counterproposals promised within seven days, but the members were wary. Some employers were sure that the subcommittees would "foul up" their intended program, for how could they negotiate with subcommittees while preparing an all-inclusive proposal? Nevertheless, the subcommittees had to meet as agreed. Would a "Boulware"-type, all-inclusive, final package prevail, particularly by November 15? Or were they on the road to a Taft-Hartley injunction with its "final offer," or to arbitration? Some were quite sure that the ILA intended to get only a partial agreement by the deadline, with the unresolved issues, including coastwide bargaining, to be submitted to arbitration. Was the ILA strong enough to take a strike in the face of a good proposal advertised to the men? How would the men react, and would the outports support New York in the event of a strike? In spite of differences of opinion and some doubts, the Conference Committee decided unanimously to offer a "salable package."

They worked vigorously and, surprisingly, drew up an eleven-point proposal on which all could agree. They included as much

[29] *New York Herald Tribune*, Nov. 1, 1956, sec. 2, p. 1.
[30] NYSA, Report No. 1338, Nov. 1, 1956.

as possible in order to make it "salable," asking Rudge, on the basis of his study, whether they could sell it. They impressed upon each other the need to avoid item-by-item consideration. It had to stand or fall as a complete settlement. Said one realistically, "If we go back to old-style bargaining, we will have a rough time. If anyone feels we are going to trade on top of this, we are off on the wrong foot."

They recognized, of course, that the ILA would try for more in the remaining week. The NYSA organized for this and prepared proper rebuttals. They would hold a press conference, once copies of the proposal were given to the ILA, to get their pitch before the public, and they would send copies to each longshoreman to let him know that they were getting more than they or their leaders thought possible, a liberal settlement. Yet, some equivocation existed among them, for—departing from the General Electric approach—they decided as a supporting argument that they would say the "package" was being submitted because of the lack of time to bargain in the usual way. Finally, if a work stoppage occurred—instead of standing as General Electric did—they would withdraw the whole thing and go back to their original demands. Consequently, they were not prepared for the new bargaining stance, which would have required the taking of a strike, if necessary, to force acceptance of their offer.

Copies of a proposal, *Three Years of Industrial Peace*, done up like a Madison Avenue brochure on fancy paper, were given to the ILA on the morning of November 7.[31] Simultaneously they were arriving in the mail at the homes of longshoremen, and copies were given to the press. An all-out effort was made to convince everyone that it was a genuine bid for dock peace, that a fair agreement was their only goal. They had to make clear that they were not presenting the traditional first counterproposal, a merely tentative offer, which would be only the starting point in the old game of trading off issues one by one. Rather, they were presenting their "best thinking as to a final contract settlement," a package in which all elements in the ILA demands

[31] NYSA, *Three Years of Industrial Peace* (n.d.; issued Nov. 7, 1956).

and the NYSA demands had been considered. It was their complete position with nothing held back.

They offered thirty-eight cents in monetary increases for the three-year period, twenty cents the first year, ten cents the second year, and eight cents the third; paid holidays for the first time, granting two, Labor Day and Christmas, for all men who worked thirty-two hours during the payroll week in which the holiday fell; Good Friday as an additional holiday for overtime purposes; a third week of vacation to men who had worked in the industry for 700 hours a year for ten years or more and who worked 1,800 hours in the qualifying year; three cents per hour added to the contribution to welfare; certain penalty rates for handling especially difficult or hazardous cargo; and a safety program, including a joint union-management portwide safety committee. Making note that productivity had not kept pace with the national average, they offered a productivity bonus in the form of a fifteen-cent-per-hour differential when only a sixteen-man gang was used on cargo arranged on pallets. Under "major improvements in our labor-management relationship," they emphasized their belief in a strong union, an enforceable contract, and industrial peace. To achieve these things, certain changes in the contract would be made: the clause on "customs and practices" was to be deleted, yet consideration of custom and practices would be specifically provided for and made reviewable by the arbitrator; the grievance procedure was to be improved and strengthened; the steward system was to be improved; rights of union and management were to be clarified; the possibility of establishing seniority was to be studied jointly; and a check-off of union dues was to be granted.[32]

When the Conference Committee met prior to the meeting with the ILA, it examined a *New York Times* story which had made an unfortunate misinterpretation of their proposal by specifically mentioning clinics. Chopin explained that he had tried to keep the press from playing up coastwide bargaining but the *Times* reporter had asked about clinics. Chopin had carefully

[32] *Ibid.; New York Herald Tribune*, Nov. 8, 1956, pp. 1, 20.

avoided mentioning clinics, which the NYSA had decided not to support, by saying that the employers were offering "a big increase in welfare which would cover many benefits." The *Times* had interpreted Chopin's statement as including clinics.[33] The Conference Committee therefore quickly called Connolly and told him that clinics were not in the "package" and that the *Times* was in error.

It is amazing that the employers had prepared and rehearsed a formal script for their meeting with the union. Various members were given roles to play and cues for entry. Rudge raised possible questions, reflecting probable ILA responses, and Chopin answered them. They were reminded not to show fear of a strike and cautioned: "Let's face it. We must be firm and make it understood that we stand on the 'package.' Don't ever propose a return to wrangling."

As soon as the meeting of the two groups got under way, Bradley characterized the proposal as only "a step in the right direction."[34] Connolly quickly said they did not like some of the proposals and wanted to find out why many of the ILA demands were not even mentioned. "All we can see here is money. We like money, but don't see how it is all to be applied." Not having had enough time to study the proposal, he suggested that they go through it "to take you apart like you took us apart" and to get to the meat of it. Chopin said that they would be glad to assist, although he said the "package" explained itself. If they needed more time that was all right, but he said, "Remember that this is an opportunity to skip the horse-trading and demonstrate to you, to us, to the men, the port, and the public that we can agree mutually." He then said, "Let others with long experience speak."

A "script drama" was launched. One of the employers whom the union liked as much as anyone said that he was disgusted with jockeying for position and that he was glad that the employers could make a good and conscientious offer which should

[33] *New York Times*, Nov. 8, 1956, p. 1.
[34] *New York Herald Tribune*, Nov. 8, 1956, p. 1.

provide a new approach to the bargaining table. But the script ran through about three spokesmen and fell flat. The ILA leaders did not get, or would not accept, the message. They had objectives of their own.

Waldman said that they had read the proposal with interest and would try to understand it, but added, "We will ignore the propaganda part of it; done well by people who know how"; adding also, "You, in effect, said 'no' to our proposals." He would discuss the "package" with them, item by item, but then try to find out why they could not grant the proposals of the union. The employers were quick to point out that careful consideration had been given to everything.

They proceeded to go through the proposal, but Waldman cautioned, "Please note, we are not now agreeing to anything, but merely exchanging information." Nicholas Kisburg, education and research director with Field's Local 856, started a speech from the floor, but he was cut off sharply by Connolly and Waldman. Yet, as they went through, topic by topic, many on the floor at times wanted to get into the act. When they got down to the increases in welfare payments, several did jump into the fray, led by Anastasia, who said in his inimitable way, "You tell in the great City of New York you got wonderful hospitals. You never talk about other crafts because they got good clinics. You no discriminate against them. We get clinic otherwise you can stop talk right now, believe me." Walter Sullivan, ILA welfare representative, asked an embarrassing question, touching on consistency and good faith of the employers. "Are you telling us that the subcommittee on clinics, now studying the problems, is adjourned as of now?" Waldman headed off an answer, saying, "We know you did not intend to cover clinics," but said that they could get back to it later.

When they came to "customs and practices" and grievance machinery, vociferous argument developed from the floor and Waldman had to assert control. He, of course, did not need help from the floor and proceeded to lambaste the request for changes in "customs and practices."

The ILA objected strenuously to the omission of coastwide bargaining and to the lack of limits on sling loads and of a guarantee of eight hours' pay. After Giardino gave all the legal reasons for not giving into the demand for coastwide bargaining, noting decisions of the NLRB, Waldman pointed out that there was no legal reason that kept the employers from agreeing to it. But Giardino, for the benefit of the ILA leaders, pointed out that Waldman forgot to say that the matter was not a mandatory bargaining issue. Waldman rejoined, "The ILA may make a demand. The NYSA may grant it. Also, if the NYSA says it will not bargain unless coastwide bargaining is withdrawn, an unfair labor practice would be committed."

When they came to the explosive subject of clinics, Connolly asked, "Why have you eliminated this from your 'package'?" Employer spokesmen outlined the reasons only to have the wily Connolly ask why they had joined the subcommittee to explore it when they knew the decision would be against clinics. Weakly, the employers said that the decision had not been final until the last day. But Anastasia, not to be denied so easily, jumped into the controversy, saying that before he started his clinic in Brooklyn he had written to the NYSA and the board of directors had agreed in principle for him to start. Chopin quickly responded, "The board of directors answered you that it was a matter for collective bargaining."[35] Gleason echoed Anastasia, "Why do you give clinics to marine unions, but not us?" Bradley stepped in, "It was almost mutually understood that we were going to get this." Connolly underscored the point that the ILA expected the employers to grant something on clinics.

Picking up the employers' verbiage, Connolly referred to the ILA's demands as "our package"; and wanted to review all eleven points. But Chopin said that they had considered all of them: "We have specified in our package that all other demands were refused." Quickly Gleason countered, "That 'package' is

[35] Without an agreement, Anastasia had gone ahead to build a clinic, believing the employers had committed themselves or would come across with the necessary funds.

getting monotonous. . . . Did you give any consideration to these demands?" Chopin was quick, too, "We did not just take our package out of the air. We considered everything. We took what we thought was best for the whole industry." Bradley interjected, "I understand that you've sent the proposed package to our membership, is that right?" Chopin replied, "Yes, and I think we are doing you a favor. In the past we have reached contracts which you could not sell to your members." But Bradley stubbornly persisted, "What I want to know is this your final offer?" Chopin replied, "Nobody has come in here with a 'take it or leave it' proposal. That's understood. But you can't just ignore it, as a package." Connolly replied, "I think you've answered Bradley; that it's not your final offer." From the floor, amid many expressions, "If they have sent it to the membership, it must be their final offer." Giardino tried to calm the situation, saying, "We tried to save time by putting it in this form. You may accept it or reject it. But if you reject it, then we go back to the original demands and renegotiate item by item. Then, you may or may not get what's in the package." "Then, in that case," said Connolly, "we should adjourn . . . study it carefully and give you an answer on Monday." Bradley interjected, "Wait, but you are no longer dealing with just this committee. This is in the hands of 25,000 men and we'll have to hear from them now. In other words, every member of our organization in the Port is now a part of this committee." Bradley also said, "We'll have confusion compounded. You have thoroughly confused us. You've helped us out so much that we might as well get out of here. Believe me, I don't want a strike. Also, I was led to believe there was no more mail [letters] going out." Chopin, finally, got to say, "No one says this is our final offer. We merely say it is *our best thinking*. We feel it covers *all we can give*. You cannot get every other item on top of money, so you will have to act on *the whole thing*."

The employers subsequently reviewed their collective judgment of events. A feeling developed that the ILA simply wanted to delay giving an answer on the "package" until the deadline was somewhat closer and then rush them into accepting changes in order to complete a contract. Others, saying they were "stuck" with the "package," felt that "If they don't buy the 'package' it's better that they refuse it at the last minute. Let them set the timetable. Let us not try to rush an answer, because they then might try to press us for another 'package,' whereas at the last minute they will either take our 'package' or go out." Still others, saying that they would know the first of the week, felt "nothing to get upset about." Over all, the consensus still was, "Let them know we are determined."

The ILA was not able, even if it had been so inclined, to put aside its customary fighting posture. Who among them could suggest that they change? They expected that the ranks of the employers would easily break and that they could push for more as they had often done on other occasions. The ILA, however, was somewhat divided, uncertain, perhaps confused. Some of the leaders thought that the "package" was pretty good. Others, feeling committed to personal objectives or fulfillment of promises, wanted some additions. Some, sensing that the employers meant what they were saying, did not like the new approach. Some were angry about the letters sent to longshoremen.

Waldman lectured the employers for sending another letter,[36] calling their statements unsound and often misleading. If they persisted they would be responsible for a blowup. He put the NYSA on notice that the letters might torpedo the negotiations and warned them that their conduct was not conducive to an agreement, that the union could not financially combat their propaganda. He reminded them that the ILA had been designated as the bargaining agent and if they persisted in their efforts to circumvent the union they would most likely end up with having to give more than otherwise.

Ambivalence on both sides accounted for much of the uncertainty in the few days before the new deadline. Some employers

[36] *New York Herald Tribune*, Nov. 14, 1956, sec. 2, p. 10.

seemed willing to give up on coastwide bargaining. Others would if they could get something valuable in exchange. Still others were adamant in maintaining their position. On the union side, Anastasia, perhaps piqued because clinics had not been made the central issue, had let it be known that "coastwide bargaining is of no importance at all." He was even trying to find his own way to settlement. Some employers suggested buying Anastasia off by giving something on clinics. Others gave them an oral spanking for even thinking of it. Two stevedores revealed another difference when they stated that they would not press for a sixteen-man gang if it meant taking a strike. At the same time, some ILA leaders seemed worried about the possibility of a strike, although they counted on a Taft-Hartley injunction being issued. Moore, at this stage, was telling them emphatically not to expect one. It was said that Gleason went to the mayor's office seeking intervention. In spite of their internal divisions the sentiment of the employers was to "let the ILA sweat a bit," too.

The ILA Counterproposals

With two days to go, the ILA surprised the employers by submitting counterproposals. It rejected the sixteen-man gang, wanted a two-year contract only, wanted a sixteen-cent-an-hour increase in wages for each year, demanded support for clinics in the amount of five cents per hour, and wanted six paid holidays with six more to be added in the second year and with eligibility based on twenty-four hours of work in the payroll week. It accepted the three-cent-per-hour increase for welfare, the three-week vacation based on its own statement of eligibility. It asked for coastwide bargaining for employer members of the NYSA only. It expected all matters then before subcommittees —which were still meeting—to be negotiated.[37]

The Conference Committee, concluding that the ILA had widened, not narrowed, the gap, was shocked and called on

[37] *New York Times,* Nov. 15, 1965, p. 1.

Moore for suggestions. He could only say that it depended on what they wanted. Reminding them that they were following the "Boulware technique," he felt they would have to see it through. But the employers remonstrated that they were not withdrawing their package; the union had rejected it. If the mediators seemed ambivalent, it was in the nature of the process of mediation that the mediators tested positions by making suggestions or observations. If they could not always be optimistic, they would not say it was hopeless.

Just before the deadline, Waldman introduced a variation in the ILA's counterproposal, saying, "You gentlemen can tell us if a contract can be worked out," but added, "There will be no further extension." When employers asked if they would be available for clarification, Anastasia said, "If you can agree in principle, we can extend for twelve hours to get a contract." From the floor, someone shouted, "Be honest, no extension," and a hassle developed within the ILA. Moore asked for control and reason, saying, "There is a midnight contract deadline, but no negotiations deadline. I'll insist we keep meeting."

In the hours to the deadline, confusion and uncertainty were compounded. The mediators worked strenuously to bring the parties into a final effort for a settlement, feeling that basically they were not very far apart. The mediators thought that there was a good chance for a settlement if Waldman could prevail upon the employers to meet the union half-way on coastwide bargaining. But the employers were hardly unified. Those for a firm stand and a showdown with the ILA were encouraged by Rudge, whose view was that the ILA was anxious for a settlement to an unexpected degree, that the employers for the first time held all the aces and could bring the ILA around by standing solidly on their position. The employers, however, held mixed views, some wanting to give a little, others saying that they always got the worst of it in last-minute compromises. One of the staunch ones said that they might bargain all night "but with the same results as last time. It is suicide. If you gentlemen will say to me right now that you definitely don't want a strike

at any price, then I'll stop my protests, go along, and give in."
When asked what he would suggest, he replied, "Tell Waldman
that if they are not big enough to control their membership,
don't look for us to bail them out with our money. To open up
the contract negotiations down the line right now is suicide."
When the mediators announced that the ILA was expecting to
meet at 8 P.M., some of the employers were dubious about joining the meeting because they had learned that the ILA had
arranged for Bradley to go on television about 11:45 P.M. and
had instructed the longshoremen to "shape your TV tonight."
Chopin said, "Let's be practical, any one or two of these items
will go far into the night, but we will stay as long as humanly
possible." Waldman appeared briefly to say that if they would
meet them half-way on coastwide bargaining it would put a stop
to representation elections every two years. He asked them to
think seriously about it, for it would be much more valuable
help to the union than the check-off of union dues they had
offered. With a compromise on coastwide bargaining a settlement of other issues would be easy.

After a quick meal they were back, meeting separately, with
the mediators shuffling back and forth between them. At 10:15
P.M., however, Bradley issued a press release calling for a peaceful strike starting at midnight. Moore then brought them into
a joint session and tried to head off the strike, but Bradley
claimed a unanimous vote of all districts, saying, "We are not
'strike happy' but we have considered and think that if there is
going to be a strike, we had better take it now." Connolly talked
against it. "But Packy," said Bradley, "we are under instructions,
I can't call it off." Chopin complained, "You are telling us now
that the only way we can negotiate is under the gun of a strike.
That's not fair play." Bradley and Chopin had a heated exchange, with Bradley saying, "We are striking with a bankrupt
organization and it's your fault." But Chopin rejoined, "Let's
knock it off. We are only getting steamed up. You marked off
the deadline, not us." The ILA did not need to threaten a strike
openly; its policy of "no contract, no work" would have pro-

duced it. Finally, the employers not only rejected the ILA counterproposals, they withdrew their own "package." In effect,
they threw down the gauntlet and challenged the ILA to go
ahead with the strike.[38]

Stalemate

At midnight the strike was on and the port shut down on
November 16. The bargaining, however, did not come to a halt,
because neither party wanted the onus of breaking off negotiations, and the federal mediators wanted to keep them talking.
There were other pressures, too. The mayor intervened, calling
the parties to his office. Chopin urged him to tell the men to go
back to work, although Bradley immediately said that it was
impossible and used the opportunity to castigate the employers
for "negotiating with the men" through letters. Both the New
York Board of Trade and the Commerce and Industry Association urged President Eisenhower to invoke the Taft-Hartley Act
if the strike ran beyond the weekend.[39]

They held a long session on Saturday, but mostly they were
trying to outguess each other as to what was ahead: a short strike
with a "back-to-work" movement or Taft-Hartley injunction,
or was arbitration down the road? Tempers were on edge but
Moore would not allow a breakoff in negotiations. When they
met after the weekend, with a request from the White House
that their differences be settled across the bargaining table,
Moore told them not to look for early governmental intervention.[40]

The NYSA then announced that it would settle the coastwide
bargaining issue before the NLRB. This, of course, complicated
the situation. "Its only purpose," said Waldman angrily, "is to
threaten the union . . . to use the NLRB as a cat's paw," an
unfortunate development, he thought, because the parties would

[38] *New York Herald Tribune,* Nov. 15, 1956, pp. 1, 17.
[39] *New York Herald Tribune,* Nov. 16, 1956, pp. 1, 12, Nov. 18, pp.
1, 66.
[40] *New York Herald Tribune,* Nov. 20, 1956, pp. 1, 18.

have to meet in court and how could they proceed in negotiations? He simultaneously announced that the ILA would not press its own unfair labor practice charge against the NYSA.

Moore warned each that neither the NLRB nor Taft-Hartley would settle the contract, that the only way was over the table. Injunctions would only postpone the inevitable. The employers, in particular, however, were not going to be stampeded. They felt that they had to be cautious, even with the mediators.

Temporarily the employers were perturbed because the NLRB did not act quickly to get an injunction against the ILA. Because Moore was trying to get them to relax their stand on coastwide bargaining—he had even suggested arbitrating the issue—they felt that the NLRB was holding back at his request and sent Giardino to Washington to investigate. There he met with both Secretary of Labor James Mitchell and Joseph F. Finnegan, director of the FMCS, only to be told that the NLRB was not being influenced. The latter asked, however, whether the employers would accept recommendations as a way of settlement. Giardino said it would be unacceptable to the employers because they would feel morally bound by recommendations but he thought the ILA would not.

In New York, the mediators were telling the employers that their impending action before the NLRB would not help them get a settlement and that they would get a Taft-Hartley injunction very soon, followed by another strike in eighty days. An employer asked, "Isn't it better to have Taft-Hartley for eighty days than to get a bad contract?" But the mediators kept trying to dissuade them from pressing the legal action with the NLRB. Chopin countered with the assertion that the ILA could have avoided the injunction had it been willing to make an offer "the employers could seriously consider."

Other events were unfolding. The ILA had made up its mind that Anastasia should have his clinic, but it was willing to wait on other clinics. Rudge submitted his resignation, revealing division in the employers' ranks and concession that "Boulwarism" had failed. City Commissioner Vincent O'Connor now moved into the act and called to tell the NYSA that if it dropped its legal proceeding before the NLRB, he understood that the ILA would go for coastwide bargaining on wages and welfare only. He wanted to meet with them. One of their staunchest members said, "It would be a terrible mistake to capitulate now. We can always do this later, injunction or no injunction. Let us save it for the best mileage." Although some objected, the consensus was that if O'Connor had anything to offer, he should do it through the mediators.

On November 21, the NLRB acted and the U.S. District Court issued a temporary restraining order preventing the ILA from pressing its demand for coastwide bargaining.[41] The mediators were sure that the employers could not now get a settlement, but employers had the assurance that they could not be coerced into coastwide bargaining. They thought the union would have to make a move. But Waldman felt that his hands and those of the union were tied because of the restraining order. The secretary of labor informed both parties that unless progress was made toward a settlement that day, a Taft-Hartley injunction would be issued the next. What chance was there to do anything?

On November 22 the President invoked the emergency procedures of the Taft-Hartley Act and appointed a Board of Inquiry, with Thomas Holland as chairman. Moore, however, was to facilitate negotiations that were to continue during the period of the injunction, which was to run until February 12, 1957.[42] The injunction, of course, brought the strike to an end, but bargaining was hardly feasible because the ILA had appealed to the courts to set aside the injunction against coastwide bargaining, and the parties were occupied with court actions. Also,

[41] NYSA, Report No. 1348, Nov. 26, 1956; NLRB, *Decisions and Orders*, vol. 118, pp. 1481–1493.

[42] NYSA, Report No. 1347, Nov. 26, 1956, Report No. 1355, Dec. 7; *New York Times*, Nov. 23, 1956, p. 1, Nov. 25, p. 1, Nov. 26, p. 1, Dec. 12, p. 1; *New York Herald Tribune*, Nov. 23, 1956, p. 1, Nov. 25, pp. 1, 28, Nov. 26, sec. 2, p. 1.

Joseph Finnegan, director of the FMCS, wanted members of the Conference Committee to meet him in Washington, but Giardino counseled that if they started then, officially or otherwise, discussing coastwide bargaining, they would lose their injunction; although once in possession of it, he said, they might bargain it away if they chose. Thereupon, the employers decided not to go to Washington and canceled all further meetings with the mediators and the ILA. Even if the NYSA had been willing to meet, the ILA was not. It said it wanted both injunctions out of the way first.

Before the NYSA won its injunction permanently, what must be seen as a comedy of errors took place. Negotiating meetings were resumed, as they had to be, with Moore shifting back to his role as mediator. The issue of coastwide bargaining was not introduced, but through inadvertence, however, the employers gave their position away without purchasing anything in return. Their "secret" about willingness to grant coastwide bargaining in exchange for something got out too soon. Knowing they would get it, the ILA leaders simply waited for it.

Meanwhile important infighting developed in the ILA. Gleason suggested governmental intervention through fact-finding—apparently wanting someone outside with power to arrange a satisfactory settlement and *force* its acceptance. He was opposed violently by Anastasia, who was afraid of losing his clinic. Anastasia also came out strongly against Bridges' proposal that the ILA and the ILWU have common expiration dates, an objective that had been sponsored in the maritime trades nationally and by the House Merchant Marine Committee. Bridges had come to New York, and some in the ILA saw common expiration dates as an aid to a broader bargaining structure. Partly because Anastasia had already come out against coastwide bargaining, perhaps seeking public favor by appearing opposed to relationships with Bridges, Anastasia openly opposed common expiration dates. Over another issue, Anastasia and Waldman came near to physical encounter. It was highly personal but was over the question of Waldman's role as spokesman.

The divisions in the union ranks frustrated, sometimes angered, the employers. Some wanted to break off negotiations but calmer ones knew they had little choice but to continue meeting. Nevertheless, the common complaint was "the constant state of anarchy across the hall, with no leadership and no coherent thinking." Their only consolation was that "the mediators now know what we have to put up with."

The ILA announced that it was standing on its fifty-two original demands and the NYSA responded that it would reinstate all of its demands. They appeared to have little to show for the numerous meetings in the previous five months. Obviously, they had not learned the route to settlement. They seemed to turn to more serious recriminations, with the ILA bitterly contending that the Conference Committee could not be trusted. But the employers thought that the ILA leaders were afraid to talk constructively in front of each other and simply made accusations for effect. Some employers thought they were in the worst position they had ever been in, for they had offered a generous package and now "had to start over and pick up the pieces."

Although the parties knew that in the absence of an agreement, a "final offer" had to be presented on January 23 for a vote within three weeks under Taft-Hartley, no progress was made over the Christmas holidays. Early in January both parties were called by the mediators, convening separately. Each submitted written propositions. The mediators then broached to the employers a suggestion, made by Waldman, that they settle all they could and submit unsettled questions to arbitration. But there was no give. Turmoil and confusion increased through January. Numerous spokesmen with no effective leadership in the union often reduced the negotiations, if the term is proper, to a shambles, and the mediators could hardly fathom what was going on. Bradley, Gleason, Connolly, Anastasia, Bowers, Field, and several others spoke out whenever moved; but the employers had more than one voice, too, although they tended to keep their differences to themselves.

At this point Field, pragmatically, charged that the mediators were not taking an active enough part, for he felt that both sides had to be told what to do. If Moore believed this he could only say that the mediators could not be expected to make the contract; yet he was well aware of the different opinions within each side, and he heard each charge the other with the lack of power to effectuate an agreement.

The "last offer" vote was just ahead. The mediators told the employers that it would be harder to get an agreement after the vote, implying, perhaps, that they should offer more. But the employer consensus was that the ILA was counting on an overwhelming rejection to use to exact much more. There would be no point in sweetening their offer at this point to attempt settlement. Employers also still rejected suggestions to arbitrate, feeling they had always got the worst of it when they had gone to arbitration. Furthermore, if they agreed to arbitrate the question of clinics, and the award was against Anastasia, would there be any peace in Brooklyn? They felt they would be trapped if they agreed to arbitration.

Should the "last offer" be explained and sold to the men? The consensus among the employers was that it would not only be futile but dangerous. They had obtained a copy of a letter Bradley had prepared to send to the men, full of lavish promises. They could not hope to offset it. What was worse, it was putting the union further into a hole of no retreat, a further impediment to settlement. It is curious that Anastasia quietly offered a "package" of his own, but the employers felt that the ILA would lift his charter if he talked openly about it. It was quite obvious that some in the ILA were sticky on their own demands because Anastasia uncompromisingly was sticking to his clinic. The situation was even more confused when delegates from the same local sometimes divided on demands, or when former enemies joined forces on some issue. The employers could not ascertain who was on top. The body seemed swayed momentarily by whoever dominated a meeting; perhaps the ILA leadership had never acted so anarchistically before.

The Mediators' Settlement

In an extraordinary move the mediators, on January 31, four days before the "last offer" balloting, called the two sides together and told them that because no atmosphere for bargaining existed, they would propose a settlement, although conceding that it was not good mediation and was risky. The proposal was given "strictly in confidence" and explicitly was not to be taken as a platform for bargaining. Both were to take it precisely as offered. Still another comedy unfolded. The next morning the newspapers published the proposal, saying that the mediators called it "a fair basis for settlement." The ILA held back. Items dear to some had been omitted. No one was willing to say, "I accept it." The employers, angry at the publicity, felt they had been done a great disservice. As they saw the proposal it was designed to get the ILA off its own hook, doing for the ILA what its leaders could not do for themselves; but, what was worse, it was tantamount to saying, just before the balloting, that the employers' "last offer" was unfair. It would obviously affect the balloting. Under criticism and pressure, the mediators, genuinely embarrassed, suspended their offer until after the balloting, and soon officially withdrew it entirely. But the damage was done and the employers could hardly be blamed for feeling they had been double-crossed. Some felt that Moore should step out, and he offered to do so, but cooler heads prevailed, because no one else could have filled the breach. As everyone expected, the "last offer" was overwhelmingly rejected, partly because union officials recommended rejection. Thereafter the parties had less than a week to work out an agreement before the expiration of the eighty-day injunction, at which time the strike would undoubtedly resume.[43]

The situation in the union seemed to get worse. Field, in a report made to his local, went so far as to reinstate the ILA's

[43] *New York Herald Tribune*, Jan. 23, 1957, sec. 2, p. 14, Jan. 29, sec. 2, p. 10, Feb. 1, sec. 3, p. 6, Feb. 2, sec. 3, p. 4, Feb. 4, sec. 2, p. 5, Feb. 6, sec. 2, p. 11.

original demands. Yet Bradley, greatly embarrassed, told the employers, "Please understand that we act as a committee and do not stand on remarks of individuals." At this juncture the employers changed their minds and made an offer of arbitration through the mediators.[44] Bradley said, "No arbitration. You have used the courts, press, every means to battle us except negotiations. We are not financially able to carry a strike, but the membership is stronger than the committee. We don't want a strike. But if you are so determined to break up our organization, I'll recommend to our officials that they may negotiate with individual companies and keep on working." In all he said he only revealed his own lack of control. He distorted reality by charging that the employers were trying to destroy the ILA, when they knew they could not do so, and did not want to. They desired a more responsible union. They had even proposed the "check-off," intending to deliver the dues income to the International to increase its power over the locals.

The employers were tired of the charge of unwillingness to negotiate and were reluctant to allow such allegations pass unchallenged, for they believed that ILA leaders made them to hide their own inability to negotiate. Anastasia echoed Bradley's accusation: "Gleason, a week ago, used some bad words to describe the shippers, accusing them of not wanting a contract. I now agree. I now make the same statement. If they don't want to negotiate the contract, I don't intend to stay here because I, for one, have a lot of individual deals to make. Let's get going, yes or no." Connolly confronted Chopin directly, "Can you negotiate a contract?" Chopin retorted, "We are fully empowered; you have not changed your position from the beginning. Now you refuse arbitration. What do you propose?" A concerted move among the ILA to walk out—Anastasia had his coat on—caused Connolly to pound for order. Moore came to Connolly's assistance; he chastized the ILA—no doubt going beyond the proper role of a mediator, but he seemed to have no

---

[44] *New York Herald Tribune*, Feb. 7, 1957, sec. 2, p. 8, Feb. 8, p. 1.

choice and was frustrated by the futility of trying to deal with the factions—saying, "You will either negotiate as a union or a howling mob. You can't negotiate with a mob, so settle down and respect your organization," and, with a mediator's reflex action, "Both sides."

Whether to startle them into sensibility, or to change the subject, Moore said that he had been visited in Washington by Bridges, who had criticized the mediators for ignoring the objective of common expiration dates in their offer of settlement. Connolly said, "We have no interest in Bridges. . . . It was Bonner who asked for the common expiration date, not Bridges. Chopin blocked it saying he had no power to agree. . . . Bridges, or any of his men, will not put the bull on us." But Gleason added, "I talked to Bridges . . . and others many times. We went to Washington at Bonner's invitation. I am for the common expiration date because I think it is best for the ILA, but not because Bridges wants it." Bradley said that there were some on each side who probably were interested in the West Coast, but he added, "I can assure you we have no deal with Bridges. We refused to sit in the house with Bridges." Then, putting his finger on a salient danger, he said, "You can't have a common expiration date unless you have a uniform national bargaining setup. You better be careful on the other side because we know what is going on. Give us the same that Bridges has on the West Coast and we'll knock Bridges off the waterfront, which is a god damn' sight more than NYSA cares to do"; and the crowd applauded.[45]

Innuendos and countercharges marked the talks. Finnegan, director of the FMCS, arrived on February 11 to try his hand,[46] working with each party. He also discovered that the ILA "had no direction as yet." Because of controversy which Connolly could not control, the ILA meeting broke up. An additional problem was that the men had been kept waiting while Finnegan was meeting with the employers; they got mad at the delay—

[45] *New York Herald Tribune*, Feb. 11, 1957, p. 1.
[46] *New York Herald Tribune*, Feb. 12, p. 1.

some no doubt drank too much and got belligerent. The next afternoon some of the employers got angry. Being pressed to make concessions, one exploded, "I'm getting mad. What we are doing is wrong and contrary to the good of the industry. We are giving away and giving away." Others joined in the demand to stop giving.

By that afternoon it was reported that men were walking off the piers in some places. Probing for settlement continued but to no avail. A rebel, dissident union group asked that all original demands be revived. When Finnegan tried again to get the employers to enlarge their offer, some wanted to tell him off to his face for putting too much pressure on them; others wanted to tell the ILA off. More moderate ones pointed out that this would only trigger retaliation. When the mediators announced that the ILA had set a deadline of 5:00 P.M. for strike, the attitude of the employers was "What the hell do we care?" The tragedy was, as one of the more moderate employers put it, "With any display of reason on the part of the ILA, a contract could be settled quickly."[47]

The Agreement

With the strike on again, progress toward a settlement was gradually made, only to have Harold Bowers, a vice-president from Local 824, inject a very local issue about porters on the luxury liner piers. He said, "These guys are voting on all this stuff and I want to get mine the way I want it."[48] In the midst of this, the Catholic Press Institute held a dinner and Secretary of Labor Mitchell was the speaker. At Finnegan's bidding Mitchell called Waldman and Chopin to a private room. The meeting produced no results. Chopin later reported to his colleagues, "I got the old 'snow job' in the public interest." On the fourteenth the ILA dissidents filibustered all day and, when they lost a motion, broke up an ILA caucus in a riot; the mediators

[47] *New York Herald Tribune*, Feb. 13, 1957, p. 1, Feb. 14, p. 18.
[48] *New York Times*, Feb. 14, 1957, p. 1; *New York Herald Tribune*, Feb. 14, p. 1.

could not get the ILA back to the bargaining table until the next afternoon. Three prominent leaders in Manhattan continued the internal squabble for a couple of days, but when Bradley threatened to leave his post if they did not stop their opposition, they decided to go along. Actually the major items had been agreed to and it was only the fringe items which continued to give difficulty. With the internal controversy "settled," the ILA and the NYSA reached a "Memorandum of Agreement" on the sixteenth. Waldman would not allow the ILA to sign it until it was ratified, but they initialed it. Although the porter clause was still not settled and the employers became angry with one of their group who was holding out on it, nevertheless, there was an agreement. When Bradley said, "If it is not the best agreement, it was the hardest fought," the ILA applauded. But Chopin was quick to add that they ought not create the impression that the workers were not getting much; he insisted that it was the most generous agreement in the history of the industry. Finally, Finnegan said, if gratuitously, "This decision you've reached tonight is your own, not that of the Mediation Service." The main terms of settlement provided for a three-year agreement with a wage increase of 18 cents the first year and 7 cents more at the beginning of the second and third years; two paid holidays in the first year plus an additional one in each of the next two years—the beginning of paid holidays in the industry; five cents per hour added to the welfare fund with the understanding that some could be used for clinics; and a three-week vacation for each man who had worked 700 hours in each of five of the six preceding years. Important, too, was the acceptance of seniority "in principle" and the agreement to continue negotiations on the subject with final referral to arbitration, if necessary. Also, there was an informal beginning on coastwide bargaining on a limited basis.[49]

But the strike did not end until ratification, and in Philadelphia and Baltimore employers balked at accepting some of the terms

[49] *New York Herald Tribune*, Feb. 15, 1957, p. 1, Feb. 16, p. 1, Feb. 18, p. 1; *New York Times*, Feb. 16, 1957, p. 1, Feb. 18, p. 1.

and had not worked out agreements on local issues. Also, no agreements had been reached for checkers and the "craft" groups, but it was not usual that such agreements were worked out until after the general cargo agreement was completed. It took a few days to settle matters in Philadelphia and Baltimore. In New York, the NYSA formally ratified the agreement on the twentieth and the ILA voted on the twenty-second. Only a couple of diehard locals voted against it, and the total vote was 6,829 to 4,017. The strike was over.[50]

A few matters still needed to be taken care of. The parties had agreed to a "check-off" and administration had to be worked out. They had to find a port arbitrator, a serious matter for both of them. But of considerable moment was the stipulation to negotiate a seniority agreement and, in the event of failure to do so, to arbitrate the matter.

The employers had offered the "check-off," suggesting it to strengthen the International as against the locals. Because the latter sent in per capita tax irregularly and for only part of the actual membership, the International office was always short of funds. If the four-dollar monthly dues went to the International through a "check-off," the International would feed money back to the locals, and so gain more control. So the employers reasoned. They did not count on the astuteness of local leaders, who concocted a unique arrangement. Instead of checking off the $4.00 monthly dues, they left the old system intact, wherein the local collected these dues, and provided for an additional "check-off" of one cent an hour, amending the ILA constitution to permit it. The one cent an hour would cover the per capita payment of the local to the International. Each thereby was better off financially, but the average longshoreman, working 1,500 hours a year, had his dues increased by about fifteen dollars. Each man had to sign an authorization card authorizing the employers to deduct one cent an hour from his wages. Any man

[50] *New York Herald Tribune*, Feb. 19, 1957, p. 1, Feb. 21, p. 1, Feb. 22, p. 1, Feb. 23, p. 1, Feb. 26, sec. 3, p. 4; *New York Times*, Feb. 19, 1957, pp. 1, 26.

who did not sign an authorization card was required to pay the money to his local. On the basis of the annual hours of work at the time, the "check-off" arrangement gave the International about $420,000 a year.[51]

By June a new port arbitrator, Burton Turkus, was selected, a forceful man who could act authoritatively when necessary.[52] By agreement of the parties he sat in as chairman of the weekly meetings of the LRC and issued rulings on all matters not resolved by the committee.[53]

As a result of the experience in the long negotiations, the NYSA revamped its organization and did away with the cumbersome sixteen-man Conference Committee. Responsibility for negotiations was placed in one man, the chairman of the NYSA, Chopin, who would function under the guidance of a new Labor Policy Committee. Of course, several of the members of the Conference Committee were elected to the new Labor Policy Committee.[54]

[51] *New York Herald Tribune,* March 15, 1957, p. 11, May 1, sec. 2, p. 10, May 16, sec. 3, p. 6; *Waterfront News,* March 22, 1957, p. 3.

[52] It may be of some interest that Turkus was suggested by Anastasia, notwithstanding that Turkus was the prosecutor of Anastasia's brother in a famous murder case.

[53] *New York Times,* April 24, 1957, p. 66, June 21, pp. 1, 15; NYSA, Report No. 1431, July 5, 1957.

[54] *New York Times,* Jan. 6, 1958, p. 57.

10 | Seniority: Protecting Jobs

The most important unsettled issue hanging over from the negotiations of 1956–1957, and of great consequence for the future, was the matter of hiring on the basis of seniority, that is, hiring on the basis of length of service as a longshoreman. In the "Memorandum of Settlement," a simple paragraph said that the parties "agreed on the principle of seniority" and that a joint subcommittee would continue working on the details, as it had throughout most of the negotiations. If settlement could not be reached within forty-five days—extendable by mutual agreement —issues in dispute were to be referred "to an arbitrator experienced in seniority matters to be designated under the auspices of the Federal Mediation and Conciliation Service."[1] But the matter was too complicated for easy resolution.

In the background were the traditional structure and practices in hiring, but as modified by the regulations and requirements of the Waterfront Commission. But also, in the immediate background, was the desire within the ILA leadership to regain some control over hiring from the commission. The Bi-State Compact explicitly allowed for the possibility of a negotiated seniority system, provided it did not conflict with the requirements of the law. Regaining a role in the control of hiring—an objective shared by some employers and hiring agents—probably was the main reason many in the ILA supported a seniority system. Some, however, had the welfare of the long-time, bona fide longshoremen in mind, for unfortunately in the hiring of men as

[1] *Memorandum of Settlement*, Feb. 18, 1957, par. 8.

214

casual workers newcomers to the industry, or less senior men, were often given preference over older longshoremen, ones who had to leave their own sections looking for work when there was little to do on their own piers. The IBL had promised a seniority system in order to give protection to bona fide and regular long-shoremen as well as to give them assurances of employment on an objective basis, not on whims of hiring agents. The ILA had to meet this challenge. But it will be recalled that the notion of seniority had been given a boost, also, in hearings before the Waterfront Commission in 1955.

Support for seniority, perhaps better described as a system of priorities in hiring, was not universal on either side, and those who supported seniority often were motivated by quite different reasons. These differences no doubt had helped to delay agreement; in fact, after acceptance "in principle" it was impossible to tell precisely who supported seniority and why. Similarly, although it was difficult to assess the opposition or to separate opposition from lethargy, some on both sides feared seniority because they thought it would infringe upon their liberty.

While the seniority issue appeared to be a new one, it had old roots. The development was a resumption, or extension, of the negotiations started in 1953, at the insistence of the AFL, to eliminate the shape-up and to establish an alternative system of hiring. These earlier negotiations, as will be recalled, were aborted by the creation of the Waterfront Commission, for the employers were not willing to complete negotiations on the matter with the ILA while the regulations of the commission were being formulated. They could not afford to become party to any move to avoid, or circumvent, the regulations which were coming. In fact, as has been noted, the employers were then engaged in conferences with the commission to develop hiring regulations. Then came the ILA struggle with the IBL and the developments under the commission.

Not until 1956 could the question of seniority be given real consideration in negotiations. At issue was the complex inter-relationships of hiring and employment and customs and practices. There was no clear image of what seniority would entail. Some of the locals practiced "equalization of earnings" in some form or other and wanted equalization of earnings protected and extended. Others thought purely of priorities in hiring under established customs and practices. It is quite likely that some on each side had been willing to accept "seniority in principle," even when they did not really want it, because they believed a system could not be negotiated or implemented.

The subcommittee on seniority, under the chairmanship of Fred Field for the ILA and Andrew Warwick for the NYSA, made steady but slow progress, exchanging programs and ironing out many differences. The forty-five days allowed was not enough, and they continued on for a year into the late spring of 1958, when they came to a stalemate on a few major and a number of minor issues. In accordance with their agreement, the parties sought an arbitrator through the services of the FMCS. The intractable issues, however, were as much issues within the ranks of the two sides as across the table, perhaps much more so.

Arbitration of Seniority[2]

The arbitration proceeding and results are interesting for the revelation of the differences internal to the parties as well as across the table and for the lack of consensus as to what was meant by seniority. In the subcommittee-negotiations stage the NYSA had proposed, "Extra gangs shall be hired in a particular area on the basis of equalization of earnings, or on the pattern of employment presently established." The ILA argued that the employers had thereby agreed that extra gang assignment would be based on equalization of earnings in all places where a definite pattern of employment did not exist. The employers disputed this interpretation, claiming that they recognized existing equalization plans only and that everywhere else the extra gangs would be hired just as they had always been hired. At the arbitration hearing the employers endeavored to preclude any consideration

---

[2] For a full discussion of the arbitration hearing, see Jensen, *Hiring of Dock Workers and Employment Practices in the Ports of New York, Liverpool, London, Rotterdam and Marseilles*, pp. 100–106ff.

of extension of equalization of earnings, arguing that it was not a seniority issue and that the only matter before the arbitrator was a seniority program. An interim decision had to be made about the scope of the agreement to arbitrate. It was obvious to the arbitrator, however, that what was being negotiated under the name of seniority was a system of priorities in hiring, incorporating principles of seniority. Hence, the question of equalization of earnings program was arbitrable.

Both parties agreed to the maintenance of existing equalization plans, but the controversy thereafter involved extension of such plans where none had existed. But, as well, it involved the insistence by the employers upon freedom to follow preferences in the hiring of particular gangs in accordance with past practice. The union opposed such free transfer of gangs because it left too much power in the hands of employers to pick and choose, thus putting undue pressure on gangs to produce, as the union described it, for fear of failing to receive future employment. Behind all of this was the variable earnings pattern from section to section, and within sections.[3] Gangs making good earnings wanted their priorities preserved, whereas others would fare better under some system of equalization of earnings or rotation in assignments. The union was not united on the question, and most employers were convinced that productivity of gangs under existing equalization schemes was lower than that of other gangs, for the most part. The employers were dead set against rotation of employment, of which they regarded equalization as a phase, because they would lose the right to choose their gangs.

Both overstated positions in some respects because no one was suggesting assignment by rotation or changing the assignment of regular gangs. The regular gangs on every pier or terminal had established hiring priorities, and no one intended to have them share their work with others. The controversy involved only the hiring of gangs as extras away from their own piers.

There were also controversy and mixed viewpoints, particu-

[3] V. H. Jensen, "Hiring Practices and Employment Experience of Longshoremen in the Port of New York," *International Labour Review*, vol. 77, April 1958, p. 363; Jensen, *Hiring of Dock Workers*, pp. 89–95.

larly in the union side, on the matter of creating seniority districts. The employers generally wanted the smallest base for establishing seniority, that is the pier or terminal. Many wanted no obligation to hire men from other sections. The union views ranged from including pier units to the entire port, or portwide seniority, as the latter was called, although there were relatively few who really wanted the latter. Pier and sectional seniority became the primary, practical bases. The committee on seniority had designated seventeen sections (as against the thirteen hiring and employment centers operated by the Waterfront Commission, reduced to twelve to facilitate administration of the seniority scheme), although the five sections in Brooklyn were to be treated as one section for the first six months. This latter point was insisted upon by the union spokesmen from Brooklyn, no doubt partly as a concession to local employers to assist them to work into it, but more likely to give them and the employers an opportunity to size up the program. The question of portwide, and borough, seniority would linger on to plague both employers and many of the unionists, even those who had rejected it.

The seniority agreement provided for a combination of individual priorities to employment at the pier, in the section, the borough, and portwide, and for succession to vacancies in gang or pier lists.[4] All men were classified as "A," "B," or "C" by sections, or they were "casuals," depending on their length of continuous service in the industry. In spite of his classification, a man's primary seniority or priorty to employment was at the pier if he was a member of a gang or had regularly followed the pier. In either event he shared the priorities enjoyed by the gang or those inherent in being on an established list. A man was not allowed to appear on two lists, either for the same employer or for a second employer.

As might be expected, the parties built the seniority system around the basic hiring arrangements. Very little change was

[4] NYSA, "Seniority Arbitration Award," Information Bulletin, Report No. 1551, Nov. 10, 1958 (mimeographed).

made in the hiring of gangs as such, but each regular or extra gang was given a seniority date at its given pier in accordance with the year in which the gang was established. As had always been true, first preference in hiring was given to regular gangs on the pier or terminal, second preference was given to regular extra gangs—if any—on the pier or terminal, and third preference was given to gangs identified with other piers or terminals in the same section. Heretofore there had been no restriction, except by custom and practice, upon an employer who might have hired an extra gang from anywhere in the port. Existing equalization schemes were continued. For example, in lower Manhattan employers were restricted to the hiring of the gangs in the area, as long as available, the gang with the lowest earnings going out first.[5] Also, an exception to the three-step priority arrangement for hiring of gangs was made in negotiations for the area north of Forty-second Street in Manhattan. The prevailing system, in which four extra "floating gangs" had priorities overall other gangs working as extras, was allowed to continue. Another exception was allowed in Hoboken where the prevailing system permitted employers, once the regular gangs at the pier or terminal were hired, to form temporary gangs made up from men available at the hiring center; although the arbitrator urged the parties to eliminate this practice in order to have hiring in the section conform to the practice prevailing throughout the port. In Brooklyn, where certain employers had been sending gangs from their own pier to other piers operated by the company, the arbitrator allowed the practice to continue, even though it permitted the bringing of gangs into a section before all the unemployed gangs in the section were hired. Special difficulties were recognized here, some stemming from the complexity of stevedoring assignments, or contract, from past practice, and from lack of enthusiasm for the seniority plan in both employer and union ranks. Even before seniority was instituted, the employers agreed to intracompany movement

---

[5] This equalization plan was given up by the local union in 1963.

of gangs only within the section. Associated with this was the shuffling of the section boundaries. At one time Anastasia wanted hiring of extra gangs to be done from a pool. Various deals were broached amid much uncertainty. On all piers where regular gangs had been assigned by hatches, the practice was to continue. On piers where assignment of regular gangs followed informal pier equalization schemes, these were to continue.

The big change with respect to employment in gangs was in the detailed provisions made for hiring fill-ins for temporary vacancies and for permanent replacements, as well as for permanent and temporary fill-ins on established dock rosters. Under Waterfront Commission regulations employers kept on file with the commission gang rosters and dock labor rosters, both serving to identify the individuals hired under the procedures. The seniority agreement caused no alteration in gang rosters, but it provided a new basis for dock labor rosters and for their maintenance, because employers were to establish seniority rosters of all men who followed the pier. To permit the use of the seniority rosters, the commission issued "variances" from its regulations, allowing the old rosters to be discontinued and supplanted by the new seniority rosters. In doing so it also permitted the hiring to follow the steps in the seniority provisions. Also, in the maintenance of the seniority rosters, permission was given to follow the steps detailed in the seniority agreement.

The scheme was administered by a seniority board composed of three representatives (later increased to four, then to six) from each side. Seniority was measured on continuous service in the industry, covered by agreements between the NYSA and the ILA, and including work as a public loader prior to December 1, 1953. The seniority board was made the sole judge of the sufficiency of the evidence of past work history. Continuous service was defined as a minimum of 400 hours of employment during the contract year. Hence, a worker's seniority reached back through all years in which he worked 400 hours to the time of his first employment. Employment for less than 400 hours in a contract year precluded the counting of earlier employment, unless an exception was allowed by the seniority board.

As noted above, all longshoremen were classified. Group A employees were those who were employed at any time prior to September 30, 1947, specifically in the period from October 1, 1945—for records of employment reach back no further. All men who had worked at least 400 hours during each of the succeeding years and whose employment reached back further than October 1, 1945, were given equal seniority. Group B employees were those who had worked at least 400 hours during any one of the contract years in the period from October 1, 1947, to September 30, 1952, and who had remained in continuous service in the industry. Group C employees were those who had worked at least 400 hours in the period from October 1, 1952, up to October 1, 1957, and who had remained in continuous service in the industry. Employees who had worked or made themselves available for work after October 1, 1957, were classed as casuals. All newcomers to the industry, of course, entered as casuals.

For assignments at the time of the opening of new piers or the reopening of piers or terminals after three years of disuse, detailed priorities were established for recognition of men and their assignments to gangs or dock labor lists. It should be noted that seniority was to the pier, not to the employer.

The seniority board had broad administrative and judicial powers. Any dispute arising out of the seniority agreement was to be referred to the board. A majority decision was final and binding. If it failed to agree, the unresolved dispute was referred to the grievance machinery commencing with the third step, that is, by reference to the Labor Relations Committee and continuing to arbitration, if necessary.[6]

[6] For a discussion of the grievance machinery under the General Cargo Agreement, see p. 162; or V. H. Jensen, "Dispute Settlement in the Longshore Industry in the Port of New York," *Industrial and Labor Relations Review*, vol. 11, July 1958, pp. 588ff.

The task of implementing the seniority agreement was difficult. A major requirement was the classification of the men and deciding upon the method of identification. Establishing the hiring date and preparing the work record of each man involved the cooperation of the Central Records Bureau of the NYSA, which alone had the necessary information. The task required much more time than the parties had allowed and contributed to a long delay in instituting the system. It would have been logical to amalgamate the information with the Waterfront Commission registration and identification card, although this was out of the question because of ILA opposition.

Once the information for classification was assembled and the identification cards prepared, they were distributed through the local unions, a procedure which contributed to confusion and delay in some areas. The seniority board was swamped with complaints of incorrect classification and claims by workers who did not get cards. This entailed a staggering job of presenting employment records of all cases appealed to the seniority board and the establishment of the rules by which exceptions to breaks in continuous employment would be allowed. Because the board wanted to be fair and the work was tedious, there was further delay. It is to the credit of the board, however, that the task was ultimately carried to completion. Yet, in the process, the acceptance of affidavits as proof of a legitimate break in continuity of employment or of work as a public loader led to considerable abuse. Men who had left the industry for a long period of time, but who had subsequently returned, saw an opportunity to get an "A" card and produced an affidavit to justify their having an "A" card instead of a "B" or "C". The board was quite liberal in accepting excuses which seemed reasonable and it preferred to err in the direction of humanity. It excused absences for time in prison if the man had reestablished himself. The practice of securing an "A" card unjustly became so rank that one of the union members of the seniority board resigned in protest, contending that it was not only violating the rights of established longshoremen but was making a shambles of the whole idea of protecting the established men's rights to employment.[7]

Another aspect of the preparations for instituting the seniority system involved conferences of the seniority board and the Waterfront Commission. Inevitably the commission was concerned with the terms of the seniority agreement. Although by the terms of the Bi-State Compact a system of hiring under seniority, once negotiated in collective bargaining, would have to be accepted, the commission had to make sure that the provisions of the system conformed to the requirements of the law and that its own system of administration of the hiring process could be adapted to the needs of the scheme. The parties had not given a great deal of attention to the details of administration, and the commission was disconcerted by the apparent lack. It initiated an exploratory conference as early as November 26, 1958, in order to discuss with the seniority board the effect the seniority agreement would have upon the hiring procedures in the employment and information centers. Thereafter in a large number of conferences the commission tried to extend its cooperation in every practicable way but only under conditions consistent with the provisions of the Bi-State Compact.

No changes in commission procedures were entailed in the mechanics of hiring gangs. But hiring from the new pier seniority lists meant, first, that the current dock lists would have to give way to the new ones established under different criteria from those set by the commission; and, second, that changes in the procedures or mechanics of hiring the individual workers would be needed. After careful consideration, the commission—as previously noted—issued variances to its regulations, which, in effect, amounted to temporary changes in the existing ones. The variances had effect only when seniority was actually

---

[7] At the beginning of 1961 there was talk about reviewing all the affidavits and correcting the card issuance according to a test of corroboration of the facts. In 1963 the checkers did agree to review classifications.

established and were restricted to the area where it was in effect. The variances were subject to renewal but also to revocation if deemed necessary by the commission. They applied primarily to the standards under which individual workers were classified as regular employees and to the prevalidation of men hired from the established rosters. No prevalidations were permissible, of course, except where employers filed their seniority lists with the commission.

It was obvious that certain procedural changes at the centers would be needed. The sequence of hiring individual workers under the seniority provisions required a hiring place for each company for each pier and a timing by the agreed priority steps, in order to assure that complaints and confusion would not arise. The commission had no authority to police the performance in terms of the requirements of the agreement. It was not given lists showing the priorities of individuals at each step. Its role was to administer activities in the centers, not to determine if hiring was in accordance with the provisions of the collective agreement. Hence, once pier hiring, the first phase, was completed, the center manager announced sectional hiring, this being set up in three stages: "A" men, or red-card holders, first; "B" men, or white-card holders, second; and "C" men, or blue-card holders, third. Of course, along the way the needs of a particular company might be filled, and its hiring agents would leave. This naturally somewhat simplified the timing of the additional procedural steps. After the sectional hiring came portwide hiring, also by A, B, and C steps. Finally came hiring of casuals.

Seniority was not instituted anywhere until November 30, 1959, after the next round of negotiations had begun; the seniority system began in Manhattan north of Forty-second Street and then place by place through the early part of 1960, but not in Port Newark until 1963. Seniority for checkers, delayed in negotiations while preparations for longshore seniority were wrestled with, but completed in June of 1959, was introduced as early as December on a unitary portwide basis, prior to introduction of seniority among most longshoremen.

The evolution of seniority is to be seen in the efforts to implement and administer it. Much was left to be desired and the problems of administering it were no less difficult to resolve than those which determined its creation. The lack of universal interest in the program compounded the difficulties. Seniority was frequently observed in the breach. There was no genuinely interested policing agency. As we have noted, the Waterfront Commission had no authority to police the system or to intervene when its terms were violated or ignored. Employers normally do not police a seniority system without pressure from a union. Hence, the union had to carry the brunt of the policing. If men whose seniority rights were not respected could not get the union to press their cases, there was hardly any recourse. There were abuses: newcomers sometimes got work when an "A" man was idle; youngsters showed up with "A" cards—either borrowed or their own—men without card classification or with lesser classification sometimes were hired even when higher-card carriers were available, and counterfeit cards were used. To control the use of cards it was suggested that the hiring agents take the card at the time of hiring and check it and the owner before returning the card at the end of the day, but often hiring agents did not want to bother.

There were problems growing from the fact that the seniority sections were not equal in number to, or coterminous with, the commission centers. In some centers, sectional hiring had to be done for each of two sections simultaneously. This required additional space and created complications. At the sectional-hiring stage, when two sections in a single center were hiring simultaneously, hiring for one section might have been still at the pier-level stage, or the sectional A, B, or C stage, when the hiring in the other section was ready to become portwide or the hiring might have been completed in one of the sections. If so, the men unemployed in the one section always drifted or rushed over to the spots where hiring was still going on. Technically, they were not to be considered available until portwide hiring began. If they pressed in upon the hiring agent they were bound to create confusion. Furthermore, even where only one section was involved, hiring agents sometimes chafed under the delays required to keep the sequences orderly. One company might have hired all "A" men at its space and was prepared to move to the "B" men in the section, while another company was still hiring "A" men. The employees of the commission used loudspeakers to make announcements and to keep the hiring on schedule. The mechanics were only part of the difficulty.

Serious differences developed in relation to hiring casuals, particularly in Brooklyn and Port Newark. In both, clamor developed for a "D" category in order to prevent men from other boroughs or sections from standing ahead of the casuals from the section. Brooklyn locals wanted to keep all the home boys (even the newcomers) ahead of outsiders. In Port Newark, the "D" category was made a condition of introduction of seniority. The problem of absorbing newcomers became a perennial problem and will come into focus later.

The Waterfront Commission was never satisfied with the way seniority worked. It knew of spotty observance and limited application of the provisions in the agreement. However, although it had doubted the merits of seniority at the outset in 1958, it came to believe that the seniority agreement properly administered would have a great decasualizing effect. Also, it came to the conclusion that the union should be made to behave more responsibly—it did not want to rescind its variances and thus prevent the seniority system from working at all—and to achieve this purpose it would write the seniority agreement into its regulations; but this is a later event and will be picked up in due course.

11 | Specter of Automation: Bargaining, 1959

Many unsettled matters, some old, some new, plagued the parties as they neared the 1959 negotiations. Seniority had taken much time and the system still had not been launched. Although the clinic in Brooklyn had gone into operation in November 1957, other boroughs had problems of financing and constructing clinics. The LRC was not always effective; the work was time consuming and, under the press of other business, it was sometimes postponed.

Another issue had come on with some force. Technological change, currently referred to as "automation" was changing cargo handling, although the dimensions of the changes coming were only partly appreciated. Certain new operations had come on, like "piggy back"—hoisting loaded truck trailers aboard—and "side port" entry—loading general cargoes through the side of the ship rather than from the deck, not just for bananas. Lumped under "automation" were the use of conveyer belts and cargo elevators in ships, but most important were containers and trailers loaded away from the piers.

The ILA held a big portwide, stop-work mass meeting at Madison Square Garden on the afternoon of November 18, 1958, to discuss increased mechanization of cargo handling and its threat to employment.[1] It was reported that some seventeen thousand attended, but this was probably an overstatement. Field read Gleason's prepared speech—Gleason was ill—and all the top leaders of the ILA spoke. Two themes got hearty approv-

[1] *New York Times*, Nov. 18, 1958, p. 66.

al: "share the benefits" and "status quo on gang size." While saying they were not against progress, the ILA leaders insisted on preserving the regular twenty-one-man gang. Captain Bradley, referring to their negotiated hiring practices, said, "We made that agreement in good faith and in a short two years we are confronted with changes that take the gang system out of the hands of the union and into the hands of the employers. This we will never allow to happen. . . . We have some good employers and we have some chiselers. This is to serve notice on all of them that we are united." Anastasia, like some others, saw changes as inevitable, saying, "We won't be able to stop automation in this great country," but he wanted to share in the benefits of greater productivity.

The Controversy over Containers

Soon after, automation became an open controversy when the ILA and the NYSA met to discuss the use of preloaded containers. The ILA wanted them barred, claiming that they took work away from longshoremen; when no agreement could be reached the union leaders walked out, Field announcing they would refuse to handle containers of any company that had not been using them prior to October 1, 1956, the effective date of the last agreement. The employers considered the ultimatum a flagrant violation of their contract, saying that cargo had to be handled the way it came to the pier and that they could not tell shippers how to send their goods. In rebuttal Field charged the companies with "soliciting freight in prepacked containers." Presumably in retaliation, Field also urged a boycott of the LRC and called on longshoremen to settle all future troubles at the pier. More important, although the meeting was stormy, the New York District Council, on December 1, affirmed the ultimatum. So aroused were some leaders that Bradley was petitioned to call a meeting in Washington of all leaders from Portland to Brownsville for the purpose of establishing industry-wide policy on automation and containerization.[2]

[2] *New York Times*, Nov. 27, 1958, p. 59, Dec. 1, p. 51, Dec. 2, p. 66.

Later in December the NYSA and the ILA reached a temporary agreement permitting use of containers by all companies that used them previous to November 12, 1958, provided that they made no effort to reduce the number of men employed in the affected operations. Turkus, the port arbitrator, hailed this as a "commendable approach [that] presages an amicable and realistic solution." They also agreed to start, on January 7, a series of talks for sixty days "with a view to arriving at broad principles on automation in preparation for future collective bargaining."[3]

They met as agreed, the ILA presenting a prepared statement on how to avoid or minimize hardships accompanying changes in technology. Citing a reduction in total longshore manhours, it claimed that "the dock worker is already the victim of changes in techniques of cargo handling." Further, "We know that progress is made at a price. But the price should not be thrust disproportionately on the shoulders of the men." A more pointed bargaining ploy: the industry "is not sick . . . it is a prosperous industry." While the union held that specific proposals would be premature, it served notice that the "unfavorable employment effects of changes in technology" had to be accepted as an additional cost to the employer who makes changes. Noting that the problem was "highly technical," it announced that Dr. Walter L. Eisenberg had been hired to compile essential facts.[4] The meetings were an alert that the issue would be prominent in the approaching negotiations; even so, they had met in reasonableness and the temporary truce was later extended.[5]

Union Difficulties

A new effort to achieve a rapprochement between the ILA and the AFL-CIO would influence negotiations. The Teamsters

[3] *New York Times*, Dec. 18, 1958, p. 48, Dec. 31, editorial; NYSA, Report No. 1573, Jan. 5, 1959.

[4] ILA, "The Problem Arising Out of Changes in Methods of Cargo Handling," Jan. 7, 1959; cf. NYSA, Report No. 1575, Jan. 8, 1959; *New York Times*, Jan. 8, 1959, p. 50.

[5] NYSA, "Extension of the Containerization Agreement," Report No. 1589, March 10, 1959.

had been expelled from the house of labor and Hoffa had become its president. Bridges and Hoffa appeared to be forming a dual federation and there was fear that the ILA might be drawn into it. Informally, some in the ILA had been told that an application to the AFL-CIO would be given serious attention, and in spite of earlier rebuffs the ILA made a formal application on January 12, 1959, for admission. Although only three top ILA officers had voted against doing so, the decision caused internal bickering in New York. Newspaper headlines revealed that Albert Ackalitis and Frank (Machine Gun) Campbell loitered outside the room at the Cornish Arms Hotel in New York while the executive board of the ILA had met. This brought the Waterfront Commission into action, to ascertain if such men were an influence in the ILA. But some ILA leaders explained that the two men had been ordered by outsiders to sit in the lobby in order to help scuttle the move toward affiliation.[6]

In June the ILA had a friendly hearing before the executive council of AFL-CIO, which made no demand that any of the present officers be dropped. At the ILA convention in July the matter was placed before the delegates. Waldman advised local unions to endorse the application to show the executive council of the AFL-CIO that the desire for admission was strong at the local level as well as among top international officers. But Hoffa was there, too, and he asked the ILA to cooperate with him and Bridges "for the benefit of all labor," saying, "There is no way that we can separate ourselves from the longshore unions as long as trucks carry cargoes to the piers."[7] But the matter of affiliation would have to wait upon action at the AFL-CIO convention in September.

In the meantime, Anastasia had opened and dedicated a new union hall in Brooklyn in March. Thoughtfully he invited

[6] *New York Times*, Jan. 13, 1959, p. 8, Jan. 14, p. 46; AFL-CIO, *Proceedings of the Third Constitutional Convention, Sept. 17–23, 1959*, vol. I, pp. 419ff, vol. II, pp. 373–375; *New York Herald Tribune*, Jan. 13, 1959, p. 8.

[7] *New York Herald Tribune*, June 13, 1959, p. 4, July 14, p. 11; *New York Times*, July 16, 1959, p. 34.

Chopin and other dignitaries, even including the two commissioners from the Waterfront Commission, to the festivities. Chopin was asked to speak and talked happily about improved labor relations. Then, in one sentence, Anastasia put him and the NYSA on notice about a completely new project, raising an issue that was to plague future negotiations: "I hope Mr. Chopin will continue to talk nice to us and we will invite him again at the end of 1960 when the Port of Brooklyn dedicates its new hospital."[8]

Anastasia's presence was felt in another matter, although it was not solely of his making. Top leadership in the ILA had never really been settled with Captain Bradley's succession to Ryan. He tried hard and meant well but, in the relatively anarchistic internal situation, with locally controlled "empires," his lack of leadership acumen or authority was pronounced. Others eyed the position. Not least of these was Gleason. Connolly, who had more qualifications than most, was no doubt contented with his role as president of the Atlantic Coast District. As chief negotiator of the general cargo agreement in New York and the common provisions in the other North Atlantic agreements, he was in a key functional position. The employers watched the internal struggle for power with uncertainty.

The situation was complicated when Captain Bradley was charged with involvement with George A. Brenner, a former Westchester surrogate and one-time attorney for the ILA, who was under indictment for forgery and theft. There were notes bearing Bradley's signature, claimed by his counsel to have been forged, but it was not clear that he was not culpable.

A move was started in March to induce a prominent "outside" unionist, Morris Weisberger,[9] to run for the presidency of the ILA. He had been port agent in New York before 1957 for eighteen years and was hardly a stranger. He had Anastasia's support because Hall and Anastasia had become cooperators in

[8] *New York Times*, March 8, 1959, p. 84.
[9] He had succeeded Lundeberg as secretary-treasurer of the Sailors' Union of the Pacific, and was a friend of Hall of the Seafarers.

affairs in Brooklyn, notwithstanding that a few years before Hall and the IBL had done their best to throw Anastasia out. The move to run Weisberger never came to fruition, largely because of bitter opposition to Hall in Manhattan.[10]

Anastasia had still other notions. He set out to woo the Negroes, not just in Brooklyn but in the South, as well. To do so he had to overcome a clash he had had with Clifford Robinson, president of all-Negro Local 968, who had denounced him when he refused to give the local a pier of its own. Anastasia had had to deny the request, for it was impossible to take a pier away from men who held it. Anastasia had simply said that to grant the request would "further perpetuate segregation" and "lead to unfortunate results." But Robinson had curtly rejoined, "Your remarks about segregating Negroes reveal a hypocrisy equaled only by your own dedication to keeping the Negro in a position apart." Anastasia later invited the Negro local to merge with Local 1814, and Robinson and the other officers agreed. When asked why, Robinson simply said, "Anastasia is the big man in Brooklyn and we don't get any support from the International."[11] Anastasia, of course, gave some jobs to leaders from the Negro local.

Almost immediately thereafter Anastasia announced that he was a candidate for the presidency, calling upon Bradley to withdraw and threatening him if he failed to do so. He said, "If Bradley runs against me and loses, he goes back to the tugboats as a deckhand." His justification for running? "I had no intention," he said, "but it is impossible to live another four years under Bradley." He charged that Bradley had been "double-crossing the union on two points: Brenner and Bridges." He said that he could excuse the association with Brenner, even if guilty, "because any man can make a mistake," but having heard that Bradley and Gleason had met with Bridges in San Francisco, he said, "I just got tired of double-crossing." He also elaborated fears that there was a power grab afoot by Bridges and Hoffa.

[10] *New York Times*, March 18, 1959, p. 61.
[11] *New York Times*, March 26, 1959, p. 54, June 23, p. 1.

Bradley would not withdraw, of course, and said, "It's up to the membership to decide between us. We have a democratic union and anybody has a right to run for president but they don't have a right to put a guy in jail," again denying that he had signed notes for Brenner. He also explained the meeting with Bridges, in Hoffa's Washington office, "so we could make it crystal clear [that] we wanted nothing to do with him," to reject a new bid for the two longshore unions to bargain jointly with employers, and to "clear the decks for clean negotiations" by settling "rumors of secret deals with Bridges." Bradley added, gratuitously, referring to the merger in Brooklyn, "We're very happy they've decided to go for integration there. The West Side has had it for forty years and it has worked out very well." (Of course, it was not universal on the Hudson River piers.) But Anastasia had a rejoinder to Bradley's explanation of the meeting with Bridges: "It wasn't necessary to meet for seven hours for such a purpose." He said that Bradley had attended the meeting against the advice of the few other union officials who had known about it and in disobedience of a resolution that forbade any official of the ILA to meet with Bridges without the specific permission of the Executive Board. Said Anastasia, "This meeting with Bridges, coming on top of the Brenner thing, made me wonder if his next mistake might not mean that we wake up one morning and find Hoffa's men running the waterfront." Anastasia, estimating that 615 votes would be cast at the convention, claimed, "Right now I am sitting on top of 272 votes of the 308 needed to win."[12]

Anastasia's move for the presidency proved to be only a diversion in his struggle with Gleason. At the July convention in Miami Beach, Anastasia suddenly withdrew from the race when it was too late for anyone else to start a campaign, thus assuring Bradley's continuation in office. Briefly explaining his withdrawal, Anastasia said he had done so "in the interest of the organization which I love and for which I work." It was clear

[12] *New York Times*, June 24, 1959, p. 1, June 30, p. 52; *New York Herald Tribune*, June 13, 1959, p. 4.

234 Strife on the Waterfront

that Anastasia had not won the support of Negro leaders in the southern ports who felt rather more at home with Bradley. Although Anastasia had announced his candidacy primarily to thwart Gleason's ambition, and deftly did so, he would have relished the post if the Negroes down the coast and along the Gulf had not maintained their allegiance to Bradley.[13]

Following the close of negotiations in 1957, the NYSA had replaced the Conference Committee, which had proved to be so awkward in negotiations, with a fifteen-man Labor Policy Committee (LPC) in order to improve the approach to bargaining. Chopin was given leadership control as spokesman and negotiator, to work within policy guidelines set by the LPC in advance. Hence, he was to be *supported* by a small body rather than directed as was the case with the unwieldy Conference Committee, which had moved by consensus of the group as strategy and tactics were evolved. However, Chopin was still dealing with a committee whose members had diverse interests. They were only relatively more unified and prepared in advance than before. They often held different notions about strategy and tactics and took many votes to get consensus.[14]

The ILA also tried to effect a change for more efficient handling of negotiations. At its convention, although continuing with its large Wage Scale Committee, the ILA voted to have negotiations handled by a committee of no more than fifteen, to be elected by the Wage Scale Committee.[15]

Negotiations

Negotiations were opened early in August, unless one could say that Chopin opened them at the Miami Convention of the ILA. As an invited speaker he had cautioned against exorbitant demands but gave assurances of sympathetic consideration of automation, saying, "No one questions your right to share in the

[13] *New York Times*, July 10, 1959, p. 42; *New York Herald Tribune*, July 10, 1959, p. 11, July 15, p. 11.
[14] NYSA, Report No. 1637, July 15, 1959.
[15] *New York Times*, July 23, 1959, p. 44.

profits—if ever there be any—gained through automation." He warned, however, against "needless strikes . . . followed in the wake of 'ask for the moon' demands in the past, because union leadership was committed to promises it could not possibly deliver."[16] Curiously, the ILA was silent on the subject of automation when it presented its demands. It laid out a mixture of coastwide and Port of New York demands, asking that wages, hours, contributions for welfare and pensions (but not the amount of benefits in either, which were to be negotiated locally in each port), and duration of the contract, be negotiated for all ports from Searsport, Maine, to Brownsville, Texas—an extension of "national bargaining." For New York, it asked for a basic six-hour day, 8 A.M. to 12 noon and from 1 P.M. to 3 P.M. at the rate of $22.40 per day and with a guarantee of a full eight-hour day; a minimum pension of $125.00 a month; eight cents an hour for clinics and hospitals in addition to the increase in welfare; a three-year contract, to be opened each year for wages and for welfare, pension, clinic, and hospital funds; deletion of cancellation clauses; all cargo gear to be tested, inspected, and certified as being in compliance with the ILO Convention, No. 32; a new vacation clause, providing one week's vacation pay for 600 hours of work, two weeks' vacation pay for 900 hours of work, three weeks' vacation pay for 1,200 hours of work, and four weeks' vacation pay for 1,800 hours of work after ten years in the industry; and twelve paid holidays for all who worked 600 hours in the previous year. In addition, numerous language changes, many of which were cost items, were sought.[17]

Bradley, at the outset, announced that no agreements would

[16] NYSA, "Address by Alexander Chopin," July 14, 1959 (mimeographed); *New York Herald Tribune*, July 15, 1959, p. 11; NYSA, Report No. 1638, July 16, 1959.

[17] ILA, Wage Scale Conference Committee, "Changes to be Made in General Cargo Agreement," Aug. 3, 1959; *New York Times*, Aug. 11, 1959, p. 54, Aug. 13, p. 54; *New York Herald Tribune*, Aug. 12, 1959, p. 11, Aug. 13, p. 11; NYSA, "Information Bulletin," Report No. 1652, Aug. 12, 1959.

be signed until all were completed. Chopin responded quickly, "We don't think you bargain in good faith if after we reach an agreement in New York you won't sign it at once." The employers had hoped, too, that they were going to get away from the huge Wage Scale Committee, but 150 were present, even more than the 135 in the previous negotiations. Connolly had tried to stop comments from the floor, insisting that the motion of the convention for a committee of fifteen be adhered to, but an internal wrangle became evident. A compromise was adopted that the committee of fifteen would serve as spokesmen, while the others could speak only through one of the fifteen. Off to themselves the members of the LPC were of one mind in describing the demands as unrealistic, impractical and impossible, but they held widely differing views as to what ILA spokesmen meant. Some were for complete rejection while others insisted on moderation to avoid retaliation and threats of strike which were bad for business. The moderate ones prevailed, and they turned to setting their own demands, the task running through the two weeks before the next joint meeting.

The employers discussed the pros and cons of greater flexibility, with eyes on developments on the West Coast, where the much-heralded mechanization and modernization agreement had just been negotiated,[18] in which the Pacific Maritime Association, in effect, bought out the work rules from the ILWU for the price of $5 million a year for the life of the five-year agreement, that is, the ILWU permitted the employers to eliminate restrictive work practices and permitted the introduction of labor-saving equipment. They knew that the ILA had had it in mind when drafting its demands and had assumed that the em-

[18] L. Goldblatt, *Men and Machines: A Story about Longshoring on the Westcoast Waterfront, passim;* W. L. Horvitz, "The ILWU-PMA Mechanization and Modernization Agreement: An Experiment in Industrial Relations," and L. Fairley, "The ILWU-PMA Mechanization and Modernization Agreement; the Union Viewpoint," *Proceedings of the Sixteenth Annual Meeting of the Industrial Relations Research Association, Dec. 27–28, 1963,* pp. 22–33 and 34–47.

ployers would be seeking more freedom in assigning men to work. Some employers thought that if they really sought flexibility they might get some. Others questioned the value of making it an issue, for they thought they already had much of what was bought in the West Coast agreement.[19]

When some worried about a strike, Chopin would often lecture them to retain a solid front and not start a "rumor factory," reminding them that the ILA leaders would carry negotiations to the deadline if they thought that the employers would not take a strike. He knew that the union leaders would exploit any break in a united front and expect the employers to surrender when the crunch came.

The employers were prepared and met with the ILA on August 17 to pass out their demands, not a counterproposal. They wanted a three-year agreement, flexibility in use of labor—both in number and assignment and in shifting gangs from ship to ship and in shifting men within gangs between hold and dock—a flexible noon meal hour, elimination of paid travel time, reduction of absenteeism, right of cancellation in the event of nonarrival of a ship, removal of restrictive customs and practices, review of pension and welfare funds, a preemployment physical examination, loss of credit toward unemployment compensation when a man refused employment, damages for violations of contract, and seniority to be reviewed six months after effectuation. They would accept the principle of job protection to offset loss of job opportunities by those regularly employed in the industry provided the ILA would ensure the unfettered right of

[19] There were differences on the West and East coasts in intercompany relationships as well as in hiring. The Pacific Maritime Association voted on the basis of ship tonnage, thereby placing a couple of large companies in control, whereas the NYSA voted on the basis of one company, one vote. The NYSA could not enforce widespread change. Furthermore, the ILWU was highly centralized and tightly controlled, whereas the ILA was not. The ILA was disdainful of any program that would have interfered with hiring arrangements or job priorities. Many thought that Bridges had sold out the men.

each employer to inaugurate and regulate automated operations.[20] It looked as much like the proverbial "laundry list" as
ever the ILA listing did.

The employers sought to have more freedom to operate efficiently, but the union felt little consideration had been given to
its demands. The range of issues suggested use of subcommittees,
as during the previous negotiations, but when it was suggested
Anastasia objected. He insisted that the convention of the
Atlantic Coast District Council had with some reluctance voted
for the fifteen-man negotiating committee. According to him it
had to negotiate everything. Actually, Anastasia was opposed
to using subcommittees because if the fifteen-man committee
was the smallest one used, he would be in on all phases of negotiations and could best protect his own interests. The employers,
however, expected to get to small committees and the ILA
eventually would have to use them, too. Connolly told Anastasia
that he had misunderstood, because, regardless, there were certain conditions, for instance, with craft agreements, which had
to be referred to subcommittees.

An interesting but relevant diversion occurred on September
1, when it was revealed that officials of the ILA were being
issued subpoenas by the Waterfront Commission. The ILA
charged harassment, designed to keep them out of the AFL-CIO
and to break up negotiations. The leaders of the ILA were irate
and lost no time in excoriating the Waterfront Commission, as
they always did at the slightest provocation. Although the employers would not join in a protest against the commission without first knowing the reason for the subpoenas, they expressed
regret that the commission would issue subpoenas at that time.
Asked if they would allow service of subpoenas in rooms at the
NYSA, they answered that their rooms were inviolate. When
it was learned that an agent of the commission was present in
the NYSA offices, asking for permission to serve a subpoena on

[20] NYSA, "Management's Proposals for New NYSA-ILA Contract,"
Report No. 1654, Aug. 17, 1959; *New York Herald Tribune*, Aug. 18,
1959, sec. 3, p. 11; *New York Times*, Aug. 18, 1959, p. 48.

Connolly—Anastasia and others had already been served—the employers became angry too. Upon investigation it was learned that the action of the commission had nothing to do with collective bargaining but was only a part of the continuing investigation of criminal activities on the waterfront. Nevertheless, they agreed to tell the commission that subpoena of members of the negotiating committee would interfere with their negotiations and asked the commission to arrange dates for return of subpoenas so as not to interfere. The commission acceded to the request.[21]

As negotiations went on, the ILA kept accusing the employers of having made no offer. The employers would say they knew there would be money involved, but they could not make an offer until they knew which demands would be removed. But the ILA demanded that the employers make a money offer and they would see what could be taken out in exchange.

The parties were meeting frequently in September, but it is difficult to say what, if any, progress was made in clarifying positions. Mediators were prepared, and waiting to get into the act, particularly the city labor commissioner. In fact, he had sent a wire to the NYSA as early as August 8, saying that the mayor wanted a settlement. The employers could not just ignore him and sent him copies of their demands. They did not want a mediator, but if they had to have one it had to be a federal mediator. The ILA, on the other hand, was more opportunistic about mediators, except that it did not want state mediators. Along in September when federal mediators suggested to Connolly that they ought to get in to help avoid a buildup of acrimony, he encouraged them. The LPC opposed it, wanting to hold the reins as much as possible, and they did not want "to start the speeches all over again," just for the mediators.

On top of the usual internal difficulties, which kept the ILA from moving toward a settlement position, was the internal fight over the question of affiliation with the AFL-CIO. Bradley announced that there would be a union-wide referendum on September 14 in accordance with the constitution. The New

[21] *New York Times*, Sept. 2, 1959, p. 46, Sept. 3, p. 41, Sept. 4, p. 34.

York District Council held a meeting on the night of September 10, where many leaders in Manhattan and New Jersey opposed the referendum because they were opposed to reentry into the AFL-CIO.[22] Some on the West Side thought reentry might give men from the IBL an upper hand. More important, how much change would the AFL-CIO force? Some were interested in an alignment with Hoffa and the Teamsters. There was a real "ruckus" at the meeting.

Connolly and Gleason, the latter being able to shift positions expediently, supported the referendum and, surprisingly to some, Anastasia wanted it badly. He and Hall of the SIU, were still working closely together. At the District Council meeting Anastasia had tried to achieve reasonableness and apparently made some headway until John Bowers broke it up with a fiery, stand-firm speech. The rebellious ones threatened to boycott the referendum, ostensibly because no one knew what terms and conditions would attach to reentry. The AFL-CIO had not yet specified conditions. Opponents urged postponement for a month of study once the conditions of affiliation were known, with the referendum, when held, being conducted by the Honest Ballot Association and not by the local unions. Field, president of the District Council, siding with other Manhattan dissenters, said, "The kind of election they have set up is the kind of election that got us kicked out of the old AFL as crooked."[23]

The balloting was postponed for one week, but turmoil continued. Anastasia was so angered by the rebels that he set attorneys to explore the ILA constitution to see if he could achieve separate bargaining for Brooklyn. He even stopped attending bargaining sessions. This was a delicate matter for the employers, because they knew they could not make a settlement without him and neither could they avoid talking with him; however, the situation did give them an opportunity to get more information from him on what was transpiring within the ILA.

The employers were in favor of reaffiliation, because they

[22] *New York Times*, Sept. 9, 1959, p. 70.
[23] *New York Times*, Sept. 12, 1959, p. 34.

thought it might make the ILA a more responsible body, and when the ILA asked for time off for balloting, they granted the men an hour, hoping to strengthen the vote.

During the strenuous campaigning, those opposing affiliation sent sound trucks all over Brooklyn. Anastasia said that they were paid for by Bridges, through Field. When the ballots were tabulated, the results showed 9,970 for affiliation, with 7,719 opposed. The bulk of the support came from Brooklyn, Staten Island, and Newark. The Manhattan and the New Jersey locals, other than Newark, voted down affiliation by margins up to ten to one. A number of Manhattan leaders mumbled about secession. Bowers said that he would wait until his men decided what they wanted to do, but Field said that the referendum was over and that he would abide by its results. Coincidentally, on the same day the AFL-CIO, at its convention in San Francisco, authorized the Executive Council to take the ILA into the federation on a two-year probationary basis. It would have to comply with any clean-up orders issued, although Meany said— most likely with tongue in cheek—there had been "tremendous improvement in the ILA since it was expelled." The ILA would enjoy all charter rights but would be subject to ouster if it did not conform. The next day, the union was in an uproar over its leadership. The employers learned that Connolly would not show up for negotiations, the rumor being that he had resigned. Gleason would lead the union team that day. This did not please the employers. They were again in the middle of disruptive circumstances unrelated to bargaining. Moore, the federal mediator, had now entered the scene and understood that his first job was to knit the ILA together. It was believed that if the situation got completely out of hand Meany might call a meeting and try to force the ILA to straighten it out.[24] A negotiating session convened the next day and Gleason announced that Connolly was sick but would be in the next day. Chopin, referring to the

[24] AFL-CIO, *Proceedings of the Third Constitutional Convention*, vol. I, p. 431; *New York Times*, Aug. 18, 1959, p. 1, Sept. 23, p. 65, Sept. 24, p. 61, Nov. 19, p. 70.

rapprochement with the AFL-CIO, said, "I don't know if congratulations are in order, I don't want to start a fire." Gleason
only said, "We are still all ILA." Some employers felt that
Connolly was not sick but just disgusted with the fighting in the
union and that they could not get very far without him, but
some thought they had picked up a signal when Gleason said
they wanted a contract and did not expect to get everything.
But the fighting within the ILA was running deep, and more
than affiliation with the AFL-CIO was involved. Many union
leaders in Manhattan felt Anastasia was getting too strong, reflected in a comment of an employer from the North River who
had been warned by a local delegate, "You cannot give Tony
a hospital without the god-damnedest strike that ever hit the
port." Another fact is that some employers liked dealing with
Anastasia and felt they would get a better break on automation
with him than with anyone else. But one checked optimism with
the question, "Can Tony get control of the union?" The answer,
"He can't control Uptown." An employer from Brooklyn rejoined, "Uptown can't control the whole port." Another said,
"We'll end up placating Tony and alienating everyone else."
The question of a hospital was rejected by the employers but
they ended up by giving more for clinics.

Just before the District Council balloting on affiliation with
the AFL-CIO, the LPC, in order to break the log jam, decided
to make a new proposal, "predicated on the *whole* contract."[25]
When the ILA simply characterized it as "a good first offer,"
the employers said, "The offer was made against our better
judgment and we won't budge unless you make a reasonable
answer." Whereupon the ILA, surprisingly, sat down in the
NYSA conference rooms and amended its proposal.[26] The LPC
saw these amendments as only a half-hearted attempt and

[25] NYSA, Report 1669, Sept. 18, 1959; *New York Times*, Sept. 19,
1959, p. 36.
[26] ILA, "Changes To Be Made in General Cargo Agreement—as
amended Sept. 18, 1959 at 80 Broad Street"; cf. NYSA, Report No. 1671,
Sept. 23, 1959, Monetary Analysis of ILA Demands."

directed Chopin to single out two or three top leaders to find out what they really wanted. But Chopin had already been feeling out Connolly, Bradley, Gleason, and Anastasia and, because of the split, found a divergence of view that kept them from agreement on anything. However, perhaps the slight movement had made for a change, for even without Connolly progress took place. But the employers had sensitive decisions to make. Believing that the ILA felt they meant business or they would not have made a move at all, some employers were for keeping the pressure on. Some felt they should make no additional move until the ILA backed up further. Others felt that the ILA should do all the moving because they believed they had reached their absolute limit. Others painted a grim picture facing them if the ILA got out of hand and felt the surest way to drive the ILA further apart was to stand firm—the sure road to a strike. The employers, too, had trouble acting in unison.

The next day some reestablished unity in the ILA was reported. Connolly returned. Both parties agreed to have the mediators step in and arrange future meetings. They continued to make progress until the employers reacted strongly to an informal passing of word on the piers that there would be no receiving or delivery of cargo over the weekend, a type of job action.[27] The employers considered this a contract violation, and because the ILA would issue no order countermanding the action, there were no meetings over the weekend.

On Monday, with three days to the deadline, Moore called a meeting. The employers felt that they should hear him out, but not listen to speeches from the ILA. As it turned out, they continued to meet well into the night, with the mediators shuffling back and forth. Moore reported "interesting discussions."[28] When meeting the next day they heard a rumor from the Gulf ports, where other negotiations were under way, that the union had insisted upon complete retroactivity for a thirty-day extension

[27] New York Times, Sept. 26, 1959, p. 36; NYSA, Report No. 1672, Sept. 28, 1959.
[28] New York Times, Sept. 29, 1959, p. 64.

of the agreement, but that those employers had refused retroactivity and negotiations had ceased. This was important because
the LPC was then nibbling at an extension and "maybe retroactivity." Nevertheless, the employers were cautious about
granting retroactivity; as one put it, "We found ourselves leaving the last negotiations thinking we had something. We found
we didn't, because it wasn't buttoned up. If we pay the price for
a contract, we want a contract and won't consider any other
situation." They did not want to grant retroactivity just for an
extension; they wanted assurance of an agreement within a
specified period of time. Some of the ILA leaders said that if a
good money offer was made they could get an agreement right
that day, but the employers were not prepared to move that fast;
there were too many loose ends. Also, in the past, when they
reached general agreement with assurances that the unsettled
portions could be settled in subsequent meetings, they always
ended up getting much less for their money than they intended.

Finally the LPC offered to grant full retroactivity on all
money items in exchange for a fifteen-day extension, but with
the assurance there would be an agreement. The ILA leaders
agreed to negotiate for ten days, but they needed five days in
which to conduct a vote in all the ports. An extension agreement
was signed by the negotiating committee, but Local 791 announced that night that it would not accept the extension agreement and that there would be a "wildcat strike" if the extension
were attempted. The "Dockers News" had also been stirring up
the longshoremen. The developments in the South, however,
was the deciding issue. At 2 A.M. on October 1, the workers in
the South Atlantic and Gulf ports went out on strike. When
Vice-President Ralph Massey called Bradley and learned of the
extension agreement in New York, he complained that the ILA
was failing to support the South. Bradley, true unionist on solidarity that he was, spontaneously said that they would stand
together, and he abruptly issued a general call to strike. The
Port of New York went down with all the others.[29]

[29] *New York Times*, Oct. 1, 1959, p. 1, Oct. 2, p. 1.

The Strike and Taft-Hartley

The strike was exasperating to almost everyone. The employers saw it as a violation of the extension agreement, and Chopin protested to Bradley, saying the stoppage was illegal and demanding that he rescind his order. Publicly the employers complained bitterly of ILA irresponsibility and pointed out that there was no connection between the negotiations in the Gulf and South Atlantic ports and their own, that the refusal of the employers in the Gulf ports to grant retroactivity was in no way connected with bargaining of the NYSA. Only the rebels in the ILA were pleased. Others thought Bradley had made a mistake, although once the call was made they respected it, all save Anastasia. He appealed to his members and they voted to work; but they stayed away in such numbers that operations could not continue.[30] Anastasia even wanted to negotiate a separate contract, but Chopin told him his best bet was to honor the agreement and continue working. The employers took the stance that unless the men returned to work they would not negotiate until October 16, the date when the extension agreement would terminate, and the condition of resumption they set would be an assurance that the ILA would carry out any contract reached, regardless of action in the Gulf or South Atlantic ports.

The basic problem was that there was no one in the ILA who could control the various factions. It was obvious, too, that the AFL-CIO could not step in effectively, for those who opposed reentry into the AFL-CIO were the fractious ones rebelling in New York. The mediators seemed to feel that nothing could be done until there was a settlement in the Gulf Ports. But employers in New York would not put pressure on Gulf employers to grant retroactivity.

With pressure upon him from many sources, President

---

[30] NYSA, Report No. 1675, Oct. 1, 1959; cf. NYSA, Report No. 1677, Oct. 5, 1959, NYSA, Report No. 1681, Oct. 9, 1959; *New York Times*, Oct. 3, 1959, p. 1, also editorial, Oct. 4, p. 1, Oct. 5, p. 1, Oct. 9, pp. 1, 18, 19; U.S. Board of Inquiry on the Labor Dispute Involving Longshoremen, *Report to the President*, Dec. 7, 1959.

Eisenhower, on October 6, invoked the emergency provisions of the Taft-Hartley Act and appointed Guy Farmer, a former member and chairman of the NLRB, to serve as chairman. Hearings were quickly held, a national emergency found, and an eighty-day injunction issued against the strike. Bradley then ordered an end to the strike.[31]

It is interesting to note that the ILA tried to persuade the judge, who issued the injunction, to have it provide retroactivity to pay increases. The union argued, "Why should the men work at the same wage rate?" But in opposition to Waldman's plea, Giardino argued, "No court has the power to enter into the realm of collective bargaining. It has no right to go beyond the status quo."[32]

With the pressure off and the new deadline set as the termination date of the injunction, no efforts to get back to negotiations were made for three weeks. The parties hardly met even in their own councils, certainly the ILA did not. There was too much dissension in the ILA ranks. It was a good question whether negotiations could even be resumed effectively. Knowing this situation, the mediators had no choice but to let things cool off. They could not let the matter drift endlessly, however, and on October 19 they brought them together again, although the southern ports were still in stalemate. Not relishing going over old issues, Moore asserted himself when the ILA, tactically, wanted to pull back, and started the parties off from the point reached at the time of the extension agreement.[33]

Because Chopin assumed that the delay in the southern ports was due to dalliance on the part of the union, he called a meeting of the employers from the other ports and urged them to file charges of unfair labor practices if the local unions refused to negotiate. The southern employers had not overlooked this as a possibility, but had concluded it was not feasible. How, they asked, could they do so while the local union representatives

[31] *New York Times*, Oct. 7, 1959, pp. 1, 32, Oct. 8, pp. 1, 20; NYSA, Report No. 1679, Oct. 6, 1959.
[32] *New York Times*, Oct. 16, 1959, p. 50.
[33] *New York Times*, Oct. 20, 1959, p. 66.

were with federal mediators in the negotiations in New York? To have a basis on which to move, they said that the employers in New York had to insist—as they had not done—that when local matters were being negotiated nobody from the outports would be present. Everyone should negotiate at the same time in all ports on local conditions.

Shortly after this meeting, when Connolly was told that local negotiations should be going on simultaneously in all ports, so that none would be held up at the end, he said, "It's not entirely our fault. The employers in the other ports all tell our people, 'Wait and see what New York is doing.'" The fact is that it was difficult to deal with local conditions until the money questions were settled and it was difficult to settle the money issues without regard to some of the local conditions. The monetary settlement in the South Atlantic and Gulf ports was hardly separable from the settlement in the North Atlantic ports. They had good reason to wait upon New York.

Reaching an Agreement

In the negotiations in New York automation—specifically, shipping in containers—became the most controversial issue, although some aspects of it were settled. The ILA demand that all containers be stripped and loaded on the piers was rejected as doing work twice. From the start the employers had agreed in principle that some protection should be afforded regular employees adversely affected by containerization, but they expected unfettered control over both the labor supply needed and the condition and manner in which containers would be utilized. The ILA was not willing to give ground on utilization of manpower, and the employers agreed to the retention of of the standard twenty-one-man gang. Realizing that it could not get the right to strip and load, the ILA demanded royalty payments on tonnage in containers. In turn, the employers proposed severance pay, seeing royalties as "a tax on containers which would just be more feather-bedding."[34]

The LPC presented its proposal on automation in writing,

[34] *New York Times*, Nov. 2, 1959, p. 52, Nov. 5, p. 62.

and the ILA, after some study, handed over its own written answer prepared by Dr. Eisenberg. This the employers found to be a gross exaggeration of the impact of containers, "so ridiculous that [they] should waste no time in throwing it back to them." They told the ILA, "it complicates an already complicated problem in an unrealistic manner."[35] Nevertheless, they talked on and recognized different problems with full containerships, partial containerships, and unitization. The employers soon got pushed off their notion of severance pay, because the ILA correctly said, "It is almost impossible to identify the guy that's displaced. . . . A man does not lose his job, automation just reduces hours." Besides, severance and a closed register would reduce a local's membership; this, some ILA leaders did not want. The employers feared that royalty payments would keep growing. The employers concluded that the ILA leaders were not sincere in their concern for displaced people and that they really wanted royalty money to administer. Chopin, to get the employers what they could for their money, then planted the notion that "there is a lot more money in any royalty fund if the employer has the right to use men as he sees fit." The employers finally offered a royalty of twenty-five cents per ton on shipper-loaded containers. The ILA wanted seventy-five cents.

As they continued bargaining, the other issues started dropping into place, and the consensus emerged that if they removed automation from the settlement, and referred it to arbitration, they might achieve agreement on all other matters. Accordingly, they set the ground rules for the arbitration on the matter of royalty.[36] But as they approached understandings, some employers reminded the others not "to accept anything in principle, but spell it out." They were opposed to leaving something open and then never settling it. By working almost three days around the clock they came to a settlement on the afternoon of Decem-

[35] New York Times, Nov. 17, 1959, p. 59.

[36] New York Times, Nov. 25, 1959, p. 47, Nov. 28, p. 42, Nov. 30, p. 46.

ber 3 on wages and contributions to health and welfare and pension plans for the North Atlantic ports, and on all other issues for the Port of New York. The news photographers were there to take pictures of the historic event—a settlement under Taft-Hartley before the injunction expired and without a last offer vote. Guy Farmer declared, "We will be pleased to report to the President that your joint efforts to reach a mutual agreement have been successful, and we extend to both parties our personal congratulations on your earnest and successful demonstration of the effectiveness of free collective bargaining in the settlement of major labor disputes." The editor of the *New York Times* said the settlement was notable because it was "the product of genuine collective bargaining" and it showed "a constructive way of handling employment problems raised by the use of more efficient methods of operation."[37]

A "Memorandum of Settlement" was signed, and the terms were ratified by the men on December 10, by a vote of three to one. But the negotiations in the southern ports did not move so rapidly and as late as December 19 there was real fear that there would be a new dock tieup in the South. Nevertheless, the New York employers said that the contract was already in full effect and that the individual companies had begun paying longshoremen under the new scale, although checks covering retroactive payments would be some weeks away. The completion of the difficult negotiations in the southern ports before Christmas was considered a personal victory for Captain Bradley and Paul Hall, who had accompanied him. Everyone in New York expressed relief at the outcome.[38]

The "Memorandum of Settlement" provided that if the parties could not settle within two weeks of negotiations the question of what royalty should be paid on containers loaded or unloaded away from the pier by non-ILA labor, it would be

[37] *New York Times*, Dec. 2, 1959, p. 1, Dec. 3, p. 1, Dec. 4, p. 1, Dec. 5, editorial; NYSA, Report No. 1697, Dec. 3, 1959.
[38] *New York Times*, Dec. 10, 1959, p. 1, Dec. 11, p. 1, Dec. 19, p. 42, Dec. 22, p. 62, Dec. 24, p. 38, Dec. 25, p. 38.

submitted to arbitration. The negotiations were not fruitful, and an arbitration board headed by Dr. Emanuel Stein, professor of economics, New York University, the impartial member, began hearings on March 25, 1960. Admiral Frank M. McCarthy was designated to represent the NYSA and Gleason the ILA.[39]

Agreements and Disagreements on Automation

The arbitration hearing put automation into perspective in the short run and, in this respect, it turned out not to be as much of an immediate issue as the ILA had made out. Yet, in setting an approach to the problem, it carried much signficance for the future. The board recognized immediately that its function was more legislative than judicial, for it had to seek a fair and equitable answer, amid conflicting contentions, where no agreed-upon guidelines had been set. There were many variables and inadequate factual data, because of lack of experience. Dr. Stein, experienced arbitrator, knew that he could do little more than arrive at an "informed judgement."

The principle of royalties had been agreed to; the question was the amount. The authority of the board did not extend to determination of the uses to which the money was to be put, because the parties had reserved that for themselves—for a future decision. Presumably the money would be used somehow to ameliorate or cover the costs of displacement of men or reduction in earnings, but neither party was prepared to make a decision at this stage, a fact regretted by Dr. Stein, who thought they might have fixed payments more confidently if the end uses of the funds had been known.

The hearings extended until August 3, 1960. Both parties gave facts and opinions on the nature of containerization, short-term trends in use of containers, labor supply and future changes, tonnage handled, labor costs, productivity—on conventional ships with only break-bulk cargo, on ships with a mix of break-

[39] "Memorandum of Settlement," see NYSA, Report No. 1697, Dec. 3, 1959, Report No. 1759, March 23, 1960.

bulk cargo and containers, and on ships devoted exclusively to containers—and the actual and prospective impact of containers upon employment of ILA members. At the request of the parties, the board visited a number of piers to observe the operations.

The ILA maintained that the conversion to containers would result in substantial reduction in the number of men employed and that the hours worked by those remaining would be substantially reduced. It was easy to paint a gloomy picture. With no drafts of cargo to make up or tear apart and with no articles to be stowed in the hold, the gangs' work would be drastically reduced. The work of checkers and clerks would also be substantially reduced and simplified—checking one container as against a hundred pieces. Also, even the sweepers and extra labor on the piers would have less work because the container operation would be a much cleaner one. Furthermore, there would be no handling of cargoes in pieces in loading and discharging of trucks. Cargoes would be lifted off or on in a container.

The employers contended that shipper-loaded containers were few and that the ILA was unduly exercised and overstated the volume. They insisted there had been no loss of jobs or decline in hours for regular employees and that attrition would more than offset any future loss. They had already taken steps to cushion adverse effects by increased contributions to pensions. They pointed out that they had even agreed to maintain substantially larger gangs for containers than were needed. Royalty payments would create a fund for a purpose that did not exist and would constitute an unwarranted penalty upon the use of containers to the detriment of the future of the industry and its ability to provide jobs. It may be noted, however, that not all employers were concerned about the issues, only those expecting to use containers. But at this stage containers were more on the horizon than a reality and most companies were not concerned about them.

It would appear that the employers argued as forcefully as they did because the ILA was pushing so hard. Even after they agreed to payment of some royalty, they argued against it. Toward the end of the hearings the ILA formulated its demands, much more than the 75 cents at the close of negotiations. The ILA asked for $1.50 per ton for containers under 17 feet, $2.00 for containers between 17 and 34 feet, and $3.00 for containers of 35 feet or more.

The board found that containerization would have an adverse impact upon employment, both in loss of jobs and in reduction of manhours, although this estimate was mostly prospective. It was clear, though, that the parties had proceeded upon the proposition that the burden of payment was to rest exclusively upon the companies using and handling containers, that payment was not to be considered as an increase in wages or as a division of the savings, or based upon the ability to pay; nor was it intended to reflect literal improvements in productivity. While the impact from container use was still small, the board found that the employers knew that large labor savings were implicit in containerization, but it did not want to set payments that would discourage the technological advance. It concluded that a flat royalty per ton, regardless of the size of the container or the nature of the ship carrying it, had the obvious appeal of simplicity and ease of administration; but it was rejected because it took no account of the ways in which the nature of the ship on which containers were carried would affect employment opportunities. A uniform rate would be only superficially fair. The board then came to the conclusion that the best single standard was the type of ship itself—a conventional one, a partially converted one and fitted out for container operations, or a fully containerized vessel—for the difference between these types of ships was more than a difference in degree, it was a difference in kind. Hence, it concluded that to levy the same royalty on cargoes from each type of ship would be to discriminate unfairly against ones which displaced less manpower per ton of cargo.

The board said that lacking knowledge as to the dimensions which the problem would assume over the next two years, and, lacking authority to make any determination as to the disposition of the payments, it had to grope for a relatively realistic and workable answer. It set up a formula as follows: (1) in conventional ships, 35 cents per gross ton; (2) in partially automated ships, in which not more than two hatches and not more than 40 per cent of the bale cube had been fitted for the handling of containers, 70 cents per gross ton; (3) in automated or containerized ships, in which more than two hatches or more than 40 per cent of the bale cube had been fitted for the handling of containers, $1.00 per gross ton. It decided that the differences approximated the variations in the degree of labor displacement. Payments into the royalty fund were made effective as of July 1, 1960.[40]

Gleason wrote a vigorous dissent opposing the royalty schedule. He argued that it would not sufficiently minimize adverse effects on employees and that he regarded the distinction among types of vessels as an open invitation to chiseling evasions of the high royalty levies, because there would be controversy over improper classification of ships. He also criticized the failure to define a "container" as including all unitized cargo, that is, cargo put up in any form to serve the purpose of a completely closed container; he argued that this failure would lead to another union-management conflict because users of substitutes for containers, or near-container devices, would be encouraged.[41]

[40] NYSA, Report No. 1840, Nov. 23, 1960, "In the matter of arbitration between New York Shipping Association and International Longshoremen's Association, AFL-CIO" (Containerization Arbitration Award).

[41] "Dissenting Opinion of ILA Arbitration Board Member," see NYSA, Report No. 1844, Nov. 30, 1960.

12 | Was It Collective Bargaining?

The two previous ordeals in negotiating led some in both parties in 1962 to try to avoid "deadline" bargaining. They were not successful. Connolly had died and Gleason succeeded him as executive vice-president of the ILA and president of the North Atlantic District.[1] Gleason thus became the chief negotiator for the union and, because the parties had been dealing very closely with each other since the last negotiations—in the LRC, in implementing seniority, and in working on safety—he was not unreceptive to a suggestion by Chopin that they reach an early understanding and avoid the long wrangling and frustrating uncertainties of past negotiations, for success might improve his own new position. Throughout 1961 the parties had averaged over one prearranged meeting per working day and many of these were long ones; they may have been the "meetingest" labor relations people in the country. The meetings produced constructive ideas about various issues although the parties did not always come to understandings. The past could not be sloughed off, and they were past masters at hearing without listening. They heard what they wanted to hear. Much of the daily give-and-take consisted of deal-like adjustments, settlements of convenience which, if they satisfied the need of the moment, did not solve major problems. Although progress was often ephemeral, it was encouraging. Gleason's willingness to cooperate, of course, could easily change if union sentiment dictated otherwise.

[1] *New York Times*, Aug. 25, 1961, p. 38, Dec. 24, p. 12.

Even before the fateful year of 1962 began, the parties were conversing informally about the prospective negotiations. Long before formal negotiations—and these were moved up to early June when the usual starting time had been late August—Gleason and Chopin had reached a meeting of minds about the settlement. It is even said that they had worked out a settlement but that Gleason could not deliver. Whether true or not, events very quickly showed that settlement was more difficult than ever.

Gleason, Anastasia, and Bowers—Union Difficulties

Gleason's acquisition of the higher post did not give him the power to put over a settlement. Actually he was less effective than Connolly, for he did not command the respect that his predecessor held from the rank and file or the coterie of local officials. Connolly had been a longshoreman and everyone knew that he knew the industry. Gleason was a checker, and even though he had been elected to his new position, some colleagues were jealous and did not trust him. His uneasy leadership is a major key to the prolongation of negotiations, leading to a long, ever-rising procession of governmental intermediaries who, if they added color, did not add dignity to collective bargaining. Gleason's lack of power to make a concession, let alone a settlement, proved costly.

After the last negotiations, the FMCS had appointed Andy Burke as Maritime Coordinator to keep close watch and maintain liaison with the parties. This he did. In mid-January 1961 Moore had joined him in meetings with both ILA and NYSA officials. They were independently trying to get bargaining talks under way early, hoping for resolution of some problems before the deadline. Soon thereafter both parties began to make factual surveys, especially on automation. It was not to be a central issue, however, because experience had borne out the employers' contention: a very small part of the general cargo handled in the port in 1961 had come in containers, less than 3 per cent.

In a fashion typical of preliminaries in collective bargaining, general speeches pointed to the beginning of negotiations. Gleason spoke in mid-April at a meeting of the National Safety Council. Top industry leaders, listening, noted his lack of belligerency and his desire for early negotiations in order to avoid deadline bargaining. Soon thereafter Chopin, at the Foreign Commerce Club, also gave encouragement, stating that since the last settlement "waterfront labor relations had continued to improve." But he also alerted his audience to the "ominous clouds" of internal dissension in the ILA; the greatest need, as he saw it, was "a strong, responsible and well-disciplined leadership" in the ILA.[2]

Even as 1962 had begun a feud inside the ILA between Manhattan and Brooklyn dock leaders had broken out into the open. At the first meeting of the New York District Council, Anastasia walked out with his delegation, protesting refusal of more voting power for his local. The Manhattan locals, particularly Local 824 led by Bowers, did not agree that Anastasia should have more votes. Anastasia threatened to go to court or to establish a Brooklyn District Council. Although Anastasia did not push this matter further, a more ominous internal difference surfaced in mid-April. Just as the Atlantic Coast District Council was to convene to draft bargaining demands, Bowers publicly challenged the propriety of Gleason heading negotiations. Because he had thought of himself as the obvious heir to Connolly's post, having come from the same local, he was unhappy about Gleason's accession to it. "My local cannot see a man who represents 5,000 checkers and who has an obligation to them to come up with a good contract," he said. But Captain Bradley deplored Bowers' remark and publicly upbraided him for "a very bad mistake," and said negotiations "will be conducted in accordance with the Constitution and By-Laws." Gleason, not one to shy away from a fight, said, "It's too bad that Bowers has to try to fight our battles in public, playing right into the hands

[2] NYSA, Report No. 2017, April 30, 1962; *New York Times*, April 16, 1962, p. 54, April 19, p. 52; *New York Herald Tribune*, April 19, 1962, p. 37.

of the operators and Waterfront Commission people who will say, 'Look, they are fighting among themselves.' "[3] Nevertheless, the Wage Scale Committee relentlessly gathered the variegated demands from the many locals and, as usual, deliberately cumulated them without winnowing, although the committee met again in New York in mid-May and took further steps in preparation for negotiations.[4]

Coastwide and Local Bargaining

At the same time management groups from the various ports were concerned with their problems of preparation. A resolution prepared at a meeting of employers in Baltimore, designed to determine whether the ports in the North Atlantic area would accept a master contract negotiated by the NYSA, was voted upon. Trouble arose because employers in Philadelphia were reluctant to let the NYSA negotiate the master contract until local conditions were settled.[5]

The demands of the ILA were presented to the NYSA on June 13.[6] Gleason did not need to say it, because the employers could see, but he pointed out that "every port in the North Atlantic is here with representatives from every local, also district vice-presidents, and representatives from the South Atlantic and Gulf ports, to report back to their locals." Although local conditions would be negotiated locally, he warned that the union would stand together even if employers in Philadelphia were balking at coastwide bargaining. He gave notice—it had to be with tongue in cheek—that "the ILA has unity at this time" and then announced that they would have "four co-chairmen" on negotiations. After sparring a little, Gleason introduced what would be a continuing theme, that the NYSA paid—as required by law—two million dollars to support the Waterfront Commis-

[3] *New York Herald Tribune*, Jan. 4, 1962, p. 33, April 18, p. 32; *New York Times*, April 18, 1962, p. 66.
[4] *New York Times*, May 16, 1962, p. 66.
[5] *New York Times*, June 11, 1962, p. 51.
[6] NYSA, Report No. 2027, June 13, 1962.

sion, as he put it, "to fight us," and the ILA demanded a similar amount with which to fight the commission. He needled the employers for not trying to get rid of the commission because of the additional cost imposed on them from having to wait to get men from the hiring halls to the piers.

Chopin was careful not to respond to this issue and simply said, "We don't want any deadline bargaining and we hope that Taft-Hartley and injunctions are not a built-in part of negotiations, but that's how you are starting out, doubling costs in New York." His quick calculation was that the union's wage demand alone, without fringes, would cost at least $100 million a year. He warned that unless they changed their minds, "We are faced with either meeting impossible demands, which would be economically suicidal for the industry, or taking an equally ruinous strike."[7] Continuing, he said, "We are thinking in terms of the guidelines [President John F. Kennedy's guideline that wage increases should be limited to 3.5 per cent], but you say you have no scissors. Well, we will just have to find them!"

As they met again on June 25, a major difference that was to become a block dominated the session. The NYSA took the stance that until local negotiations were settled, no money offers could be made on the master contract; Chopin said, "We must know what we are buying before we set up the money." But ILA spokesmen, one after another, indignantly insisted that there would be no local negotiations until money for the master contract was agreed to, and that this was traditional. The matter of a payment equal to the money required to support the Waterfront Commission also came forward, with Gleason frankly saying, "We want to knock out the Waterfront Commission and we need funds to do it."

The most immediate problem for the employers was the ILA's insistence on negotiation of the master contract before turning to local negotiations, because Philadelphia employers would not give New York the authority to negotiate a master contract until

[7] *New York Times*, June 12, 1962, p. 63, June 14, p. 55.

local settlements were made. Their view, generally, "It was the time to band together to stay apart." Chopin felt that this might have been possible if the Philadelphia Shipping Association had supported the Baltimore resolution not to *conclude* a master agreement (not that there would not be negotiations on the master contract) until local conditions were negotiated. At this stage he felt it was too late inasmuch as they were faced with the necessity of offering counterproposals on the master contract. The employers, however, discussed the practicality of bringing employers from the other ports to New York to participate in proposals on local conditions. But the Philadelphia employers did not want this either, although they finally authorized New York negotiations on the master contract if the ILA would submit local demands in each port and "endeavor to negotiate." Chopin believed he could now hold the ILA in negotiations and insist that no final settlement be made until the ILA entered serious negotiations in the outports. Both master contract and local negotiations could be concurrent.

During the first two weeks of July, Gleason was away and negotiations marked time. The employers did not want to bargain with Bradley and the latter felt he should not negotiate without Gleason. Meanwhile, Anastasia, very unhappy with Gleason's leadership and accusing him of a one-man operation, was clamoring for a meeting. He even publicly criticized the ILA demands as ridiculous. Although this of course pleased the employers, ironically, much earlier, Local 1814 had set out its demands in its own "1962 Policy Statement," and the employers had considered these very outlandish, too. Lumping Bradley with Gleason, Anastasia charged, "They completely ignored our repeated demands for a more realistic list of items."

Anastasia's outburst revealed that differences between Anastasia and other ILA leaders were more serious than ever. In comparison, the earlier spat between Bowers and Gleason was trivial. When negotiations resumed, in mid-July, Anastasia boycotted them and petitioned the NLRB for certification of Local 1814 as the bargaining agent for Brooklyn. The ILA called a special meeting on July 17 to close the breach and head Anastasia from his breakaway course. But Anastasia was adamant and threatened to withdraw his local from the ILA.[8] The employers watched the battle with interest and saw it "strictly a union internal problem," but a serious obstacle to negotiations. Some employers in Brooklyn would have preferred separate bargaining, but those in Manhattan would not. One said, "We certainly don't want a split within the port" and another added, "whether or not Tony likes it." Collectively, they knew they had to avoid appearing to favor either side, not an easy thing to do. Their problem was how to approach negotiations "as though normal" when they knew they were not, although they expected Anastasia's efforts would most likely fail. To protect their impartiality they avoided separate talks with Anastasia. The employers were aware, too, that all the "outport leaders" supported Bradley and Gleason, spurning Anastasia because "no man is bigger than the ILA."

The NLRB promptly called the parties to a hearing. The ILA, of course, asked the NLRB to refuse Anastasia's request. Waldman warned that if the proceedings were allowed to interfere with negotiations, or if the board gave cognizance to fragmentation, there would be "chaos run wild." He argued that Anastasia's participation in ILA strategy meetings and in the first stages of negotiations precluded consideration of his petition. When Waldman said the breakaway was "tainted with illegality and immorality," Anastasia interrupted, "We dissent to that." Anastasia's attorney said they were "not talking of a minority group trying to break away . . . what we are talking about is a self-determining election."[9]

Anastasia, most likely sensing the impossibility of a decision favorable to him, abruptly withdrew his petition, announcing that he was doing it in the interest of presenting a united front in negotiations; but Gleason would not forgo saying that it was

[8] *New York Times*, July 15, 1962, p. 62, July 16, p. 38, July 17, p. 43, July 18, p. 46, July 19, p. 45.
[9] *New York Herald Tribune*, Aug. 9, 1962, p. 21.

"a complete victory for the ILA." Union men from some other ports, as well as some in New York, threatened to leave the bargaining if Anastasia returned to the four-man committee.[10] Union antagonism toward Anastasia was strong, and the Wage Scale Committee ousted him as one of the cochairmen and voted to institute charges against him for violation of the constitution on two grounds, for moving to secede and for making angry, public accusations about the committee and its bargaining demands. Of course, only the Executive Board of the ILA could oust him. Apparently, they were not prepared to go this far, because they did not know what the consequences would be in Brooklyn, but in his place on the negotiating committee, Field was appointed a cochairman.[11]

[10] *New York Herald Tribune*, Aug. 14, 1962, p. 25.
[11] *New York Herald Tribune*, Aug. 21, 1962, p. 29, Aug. 23, p. 62. The truth, the irony, and the humor in the situation were skillfully laid out by Murray Kempton in his column in the *New York Post*. Describing the "ILA Purification Rite," he wrote:

"The surviving heirs . . . met . . . for the ceremonial beheading of Tony Anastasia . . . an action entirely symbolic, the excommunication of an enemy whose citadel is both distant and bristling with armor. Anthony Anastasia still holds Brooklyn; the ILA officers talk wistfully of dislodging him, but there are no real candidates for the assault upon his dark tower. He will not be drummed out as a vice president of the ILA as a prelude to his ouster from the waterfront; . . . the public struggles in the ILA have always had this particularly empty character. . . . It is the only anarchist union. No strong man seizes all power; no strong man is ever stripped of any power. They depart by death, age or jury verdict, but they are never defeated.

"Tony Anastasia bears the only name redolent of the ILA's middle barbaric period, and is the only muscle man left in its old age. His colleagues seem weak beside him, and he makes the mistake of underrating them. . . . Tony Anastasia's brothers in the leadership loathe him primarily because his only debating device in their inner councils is the bellow, and now they have him at last.

"Their decision to remove him [from the bargaining committee] . . . does have some aspects of the unprecedented . . . the first ILA official ever to be disciplined for doing the work of the employers . . . the first . . . to perform this service for nothing and thus to have some claim to be a labor statesman. No national career is shorter in the ILA than the career of a labor statesman.

Money and Productivity

Anastasia, absent from negotiating sessions for a short period, was soon back as a power to be considered. The episode did not help the bargaining situation for any of the parties. The employers thought that it would harden the core in the ILA, who would now fight to prove that their demands were not ridiculous. Bargaining sessions had continued; in fact, the employers had prepared their counterproposals,[12] and had given them to the ILA. Almost immediately one of the union spokesmen said, "I don't see any money in this." Chopin responded quickly, forcefully letting them know that when the employers learned what they were buying then they could set a price.

In the rolling way that issues follow one after another without resolution, or even complete discussion, they were soon on the issue of a payment to the ILA equal to the sum the em-

---

"Tony Anastasia has, of course, always been an employer at heart. . . . With age, Anastasia has taken on a weakness for good works; but they are the good works of a padrone; he gives in the same rough tone with which he used to take.

"He is hobbled by his strength as his peers in the ILA are rescued by their weakness. . . . If any one of them had been asked what he had done in the ILA, he would have had to answer, honestly and fervently, 'I survived.' . . .

"After they announced their purgation of Tony Anastasia, the television cameramen pulled the survivors together . . . a young man from the network asked: 'Does this have anything to do with Anastasia being a lone shark?' He had meant of course to say 'lone wolf.' Gleason thought naturally that he had said 'loan shark.' He answered . . . with calm decision that no such charges had ever been brought; afterward he fairly yelled, 'What are you trying to do to us?' and enforced the excision of the colloquy. 'Loan shark is a criminal word on the waterfront,' he said. One of the survivors kept saying, 'This is a trade union matter.' The distinction was delicate; loan sharking, you understand, is a matter of local autonomy. Tony Anastasia is not a loan shark. . . . What got him in trouble was ambition which means not minding his business" (New York Post, Aug. 23, 1962, editorial; Reprinted by Permission of New York Post © 1962, New York Post Corporation).

[12] NYSA, Report No. 2041, July 16, 1962, "Management Proposals for New NYSA-ILA Contract."

ployers had to pay to support the Waterfront Commission. Some employers simply responded that the commission was no pleasure for them and they were saddled with it by law. The ILA leaders usually pressed the employers to join with a committee from the union to go to Albany and Trenton to have the law rescinded or at least require the commission to close the longshore register and prevent new entrants from coming into the labor force. The employers were favorable to freezing the register and would have been happy to have the ILA join them in having the cost of the commission paid for by general taxes. But the employers were not prepared to go with the ILA to try to abolish the commission.

When ILA leaders, as justification for their demands, mentioned what Bridge's ILWU got on the West Coast, the employers countered with, "Let's also read what they got for the money." But the ILA was not prepared to talk about changing work rules or giving management concessions in exchange for benefits.

Meeting again two days later, the employers were told that their counterproposals, characterized as not real offers but only requests to take away, were turned down. In response to insistence of ILA leaders that they could not negotiate without getting an offer of money, the employers repeated their position, that they would not put money on the table until they knew what they were buying, that is, what was the ILA willing to give for it. But an ILA spokesman countered, "You can't get men to give away a condition until they know what the money is." Others supported him: "We stand firm on our request for a master agreement now and, afterward, a turn to local bargaining. If we have no offer, we have no place to start." They asserted that the proposals of the NYSA offered nothing and were insistent that the employers make an offer.

The employers had mixed views about pushing for changes in working practices, some fearing that they might lose some which were favorable to them if the subject was really opened up. But the majority view seemed to be that some relief had to be obtained, hence, the insistence on no offer of money until they knew more about what the ILA was willing to concede. What the employers had in mind was: flexible meal hours without payment of penalty rates, elimination of travel time in those places where it still prevailed, revision of the cancellation clause, assurances of gangs for work at night, modification of the weather clause, and elimination of absenteeism in gangs. On the last one the ILA would simply say they could do nothing because they had no control over hiring, and turned immediately to a request of the employers that they join with the ILA in getting the Waterfront Commission to permit them some control over hiring. Also, whenever the employers stressed the need for productivity, the ILA would assert that the greatest loss of productivity was directly traceable to the commission, because men hired as extras and fill-ins had to travel from the hiring centers to the piers after being selected, which took an hour or more. To the employers, however, a more costly factor was "frozen details,"[13] but this touched many in the ILA sensitively, particularly Gleason, for it was his checkers who held the greatest sinecures from them.

In the latter part of July, negotiations were as though a cracked record was playing: "No offer until we see the give," and, "No give until we see the offer." Gleason offered to let subcommittees work on demands if the employers would put the money on the table. The employers, even though they did not want the old contract unchanged, wondered if a money offer and the continuation of the old contract would suffice to break the stalemate, but union spokesmen quickly let it be known that they wanted the money offer first, then they would go on from that. As negotiating sessions dragged on, there was increasing restiveness from the floor which was difficult to control.

In an effort to get negotiations off dead center, the NYSA, on August 1, made a money offer.[14] As copies were distributed it

[13] Limiting a man's assignment to only one type of task.
[14] NYSA, Report No. 2048, Aug. 1, 1962, "Management Proposals for

was announced that the offer was worth $22 million; twenty-seven cents an hour over three years, that is, nine cents an hour in each of three years of the proposed agreement. In return they wanted rights of cancellation of orders of employment whenever a ship failed to reach its berth or when weather was adverse, clarification of a night-shift differential, obligation of ILA to provide labor for overtime work, obligation of a gang to give notice by 3:00 P.M. of its desire not to engage in night work, assurance of full and more efficient work force, extensive revision of the seniority article, and improvements (not cost reductions) in pensions, welfare and clinical benefits. Gleason immediately conceded that it was the "highest initial offer ever made by the steamship companies" but was quick to add, "We don't think this is all that's in the pocketbook."[15] It did not take long for the ILA to say that the money looked good but that the employers were taking four times more than they were giving. Gleason said, "We don't expect you to cut your throats but don't expect us to cut ours. The strings attached to the twenty-seven cents is a $107 million reduction to longshoremen. We won't sacrifice jobs for nine cents an hour and we won't give up, for a paltry sum, conditions which we fought for years to get." The ILA stood pat. The employers kept saying they would not buy themselves out of a strike with money. They had concluded that the rank and file was worried about a strike, fearing that the employers would take one this time. The employers, therefore, felt that their best tactic was to stress that their demands for relief from burdensome work practices would have no adverse effect on any bona fide longshoremen.

In the meeting on August 14, the ILA presented Dr. Eisenberg's twelve-page analysis of the NYSA offer which concluded that the industry would save over $144 million during the three-year contract—an even higher estimate than the ILA previously

New NYSA-ILA Contract"; *New York Herald Tribune*, Aug. 2, 1962, p. 23.

[15] *New York Times*, Aug. 2, 1962, p. 52.

made—while giving to the union only $22 million.[16] Some employers felt that the Eisenberg estimate of the value of the things they wanted the ILA to give up, things for which the employers felt they had been getting no return, was an acknowledgment that "the ILA was lying on a $144 million dollar featherbed," and was more supportive of their need for relief than a justification for the ILA.

The Mediators Enter

September was the mediators' month. William E. Simkin, director of the FMCS, directed Moore to join a special four-man longshore mediation team, headed by Burke. The addition of Moore was satisfying to both the ILA and the NYSA because he was familiar with their problems.[17]

After hearing the parties jointly on August 27, more to provide an opportunity for catharsis than to get the sense of the negotiations, they met with them separately. The ILA remained adamant that the employers wanted much more from the union than they were offering. In turn, the employers tried to convince Moore that their offer of twenty-seven cents was absolutely contingent upon improved productivity. Because positions were being so firmly held, the mediators were well aware that a strike was very likely. They were aware, too, as the employers were, that the political problem in the union made Gleason's task difficult. The employers, of course, were not averse to telling the mediators that Gleason's problem was his own, not theirs, and they were not prepared to bail him out by making concessions; they had to protect their own bargaining position. The

[16] NYSA, Report No. 2053, Aug. 21, 1962, "Analysis of NYSA Proposals of August 1, 1962"; cf. New York Herald Tribune, Aug. 15, 1962, p. 36; New York Times, Aug. 15, 1962, p. 52, Aug. 18, p. 50, Aug. 21, p. 1, Aug. 23, p. 47; Journal of Commerce, Aug. 15, 1962, p. 1.

[17] New York Times, Aug. 28, 1962, p. 50; shortly thereafter, Joseph Finnegan, then chairman of the New York State Board of Mediation, named Harry Silverman to work with the federal mediators, and the city's commissioner of labor, Harold A. Felix, assigned Morris Tarshis to help. But it was the federal mediators' job, not theirs.

employers made it clear to the mediators, also, that there was no use trying to soften them up unless they could soften the ILA.

The mediators worked hard to break the impasse. Even without the deep political divisions within the ILA, the questions of size of gangs, utilization of men, and the elimination of practices which affected productivity would have been difficult ones to resolve. Under the circumstances they were probably unresolvable. The more the employers pushed on these issues the more adamant Gleason became. He knew full well that on these issues he could command widespread support from the men, that is, they could easily be moved to strike to protect jobs. He said, "What union official is going to step up to any of the 560 gangs listed in the port and tell four men, 'You are no longer going to work.' . . . There would be a whopping wildcat strike if our committee ever agreed to any gang reductions." The employers countered with the contention that "the four men are not even in the gang," meaning that with absenteeism being what it was and the union's insistence that the gang complement be filled out, employers had to go to the hiring centers and hire men when it was known at the time of hiring that there was no possibility of putting all twenty men in the gang to work. One prominent stevedore said, "The ILA does not work with a twenty-man gang. It only insists that the men be hired. A maximum of fifteen men can do all the work that is required." (He was obviously referring to stowing of cargo, for in the discharging of cargo extra men were sometimes added to the gang.) Chopin insisted that men drew pay for no work performed. However, Gleason more than once countered with the assertion that the charge by employers of featherbedding was a "phony" one and said emphatically that the union "will not budge from its twenty-man gang that was bought and paid for dearly over a period of thirty years."[18]

[18] NYSA, Report No. 2060, Sept. 11, 1962; *New York Herald Tribune*, Sept. 11, 1962, p. 29, Sept. 12, p. 30, Sept. 16, p. 65; *Journal of Commerce*, Sept. 12, 1962, p. 1; *New York Times*, Sept. 11, 1962, p. 55, Sept. 12, p. 65, Sept. 18, p. 65.

The employers felt the gang-issue was being pushed by the union beyond all proportions, because the employers certainly were not trying to get rid of any productive men, only non-productive ones. What the employers were seeking was not "reduction of the working force but reduction of the nonworking force," particularly the "frozen details" which primarily involved checkers. To submerge this matter, Gleason had always emphatically seized every opportunity to defend the twenty-man gang and to cast the employers in the role of callously destroying jobs and "work practices which the union had fought for years to obtain." The simple fact is that the practices had just grown from pressures from the pier, not from any ILA program, although the ILA would defend them to the hilt. Besides protecting checkers, Gleason's stance was dictated by his lack of power to lead; all he could do was defend the status quo; sometimes his vitriolic language was in proportion to the political pressures from within.

When the mediators warned that if the stalemate continued the government might have to exert pressure on the parties, it had little effect. The employers, generally, said, "We do not care anymore." In fact many of them would have welcomed a governmental fact-finding board, perhaps even compulsory arbitration, provided there were assurances that the questions of manpower and productivity would be arbitrated. The employers did not fear the Taft-Hartley Act; they only disliked the uncertainty that the prospect of a strike created for business. Whatever, they had little choice but to wait things out. The ILA did not fear the Taft-Hartley Act, for the officials knew they could go the route of a strike without suffering the costs of a strike, they would retain their old conditions, and the Taft-Hartley board would be able to make no recommendations for change. Of course, the possibility of a strike after the eighty-day delay under a Taft-Hartley Act injunction was another matter. When Gleason delivered a speech on the night of September 10 before the World Trade Club, reviewing the dispute as he saw it, seizing the opportunity for its publicity value to criticize the Waterfront Commission in connection with the controversy over manpower and stating that the ILA would not "sell out jobs like Bridges did," some employers in the audience read indications that he was bothered by the prospects of a strike more than he was admitting.

The employers concluded that if they simply waited for the deadline, all they would get was Taft-Hartley, whereas they needed more. Therefore they prepared telegrams to Secretary Wirtz and President Kennedy, being careful not to allege bad faith on the part of the ILA for fear the dispute would be shunted to the NLRB to test the good faith issue and that this would prevent them from "going right to the summit."[19] Shortly afterward Assistant Secretary of Labor James J. Reynolds was in New York City. He spent a day conferring with the parties, primarily to dispel the notion that Secretary Wirtz would enter the dispute or that anyone other than the mediators would do so.[20]

The mediators continued with their efforts, although to break the deadlock seemed hopeless to them. Neither side was responsive to their overtures. The employers concluded that the mediators were putting too much pressure on them to modify their position and not enough on the ILA to change its position. They made it clear to the mediators that if they were to attempt to appease Gleason they would only get more pressure from his opponents within the union regarding their favorite demands. The fact is that no one on the union side was in a position to make concessions in order to start movement to a settlement. Gleason always remained adamant.

Moore knew that Gleason would not, or could not, change his position. When the employers pressed for fact-finding before a strike, Moore said that study of the situation would only throw out any possibility of getting together. The employers tried to impress him that the rank and file were not solidly behind their

[19] NYSA, Report No. 2061, Sept. 12, 1962.
[20] *New York Herald Tribune*, Sept. 14, 1962, p. 33; *New York Times*, Sept. 14, 1962, p. 50.

leaders. One said, "Talk to the men in the hold, the only true working gangs." But Moore could hardly bypass the leaders, in any event.

After another joint meeting, on September 18—where Gleason was even more vituperative and assertive than ever, declaring, "We won't discuss the disintegration of our Union. We are not giving in," and a chorus from the floor echoed, "That's right," and the employers insisted that they had to have relief—Moore adjourned the meeting and announced that the mediators were pulling out. He said that the efforts of the mediators were not only failing to serve any purpose but were actually "a disservice by leading the public to believe that progress can be made when it cannot be."[21]

The mediators returned to Washington, prepared their own proposal, and were back in New York again on September 24, after what had turned out to be a week's recess. It was only a week to the deadline. Accusations again punctuated the discussions from the outset. After explaining that the week's recess was due to the hopelessness of the situation, Moore asked if there were any change in attitude. Gleason spoke up: "Since you always request the union position first, nobody on our side has made any change in attitude; the rank and file is adamant. You called the meeting. I thought you might have come up with a formula." Chopin followed, "Gleason reads us very well. There's been no change in our position." After about an hour of wrangling, when Moore found no change in positions, he announced that the mediators had a proposal and he passed out copies.

The proposal reviewed the situation in considerable detail, noting that very few demands had been discussed seriously, other than productivity and gang size, that the long-range impact of containerization was upon them, that in spite of their early preparations for negotiations no realistic approach to a solution of their problems had been developed, and that what

[21]*New York Herald Tribune*, Sept. 19, 1962, p. 38; *New York Times*, Sept. 19, 1962, p. 65.

they needed was a framework within which they could "honor- ably and in good faith prevent a strike," but that now there was insufficient time to develop it. Therefore they recommended a one-year contract "with only those changes that are immediately and absolutely essential to each party." This would avoid the necessity of carefully reviewing the whole contract but "the union and the association would provide for a joint study of the entire problem of changes in cargo handling and operations and what is to be done to protect the labor force and insure its continuing opportunity for full employment and increased earnings."[22]

The employers accepted the proposal, provided that any issues left unresolved would be submitted to binding arbitration. When Chopin read his prepared statement, there were groans from the floor and Gleason said, "We could never go for that." The ILA did not want a study and would not agree to arbitra- tion. While the employers were willing to have the study they knew they did not really need one. Both parties knew the facts. The proposal by the mediators, as it turned out, only served to freeze the positions of the parties even tighter. With this turn of events, Moore, who had been opposing governmental action, now became favorably inclined to recommend quick use of Taft-Hartley.

At this juncture, Simkin arrived in New York to use his in- fluence with the parties. Experienced mediator that he was, he tried several ploys, including references to the viewpoint in Washington that negotiations should be allowed to continue, letting both parties sweat it out for a while before invoking Taft-Hartley. The employers made doubly sure that he under- stood what to them was the glaring fact that politically a strike was inevitable because the ILA leadership was neither powerful nor capable enough to avoid it: "The leaders could not satisfy

[22] Federal Mediation and Conciliation Service, "Recommendations to the New York Shipping Association and the International Longshore- men's Association," Sept. 24, 1962 (mimeographed); *New York Times*, Sept. 25, 1962, p. 62; *New York Herald Tribune*, Sept. 25, 1962, p. 39.

all factions, nor quell them." The employers wanted no more joint meetings because they felt such would be more disruptive than beneficial. They stood firmly on their position that the impasse involved many more issues than the twenty-man gang, the issue which Gleason always emphasized was the only real one and which the union insisted be removed from the table, always asserting, too, that it was the obstinate refusal of the employers to remove the issue from the table which was responsible for the stalemate. He lost no breath in laying the blame for the strike on the employers. Chopin was equally dogmatic that it was the intransigence of the ILA which was causing the strike. After hearing the parties out and reviewing the situation, Simkin seemed only able to say, "There are no grounds for optimism."[23] The employers made it clear that there were to be "no eleventh-hour deals this time," they were taking the strike because they had to, in order to gain flexibility in the use of manpower necessary to efficient operations.

The inevitable strike came followed by the inevitable governmental intervention. It would be interesting to speculate what would have happened if there had been no sanctuary of governmental action. The old adage that a strike is a dispute looking for some place to go would have required a different search had not the government sanctuary been the easy option. Of course, one of the options—some thought a necessary one for fundamental change—was a long strike; long enough to crush false positions. The long strike the government would not permit—local, national, and international pressures were too great.

The Taft-Hartley Board

President Kennedy, on October 1, promptly invoked the emergency provisions of the Taft-Hartley Act, saying somewhat extravagantly, "If this strike is allowed to continue for any length of time, its effects will have such grave and far-reaching repercussions on our total domestic economy and upon our

[23] *New York Herald Tribune*, Sept. 28, 1962, p. 37; *New York Times*, Sept. 25, 1962, p. 62, Sept, 29, p. 36.

ability to meet our urgent commitments around the world that the national interest would be gravely jeopardized." The *New York Times* described the situation in the industry as "a solemn farce," a "travesty on bargaining." The Board of Inquiry, responding to the President's instruction to mediate, convened quickly. The mechanics of the statute produced the eighty-day injunction in due course, but there was slight hope from the outset that the board could do what the mediators had failed to do. Some employers were perturbed to learn that the board had no power to arbitrate the dispute.[24]

When the board, composed of three professors who had classes to meet, did not convene follow-up meetings as promptly as Gleason desired, he called for the federal mediators, in mid-October, to take over once more and criticized the board for planning no meeting until the end of the month, hardly the truth because meetings were held in five days. Also, the mediators were never very far outside the dispute and the board from the beginning worked closely with Moore and Simkin, although it had requested Moore not to sit in during sessions with the parties for fear that his presence would make the parties even more rigid. Gleason no doubt had no confidence in the board members; the chairman, naively, was seeking a reasonable settlement, where one was not possible. Gleason publicly criticized the board for "wasting time rehashing everything," whereas the mediators "know the story, they are not going to waste time going back over the same details and maybe we can move ahead." After careful consideration, the board concluded that the only possibility of breaking the impasse was to separate out the issues of manpower utilization and security and postpone them for future study and subsequent negotiations. It therefore prepared a statement and made recommendations to this effect,

[24] *New York Times*, Oct. 2, 1962, pp. 1, 66, Oct. 4, p. 65, Oct. 5, p. 1, Oct. 6, p. 26, Oct. 8, p. 34, Oct. 11, p. 70; *Journal of Commerce*, Oct. 2, 1962, editorial; NYSA, Report No. 2070, Oct. 2, 1962, "Review of Association's Position"; ILA, "Statement on Behalf of ILA, AFL-CIO," Oct. 2, 1962.

suggesting that a three-year contract be negotiated on other matters, retroactive to October 1, 1962; that a five-man special committee, composed of two from each side and a mutually selected neutral, conduct a study on the use and security of manpower and make recommendations to the parties not later than October 1, 1963, which would then be subject to negotiations for a period of thirty days and, if an agreement was not reached, either party could terminate the agreement on sixty days' notice.[25]

Each member of the board tried to persuade the parties to give the statement serious consideration and to return with their reactions. But Gleason lost no time in launching a tirade against it, and the next morning the NYSA rejected it. The employers did not mind the study but would not accept it without the inclusion of compulsory arbitration of unresolved disputes. Gleason continued his tirade, damning the employers for not bargaining in the traditional way, for rejecting the proposition to rid the industry of the Waterfront Commission "to save millions of dollars," and for endeavoring to let cheap labor take over work longshoremen had done for thirty years. Also, he said, "We don't want a strike but we won't be frightened by a threat of strike. We don't want to sell jobs either. . . . The West Coast sold their men out, but here on the East and Gulf Coast, we don't do that . . . if we have to fight, we'll do so. Either you knock our brains out or we knock yours out . . . this committee [Wage Scale Committee] is solid now. We aim to get a good contract." With strange logic, he added, "Something's going to be done, either by Washington, or someone else."[26] In his anger and frustrated state he revealed his own inability to get to a settlement without outside assistance.

---

[25] Board of Inquiry, "Statement of Board of Inquiry," Oct. 30, 1962; cf. Board of Inquiry, *Report to the President*, Oct. 4, 1962; Board of Inquiry, *Second Report to the President*, Dec. 3, 1962; ILA, "Statement to the Presidential Board of Inquiry," Oct. 30, 1962.

[26] *New York Herald Tribune*, Oct. 31, 1962, p. 41, Nov. 1, p. 33; *New York Times*, Nov. 1, 1962, p. 61.

Because neither party accepted the recommendations of the board and offered no substitutes, the board, having had an understanding with Moore and Simkin, withdrew; it left the dispute to the federal mediators, saying there were no further functions that it could perform at the time. They reported to the President the "unwillingness of the parties to do any serious bargaining until more of the time allotted within the Taft-Hartley injunction has passed . . . and that both parties believe that the government cannot, and will not, permit a strike to occur or long continue."[27]

Gleason promptly said he preferred government mediators to university professors: "The egg-head approach is not adequate: they are good men, but the answers to our problems are not in books and the federal mediators have been in close touch with our controversial clauses for many weeks." The employers remained silent, but the *New York Times* poked fun at "academe on the docks."[28]

Federal Mediators Again

Moore, with about two months to go to the expiration of the eighty-day injunction, with no public fanfare, held bargaining sessions daily for most of a week because the parties assured him they were willing to start negotiating "without any ultimatums by either side" and to go through the contract and bargaining demands item by item. It appears that pressure in the ranks of the ILA forced Gleason to try to work something out. If true, it was only transitory. Confrontations and acrimony remained typical. Each topic brought out the old arguments. Although Gleason had publicly complained about rehashing issues before the board, he now rehashed again before the mediators and, this time, with more acrimony, although acrimony was found on both sides. Manpower utilization, as already noted, was always the big issue—saving jobs, on the one hand, and eliminating restrictive practices, on the other.

[27] "Letter from Board of Inquiry to the President," Nov. 1, 1962.
[28] *New York Times*, Nov. 5, 1962, p. 53.

By mid-November, Moore felt that they had made some progress, but the employers, among themselves, did not agree. Moore kept telling them to go on through the contract, letting the ILA "get rid of their steam" and "then, be ready to negotiate." The employers had trouble convincing Moore that the more tolerant they were of Gleason's needling, the more intolerant his own committee became. They felt better when Moore suggested they continue bargaining through separate sessions, instead of further joint meetings.

At this time, in mid-November, the Waterfront Commission opened a new hiring center in South Brooklyn—at the request of Anastasia—to relieve overcrowding in the other centers in Brooklyn. This supplied Gleason with another opportunity to vent his feelings about the commission and, led by him, longshoremen refused to enter the new center, being directed to go to the old centers instead. This was an open attack on the commission's control over hiring and Gleason charged the commission with interfering with collective bargaining, because, referring to an ILA proposal on the bargaining table, he said, "They know that we are working closely with the shipping association to open jointly operated hiring halls. . . . We want labor-management hiring, just the way the men are hired in the rest of the maritime industry." But, Myles Ambrose, executive director of the commission, simply asserted the commission's right under the law to control hiring and said unless the men went through the new center "nobody gets hired for work" in the area it was designed to serve. He also said a joint hiring hall would be illegal because the law required hiring be done through the centers operated by the commission. The employers, of course, were opposed to a joint hiring hall, in any event. The new center was opened and the next day longshoremen entered to be hired, but Gleason called the centers "concentration camps, operated like slave markets."[29]

Moore tried to get the employers to make a move to get the

[29] *New York Times*, Nov. 19, 1962, p. 58, Nov. 21, p. 21.

deadlock broken, but Chopin asked, "Why is it always incumbent on the industry to move? We did so with the wage offer, took a long chance, but all their outrageous demands are still there." When told that they could expect no further help from the government once the Taft-Hartley injunction expired, the LPC still was determined to get some productivity for the wage increase offered. The employers were not going to bail Gleason out of difficulty within his union. But, within their own caucus, they concluded they would never get to the trade-off stage, that "some new formula was needed." It would probably have "to come from some outsider . . . depending on his prominence, influence, and impression on the ILA." Some wanted to get President Kennedy into the picture: "He is the only one with enough weight to frighten the ILA into line." When some employers told Moore that they wanted to be heard in Washington, he replied, "Put yourself in Wirtz's role, all you would do is transfer the stymie to another office." Unless they had a formula for breaking the stalemate there was no use in trying to involve the administration in Washington. Other employers felt that raising the question of governmental intervention reflected a sign of weakening and that Moore would press harder to get them to compromise. The rebuttal was that they had not withdrawn anything and the mediators are "firmly convinced that the LPC must hold its line."

In the latter part of November the employers had to make their "last offer" presentation to the Board of Inquiry. In it they had modified their position only with respect to the gang-size issue, proposing that the reduction be effectuated by one man a year in each of the contract years.[30] With the "last offer" proposal in the hands of the union and the balloting set to be concluded on December 18, no bargaining sessions were convened early in December. It was a foregone conclusion that the proposal would be rejected.

[30] U.S. Board of Inquiry, *Second Report to the President*, Dec. 3, 1962; NYSA, Report No. 2081, "Last Offer of Settlement."

Wirtz Enters

Secretary Wirtz convened a meeting of twenty-six ILA and eighteen employer representatives in Washington on November 14. He considered it a simple transfer of negotiations to Washington. After opening speeches, Wirtz learned that the ILA was not prepared to negotiate without its whole committee, but he queried the parties on their positions and set a meeting after the weekend in New York City. Wirtz and Simkin over the weekend worked out a recommendation for settlement, a variation of the one presented by the Board of Inquiry. Manpower problems were to be studied by a Manpower Utilization and Job Security Committee, composed of an equal number of representatives of each party and a chairman "of independent stature, experienced in such matters" appointed by the secretary of labor and the director of the FMCS. The parties would negotiate all other issues with the assistance of the secretary and director. The recommendations of the committee on manpower would be due on or before August 1, 1963, and the parties would have thirty days for negotiations with the assistance of Wirtz and Simkin, "with the further understanding that the Secretary and the Director may recommend to the parties special procedures for the reaching of agreement."[31] Both parties rejected the recommendations. On the twentieth, with three days to go to the expiration of the eighty-day injunction, Wirtz announced that at a meeting the next day "we will ask each side for movement," commenting, "Thank heavens this is a country where men can refuse governmental suggestions"—although he underscored, "This offer in various forms has now been refused for the fifth time," and, "This is a complete breakdown in collective bargaining." Wirtz and Simkin met with the parties separately and,

[31] W. Willard Wirtz and William E. Simkin, "Recommendation for Settlement of the Dispute between the New York Shipping Association and the Atlantic Coast District, International Longshoremen's Association, AFL-CIO," Dec. 19, 1962 (mimeographed), pp. 1–4.

while the employers proposed various alternatives on the original recommendation, no proposal was obtained from the union.

On the twenty-third, President Kennedy intervened with a proposal which he telegraphed to the parties. After briefly describing the stalemate, he said:

I therefore propose, in the national interest, that the parties agree to accept the following procedure:

1. That all disputed manpower utilization, job security and related issues be referred to a study which I shall direct the Secretary of Labor to undertake at the earliest possible time.

2. That all other disputed contract issues, including the question of contract period, be presented to a board composed of Judge Harold R. Medina of New York City, Chairman; Emanuel Stein of Long Beach, L.I., and James C. Hill of Pelham, N.Y. which I am appointing for this purpose; this board to hold hearings on these issues and questions, to make recommendations to the parties regarding them on or before February 15, 1963, and to assist the parties in reaching agreement on these issues and questions.

3. That operations be continued under present employment terms and conditions for a period of 90 days.

I request that you advise me, through the Secretary of Labor, at 12:00 o'clock, noon, today, December 23, regarding your acceptance of this proposal which the national interest so urgently demands.[32]

The employers pledged "complete cooperation to the President and his Board," but the union rejected the proposal.

The Strike Renewed

With the strike on and the Christmas holidays over, Wirtz, James Reynolds, and Moore shouldered the task of achieving a settlement. Wirtz, however, also had to attend to the newspaper strike in New York City; a good part of the load, therefore, fell on Reynolds. The mediators met the parties separately almost every day up to New Year's Eve. Wirtz wanted a procedural plan developed, good for the future, too, but was not successful,

[32] NYSA, Report No. 2092, Dec. 27, 1962.

although after a couple of weeks he was optimistic, even saying the talks were "fluid" again.[33]

No doubt some of the "fluidity" in the situation, if there was any, was related to a controversy between Bradley and Gleason. Gleason was openly challenging Bradley for the presidency of the ILA and he treated Bradley cavalierly, possibly because Bradley, appearing to criticize Gleason, indicated publicly that thirty-five cents could settle matters.

On January 15, Reynolds said he would make one further attempt to narrow the issues and, failing to do so, would ask that President Kennedy take action,[34] which, under Section 210 of the Taft-Hartley Act, the President could do whenever he desired, by reporting to Congress with such recommendations as he might consider appropriate. Reynolds failed and became angry with the parties, saying,

It seems to me that the whole history of these negotiations is a sorry chapter in the history of collective bargaining in the country. . . . I think both positions are unrealistic under all the circumstances and must be modified substantially if we are to get a satisfactory settlement. . . . In view of all the meetings we have held and all the efforts we have put into developing some accommodations between the parties, the fact that both sides adhere to these positions is unrealistic and a complete negation of any real concept of collective bargaining.[35]

The Presidential Board—Mediation or Arbitration?

Wirtz carried the problem to the President, who acted by issuing a public statement, reading in part: "All statutory procedures have been exhausted. . . . Intensive mediation . . . has been unavailing. The point of public toleration . . . has been

---

[33] *Wall Street Journal*, Jan. 10, 1963, p. 6; Bureau of National Affairs, *Daily Labor Report*, no. 6, A-1, Jan. 9, 1963.

[34] *Wall Street Journal*, Jan. 16, 1963, p. 1.

[35] Bureau of National Affairs, *Daily Labor Report*, no. 11, A-7, Jan. 16, 1963.

passed . . . public action is required." He established a special presidential board comprised of Senator Wayne Morse, chairman, James J. Healy, Harvard University professor, and Theodore Kheel, well-known arbitrator in New York City, and charged the board with "the responsibility of making a necessarily quick and summary investigation and review of this controversy, and the prospects for its prompt settlement without further injury to the public interest, reporting to me no later than January 21, five days from today." This board was also instructed to assist the parties "by mediation or recommendation" and if the board failed to produce an agreement, it was "to recommend a procedure which [would] assure immediate resumption of operations . . . on a basis and by a procedure limited to the circumstances of this particular case." The President made it clear that he was prepared to report to Congress with his own recommendations as the next step, if necessary, and called upon the parties "to exercise their responsibilities" not only to their own private interests "but also as stewards of the essential institution of free collective bargaining."[36]

At this very time congressional hearings began on maritime labor problems—not occasioned by the fact of this strike, but certainly made more timely by virtue of it, for the hearings had been conceived for the purpose of investigating the offshore part of the industry. It was a foregone conclusion that a bill calling for compulsory arbitration for the maritime industry would be forthcoming. President Kennedy, and the administration, were very reluctant to go the route of compulsory arbitration.

The President's board went to work with dispatch. After hearing the parties out, it directed them to stand by to receive a set of recommendations, without discussion or debate. Senator Morse said that the President wanted a voluntary settlement but added, "What we offer to the parties is their last opportunity to

[36] Bureau of National Affairs, *Daily Labor Report*, no. 11, A-5, Jan. 16, 1963; NYSA, Report No. 2133, Appendix A, April 5, 1963.

settle their disputes before the President reports to Congress."[37] Morse made it clear also that the board would make but the one proposal of settlement, saying, "It will be up to you, then, to decide whether or not you wish to accept or reject that offer, for we will leave Monday morning at 7:30 to lay the matter before the President." He added, "We will not appear before you . . . to defend our proposals, but to recommend them to you. But let me make very clear . . . that once we make them and return to Washington, we shall defend them to the hilt."[38]

Sunday afternoon the parties were given the gist of the proposal, so as not to be taken by surprise upon formal delivery the next morning. No discussion was entertained. Gleason afterward said that the proposal was limited to the general cargo agreement (it will be recalled that this was only one of a half dozen agreements negotiated, although always the first one) and that the checkers' demands were still intact. Catching wind of this, the employers were as quick to point out to the board that, if so, the strike would continue. The employers were worried, also, because the proposal was addressed only to the situation in New York and not to the South Atlantic and Gulf Coast ports. Many employers, however, hearing the preliminary revelation, thought the ILA would buy it. Expecting that the ILA, after acceptance by the Wage Scale Committee, would submit the proposal to its membership for secret ballot vote, many employers hoped that this would "take the monkey off Gleason's back." They, of course, would want to refer the proposal to the membership of the NYSA, too. Some were quick to point out, however, that "because it does not achieve manpower utilization on the docks, it's ransom; we are paying in advance but will still have to bargain on it for a high price at the end of the second year."

[37] Bureau of National Affairs, *Daily Labor Report*, no. 12, A-11, Jan. 17, 1963.
[38] *Congressional Record*, Jan. 22, 1963, pp. 700–703; Bureau of National Affairs, *Daily Labor Report*, no. 16, D-12, Jan. 23, 1963.

When the parties convened to receive the proposal of the board, Morse said, "We come before you as your servants . . . as pleaders . . . in no capacity other than to urge you to recognize that both sides to this dispute have the responsibility of being responsive to responsibility."[39] The main points of the proposal were: the agreements (six, not just the general cargo agreement) previously in effect were to run for two years, until September 30, 1964; basic wages increased 15 cents per hour effective October 1, 1962, another 9 cents per hour effective October 1, 1963; pension contributions increased by 4 cents and 5 cents (on the dates listed above) and with an increase of pension to $100 per month, an increase in death benefit by $500 and vesting after twenty-five years' service; a 2-cent increase in contribution to clinics and a 2½-cent increase for health and welfare; one additional paid holiday; joint management of welfare and pension funds; a manpower utilization and job security study, plus study of all other related issues, to be conducted by the secretary of labor, and upon completion the parties would bargain with respect to the implementation of findings, and if no mutually satisfactory agreement could be reached by July 31, 1964, the parties would select a neutral board to study the areas of disagreement and make recommendations.[40]

It is of some interest that when the proposal was informally offered Sunday evening, Curran, president of the NMU, sat on the stand next to Gleason. The employers thought that he did so to intimidate the representatives of the American steamship companies. When word came later that the ILA committee had accepted it without reservations, the reaction among the employers was, "Then, let us reject it and make the government force us to accept it; then maybe we can force the government to put some starch into the study." One among the less happy

[39] *Congressional Record*, Jan. 22, 1963, p. 700.
[40] "Statement by the Mediators" and "Mediators' Proposal," signed by Healy, Kheel and Morse, "Memorandum of Settlement," Jan. 20, 1963 (all mimeographed).

employers said, "We should show up this board for what it is, a sellout, and I am going to vote against it and force the government to make me accept it." Another added, "We have no alternative, we have to recommend against acceptance." They decided to sleep on the matter overnight, feeling that they should let Washington know formally that the LPC would not recommend buying itself out of a strike and that it would have to have some assurance on the study before submitting the matter to the membership. Also, before going to the membership they wanted to establish that "we got our shellacking, not from the ILA, but from the U.S. Government." The feeling was that "Morse had bailed Gleason out," that "we got the 'or else' treatment, at a high price, which seems to have bought us nothing." They took some consolation when Morse insisted on immediate removal of pickets at each port that accepted the settlement. The employers' final view of the settlement was subsequently given by Chopin in a speech given in September at the Rudder Club. He said, "Under strenuous pressure of a rather compulsory nature we swallowed hard another Presidential Board's recommendation to end the strike by paying a substantial price in advance for whatever later benefits might come out of the unresolved issues."[41]

On national television, Morse defended the board against the charge that the settlement was tantamount to compulsory arbitration. He insisted that it was mediation, that the parties were given the right to choose: "We simply told the parties that this was it, or else." It is interesting, too, on the same broadcast, Gleason was so delighted that he quipped, "I guess we'll take the extra holiday on Kennedy's birthday."

Argument might continue as to whether it was really mediation, but it is interesting that spokesmen in management thought it was arbitration, as expressed by General John M. Franklin, U.S. Lines, in the hearings on the Bonner Bill: "This mediation was in effect arbitration, although the proposals were accepted

[41] NYSA, Report No. 2183, Sept. 18, 1963; cf. *New York Herald Tribune*, Sept. 12, 1963, p. 27.

by the parties rather than being binding." But in the same hearings, Bridges put it down a little more strongly: "While the board's report and recommendations were not binding upon the parties, we saw the action as an ultimatum. A take it or else deal. The parties had to go along. It was compulsory arbitration *defacto* though not *de jure*." Gleason described it as "mediation by dictation" and said, self-servingly, he did not like the settlement but took it.[42]

Morse, partly because he was expected to do so but mostly because of the widespread public criticism of the settlement and the method of achievement,[43] defended his board and the settlement before Congress. Wirtz, on the other hand, was privately critical, for had he been able to justify terms more generous than the 22 cents he had in mind over two years, he too might have produced a settlement, provided he could have exerted leverage on the employers. Morse claimed the settlement cost only 37 cents, not 39.9 cents as had been stated in the press. He argued that the board had not broken the antiinflationary program of the government, insisting that the increase was less than 4 per cent, and when inequities and cost-of-living were considered, the increase was even less. He held that the criticism that the settlement was much nearer the proposals of the ILA than the employers' was completely irrelevant, nor was it true.[44] Furthermore, he argued, the settlement was less, because it was mediation, than it would have been in arbitration. He said they achieved a "conscionable compromise" between the positions of the parties and ignored many of the demands, whereas an

[42] House of Representatives, Committee on Merchant Marine and Fisheries, *Maritime Labor Legislation, Part 2; Hearings on H.R. 2004 and H.R. 2331*, 88th Cong., 1st. Sess., 1963; Bureau of National Affairs, *Daily Labor Report*, no. 44, F-1, March 5, 1963, and no. 55, F-1, March 20, 1963.

[43] For example, *Wall Street Journal*, Jan. 24, 1963, p. 12, Feb. 20, 1963, p. 18.

[44] Actually the settlement was nearer to the figure the employers had agreed to give than it was to the union's original position, but the employers had expected improvement in productivity, of which they got none.

arbitrator, as he said, "as a judicial officer" would have had "to consider all the issues." He concluded by reading the statement that the board had read to the parties, which contains the following statement: "We wish . . . to emphasize our strong belief that the capacity of this industry to support wages and benefits to which employees are entitled cannot continue without serious impairment in the absence of marked improvement in manpower utilization." He then held out the promise of the study of manpower utilization and job security, and the use of a neutral board if there were "any refusal to negotiate," with the shipowners being given "the opportunity to present their proof." He ended on the note that "the time has come for all involved to relax their visceras and let their intellects take over. They [the parties] should recognize a responsibility for being responsive to the great national welfare responsibility."[45]

But who would make sure that the parties would be "responsive to responsibility?" The forthcoming study offered a hope, even a promise.

[45] *Congressional Record,* Jan. 22, 1963, pp. 700–703; Bureau of National Affairs, *Daily Labor Report,* no. 16, Jan. 23, 1963, D-1 to D-4.

13 | The Department of Labor
Study and the Next Round

If the "Morse Settlement" was not actually an arbitration award, the possibility that the next settlement might be subject to arbitration was on the horizon. While the Morse board was at work, the House Committee on Merchant Marine and Fisheries began hearings on a bill proposing a procedure which could terminate in compulsory arbitration by a decision of the President. The hearings had been designed to come to grips with a problem in the offshore part of the industry, yet the longshore strike added further pressure for them. Many longshore employers as well as offshore employers testified at length about the state of maritime labor relations and the need for compulsory arbitration. In their view, collective bargaining had failed and the Taft-Hartley Act was inadequate and a farce. Union officials, in turn, opposed the bill, because they said it would destroy collective bargaining. They accused the employers of only desiring to weaken or destroy the unions. Captain Bradley and Gleason testified against it while Chopin joined the chorus of employers from the shipping companies. The latter said he did not endorse compulsory arbitration with any relish, only as a desperate last hope in the face of a union which he said had been irresponsible several times. "We have no place to go any more. We have no alternative. In the national interest we can't go through again what we have been through. . . . With a recalcitrant union, there is nothing else we can do about it. We have urged the ILA to undertake collective bargaining the way it should be."[1]

[1] Bureau of National Affairs, *Daily Labor Report*, no. 50: D-1, March

The nation did not view the matter, however, as an issue limited to the maritime industry. Employers in other industries and other unionists testified against the bill. It would destroy free collective bargaining and private decision-making. In August, the compulsory arbitration section was deleted from the bill in order to make it more palatable, but it subsequently died in committee.[2]

The Struggle for Union Leadership

Meanwhile, the struggle for leadership between Bradley and Gleason punctuated affairs in the ILA. Destined to be settled at the annual convention in July, it generated considerable heat late in the spring. Of related significance was the untimely death in March of Anastasia, due to cancer of the throat. This led to the placing of his son-in-law, Anthony Scotto, into the vacated position as head of Local 1814 in Brooklyn and, as well, into a vice-presidency of the ILA.[3] One outcome was to thrust Scotto into a bid for the top vice-presidency in opposition to Bowers of Local 824 in Manhattan and George Dixon, Negro president of the local in Mobile, Alabama. Hence, two bitterly fought battles for position enlivened affairs within the ILA.

In June massive opposition developed against Bradley on the ground that he was inept. His supporters, in turn, charged that Gleason "holds at least a dozen jobs in addition to the post of Executive Vice President and General Organizer of the International Union, and he should not have the presidency." Bradley, who was normally taciturn, spoke angrily about Gleason and the campaign of derogation he was conducting. When Bradley was asked if he might concede defeat in the Port of New York, he said, "Probably, because the ILA Constitution provides for

---

13, 1963; NYSA, Report No. 2133, April 5, 1963; *New York Herald Tribune*, April 2, 1963, p. 45; House of Representatives, Committee on Merchant Marine and Fisheries, *Maritime Labor Legislation; Hearings*, 88th Cong., 1st Sess., Part 2, pp. 934–935.

[2] *New York Herald Tribune*, Aug. 21, 1963, p. 27; *New York Times*, Oct. 14, 1963, p. 50.

[3] *New York Times*, April 13, 1963, p. 28; *New York Herald Tribune*, April 21, 1963, p. 47.

election by the delegates to the convention. I challenge Teddy Gleason to a referendum, supervised by the Honest Ballot Association. Let the rank and file decide who they want as President." Even Scotto, saying that aggressive leadership was needed to bring the ILA to solvency, endorsed Gleason; in spite of the fact that his father-in-law had always been a bitter opponent.[4]

Bradley made a vigorous bid for the support of the twenty thousand Negro members in the South. He toured the ports in the Gulf and South Atlantic and made a point to assure President Kennedy that he would continue to endorse his policy of supporting Negroes, "not only for employment on our docks, but as officials." He said that if reelected, "I shall fight for the election of a Negro to either the Executive Vice Presidency of the Union or as the General Organizer of the ILA." Gleason, in turn, also visited the southern ports. As part of his candidacy he gladly accepted "any criticism," as he put it, for "holding out on last year's negotiations until the ILA won its point on the matter of gang sizes and speedups." Bradley rejoined, "At least Teddy Gleason admits responsibility for what I consider an unnecessary strike. Gleason's refusal to bargain resulted in a government study on manpower and gang size which could very well force reductions in work gangs or provoke another strike at great suffering to our members and our families."[5]

Bargaining relations in the industry would hinge on the outcome of the election. The delegates in Miami elected Gleason unanimously when Bradley, after a caucus, agreed to accept a newly created post of "President Emeritus." Bowers was elected to the post, vacated by Gleason, of executive vice-president, when Scotto "stepped out" of the race, announcing that the 111 votes of his local were for Bowers.[6] It was evident that Dixon

[4] *New York Times,* June 11, 1963, p. 62, June 12, p. 69; *New York Herald Tribune,* June 11, 1963, p. 42, June 12, p. 40.

[5] *New York Times,* June 20, 1963, p. 53, June 26, p. 63, July 2, p. 46; *New York Herald Tribune,* June 20, 1963, p. 25, July 18, p. 15.

[6] There is a story that Scotto was very unhappy about the arrangement (said to have been made elsewhere) that he step out to let Bowers in.

would be defeated, although Bowers had to turn back a determined bid to break the New York monopoly of the top leadership. What the challengers got was the ILA's first roll call vote
of any convention, although Bowers won by a vote of 580 to
242. But delegates from South Atlantic and Gulf ports left with
mixed feelings of bitterness and pride. Dixon, satisfied that he
had put up a good fight, said, "I'll be back." Other Negro leaders
said they would plan a better campaign when the union held its
next convention in Montreal in 1967.[7]

Waterfront Commission Regulations and Seniority

Problems of implementation of seniority and administration
were mentioned in an earlier chapter. Note was made that the
Waterfront Commission, which had only with reluctance issued
variances so that seniority could be introduced, came to see it as
a protector of the men as well as a great decasualizing device.
Poor, slovenly administration by the union, as well as by employers, led to a decision, in the early part of 1963, to write the
provisions of the seniority article of the collective agreement
into its regulations. This would make the provisions enforceable
by the commission. It could have refused to extend the variances
but this would have disrupted the whole program. What it
wanted to do was simply guarantee the hiring rights of longshoremen.[8]

The commission had come to realize that vacancies in gangs
were not being filled in many places. This gave hiring agents
the opportunity to hire fill-ins and to dispense the favor of jobs.
Also, when vacancies were filled permanently, it was easy for
a hiring agent to contrive to have a favorite present in the center
at the time, and no others who were eligible. The union could
influence hiring by prearrangement. The commission would re-

[7] *New York Times*, July 14, 1963, p. 62, July 18, p. 44, July 20, p. 34;
New York Herald Tribune, July 18, 1963, p. 15.

[8] Waterfront Commission, "Proposed Revised Hiring Regulations,"
Feb. 1, 1963 (mimeographed); Waterfront Commission, *Annual Report*,
1962–1963, p. 14.

quire posting and filling of vacancies and it would also control absenteeism. The latter would be achieved by requiring a man to be in attendance with his gang or have his name deleted on the same basis as the men on dock labor lists: he had to work in the gang twelve days a month or 80 percent of the time the gang worked, which ever was less.

When the commission announced its intentions, the parties took umbrage at the notion that the terms of the collective agreement should be enforceable as a matter of law. Both insisted that the procedures for enforcement rested in the Seniority Board, the LRC, and the port arbitrator.[9] Both thought it an interference with collective bargaining. But the commission knew that provisions of the seniority agreement, in many instances, were not being enforced by the union, and it would not allow lax administration to serve as a blind, or cover, for illegality. The NYSA took exception to the five-day posting requirement set by the commission, insisting that a condition not agreed to in collective bargaining was being imposed, whereas the only requirement, contractually, on the employer was to make replacements from among those physically present in the center at the time the employer desired to fill the vacancy.

While this controversy was running, the ILA and the NYSA still had a bargaining problem about seniority to settle. The matter had become lost in the shuffle of the "Morse Settlement," mostly because many on each side did not give it a high priority or considered it settled. An anomaly existed. The employers knew that many of the ILA leaders did not want seniority and most of them did not want it either. But some employers believed that seniority was a good thing and reminded the others that "there were 10,000 A-card holders who won't let it go. There is no man big enough to take it away from them and there would be all hell to pay if it were tried." The fact is that most longshoremen wanted seniority very much.

A difficulty had grown out of the fact that the seniority article

[9] "Comments of the NYSA on proposed Revised Regulations of the Waterfront Commision," March 8, 1963.

provided for three classifications by length of service, "A," "B," and "C," but during the time it took to implement seniority a large number of newcomers had entered the work force and held no classification. In some parts of the port, notably in Brooklyn and Port Newark, the leaders felt that all men in their areas should have claims to employment prior to those from other boroughs. Because men without classification in their localities stood behind seniority men from other boroughs in the hiring of casuals, they demanded that a "D" classification be added along with recognition of the concept of borough seniority. In fact, Port Newark had made a "D" classification a condition of introduction of seniority.

The Seniority Board tried to settle the matter by agreement in August 1961, approving two amendments to the seniority article, one providing for a "D" classification for those who had worked 400 hours in the preceding two years and, the other, providing for borough seniority.[10] The matter would have been settled except for the fact that Field threatened to go to court to block the changes because the amendments had not been ratified as required by the ILA constitution.[11] Field would have none of it because work in his area of the port was slack and the men had to travel to get employment. The "D" category and borough seniority would have placed his men behind "D" men in casual hiring in Brooklyn. He knew no reason why an "A" man from his local should stand behind a "new mickey" in the industry. His threat of court action stymied the matter until negotiations in 1962. It could have been settled then but was not included in the "Memorandum of Settlement."

Another related matter, preemployment physical examinations, once agreed to but not settled, was before them, too. An agreement had been made in 1959 but had not been implemented with the large number of unclassified men working in the industry; it had to wait on the "D" classification. The matter now came up again. These examinations would serve the employers by

[10] NYSA-ILA, Seniority Board, "Minutes," Aug. 16, 1961; NYSA, Report No. 1934, Aug. 18, 1961.
[11] New York Times, Oct. 11, 1961, p. 76.

assuring that only able-bodied men would come into the industry and help to minimize future liabilities. They would serve the union by instituting a control over entry not otherwise available under the Waterfront Commission program, a device to deter, or check, entry in the face of commission refusal to close the register.

The parties entered into negotiations in February 1963 to take care of these matters but also to counter the new amendments of the commission. The ILA proposed that there be no additions to pier lists except by "agreement between union and management" and that any vacancy in a gang be "offered to the most senior man on the pier, subject only to his capability where special skills are required" and that any vacancy on a regular pier list "must be offered to the most senior man in the section by A-B-C-D" and no additions be made "unless there [was] a prior written approval of the seniority sub-committee in that section."[12] Obviously, this was designed to offset the kind of surveillance intended by the Waterfront Commission in its proposed amendments. The parties easily agreed to a "D" category, and to borough seniority, and to a preemployment physical examination for which the employee paid a fee of fifteen dollars, refundable by the seniority board provided the new employee completed a total of 700 hours of work in the industry during the ensuing twelve months. In addition, they agreed to "freeze all pier lists." They were hoping, certainly the ILA was, that they could get out ahead of the commission through a collective agreement and negate its efforts to amend its existing regulations, perhaps regain some control over hiring. They also provided for annual upgrading, "A" cards for fifteen years' consecutive service, "B" cards for ten years' but less than fifteen years' consecutive service, "C" cards for five years' but less than ten years' consecutive service; and "D" cards for two years' but less than five years' consecutive service.[13]

It is curious that this agreement was not submitted to the men

---

[12] NYSA, "ILA Seniority Proposals," Report No. 2120, Feb. 20, 1963.
[13] "Longshore Seniority Amendment," April 11, 1963, see NYSA, Report 2137, April 15, 1963.

for ratification, either, but no one made an issue of it. Field remained silent. Perhaps it was because the matter should have been a part of the "Morse Settlement." There is very good opinion that had the men voted on the "D" card question, it would not have passed. Why, it was asked, should men agree to let newcomers to the industry have priorities to employment that might result in less employment for themselves if they went to another section or borough? Of course, men who felt confident in their employment on their own piers or section might have voted in loyalty to their own kin and friends to give them employment rights over men from other sections or boroughs.

The "Voice of the Rank and File," an anonymous throwsheet that appeared irregularly on the waterfront, called on "all A-B-C Rank and File Longshoremen" to "Wake Up" and contest the claim of delegates that the rank and file wanted the "D" card. "Call your local delegate," it was urged, "Call the International"; "No 'D' Cards without a closed vote by all the men, by Honest Ballot. It is too late in the game for some officials to make fools of us 'old timers,' we are now too smart"; "Protest and be heard." "Demand Port Seniority—A-B-C all the way."[14] But the ballot was not offered.

After receiving a copy of the new agreement, the commission asked for the meaning of "freeze all pier lists." It wanted to know whether the lists were to be in conformity with the original seniority articles or with the negotiated amendment. It desired a clarification "since our surveys show that many persons on the present lists have been added in violation" of the 1959 provisions. Further, "We assume that the parties do not intend to freeze improper classifications obtained by fraud or issued by mistake."[15]

The ILA and the NYSA made a joint response: "Freeze all pier lists" was "explicit and clear," and "completely current listings" would "facilitate the resolution of questions regarding

[14] Handbill of Voice of the Rank and File, early April, 1963.
[15] Letter to Chopin and Gleason from Waterfront Commission, April 18, 1963.

the status of any employee," but also these "new lists—should reflect the seniority rosters in effect under the original seniority provisions. . . . Accordingly, our position is that the persons who were placed on the seniority lists . . . are properly on those lists." New hirings and additions were to be made in conformance to the new agreement. But to affirm their rights and intentions they went on to say, "If a complaint is made, the parties intend, and have provided, that the Seniority Board consider the matter and make a decision under the grievance procedure previously established. . . . Any employee who believes there has been a violation . . . has a right to present a grievance. This has been true in the past and will be true in the future."[16]

This hardly satisfied the commission, and while it said it gave "considerable weight" to the existing agreements in preparing its final regulations, it adopted its proposed amendments on March 26, 1963, to become effective on May 6, 1963. It did not delete the requirement of posted notice, although it permitted the employer to interview applicants prior to selection at the center, provided the applicants first registered at the center; it was explicitly made a violation for an employer to interview applicants before he filed an application with the commission and posted the vacancy. Obviously this was designed to check, as far as possible, predetermination under pressure from the union.[17]

It can probably be said that if the letter of the new agreement were followed—and, even had the letter of the original agreement been followed—the amendments to the Waterfront Commission regulations would not have been needed. No such confidence was held in the parties, and the regulations were put into effect as scheduled, on May 6, 1963.

In August the NYSA and the ILA were ready to implement the agreement reached in April, that is, they were prepared to give the preemployment physical examinations and had already

[16] Letter, Chopin and Gleason to Waterfront Commission, April 23, 1963.

[17] Waterfront Commission, "Revised Regulations," May 6, 1963, *Annual Report, 1962-63*, p. 14; NYSA, Report No. 2142, May 3, 1963.

issued the "D" cards. Other questions had to be settled. Most were not difficult. It is interesting that the posting requirement stayed alive as an issue and was being discussed with the parties at the commission offices in October. The commission would call it a violation if a man went to the employer before a job was posted, but the employers thought they had convinced the commission that filling vacancies should be solely in the hands of the employers under the terms of the collective agreement. The commission could enforce the law wherever it was found to be violated, that is, wherever the employer's selection was being pressured. The commission could hardly be convinced that the union was not exerting an influence in the hiring.

Many dockworkers looked to the commission for objective consideration and protection of their employment rights, a fact that may have been a problem for both the union and the employers. But the employers thought the commission was taking on the role of an employment agency, which it was not authorized under the law to be. The law placed full authority and responsibility for hiring in the hands of the employers. The NYSA, therefore, thought that the commission should limit itself to enforcement of the law. They were not going to let the commission select the men, nor did they want the men to think that their jobs came from the commission. If the men gave the employers the credit, discipline would be more effective. The employers insisted that seniority was to govern in selection and if an employer violated seniority the union could file a grievance. If the union exerted any undue pressure the commission had a defense for that. But the commission was determined to play its role of surveillance and was not willing to allow practices which it felt might give the ILA an opportunity to influence the selection of men.

The Department of Labor Study

A study of the magnitude contemplated in the "Morse Settlement"—even in the absence of complexities such as bedeviled the docks industry—would not have been easy. Considering the deadline—which had to allow sufficient time to allow the parties to bargain to an agreement before July 31, 1964—research would have to be finished in not more than one year. The Department of Labor and its primary research department, the Bureau of Labor Statistics, had experienced research planners and researchers, but none thoroughly acquainted with the industry, and experts agreed that the major difficulty in doing the study was the lack of knowledgeable researchers about the industry, its complexities, and its people. There was not time to make the type of contacts needed to get into the nuances that make judgments meaningful.

The "Morse Settlement" provided only a general guide to study "the problems of manpower utilization, job security, and all other related issues which affect the longshore industry . . . a comprehensive . . . analysis of and findings with respect to gang size, work-force flexibility, severance pay, register closing, automation, and such other manpower utilization–job security items as the Secretary of Labor shall determine." He would "be guided by advisory panels to be selected by each party." Similar services would be available to other ports (other than New York) with manpower utilization–job security problems.

The NYSA wanted to make sure, in talking with Wirtz, that the study would be his and was not to be farmed out. As it turned out, the NYSA had to hold the ILA to the study; the latter tried to avoid it by ignoring it. Gleason said that the study would not amount to very much, and even said publicly—a campaign gesture, to be sure—that he had no intention of accepting any adverse government recommendation. This was because Bradley had charged him, through his unwillingness to bargain, with causing an unnecessary strike and, then, to get it settled, with accepting a governmental study that was bound to end up in loss of jobs to longshoremen. Gleason had rejoined, "I held out last year for job security and I pledge right now that I will never surrender the right of our union in joint talks with the shippers to determine our work rules."[18] The NYSA did not think the study would amount to very much either, but it was the major promise and the employers wanted it done seriously and cooperated all the way.

Wirtz assigned Reynolds to head the project, but the veteran careermen, Nelson Bortz, deputy assistant secretary, and John N. Gentry, planned and coordinated it in the early stages, at least. Later, David H. Stowe, a veteran arbitrator and mediator and one time aide to President Truman, was designated as the director.[19] Stowe was not primarily a researcher; his role was to prepare himself to mediate once the report was finished. He was to learn about the industry and ingratiate himself with the leaders on each side so that he could more effectively produce whatever compromises would be needed. One of the partisan spokesmen, in the autumn of 1963 while the study was in progress, surmised, "Stowe thinks he will be able to knock our heads together."

The study got under way in April. The staff from the Department of Labor started gathering data promptly and held meetings with representatives of the ILA and the NYSA and toured the New York waterfront. Captain Mossman coordinated the visits for the NYSA; but no ILA representatives showed up because none had been appointed, even though the ILA knew that government researchers were coming to Brooklyn to observe operations. Only when called upon explicitly did the ILA send representatives to accompany the tour. The ILA then acted promptly from embarrassment because the observers saw the winches being handled quite adroitly by two winchmen, and sometimes only one, whereas the ILA had demanded that the use of four be continued.

It is interesting that Waldman, at the Atlantic Coast Convention in July, felt impelled to give solemn warning of the import

[18] *New York Herald Tribune*, July 2, 1963, p. 64; *New York Times*, July 22, 1963, p. 22.
[19] *New York Times*, April 13, 1963, p. 28, Aug. 5, p. 38.

of the study and of the ILA's need to cooperate in order to get its position properly considered. He told the delegates that "flexing of the union's economic muscle" after the study was completed would do the union no good. "Settlement of last winter's ILA strike has left the big questions in controversy to be determined during the year 1964." He said the findings would not be "a mere exercise in intellectual curiosity," and the investigators "can only find what they see and hear and are told." The study "opens up golden opportunities" for the employers, he emphasized, and suggested that the ILA should not sit idly by, "prepared only to cry to the heavens if the results seem unfavorable. . . . Those findings, if adverse to the ILA, may spell disaster to dockworkers . . . and a sanction of the Labor Department may well impel Congress to restrict your economic action where it is now reluctant to do so."[20]

At the dedication of the Anastasia Memorial Wing of the Brooklyn Longshoremen's Medical Center, Reynolds explained that the study was ready to go into high gear and also prepared the parties for some possible consequences. He compared the study to the diagnostic examination, which was a main feature of the clinic's service, and said that the study might turn up faults on the piers which could be cured by management and labor cooperation.[21]

The Department of Labor studied all the major ports and produced eight separate reports covering ten ports in all.[22] The report on the Port of New York was formally delivered to the parties on July 1. Evaluation of the impact is difficult. It no doubt had greater influence than some in the industry or union

[20] *New York Times*, July 10, 1963, p. 58.

[21] *New York Herald Tribune*, June 4, 1963, p. 33.

[22] U.S. Department of Labor, *Manpower Utilization—Job Security in the Longshore Industry—Port of New York*, July 1, 1964; issued subsequently were reports on the ports of Boston, Philadelphia, Baltimore, Jacksonville-Charleston, Mobile, New Orleans, and Houston-Galveston. Cf. Phyllis Groom, "Hiring Practices for Longshoremen," *Monthly Labor Review*, vol. 88, Nov. 1965, pp. 1289–1296.

had anticipated, yet it contained little that was not known—certainly to the parties. The fact that the report spoke with the voice of the government gave weight that could not be ignored. Nevertheless, one would have thought that with the expenditure of a half million dollars something more would have been reported. Perhaps the base of the iceberg is in the Department of Labor files. The report focused only on major problem areas and was designed to help the parties reach "the best mutual accommodation." This objective set the style and made it less a research report than one to facilitate negotiations. Too much detail might have been too controversial. In any event, broad brush strokes, so to speak, are the chief characterization.

The report clarified one important matter that a nongovernmental researcher would have had difficulty establishing, that is, the extent to which dock workers in New York, whose earnings are low, supplement them by work in other industries. By taking earnings for 1962 from the Central Records Bureau of the NYSA for all longshoremen who worked less than 700 hours and comparing them with earnings by social security numbers as revealed in the records of the Social Security Administration, it was demonstrated that 3,500 who received less than $1,500 in earnings from longshore employment earned no less than $4,500 in covered wages. Obviously many casual longshoremen found their primary earnings in other industries, or, in fact, used longshoring, on a so-called "moonlighting" basis. The report, of course, included other statistical characteristics of the labor force. It included sections on hiring and seniority; customs and practices affecting manpower utilization and workforce flexibility, that is, the facts concerning gang sizes by different types of operation and "frozen details"; job security and the relationship of it to control of the register and the extent to which entry to the industry was already under control. It included results of observations at the piers, suggestions made by both parties, and a discussion of future technological changes in the industry which, in retrospect, were portrayed as modestly—and as incorrectly—as the views prevailing generally. The researchers, like others at the time, failed to see the extent of the technological revolution ahead.

Some of the major findings: labor force supply was much nearer to demand than formerly; the large majority of long-shoremen obtained rather sufficient annual income as reflected in hours worked; many low income longshoremen got a substan-tial, if not principal, part of their earnings from other industries; controlled entry into the work force was desirable; any move to establish a more permanent work force would involve adjust-ments in the seniority system and related rules, but complete mobility was not feasible; the inability of management to utilize all men in the minimum gang size—hence there were problems about numbers in gangs for different types of cargo, whether palletized or not; there were problems about restrictive practices and in the use of so-called "special details"; attention to early retirement was needed as well as to alteration of sectional sen-iority.

Gleason, in a highly diplomatic tone, but with his eye on the pending negotiations, praised the report and said that the ILA welcomed it. "We are gratified," he said, "to note that the report agrees with the ILA that too much of the work in this port is taken up by casuals," that the intake of new men should be limited and that longshoremen should not be expected to change prac-tices "unless major steps are taken by the industry to assure broader guarantees of employment and satisfactory levels of earnings to regular longshoremen." He suggested, significantly, that "the time may well be ripe to institute in this industry a guaranteed annual wage." He felt that the report played down "featherbedding" and that changes in work practices had to be accompanied by "benefits to the workers which the employers in this port have consistently refused to accord." He explained that prepalletization had little to do with technological change, saying, "This is simply a case of transferring the function of palletizing cargo from longshoremen to other workers—usually nonunion or poorly paid—at other places." He took solace, too, by saying, "The Department of Labor did not offer a pat solution to all problems. It recognized their complexity and acknowledged that lasting and meaningful progress can be made only through the efforts of the parties in collective bargaining."[23]

Negotiations—Flexibility and Guaranteed Wages

The ILA had submitted demands to the NYSA on June 26, before the report was issued and talked about the need for a common program for the whole union. Gleason was saying, "The government has given us national bargaining by virtue of the study." The principal demands were: a three-year contract with wage increases of 15, 10, and 10 cents, respectively, and with an additional paid holiday in each of the years; pensions increased to $175 monthly and half pensions for widows; vacations of one, two, three, or four weeks for work in the previous year of 700, 1,100, 1,300, or 1,500 hours, respectively, the four-week vacation being limited to those who had received a vacation check in nine out of the ten previous years; welfare and clinic programs to be worked out; gang sizes to remain the same; guarantee of eight-hour day, with two of the hours at overtime; the cancellation clause to be eliminated; guarantee of two hours' pay for each man who "shows up" at a center; labor-management hiring halls; all prepalletized, unitized cargo to be stripped and loaded at pier and all such cargo unloaded on piers to be subject to a royalty payment; and complete studies to be conducted of severance pay and the seniority system.[24]

As the parties met for the first time after the report was delivered, they got off to a fractious start and never got to the key demands of the ILA. Chopin wanted to begin by taking up the findings of the study, but Gleason refused, saying, "I regret that the shipping association has not seen fit to have a set of counterproposals." After a little argument, the employers agreed, reluctantly, to have counterproposals by their next meeting.[25]

[23] *New York Herald Tribune*, July 6, 1964, p. 25.
[24] NYSA, Report No. 2254, June 26, 1964.
[25] *New York Times*, July 8, 1964, p. 59.

In mid-July the employers submitted their proposals, primarily based on the study. Like the ILA, they stressed the points in the report favoring their demands, the need for flexibility in assignment and reduction in size of gangs. Citing the conclusions on manpower utilization, they proposed that a joint committee "be immediately constituted for the purpose of reviewing gang-size needs for palletized, pre-palletized, unitized and containerized cargo, for unboxed autos, and for vessels equipped with special cargo handling devices" to report back "on or before July 21." All "frozen details" among checkers and clerks should be eliminated, with the employer exercising the right to deploy and reassign employees to perform any work within their craft. Freedom to make technological changes without restriction. In exchange, the employers proposed a variety of protections: restricted entry to the labor force; increased pension benefits and earlier retirements; guarantee of eight-hours' work a day with appropriate exceptions; severance pay to men permanently displaced by reason of changes in work practices; a minimum guarantee for a basic work period or some form of guaranteed wage for regular men; and a "Human Relations Committee" to advise on major policies or relationships. Work practices were to be modified extensively. Wages, vacations, and holidays would depend upon the outcome of negotiations on the proposals made. Seniority and pension, welfare, and clinic benefits were to be studied. Royalties were to be eliminated. The contract was to run five years.[26]

When the ILA indicated that it was willing to consider a reduction in gang size, it appeared that a change had taken place. At least the ILA agreed to the establishment of a joint committee to consider the matter. Gleason said that although the union was pledged to keep the twenty-man gang, inasmuch as the employers were willing to offer increased benefits in a barter deal, the way was open to a reduction. A twenty-eight-man committee would work on the matter and report by July 27. As

[26] NYSA, Report No. 2258, July 14, 1964.

it turned out, the dock workers' negotiating committee continued adamant on the twenty-man gang. Consequently, toward the end of the month the federal mediators made a brief entry; a three-man team comprised of the veterans Moore and Burke, plus Herbert Schmertz, special assistant to Simkin, began meeting with the parties.[27] They did not do much and the July 31 deadline was upon them.

The parties appealed jointly to President Lyndon B. Johnson, asking for intervention. It is reported that Gleason said, "The government got us into this mess, let it get us out of it." But it is to be noted that they were still sixty days to the expiration of their agreement. The President reappointed Morse, Healy, and Kheel. Morse soon bowed out, owing to senatorial commitments, and Reynolds, by unanimous choice of the parties, took over the chairmanship. Stowe was assigned to serve as executive secretary.[28]

This board went to work in earnest, looking ahead to its task of making recommendations and feeling the parties out on the various issues. A guaranteed annual wage was discussed, the ILA offering to abandon the twenty-man gang in exchange for it. But the ILA became angry when the PNYA (Port of New York Authority) urged that the negotiators equalize cargo handling costs between New York and the other ports by eliminating surplus men and achieving flexibility of assignments. Gleason charged, "I resent the interference in negotiations by this type of pressure." Nevertheless, hiring and manpower problems got sufficient discussion that the ILA was willing to name a committee to study problems that would arise if legislation were obtained to remove the Waterfront Commission from the hiring process. They discussed changes in seniority, too. But they really never got far away from stalemate. In mid-September the

[27] *New York Times*, July 15, 1964, p. 54, July 29, p. 54; *New York Herald Tribune*, July 15, 1964, p. 35.

[28] *New York Times*, Aug. 3, 1964, p. 44, Aug. 12, p. 58; *New York Herald Tribune*, Aug. 3, 1964, p. 25, Aug. 12, p. 26; ILA, *Fact Sheet*, vol. 1, no. 2, Aug. 1964.

employers proposed that all issues be submitted to arbitration by the board, but the ILA refused.[29]

On September 25, the board submitted its recommendations covering all aspects of the dispute. Unfortunately, the board was not unanimous on all recommendations; Kheel departing from Reynolds and Healy on one major and one minor matter. Without a doubt the recommendations on "Income Guarantee" were the most significant. Reynolds and Healy thought that there were two fundamental problems, income assurance and income stability. The latter, they felt, was a long-range problem whose solution hinged upon strict control of entry of new employees into the work force, greater mobility, control of absenteeism, and more efficient utilization of manpower. They did not think the parties had the time to resolve the issue. Accordingly, they addressed themselves to only the former and recommended that all holders of seniority be guaranteed an annual income no less than 75 per cent of the employee's gross annual earnings, including vacation and holiday pay and unemployment compensation. The guarantee would be computed and paid quarterly but, in the calculation, eight hours would be deducted for each failure of an employee to report when ordered or failure of an employee to make himself available at a center, on Monday through Friday when not employed, to accept work "on a port-wide basis" for which he is qualified. Kheel recommended a guarantee of earnings of 1,600 hours a year multiplied by the existing hourly rate, also inclusive of vacation and holiday payments as well as unemployment compensation and subject to the same deductions specified by Reynolds and Healy regarding availability of employees. Both carried an effective date for introduction of April 1, 1966, coincident with manpower changes to be effective on that date. Because many complex details would have to be worked out, Kheel also called for nego-

[29] *New York Times*, Aug. 13, 1964, p. 58, Aug. 19, p. 62; *New York Herald Tribune*, Aug. 14, 1964, p. 29, Sept. 4, p. 32, Sept. 16, p. 25, Sept. 22, p. 32.

tiation by the parties for twelve months with arbitration on matters on which they could not agree.[30]

The board recommended a number of measures for flexibility, the most important being that employers should be required to hire only the number of men necessary to perform the work, with "frozen details" eliminated; distribution of members of a gang to any assignment within the gang for which the men were qualified; adding extra men to a gang, to be transferable from gang to gang as needed; and allowing gangs to be transferable from hatch to hatch and from ship to ship within the same terminal provided such transfer did not cause displacement of another gang. On "Gang Size," they recommended:

A. Effective April 1, 1966, the present minimum gang size of 20 for general cargo shall be decreased to 18. Reductions from the gang should be on the basis of gang seniority.
B. Effective October 1, 1967, the minimum gang size of 18 for general cargo shall be decreased to 17.

Wage increases and increased pensions were offered. Reynolds and Healy recommended a general increase in wages of ten cents per hour effective October 1, 1964, and, additionally, improvements in the value of twelve cents effective October 1, 1966 and a like amount a year later. Kheel recommended an alternative to the latter by recommending a five-year, rather than four-year, contract with one reopener on wages for the fourth or fifth year, with arbitration if the parties failed to agree. "Mobility" and "Absenteeism Control" should be subjected to study, the register should be subjected to control "consistent with law and the authority" of the Waterfront Commission, and a Labor-Management Employment Cooperation Committee was recommended.[31]

[30] James J. Reynolds, Chairman, Theodore W. Kheel, and James J. Healy, "Recommendation on Manpower Utilization, Job Security and Other Disputed Issues for the Port of New York," Sept. 25, 1964; NYSA, Report No. 2272, Sept. 26, 1964.
[31] *Ibid.*

A joint meeting of the parties scheduled by Reynolds for September 26 was cancelled at the request of management. Gleason expressed anger, wanting a contract without a strike in his first term as president, and based on Kheel's recommendations. The employers felt that the board's proposed cut in gang size was not enough, but, in spite of verbal castigations, the parties were very close to a settlement until the checkers balked over the language eliminating "frozen details." It was claimed that employers were being given a blank check to decide on the number of checkers without regard to the need. When the checkers backed off, the longshoremen backed off, too.

On October 1, the strike was on. Never before was a Taft-Hartley Board appointed so quickly. Schmertz, a member of the mediation team, was named chairman, and Healy and Kheel were the other two members. Reynolds, perturbed by the failure to achieve a settlement, ruefully said that no labor negotiations in history started off "with such a body of information"—as though the amount of information makes the difference in the bargaining outcome—and added, "Every possible tool was at their command and they failed to agree. To anyone interested in preservation of free collective bargaining this is a matter of grave concern." If Reynolds would not place blame, Chopin would. He was bitter about Gleason, who would never do anything the checkers did not like, and about the ILA committee, which, to him, had "simply refused to bargain. . . . I still have faith in collective bargaining; but in this case there was no bargaining." Likewise, the *New York Times* would assign blame, "There is less justification for the union's stubbornness this year than ever before. . . . The ILA, after some initial gestures of willingness to bargain, reverted to its classic posture of total rejection."[32]

The truth was not that Gleason would not bargain but that he was still in a position where he could not deliver. He was secure, as the newly elected president, although some thought that Kheel's recommendation of a five-year contract was de-

[32] *New York Times*, Oct. 1, 1964, pp. 1, 32 editorial.

signed to give Gleason an additional year before another round of negotiations. He did not have the power to oppose local leaders; he certainly was not willing to cross the checkers, who, some thought, might have removed him as their local president, thus depriving him of his base.

The Taft-Hartley Board requested an injunction the day the strike was called, and it was quickly issued. The ILA leaders expressed anger, and although Waldman said he would not oppose the injunction he intended to fight it as he would a narcotic because it was getting to be a bad habit. He attacked the speed with which the legal action was effectuated and the fact that only one member of the board had held separate sessions for the ILA and the NYSA, procedures he saw as illegal. He argued that the judge should specify that any benefits agreed to would be retroactive to October 1. Judge Irving Ben Cooper upheld the injunction for the eighty-day period and rejected both the contention that no hearing had been held and that there was no basis for the order; because the members of the board were intimately familiar with the dispute and its possible consequences, this was enough. He also rejected the notions of retroactivity or continuation of all terms of the old contracts, because the law sought to produce settlement, and to grant either might deter this prospect.[33]

With the eighty-day injunction, the new deadline became December 20. Reynolds urged the parties to get back to bargaining, but he continued to mediate. It is interesting to note, because of events ahead, that Chopin said, "Part of our job now is to try to inform the rank-and-file . . . of just how far we have gone in job security . . . , and how much we have offered in caring for the basic work force. . . . We just don't think the men know."[34] But they could not effectively do it.

By early November negotiations had bogged down to the

[33] NYSA, Report No. 2276, Oct. 15, 1964, for a copy of the court order; cf. New York Times, Oct. 11, 1964, p. 1; New York Herald Tribune, Oct. 6, 1964, p. 1.

[34] New York Times, Oct. 15, 1964, p. 65.

point where Wirtz felt compelled to call the parties to Washington. The checker issue effectively blocked progress. Reynolds then proposed a one-year extension of the contract with a 10-cent-per-hour increase in wages retroactive to October 1, an increase in the pension from $100 to $125, and improvements in welfare. The ILA leaders accepted with alacrity, but not the employers. Chopin explained that there was nothing in it "except to continue discussions for another full year of the featherbedding issues already postponed two years"; they would accept no extension "without some form of terminal arbitration."[35]

The *New York Times*, editorially, found Reynolds' proposal astounding: "dismaying evidence of the extent to which considerations of peace at any price often banish both principle and good sense when Government intervenes in labor-management affairs." It was thought puzzling that Reynolds, who had proposed a four-year contract, was now proposing, "a one-year settlement on the basis that would again give the ILA more money with no commitment ever to face up to the necessity for lopping off any of the manpower fat." It was felt that the two brightest young leaders, Bowers and Scotto, who had "shown genuine receptivity," were being ignored in favor of "the troglodyte elements in the union leadership [who] are jubilantly embracing the extension plan as a new excuse for doing nothing —to the lasting hurt of the longshoremen, the industry and the country."[36]

The "last offer"[37] was rejected, two to one, a foregone conclusion.

With the December 20 deadline ahead, progress was made toward the middle of the month when Scotto and Bowers assumed more active roles, and work rules for checkers were thrashed out. Discussions then moved conclusively to a settle-

[35] *New York Times*, Nov. 5, 1964, p. 89, Nov. 11, p. 74, Nov. 25, p. 65; Bureau of National Affairs, *Daily Labor Report*, no. 232, Nov. 30, 1964, p. A-6.

[36] *New York Times*, Nov. 27, 1964, p. 34.

[37] NYSA, Report No. 2285, Nov. 27, 1964; *New York Herald Tribune*, Nov. 29, 1964, p. 12.

ment on December 16, four days before the deadline. The other issues fell into place quickly, having been more or less agreed when the checkers action precipitated the strike. Amity marked the final negotiations. Great credit is no doubt due to the efforts of Reynolds, but Scotto and Bowers were instrumental, although they did not displace Gleason, who also participated in the settlement.[38]

The 1964 Agreement

The agreement was set to run for four years and provided a package worth eighty cents, inclusive of a thirty-six-cent-an-hour increase in wage rates over the four-year period, and a twenty-four-cent-an-hour increase in contribution for pensions. There were three additional paid holidays, one to be added in each of the first three years of the agreement. Vacations were extended to four weeks per year for all employees who worked 1,500 hours in the year and who had worked for no less than 700 hours in each of the preceding twelve years. The income guarantee, of course, was the central feature, but the plan adopted was the Kheel proposal, not the Reynolds-Healy proposal. In exchange the ILA agreed to adjustments in manpower and flexibility in assignment and employers were required to hire only the number of clerks and checkers "as may be necessary to perform the work" and "frozen details as now constituted shall be eliminated." The palatability of this language was due to the implementation provided. Gang size for general cargo was reduced by two men, effective April 1, 1966, and by a third man, effective October 1, 1967, with certain rights in assignment of gangs.

A Human Relations and Implementation Committee (HRIC) was provided for, to "review existing seniority arrangements for the purpose of enhancing mobility of longshoremen within each borough and within the New Jersey area and the availability of longshoremen on a portwide basis . . . to work out a system

[38] *New York Times*, Dec. 9, 1964, p. 35, Dec. 11, p. 42, Dec. 17, p. 1.

of penalties for consistent absenteeism and tardiness along with portwide machinery for administration and enforcement"; to establish standards for applying and defining "qualified" under the guarantee of income, as well as the phrase "continuously fails to make himself available for employment"; and other issues dealing with implementation of the agreement with Kheel designated as arbitrator in case of failure to reach agreement. They also agreed that the register should be closed, with appropriate methods for reopening, and agreed to meet jointly and cooperate with the Waterfront Commission to seek the necessary legislation. In addition, they established a Management-Labor Employment Cooperation Committee to make "arrangements to have union representatives at the Waterfront Commission Hiring Centers to monitor hiring and to carry out the provisions of the agreement, including those dealing with the income guarantee."[39]

The great happiness was promptly shattered. Provision had been made for a thirty-day extension of old agreements in order to give an opportunity in New York for a referendum and to permit settlements in other ports. But at the expiration of the injunction a wildcat strike started in New York and troubles developed in other ports, particularly in Baltimore and Galveston. Coming as it did, just before Christmas, the situation was confused. At first it looked like an incipient walkout that was fizzling. By Christmas, it seemed over,[40] but was not.

Was the strike disaffection with the leadership, anticipation of undesirable terms, or a result of ignorance about the terms of the agreement? The ILA leaders, thinking it was the latter, called on all locals to hold membership meetings to explain the agreement, one expressing conviction "they will go for it." Balloting took place on January 8, 1965, under the auspices of the Honest Ballot Association, and the agreement was rejected by a vote of

[39] NYSA-ILA, "Memorandum of Settlement"; *New York Times*, Dec. 17, 1964, p. 1.

[40] *New York Times*, Dec. 22, 1964, p. 1, Dec. 24, p. 40; *New York Herald Tribune*, Dec. 23, 1964, p. 1.

8,633 to 7,703, with only two locals voting for it, Scotto's and Bowers'; where it had been fully explained. Elsewhere, so Chopin charged, no efforts were made to sell it, "a wretched job of informing members." Chopin warned that if the strike continued the employers would have no alternative but to request President Johnson to seek congressional action on compulsory arbitration.[41]

Whether or not the rejection was caused by lack of an educational effort, it was an important factor. However, some men were angry because tucked away at the end of the agreement was a "check-off" of an increase in dues from one cent to two cents per hour. This not only diminished the wage increase to nine cents, but the men felt that it was improper to increase dues without raising the matter in the union, or submitting it for a separate vote.[42]

The ILA belatedly sent a statement about the settlement to all members on January 13. The union got support, too, from Senator Morse's publicized statement to his colleagues in the Senate. Two years before he had helped set up the study by the Department of Labor, and now he pled with the rank-and-file longshoremen "to take another look," convinced that if they took time to study the agreement they would accept it. But he was critical of inclusion of the increase of dues deduction, "a gross error." He knew that in some locals there was more talk about this than anything else and he urged that at the next vote it be separated for a second ballot because it dealt solely with an internal union affair.[43]

A date for another vote was set and the ILA leaders this time put on a drive to sell the agreement, including an explanation of the need of the union for more money. It was also made clear—as had been made clear by Reynolds—that the government was taking no further hand in the affair and that the ILA leaders had

---

[41] *New York Times*, Jan. 10, 1965, pp. 1, 12, 40.

[42] *New York Herald Tribune*, Jan. 11, 1965, pp. 1, 27.

[43] *Congressional Record*, Jan. 12, 1965, pp. 580–583; cf. NYSA, "Memo to Members of the Labor Policy Committee," Jan. 14, 1965.

no intention of reopening negotiations. They were standing on the agreement. This time the men accepted the agreement by a vote of 12,171 to 5,649.[44] Even so, the strike went on, awaiting the outcome of the negotiating and balloting in the other ports. Chopin, however, called upon the ILA to return to work in New York, declaring the strike senseless because the only issues in other ports were local ones: "It is inconceivable, under these conditions," he said, "that the ILA leadership should stick dogmatically to its position that settlements must be reached everywhere." The next day the Baltimore dockers added confusion by rejecting the agreement. Reynolds charged that "Communist-allied" activities were behind the rejection. The NYSA then sent a telegram to President Johnson asking him for "immediate action to terminate this senseless, suicidal and unjustified strike and reopen our ports pending congressional action towards compulsory arbitration." A settlement in New Orleans and one in Mobile were the only signs of a change. But President Johnson refused to act. Key trouble areas were Baltimore, where a second vote was scheduled, Philadelphia, and Galveston.[45]

The situation remained confused. As pressure continued for a return to work where agreements had been negotiated, Gleason kept insisting that the ILA could not desert any ports: "I run an international union and I must protect every member in this union." It was possible, however, that resumption of work in the ports where agreements had been reached would put employers in other ports under pressure to settle. Some thought that the ILA was wrongly advised to continue its policy of "none back until all are back," but not the ILA officials. In southern ports union leaders said they could not break their ranks, for Galveston would be let down and, in a future time, none would have confidence in the national leaders.

[44] *New York Times*, Jan. 14, 1965, p. 62, Jan. 16, p. 13, Jan. 22, p. 1.
[45] *New York Times*, Jan. 27, 1965, p. 58, Jan. 28, p. 1, Jan. 30, p. 41; *Baltimore Sun*, Jan. 29, 1965, p. 1; telegram, William B. Rand to President Lyndon Johnson, Jan. 28, 1965, see NYSA, Report No. 2301, Jan. 29, 1965.

An unusual request to President Johnson was made by the Commerce and Industry Association in New York, whose members were chafing under the hurts of port idleness. They urged that he again invoke the national emergency provisions of Taft-Hartley—an unprecedented suggestion—because the current strike involved issues entirely different from those in the earlier dispute. But through Wirtz, President Johnson pled with the ILA to send the men back in all ports where settlements had been reached. There was also encouraging news from Baltimore, where the men, in the second balloting, voted 1,879 to 468 to accept the agreement they had rejected in the balloting the previous week by a vote of 1,371 to 1,016.[46]

But the lack of agreement in Philadelphia deterred the ILA leaders. Gleason wanted to see what developed there, and although his associates were aware that the men in New York were willing to return to work, they would not break traditional policy. Scotto devised the proposition that the men should go back to work but refuse to handle any cargo for companies which had not contributed to settlement. The ILA pondered seriously "selectively striking companies . . . in the stalemated Gulf dispute." Getting exasperated, the NYSA sent a more strongly worded telegram to President Johnson, expressing "bitter disappointment" at the "flaunting of your high office" and appealing for "personal intervention in taking whatever action is necessary, either through Congress or any other measure at your command, to end this strike." Noting that both Wirtz and Reynolds had "worked tirelessly" and that their efforts were appreciated, "but with the ablest men in the Labor Department still frustrated and all facets of collective bargaining now exhausted, we have no other recourse but to petition you for your personal intervention."[47]

Hope for a settlement picked up in Philadelphia and almost as

[46] Bureau of National Affairs, *Daily Labor Report*, no. 21, Feb. 2, 1965, p. A-11; *New York Times*, Feb. 2, 1965, p. 1.

[47] *New York Times*, Feb. 3, 1965, p. 58, Feb. 4, p. 54, Feb. 5, p. 53, Feb. 6, p. 1; NYSA, Report No. 2306, Feb. 5, 1965.

quickly abated. The guaranteed annual wage seemed to be the biggest hurdle; the employers claimed they could not survive with a guarantee of 1,600 hours, had offered only 1,300, and wanted the right to shift men from one pier to another, whereas the rule for a dozen years had been that gangs worked only a single ship for a full day.[48]

The employers in New York would wait no longer. They turned to the NLRB and petitioned for an injunction, charging the ILA leadership with bad faith in bargaining, having come to an agreement accepted by the membership on both sides, and not abiding by it. The delay in coming to the NLRB was "because we had been encouraged by the Administration in Washington to believe that settlement in Philadelphia would bring about reopening of these ports which have concluded contracts."[49] The NLRB thereupon sought and obtained an injunction. A similar action was taken in Baltimore. Naturally, the men returned to work in these ports.

Concurrently, President Johnson took action to settle the South Atlantic and West Gulf Coast disputes by appointing a special informal committee comprised of Wirtz, John Connor, secretary of commerce, and Senator Morse to seek a settlement and report to him within two days. But, as the negotiations in Galveston remained in stalemate, a top federal mediator blamed the impasse on "a deep sickness in labor management relations." Labor leaders in Miami, however, attributed the failure to "unwarranted interference" on the part of the government. The Maritime Trades Department of the AFL-CIO adopted a sharply worded resolution criticizing Wirtz for bolstering the resistance of employers. Gleason, who attended the meeting on the Galveston and Miami situations, said that the stalemate needed "new brains and new thinking." Tempers flared further as Reynolds, commenting on Gleason's statement, said, "I fully agree with Mr. Gleason on the need for new brains, and I think the best

[48] *New York Times*, Feb. 6, 1965, p. 11, Feb. 9, p. 62.
[49] NYSA, Report No. 2307, Feb. 9, 1965; *New York Times*, Feb. 10, 1965, p. 1M, Feb. 12, p. 1M.

place to begin is in the chair he occupies." Some of Gleason's colleagues immediately expressed regret that the dispute had come to name calling. Scotto said, ruefully, "At this point in our troubles it would be insane to ask for new people, new mediators. And we have no business in offending the Federal officials who have spent so much time and tried so hard in this dispute. We need all the friends we can get."[50] Finally, early in March, the stubborn dispute was settled.

[50] *New York Times*, Feb. 13, 1965, p. 1M, Feb. 20, p. 1M, Feb. 21, p. 1M.

14 | Guaranteed Income—the GAI

Relevant to the Guarantee of Annual Income (GAI) are some episodes in the ILA's fight to oust the Waterfront Commission. In the immediate background was the unsuccessful legislative effort in 1964 to wrest control of hiring from the commission and place it in union-management operated halls. The New York State AFL-CIO, with substantial urging from Paul Hall, supported bills introduced by state Senator Thomas Mackell, a friend of the ILA. Meany had written a letter which Waldman presented in the legislative hearings, but it is of interest that Meany opposed only the concept of governmental control. He did not condemn the commission outright: "The establishment and maintenance of far reaching state control over the details of employment in this or any other industry is not compatible with the concepts of a free society. It can be justified, if at all, only as a temporary expedient." However, with organized labor of the state behind the bills, giving the ILA more support than it previously had in its fight on the commission, prospects for passage looked encouraging. The commission launched a very strong counterattack, with the support of the PNYA and several management groups. The commission charged that the law would create "an indoor shape-up" and permit "many evils of the past to recur." It contended that the labor supply was in balance and closing the register was not in the public interest. The NYSA, too, was opposed, saying, "There is no need to close the register" and that it was dead set against a labor-management hiring hall, which it believed would simply become a union hiring hall. The attacks kept the bills in committee and they never came to a vote in the legislature.[1]

But in 1965 the situation was somewhat different. The NYSA, having agreed to the GAI, had changed its position, desiring to minimize the cost of the guarantee by keeping the number of longshoremen as low as possible. It had committed itself to a joint effort with the ILA to get legislation if the commission would not cooperate to close the register. Also, the Department of Labor study had stated that early curtailment of new entrants into the labor force was essential, and orderly entrance of new employees was required.[2]

The commission had its own views of the needs in the situation and of the motives of the ILA. Instead of working with the parties, it challenged their "closing of the register" by their refusal to give physical examinations. It went to court alleging usurpation of a commission function. The court called upon the ILA and the NYSA to show cause why they should not be enjoined from blocking entry into the work force. Both charged, in turn, that the commission was interfering with their collective bargaining agreement. Because the GAI had just been negotiated, the judge deferred decision to give the industry an opportunity to get its "mobility" machinery in operation.[3]

Legislative Action in New York

In the meantime, bills to close the register had been introduced into the legislature and a heated fight turned to these, the arguments being the same as the year before.[4] Again the New York

[1] *New York Herald Tribune,* Jan. 3, 1964, p. 30; *Local 824 Bulletin,* Feb. 1964, p. 1; *Seafarers Log,* June 26, 1964, p. 2; *New York Times,* June 23, 1964, p. 34M.

[2] U.S. Department of Labor, *Manpower Utilization—Job Security in the Longshore Industry—Port of New York,* p. 11; cf. Waterfront Commission, *Annual Report, 1964–65,* p. 15.

[3] *New York Times,* April 8, 1965, p. 66, April 26, p. 58.

[4] "Memorandum of ILA in Support of Bill to Close the Longshoremen's Register and to transfer the Waterfront Commission's Hiring

State AFL-CIO endorsed the bill while the PNYA opposed it. The New York State Conference of the NAACP also opposed it, fearing racial discrimination.[5]

In May the NYSA, appearing to renege on its agreement of cooperation, opposed the Mackell bill, the one the ILA was promoting, characterizing it as a union bill. The NYSA held that it was an error for a single bill to provide for closing the register —which it favored—and for turning hiring over to joint union-management control—which it opposed. Although wanting to close the register, the NYSA did not want to limit the commission in any other way. With organized labor behind the bill, chances of passage looked good; yet, because of the NYSA stance, a major change was made. Instead of mandating labor and management hiring halls, the bill was changed to permit them through collective bargaining. With the change, the NYSA again endorsed the legislation, but Chopin made it clear that the NYSA, at the bargaining table, would vigorously oppose joint control over hiring. It is of interest, too, in view of the role he had just played in the industry and the role he would subsequently play, that Kheel publicly urged passage.[6]

On a first try the State Senate rejected it by a narrow vote, but the bill, following some bitter debate, was reintroduced, as was possible under New York legislative procedures, and was approved. The Assembly voted overwhelmingly for passage. Editorially, both the *New York Times* and the *New York Herald Tribune* thought it was "back to the dock rackets" and "back to the shape-up." When the bill reached Governor Rocke-

---

Centers to Joint Labor-Management Operation," April 27, 1968; Waterfront Commission, "Memorandum in Opposition to Senate Bill Intro. No. 3067, Print No. 3253 and to Assembly Bill Intro. No. 4922, Print No. 5083."

[5] N.Y. State AFL-CIO, "Memorandum—S.1. 3067—Mackell, A. I. 4922–Rice"; letter, PNYA to [Senate and Assembly Committees], March 30, 1965; letter, W. Eugene Sharpe, NAACP, dated May 18, 1965.

[6] *New York Times*, May 3, 1965, p. 57, May 17, p. 57, June 1, p. 62.

feller's desk, he vetoed it.[7] But this was not the end of the matter, for the GAI eligibility year had been set so as to begin the guarantee on April 1, 1966. Before that date another legislative session would convene and Senator Mackell promised to introduce a modified version of the bill the next year, and he did.

The 1966 legislative battle was, in part, an echo of the previous one, with the difference that matters on which the ILA and the NYSA held different views were placed in separate bills, while the commission itself introduced a bill to empower it to close the register whenever it thought it was needed, designed, in part, "to remove any impediment to an orderly transition to the new work rules." In fact, the commission had held meetings in the latter part of 1965 with the NYSA and the ILA to implement hiring procedures and to achieve workable understandings about proposed legislation.[8] These did not weaken the ILA's fight against the commission, however. Gleason and Scotto warned that there would be trouble on April 1, when the GAI was to commence and two men were to be removed from each gang, if the commission did not accede to the closing of the register. In fact, Gleason said, "I will not allow the Waterfront Commission to say how many men will work and when they will work. Furthermore, if there is a strike I will lead it." Scotto added, "If any new men are permitted to come into the industry in violation of our collective agreement, we will have a work stoppage on April 1."[9]

The NYSA and the ILA, of course, had been working through their newly created HRIC to effectuate understandings needed to implement the guarantee. They agreed on plans designed to overcome the reluctance or refusal of longshoremen to take employment outside of their local areas or jobs customarily shunned. A typical disciplinary procedure with a schedule of

[7] *New York Times*, June 2, 1965, p. 61, June 10, p. 57, June 16, p. 70, June 25, p. 54.

[8] Letter, Louis Waldman to William P. Sirignano, Dec. 28, 1965.

[9] *New York Times*, Dec. 20, 1965, p. 69, Jan. 23, 1966, p. 61, Feb. 25, p. 50.

penalties for nonperformance, running from warnings to layoffs, and possibly ultimate discharge, were agreed to. In addition, they agreed on several other matters, such as a new type of seniority card to facilitate administration of the guarantee and to place union delegates in the hiring centers to observe hiring under the guarantee.[10]

An important unresolved issue between them was submitted to Kheel, the special arbitrator of disputes under the GAI. They held different notions of the meaning of the word "qualified" in the clause that a man had to make himself available and accept "work for which he is qualified" or be debited on his guarantee. The nature of this obligation bothered longshoremen, particularly the older ones. At the time of voting on the settlement, the question was raised, "What do you mean by qualified?" Gleason's answer, in the leaflet circulated in the effort to get them to reverse the vote, was, "You are required to do only the specific type of work you normally do; for example, if you are a deckman, you'll be required to take only a job as a deckman." The leaflet had been submitted to the NYSA before it was distributed and, while the NYSA neither approved nor disapproved, Gleason took the position in arbitration that silence amounted to consent. The ILA contended, therefore, that a man, to protect his guarantee, had to accept work only in his classification, although he was free, if he chose, to accept other work. The NYSA insisted that a man was required to accept any work he was capable of performing or lose the guarantee for the day. Kheel, aware that the parties had discussed the meaning of "qualified" at great length in negotiations, and had left definition in the hands of the HRIC, concluded that the contract could not be amended "by a leaflet unilaterally distributed." He thought that employees who had accepted various types of work in the past were not justified in insisting on working only in their own classification. On the other hand, he did not feel that employers achieved the right to make any assignments whatsoever

[10] *New York Times,* Oct. 18, 1965, p. 62.

without regard to a man's past work experience. Consequently, he ruled that employees could not reject work of the types previously accepted and employers could not demand more.[11]

Meanwhile, the legislative battle over the register took a new turn. The commission's bill was sent to the legislature by Governor Rockefeller. It had been drafted in consultation with the governors of both New York and New Jersey, with the PNYA and others. The commission introduced other bills, too. It had informed the parties of its bill on closing the register. It had said nothing at all about the other bills: bills to broaden coverage of the Bi-State Compact, to give the commission authority to set standards of proficiency for longshoremen and checkers and seek funds from any governmental agency—including the federal government—for establishment of vocational training, and to authorize the commission to set standards of physical and mental fitness. These other bills made both the ILA and the NYSA angry.

The ILA called for a one-day strike for March 15 to demonstrate legislative support for the bill to close the register—a matter on which there was a great deal of rank-and-file support. Scotto said, "We will stage a massive all day demonstration to prove to Governor Nelson A. Rockefeller and to every Assemblyman and Senator that the ILA rank-and-file has unanimous labor support in its efforts to democratize the Waterfront Commission." They got a delegation to travel to Albany; Paul Hall joined the demonstration and, along with others, attacked Governor Rockefeller for supporting the commission, charging him with showing disrespect for dock workers. The commission reported, however, that 16,195 men worked on the piers on March 15 and said there was "not even a slowdown."[12]

When Kheel publicly supported the ILA's legislation, Joseph

[11] NYSA-ILA, "In the matter of arbitration between International Longshoremen's Association and New York Shipping Association"; see NYSA, Report No. 2434, March 10, 1966; *New York Times*, March 6, 1966, p. 19.

[12] *New York Times*, March 9, 1966, p. 65, March 16, p. 72.

Kaitz, New York Waterfront Commissioner, challenged him to cite a single instance of an improvement or reform in the ILA in which the union had moved "without prodding by the Waterfront Commission." He even attacked Kheel's role in settlement of the dispute which had resulted in establishment of the GAI, saying that Reynolds and Healy had spent several hours in acquainting themselves with the commission, whereas "Kheel did not spend a minute of time with us." Implying conflict of interest he derided Kheel for lobbying for the legislative proposal "despite the fact that he [was] named in the NYSA-ILA contract as an arbitrator." He challenged Kheel's criticism of the commission for promoting legislation and wanted to know why the commission should not be permitted to lobby: "It is the place of government to inform the legislators of its position" and defend "the public interest." He accused Kheel with not having done his homework and asked "who is going to watch" the ILA "to see that the workforce is not cut below the legitimate needs of the port," citing the experience under seniority as evidence of lack of responsibility on the part of the ILA, because "true seniority was never honored, and favored workers and relatives were given assignments ahead of senior men."[13]

While the legislative battle was at its height, Kheel again spoke out in favor of closing the register, echoing the refrain that there was a real possibility of trouble among longshoremen on April 1. He expressed concern about whether the governor or the legislature were "fully aware of the extent that the closing of the register [was] necessary psychologically and contractually to bring the new system into effect," and argued that there were ample reasons inherent in the longshore industry for both management and labor to maintain a work force neither too large nor too small, whereas, "The Commission is taking a 'big brother' approach to the problem, and perhaps it is unkind to say that it is interested in its own job security, but it is hard to avoid that conclusion."[14]

[13] *New York Times*, March 13, 1966, p. 88.
[14] *New York Times*, March 21, 1966, p. 53M.

The give-and-take of the legislative process produced a deftly worked-out compromise, which was written into Governor Rockefeller's bill, leaving the commission in control of the register but permitting the NYSA and the ILA jointly to request opening or closing, depending upon work force needs, that is, on the basis of a factual showing and public hearing. With the compromise, the bill unanimously passed the Senate and the register was closed.[15]

The GAI and the Seniority System

Implementation of the GAI was the most important development in 1966. In addition to all the understandings and rules worked out by the HRIC, and the arbitration decision, there were many problems related to the mechanics of administration. This was largely, but not exclusively, an assignment falling on the NYSA. It had the task of policing the GAI and making sure that each eligible worker was properly credited with hours worked and debited for absenteeism or refusal to take jobs. Existing methods of reporting data to the Central Records Bureau would not suffice, so it installed computers for recording information and for facilitating assignment of employees.

The GAI could not have been introduced had not the seniority system been developed previously, even with its imperfections. The parties were committed to improve the system, but did not. Also, the GAI could not have been administered without the computer. It had to be programmed to give instantaneous informational retrieval on each individual employed. The computer held the data about each member of the work force in its memory bank, comprised of the information on the revised seniority card—name, status, pier including list position, section, and social security and waterfront numbers.[16]

The computer had to be programmed, also, to record daily

[15] *New York Times*, March 19, 1966, p. 58, March 25, p. 20, March 31, p. 65M; *Longshore News*, March 1966, p. 1.

[16] The data in the Central Records Bureau had to be checked for 23,000 men, a monumental job.

hiring orders of employers, worker acceptance of such orders, physical presence of men at the hiring centers—including a check as to whether they had already been hired on their own pier— acceptance of work, and failure to obtain work. Since the computer could also facilitate the hiring process and enhance mobility of the men, the program of hiring had to be pro- grammed—done actually in conjunction with the commission— around the priorities in the seniority system. This was a monu- mental task.

A "Real-Time-On-Line Electronic Data Processing System" was set up in the office of the NYSA, to be the nerve center of the program. It was comprised of two IBM System 360, Model G-40 computers. Locked in these duplexed computers was a com- plete file of all men by gangs and various dock labor lists. By using leased telephone wires, the computers were connected with fifty-six input and output units located in the thirteen hiring centers maintained by the Waterfront Commission.

The GAI was launched with some difficulties, but the pro- tests, which led to "wildcat" strikes, were over changes in work rules, particularly with respect to assignments of men in gangs. The reduction of two men from the dock complement led to the most serious problem. The men were resigned to the reduc- tion; what bothered many of them was the possibility of changes in customs and practices, that is, the usual ways of doing things to which they were accustomed. The first week saw several spot work stoppages. It appeared that 10 per cent of the men either did not understand or were defying the new rules. A special meeting of the LRC voted to order the men back to work and Turkus, the arbitrator, ordered an end to the walkout. Just when the "wildcat" strikes seemed to be fading, more broke out and an injunction was obtained, whereupon the ILA asked un- successfully for reconsideration of the rules.[17] At first no one had known precisely what the trouble was, but it soon became obvious that it was more than that a few men did not understand

[17] *New York Times*, April 3, 1966, p. 1, April 8, p. 46M, April 14, p. 66M.

the agreement. In fact, the employers had not prepared themselves for the problem beyond the problem of the reduction of two men.

It will be recalled that the employers had made a big case for reduction of one man from the deck, because they claimed that he was never needed. The normal distribution of the twenty-man gang was eight on dock, four on deck, and eight in the hold. The employers would have started the reduction in the size of the gang by first removing the fourth man from the deck and one from the dock. The union had had different notions, and Gleason had told them as early as April 1965 how the agreed-upon reduction of three men in the gang—two men on April 1, 1966 and one man on October 1, 1966—would take place. The first two would be from the dock complement. It was thereafter generally understood that the general cargo gang was first to be reduced by removing two from the dock complement. Hence the men did understand the agreement; it was the application of it in some areas that caused trouble, and perhaps had all employers removed the two dock men to implement the agreement, the "wildcat" strikes would have been more like a portwide strike. All the employers did not act in the same way, because the fact was that on discharging operations a reduction of two men from the dock complement was no saving at all, for the necessary sorting required more men in the dock complement than was usually the case while cargo was being stowed. Hence, reducing the dock complement by two was not a saving of two men all the time, not even half the time, because extra men were sometimes hired. To some employers the reduction was not worth the trouble, and others had decided to delay and see.

The troubles arose in those parts of the port—generally not in Manhattan but prominently in Brooklyn and Port Newark—where union leaders had, for some years, permitted the transference of four men from the dock to the hold while loading palletized cargo, leaving only four on the dock. In these areas when two men from the dock complement were eliminated, some employers attempted, while working on palletized cargo, to transfer four men to the hold as they had been doing, leaving only two on the dock. The men and the union took the position that four men had to be left on the dock.

A "powder-keg" condition developed because employers differed in their approaches to this problem. Following the termination of the "wildcat" strikes, slowdowns on the part of some men took place, and there appeared, to the employers at least, deliberate efforts on the part of some leaders in the union to abrogate the agreement. No doubt the employer who said, "It is the biggest mess since I have been on the waterfront," was near to being right. Scotto charged that "everyone knows that four men are used on the dock everywhere in the Port." But employers charged the ILA with blocking compliance. One said, "This contract may be more revolutionary than we thought," as one after another employer surrendered and resumed use of at least four men on the dock. Another added, "If this keeps up, the union gains will remain and the *quid pro quo* will flow down the river and out to sea." Admiral George Wauchope, of the Farrell Lines, said ruefully, "We were the last holdout [but] someone had to stand up and protest this outrageous situation." The issue led to acrimonious arbitration. There was even a bitter controversy over who was to arbitrate, that is, whether it was a matter falling under the HRIC or the LRC. They went to court and got a decision that it was an LRC matter.[18] The arbitrator, therefore, was Turkus rather than Kheel.

The arbitration would be of more interest had the employers not capitulated before the hearing commenced. Turkus chastized both, the employers for trying to force a rigid universal rule where their only right to reduce the dock complement was "when the operation permits it" and the men for resorting to self-help rather than the grievance machinery. He upheld neither and gave the parties guidelines for future settlements. But, as has

[18] *New York Times,* April 15, 1966, p. 66, May 3, p. 55, May 5, p. 94, May 6, p. 94, May 7, p. 63.

been noted, the union had won its case at the docks and it was not likely that employers would try to assign less than four men on the dock under any circumstance.[19]

Computer Hiring

Hiring by utilizing the computer became a reality on April 1, 1966. The new ordering program can be briefly described.[20] Between 2:00 and 3:00 P.M. on a weekday, the company hiring agents appeared at the hiring centers and ordered their regular employees, that is, their gangs and the men from their various dock lists for the next day's work. Each hiring agent had IBM port-a-punch cards, one for each gang and one for each longshore group of twenty-five men or less, that is dock labor, drivers, checkers, carpenters, coopers, or maintenance employees. The cards contained the ordering information and were fed, via the input devices at the centers, into the computer by the hiring agent who had inserted his own special identification card. By the insertion of the identification card and the gang or dock lists, the men were automatically hired, and the computer stored this information. If gangs in addition to those on the employer's own pier were desired, they could be hired after this first phase of the hiring was completed. It was intended for the computer to supply lists of available gangs in the boroughs; but although it printed them out at the rate of twelve gangs per minute, these gang lists usually were not very realistic, for the reason that in the hour up to 3:00 P.M., the hiring agents who were anxious to hire particular gangs resorted to use of the telephone to secure gangs from other piers; this practice had developed under the Waterfront Commission before the introduction of the computer.

When additional gangs were selected, the hiring was con-

[19] NYSA-ILA, "In the matter of arbitration between the NYSA and the ILA," LRC Report No. 156, July 11, 1966; *New York Times,* July 15, 1966, p. 50.

[20] For a more detailed description, see the author's "Computer Hiring of Dock Workers in the Port of New York," *Industrial and Labor Relations Review,* vol. 20, April 1967, pp. 425ff.

summated when the hiring agent inserted a gang-order card supplied by the center manager into the computer, which recorded the hiring. At the completion of gang ordering, the hiring agents then turned to the task of assuring that extra men who had been hired previously, who were currently at work and whom it was desired to retain, were continued in employment. Their engagement could be extended by the insertion into the input unit of their seniority cards, which the hiring agent still held. (If an individual who had been working as a casual did not want to continue in the employment, he asked for his seniority card after the lunch break.) As the hiring agent inserted the seniority cards into the input unit, the computer checked to determine if the men had been ordered back to their own piers by their primary employers in the earlier phase of hiring. The computer notified the hiring agent which of them, if any, were not available for another day or else recorded them as continuing in employment. At that time it was not possible to hire additional individuals for casual employment for the next day, but experience showed that 90 per cent of the men at work on a given day had received their orders the day before. (It would be a few years before prior-day-ordering of casuals would be effectuated.)

The next activity in the hiring process—the so-called casual hiring—occurred the following morning at the hiring centers, when men were hired to fill in for those who were absent or to supplement those hired the day before. The men who appeared at the hiring centers on any day were individuals who had no assignment for the day from their regular employers, plus men who had not been established in a gang or on a pier list, usually men with low seniority who had only recently come to the labor market. There were, however, always a good number of high seniority men from the section available, particularly if they anticipated a good employment opportunity. They usually were not willing to accept any employment whatsoever and could pass up employment that was not to their liking. Also, many of these men were unwilling to travel to other sections.

Men who were eligible for the GAI had to report for employment at their own hiring centers or suffer debits to their guarantees. (Some men resented this requirement to report to their home hiring center, because they had always gone where the work opportunities looked best.) As the men arrived at the hiring centers, they "badged in," and the information on the seniority card was transmitted to the computer, which made an instantaneous check to determine whether or not the man already had been given orders and was expected at some pier. If he had been given orders, a message was printed in red, telling the man where he should be and making him ineligible, technically, for hiring at that time at the center. In spite of prior orders some hiring agents would hire such men because they liked to employ men whom they could see. Nothing was done to prevent such hiring if it conformed to seniority steps.

Practice varied, because men started "badging in" at some centers as early as 7:30 A.M., whereas in other centers the local union would not let them do so until 7:55 A.M. The early "badging in" occurred in those hiring centers where employment opportunities were meager. Many of the men attached to these centers went immediately to other centers where they knew hiring that day would be heavy. In doing so, they ran the risk of getting a debit in case they were not hired, because they would be counted as unavailable in their home centers at the conclusion of the hiring process. But the risk was offset by the fact that a hiring agent would take them on if hiring reached down to their seniority status, because he would rather employ a man standing in front of him who was relatively near the pier where he was to go to work, than to hire impersonally through the computer.

In casual hiring, foremen selected men in accordance with the seniority-priority system. When an individual was chosen the hiring foreman handed him a slip containing his assignment. In turn, the worker surrendered his seniority card and the "okay" slip he obtained from the output unit and proceeded to the pier to check in.[21] When the hiring agent had completed his selections, he inserted his own identification card into the input unit and fed in the seniority cards of the men hired in order to record their employment. The computer simultaneously stored the knowledge that they were no longer available for employment, which was important for the next stage in the process—intercenter or borough hiring. When a man checked in with the timekeeper at the pier, he surrendered his assignment slip. His seniority card was retained by the hiring foreman until the end of the day or until the employment stint terminated.

If all the men available at a center were hired, and the hiring agents there still needed men, a listing was requested of the men available in adjacent centers. This feature of the program was designed to increase the mobility of the men. The computer printed out the lists, by seniority classifications, but the lists left something to be desired. It was intended that hiring agents would select men from the lists, entering manually into the input unit the identification numbers of the men employed; following which the computer would send the information to the center where the man was based, and the output unit there would print and issue a job ticket, which was delivered to the man who was to go to the pier as directed and check in. The problem in utilization of the lists of casuals in intercenter hiring was one of availability. Although "badged in," a man might have left if he did not get employment in his section, not caring about the debit of his guarantee.

Another problem with intercenter, or intersectional, hiring was a bottleneck. Intercenter hiring followed sectional hiring and was programmed to begin only when all sections had completed their hiring. This caused both the hiring agents and the

---

[21] For some time the Waterfront Commission had the men check past its counter before leaving for their work and kept a second set of records just as it had always done. It did not eliminate its validation procedure until it was satisfied that the data produced by the computer were reliable.

men in other centers to stand around idly until the last hiring center had completed sectional hiring. The man who eventually got hired did not mind, because he got paid from 8:00 A.M. on, but the employers were unhappy, and the men who did not get hired complained not only because they did not get employment, but also because of the long wait imposed upon them.

At the completion of intercenter hiring, the manager of each center inserted into the input unit information about the level of seniority reached in the hiring. The identity of the men who shaped and refused work, as well as those who reported, but were not hired, was then determined by the computer. The latter, of course, got credit for reporting, whereas those whose seniority was greater than the seniority of the last man hired had their guarantee debited, because they obviously had passed up employment offered.

The casual hiring procedure was repeated again at 1:00 P.M. each week day. The computer maintained weekly activity files on each individual. A record of all orders given him and information about his reporting for the shape-up, or failure to do so, were included in each individual's file. Payroll information received from employers, showing hours worked each day, was given to the computer, and information about his working time was placed in the file of the individual, thus completing his employment and shape-up history. Each week every worker's record was cumulated, showing all hours worked and all hours debited to date.

At the completion of each quarter, each man's vacation, holiday, and unemployment compensation payments were included in his record.[22] The quarterly record determined whether an individual was entitled to a payment under the guarantee.

In granting the guarantee of annual income, the employers not only expected great flexibility in deployment of men and the

[22] An arrangement was worked out with the unemployment insurance agencies of New York and New Jersey so that information on unemployment compensation was obtained and entered into the computer, and the two state bureaus were supplied with unemployment information.

elimination of certain work rules or practices, but they also hoped for greater mobility in the work force. Mobility, however, was not increased with the use of the computer. The debits to the guarantee of annual income did not have sufficient impact to overcome the reluctance of many men to accept work away from their own sections or piers. This reluctance to "travel," as it was called, was one of the most pervasive attitudes found on the waterfront among the older and well-established longshoremen and was of long standing. It was characteristic both of gangs and individuals.

A negative kind of mobility was observable in some sections when men defected from their gangs in order to take more attractive assignments elsewhere, or to avoid cargo whose handling was distasteful. The commission did not police the computer system, and it was not illegal for a bona fide longshoreman to be selected by a hiring agent. It would have been up to an employer, the NYSA, or the ILA to prevent such practices. Also, men sometimes defected from gang assignments when they knew that the assignment of the gang would last for only four hours.

The Labor Force and Seniority

As the GAI went into effect, hiring priorities created continuing problems and controversy. Strange as it must seem, in view of the long and bitter battle to get the register closed and the claims that the commission was inundating the waterfront with newcomers, within four months Gleason joined Chopin in asking the commission to open the register, because there were serious shortages of men in some sections of the port. Perhaps to set a procedural precedent but also, perhaps, to make the ILA eat its words, the commission asked for a factual showing of the need. The parties came back with a request that 2,066 men be added, saying shortages were "disastrous" and "damaging" to the port. The commission held a hearing on August 18, then set August 30 as the date for receipt of applications. Because a large number might apply, the National Guard Armory was used. Applications were received from 2,598, and approximately 1,600 were added to the register subsequently.[23]

It will be recalled that the NYSA and the ILA had agreed between themselves to give physical examinations to all new longshoremen and, as a part of the running battle to get the register closed, had suspended giving them in April 1965. Of course, the commission had not discontinued registrations and if a man was able to get sufficient employment not to be discouraged or decasualized, he was a member of the work force. Neither the "1966" entrants or the others carried seniority.

The question of strengthening portwide seniority was brought to the fore, following negotiations in 1965, by those whose employment was falling off or was threatened by changing patterns of work, but the opposing interests were stronger. Yet, supplemental agreements were finally worked out and recognition of new seniority classifications were made. It will be recalled that a "D" category had been in effect for some time, the lowest rung in the longshore seniority system. With the opening of the register, the parties gave seniority to the men who earlier had been given physical examinations above those who had simply been registered by the commission and those who were entering the work force. The upshot—even though the terms of the supplemental agreements were not put to a rank-and-file vote, although they probably would have been accepted—was recognition of "medical" and "1966" seniority, but, of more significance, perhaps, was injection of "borough seniority" above portwide seniority. Also, all the "medical" men were assigned to sections. The "1966" men were assigned only to boroughs.

The order of hiring longshoremen thereafter beyond pier-level hiring was as follows, although the hiring was done through the dozen commission centers:

[23] *New York Times*, July 18, 1966, p. 41M, Aug. 12, p. 50, Aug. 22, p. 54M, Sept. 3, p. 37M, Sept. 11, p. 88; Waterfront Commission, *Annual Report of the Waterfront Commission of New York Harbor, 1965–66*, pp. 14–15.

Manhattan
> A, B, C, D, medical in the section
> A, B, C, D, medical in the borough
> 1966 Manhattan
> A, B, C, D, medical in the port
> 1966 portwide

Brooklyn
> A, B, C, D, in the section
> A, B, C, D, in the borough
> Section medical
> Borough medical
> 1966 Brooklyn
> A, B, C, D, medical in the port
> 1966 portwide

New Jersey
> A, B, C, D, medical, 1966 section in the section
> A, B, C, D, medical, 1966 borough in the borough
> A, B, C, D, medical in the port
> 1966 portwide

Staten Island
> A, B, C, D, medical in the section
> 1966 Staten Island
> A, B, C, D, medical in the port
> 1966 portwide

Checkers and other crafts had their own hiring sequences. The order for hiring of the most important group, the checkers, was portwide from the outset, although the actual hiring was done in only three centers. In 1966 it ran, A, B, C, D, E, F, "medical," and "1966" seniority.

The controversy about portwide seniority would not die. In fact, it was exacerbated by injection of borough priorities. It frequently came into the headlines late in 1966 and throughout 1967. An earlier agreement to overhaul the seniority system could not be fulfilled. The irony is the fact that the problem had been created, in large part, by some of the very ones then suffering. More farsighted ones in the union at the outset—

although one could be cynical and say "those whose economic interest lay in having broad seniority"—had urged portwide seniority. They had wanted to enhance the employment of their underemployed members. These were opposed by those who wanted to keep jobs in the section regardless of length of service. Employers had even urged that seniority be limited to the pier to keep administration simple. Provincial interests based on territorial considerations, as in Brooklyn, were the ones who promoted "borough seniority," a deterrent, even a barrier, to portwide employment.

The problem was made acute in 1966 and 1967 by the fact of technological change and the creation of new port facilities, which caused important geographical shifts in the cargo business, notable in the loss of employment in Manhattan and the rapid gain in Port Newark. For a time employment in Brooklyn remained stable. Brooklyn, shortsightedly as it turned out, thought that break-bulk cargo would continue in large volume and that it would retain its share of work—then about half in the port. "Medical" and "1966" classifications in conjunction with borough seniority put the problem of older seniority holders, in those areas of the port that were in decline, in bold relief. It caused dissension and problems that rocked the industry.

The checkers and clerks, having achieved a consolidated local before the appearance of seniority and for quite another reason, established portwide seniority from the outset and, unlike the longshoremen, added seniority classifications periodically. The type of problem confronting longshoremen did not plague them. Their seniority system made it easy for Gleason to come out, probably forced him to come out, for a portwide seniority system for longshoremen and put him in the role of defender of men who had put many years into longshore work.

In Manhattan, it was not just Local 856, at the lower end of the island, that carried the battle this time, as it had originally, but Local 791 also. The men in this local had pushed vigorously for narrow sectional seniority rights at the outset, but now that work was fading away, the security of many of them depended upon their ability to get work elsewhere. If they traveled to other boroughs they would find themselves standing and waiting for jobs while local youngsters got them. Nor was this limited to men from Manhattan, for, as Bayonne work boomed, men from Jersey City became angry when they had to give way to youngsters in the section.

It may seem ironic that the Waterfront Commission received a petition in December 1966 from longshoremen in Local 856, asking that it review and seek amendment of the seniority system in order to provide for portwide seniority. This was the first of a series. Similar petitions were given to Gleason, who said that if longshoremen could vote on the question "we would have portwide seniority." But Scotto and the young men in his local were opposed to it because they held priorities in employment over men from Manhattan, even over twenty- or thirty-year men. Scotto would be loyal to his own. The longshoremen were split between "have nots" and "haves"—mostly a division controlled by geography—but, seasoned longshoremen, largely in Manhattan, Staten Island, and Jersey City, were not happy.[24]

With regard to a cognate matter, the ILA in December 1966 asked management to renegotiate the contract in light of the rapid developments in the use of containers, but the employers would not. The issue was up again in a new form next May. The ILA became exercised over a belief that consolidation points, where workers other than longshoremen would do the work, were springing up. Gleason said, "We are going to stop it, and we aren't going to wait for the next contract negotiation." It was not an attack on pallets and containers coming fully loaded from the factory but on concentration or forwarding depots, where cargoes were being received and loaded into containers and then taken to the piers. Scotto said, "The ILA wants no compensation for lost work [meaning royalties] but the preservation of the work itself."[25]

[24] *New York Times*, Dec. 15, 1966, p. 86M, Jan. 3, 1967, p. 58M, June 9, p. 78M, June 15, p. 93C; *Local 824 Bulletin*, June 1967.

[25] *New York Times*, Dec. 8, 1966, p. 85M, May 15, 1967, p. 85.

The fight for leadership in the ILA was still on, although it had different dimensions. Gleason was too secure to be ousted, although Bradley again placed himself in contention and tried to pull Scotto to his side. The latter had had his own designs on the presidency until he convinced himself that he could not beat Gleason; and he did not want to tie in with Bradley. He had, as early as October 1966, started a course designed to lead to the presidency, when he bid for the support of the Negro membership, asserting that racial bias was hindering the organization. He proposed a biracial committee to draw up plans for total integration in every port. Citing the existence of black and white locals side by side, he said, "that guarantees mistrust, disunity and bitter competition for work." As the struggle shaped up in mid-1967, Scotto shifted to attack Gleason for holding two top offices, the presidencies of the International and of the Atlantic Coast District. Scotto decided to run for the presidency of the latter, although some thought he would change course and try for the executive vice-presidency held by Bowers. In any event, the close working harmony that had developed between Scotto and Bowers at the conclusion of the previous port negotiations had faded.[26]

Increasing unrest among high-seniority men, growing out of the "1966 Seniority Amendment," led the Waterfront Commission, in October, to file suit to test the validity of the amendment. Commission lawyers contended that it was illegal because it had never been voted upon by the membership. Many longshoremen, invited at some of the hiring centers to do so, signed affidavits to support the suit. Gleason was furious, charging "intrusion" into collective bargaining. When the commission obtained an injunction on October 10, temporarily barring hiring of "1966" men prior to hiring men with greater seniority from other sections, "1966" seniority men protested with walkouts. Another injunction against these protests was obtained. But as the walkout persisted in Port Newark, Governor Richard J. Hughes asked the commission to petition the court to lift the

[26] *New York Times*, Oct. 13, 1966, p. 78M, June 30, 1967, p. 61M, July 9, p. 62.

temporary injunction. Instead, the commission tried to appeal to the men with "1966" seniority, trying to convince them that they might "disagree with the Commission on seniority practices today" but added that the rule that changes in seniority had to be approved by the men "will help you in the future."[27]

Kheel's Arbitration on Debiting

The operation of the GAI meanwhile produced disputes that had to be submitted to arbitration, concerning computation of the guarantee and the application of the award Kheel had made in February. The matter of debiting under the guarantee was still in controversy.[28] In the new arbitration, Kheel reaffirmed the ruling in February by saying that "an employee who [had] accepted work from the hiring center in the past, prior to GAI, should within the meaning of [the] February 1966 award be expected to continue to accept such work." Of most importance in the new decision was the rejection of the method of debiting employed by the NYSA, that is, whenever hiring in a particular classification proceeded beyond a man's seniority group, whether "A," "B" or "C," he was debited on the theory that he had failed to accept work in the classification. If hiring in a classification reached to "B" men, for example, any "A" man in the classification who had "badged in" and was not employed was debited, because he must have refused work. This the union challenged. The ILA's position was that no longshoreman should be debited when the employers filled all their needs. Only in the event needs were not filled should debiting take place and then only to the extent of jobs remaining unfilled and, besides, in reverse order of seniority, starting with the last man to reject work.

Kheel rejected the NYSA method of debiting and accepted the ILA contentions, reasoning that the purpose of GAI was to

[27] *New York Times,* Oct. 5, 1967, p. 70M, Oct. 6, p. 69M, Oct. 11, p. 77M, Oct. 13, p. 77C, Oct. 14, p. 42M.
[28] NYSA-ILA, "In the matter of arbitration between International Longshoremen's Association and New York Shipping Association," Oct. 6, 1967; see NYSA, Report No. 2565, Oct. 9, 1967.

provide compensation to employees who did not obtain work because it was not offered. He also reasoned that the current practice of debiting a large number of men when only a few jobs were not filled did not conform with the purpose of the GAI, saying, "Under the method now employed by the NYSA, 100 employees could be debited for refusal to accept work when, in fact, there was only one or a few jobs available." Kheel held that debits should be limited to the number of jobs not filled. Accordingly, if the employment objectives of all employers were filled on a given day, even though numerous high-seniority men had passed up the opportunity to work, none were to be debited.

There was no more justification for holding, as Kheel did, that the purpose of the debiting was to assure that employers' needs were filled, than to hold that debiting was intended to deter men from rejecting employment under the penalty of loss if they did not accept it when offered. Kheel quoted the contract language and underlined this clause, "fails to accept such work for which he is qualified, as is offered on a portwide basis," and said, "While a literal reading of the above provision might at first blush appear to support the employers' position, it is obvious that the contract provision does not reach the issue raised by the ILA here—does the above provision apply where all the employer needs have been met?" Why it is obvious is not explained or justified. He simply said, "I do not believe that such a clause is operative unless and until there is a showing of shortages of men to fill available jobs." This is obviously a belief which the employers never held, for they could not be branded as stupid, and in providing for debits it was their obvious intent to minimize the cost of the guarantee. It is most significant, as will be seen from the consequences, that Kheel added, "This does not mean, of course, that the employees can arbitrarily or capriciously refuse to accept work in the hope that all of the work needs will be filled," gratuitously adding, "At all times there must be a vigilant effort to prevent any abuses. . . . And any such abuse, is of course, subject to the grievance and arbitration procedures of the contract." What he said did not mean exactly what it meant to many men, and they were not stupid either, and many arbitrarily refused to accept work, not just in the hope, but in the pretty sure gamble, that all work needs would be filled. Perhaps no decision was ever made which aided and abetted malingering to the extent that this decision did. Kheel must have known full well, too, that malingering was not amenable to check in the grievance machinery in this industry. The decision cost millions of dollars and instead of holding the employers to an obligation—one which they had never accepted—it gave many longshoremen with seniority an opportunity to collect their guarantee and work on another job.

Kheel's justification of the reverse order of debiting—limited to borough-wide pools, because the seniority agreement would have had to be changed to provide for portwide availability of men—is interesting, too. He reasoned that "a system of seniority is intended to protect the older and more senior men" and observed that the NYSA debiting made "it more likely that the less senior men [would] first receive the benefits of GAI payments." Therefore, he held that the least senior man be first debited, moving upward in reverse order and stopping debiting completely when the number of men debited was equal to the shortage.

A revealing interlude, reflecting a fundamental attitude prevalent in the ILA, occurred when Gleason, in speaking before the NMU convention, said that the ILA would like to work out a merger with Bridges' union on the West Coast: "If we can accomplish that, then we will have a nationwide longshore union," he said. Other ILA officials were violently opposed. Scotto said that a merger with Bridges' union was "utterly fantastic, autocratic and unconstitutional," while Bowers was "amazed" but, more cautiously, said, "I think he had in mind something about developing a uniform contract with uniform working conditions in the country. To talk of merger, however—that's the last thing in the world we would do."[29]

[29] *New York Times*, Oct. 5, 1966, p. 77, Oct. 6, p. 85M.

15 | Bargaining and the Container Revolution

The container revolution came on faster than most experts anticipated. Differences in adjustment among employers and between sections of the port altered relationships and created serious problems: the shifting geographical location of work affected the men and made sectional difference in the union more intense, and the employers, who already had old differences, were now divided between conventional and container operators.

A number of manpower problems were intertwined with the new demands and problems accompanying the growth of containerization: the presence of the Waterfront Commission; the seniority system and the amendment which placed borough seniority ahead of portwide seniority (and the refusal to reconsider and accept portwide seniority); the closed register and its reopening in 1966; contractual provisions protecting customs and practices; and, not least, the travel-time requirement. Politics in the union grounded in the self-service which autonomous units had long exploited and the politics among the employers made these issues even more complex. Add to these the pressures coming from groups outside but associated with the industry, like the PNYA, which had developed and promoted use of container facilities at Port Newark and the adjacent Port Elizabeth—just opened—and pressure from local communities and politicians who saw opportunities to ease local problems if certain arrangements on the docks could be achieved, one sees additional complexities. The problems emanating from this

342

mixture of things did not intermesh. They just existed side by side in a confused way, a solution to one making the others, or at least some of the others, even more difficult.

The Labor Shortage in Port Newark

Port Newark had long been the most important focal point of expansion in the industry, gaining as a result of its facilities— more modern and spacious, and adjacent to major highways— whereas Manhattan had long been in decline, and the rate was increasing.[1] With the opening of Port Elizabeth, the need for longshoremen in the area of Port Newark increased. The PNYA had induced employers to move operations to the area, and those converting to container operations were the most anxious to do so. Upon very short notice employers transferred operations from piers in Manhattan to the Newark-Elizabeth facilities.

The result was a shortage of gangs and men in Port Newark. With a closed register new men could not be brought into the industry, and the new surplus in Manhattan could not work in Port Newark for two reasons. First, the collective agreement had long provided for travel time and the employers in Port Newark did not want to pay it. Second, many of the men in Manhattan did not choose to travel. They hardly ever had traveled; and with GAI payments they were even less inclined to do so.

The PNYA, because of the huge investment in new facilities, became concerned when employers in Port Newark complained about shortages of men. The concern increased when some employers concluded that their rush to Port Newark was probably premature or ill advised and talked about moving away. Austin Tobin, executive director, publicly stated there were "widespread and alarming complaints" from employers demanding relief. He called upon the Waterfront Commission to open the register, enlisting the aid of both local and state politicians who saw the opportunity to absorb unemployed men through the creation of jobs for local men; Newark, at the time, had a very

[1] Port of New York Authority, *Metropolitan Transportation—1980* (New York, 1963), pp. 147ff.

high level of unemployment. Governor Hughes of New Jersey added his voice, asking the commission to hold a hearing to determine the labor needs and how best to meet them.[2]

Waterfront Commission Hearing on Labor Shortage

Since records of the commission had shown daily shortages in Port Newark for some time, it hardly needed a hearing to establish the facts, but the law required a hearing. Following the announcement, a great protest was made immediately by the NYSA and the ILA. The NYSA had become deeply concerned about the increasing cost of the GAI and saw an even larger burden if men were added to the work force while there were idle men in Manhattan. The ILA saw a move simply to avoid, or evade, travel-time payments. Gleason's refrain was, "We have enough men now," and he kept insisting that sectional imbalances in manpower could be adjusted if the employers "would stick to the contract." He explained, "This pressure for a reopening of the register is just the employers trying to buy mobility without paying for it." This was not the whole truth, for when employers in Port Newark on rare occasions ordered Manhattan gangs, they were confronted with the almost certain fact that the gangs would come shorthanded, decimated by the refusal of many men to travel. The employer then was required to go to the trouble of hiring fill-ins; this was costly in the time it took to get the fill-ins to the pier and functioning in the gang. Furthermore, the cost in delay in getting men to accept work and travel, plus the cost of travel-time pay, was no small thing.

With the prospect of an opening of the register before them, the LPC and officials of the ILA met in February to discuss the matter. Chopin's view was that they needed a simple method whereby men could go directly to where the work was available and that men should not hide behind the GAI. Reminding the ILA officials that they had said there would be no abuses of the GAI, he asserted that there was considerable evidence that some

[2] *New York Times*, Feb. 16, 1968, p. 74C; *Journal of Commerce*, Feb. 23, 1968, p. 1.

men were really abusing it. The employers earlier had responded favorably to the request of the ILA to allow men to "badge in" at any center without penalty against the GAI, but only then had they moved to effectuate it by setting a date of February 19 to implement it. But this was only a partial solution, at best, simply facilitating hiring of fill-ins with men willing to travel to the center where they expected employment. Gleason said the union did not want shortages but it wanted the contract observed. With some anger he said that if the union was not called in when companies made agreements with the PNYA to place work in Port Newark and Port Elizabeth, the union could not be held responsible for inadequate manpower. Furthermore, he emphasized to the employers that they had the right to give prior-day orders for gangs throughout the port but that they were refusing to call gangs to Newark because they did not want to pay travel time, something the union insisted on preserving. Gleason argued, too, that payment of travel time would be less than cost of the GAI. Whether true or not, the cost of the GAI was a charge on the whole industry, while the payment of travel time was only a cost to the employer calling for the labor. The NYSA as a group was concerned more with the former than the latter, and Chopin emphasized that gangs in Manhattan actually refused orders to go to Port Newark, and said, "We can't force them." Gleason insisted, however, that the complaining employers in Port Newark live up to the contract. He added, "We will do nothing to hurt companies that are honest," meaning the conventional operators. Gleason took the occasion to remind the LPC that during previous negotiations he had asked the NYSA to cooperate in giving the ILA control of the hiring halls and said, "I honestly believe it would have saved companies millions of dollars, but you chose not to join us. I can't understand why." Another ILA leader added, "Give the hiring halls back to the ILA and we can cure your troubles."

Regarding this broader issue, some employers had long concluded that the commission had cost the industry much more than the annual assessment. One forthrightly said, "I am 100 per cent in accord with turning the hiring back to the ILA and giving the gang foreman the right to fill in his own gangs," adding, "There are people in this industry deliberately wearing blinders about the commission, who refuse to consider the real cost versus the assessment. It is as one to ten, because of the delays in getting manpower to the docks, not to mention the shortages." Others, not willing to go so far as to put the ILA back in control of hiring, wanted the commission "to remove some of the 'handcuffs' to mobility of the work force and allow the hatch boss to fill out his gang prior to the shape." This was not a new notion. Repeatedly, some employers had urged the commission to establish the "gang carrier" system, which had been used in some parts of the port in the past—and such as was in existence in the Port of Baltimore—where the hatch boss brought a full gang to the pier. The commission had always taken the position that this would be a reversion to the open shape-up. Yet not all employers agreed that the commission's control of hiring should be abolished, although the sentiment for it had increased; almost all would have preserved the policing and investigative functions, yet many would have liked to get it out of hiring. Probably most members of the LPC blamed employers who had moved for the situation in Port Newark, because, as one put it, "they made decisions to move, with full knowledge of the existing labor shortages"; that the problems existed before they decided to move was evidenced by the controversy over portwide seniority.

The commission would not be dissuaded from its plans to hold a hearing. Probably because he had assumed leadership to have the register opened, Tobin testified at the outset. He agreed with the preliminary findings of the Waterfront Commission that there was an urgent need for hundreds of additional workers, and he contended that the law required opening of the register whenever the number of eligible longshoremen fell below those needed. He cited excerpts from letters submitted by shipping companies, agents, and stevedores in Port Newark, including some important ones in the NYSA. He said that one thousand new jobs were going unfilled, calculated to represent an additional payroll of $7,500,000, "available to many who are now unemployed." He noted that the shipping companies were willing to employ the men; that the Port Authority had provided the physical facilities; that men were available locally; that new ships had been built and importers and exporters were anxious to move their cargoes through the new, modern, efficient docks. Emphasizing that neither the ILA nor the NYSA had come forward with any constructive solution, "It would be a calamity," he said, "to lose the opportunity to use the new facilities because of the lack of men barred from jobs by the closed register."[3]

The next witness, Jesse Langston, director of the Waterfront Commission's Employment Information Centers Division, introduced statistics and charts to show the extent of shortages which had risen very rapidly during the latter part of 1967 and through January and February of 1968. His facts were based on the actual figures of shortages reported by hiring agents, but shortages reported by hiring agents were always understated for the reason that hiring agents made their plans on the basis of the gangs they expected to get, not on what were needed. He explained: if forty gangs were desired but the hiring agent, because of his knowledge of general availability of gangs, expected to get only thirty, he would go to the center to get thirty. Perhaps he would not get thirty, but only twenty-seven. The next morning he would be at the center to hire fill-ins, not for the forty gangs he would have taken, not for the thirty he had expected to take, but the number needed in connection with the twenty-seven he got. If he failed to meet his needs on this limited basis, this would be the shortage reported. Langston also explained that if a hiring agent could not get enough checkers to check the merchandise, he would not need terminal labor or

[3] Waterfront Commission, "Public Hearing to Determine Whether Applications for Inclusion in the Longshoremen's Register Should be Accepted," Feb. 20, 21, 1968, pp. 10–42; *New York Times,* Feb. 16, 1968, p. 74C, Feb. 21, p. 94C, Feb. 22, p. 62C.

drivers he would have hired. Hence, his visible need was set by his expectation of fulfillment, not by the number he might have taken.

Waldman tried to undercut Langston's testimony by asking him if he had any statistics on unemployment, or surpluses, on a portwide basis. Langston continued and did not neglect the matter of portwide surpluses or the fact that men were not being hired in all areas. He pointed out that over five hundred men a day who sought work in other parts of the port, but who did not receive employment, were given show-up cards. But he observed also that the men were not obligated to travel from one borough to another in order to be eligible for a show-up card; they were only required to travel within their own borough. Hence, there could be shortages in Jersey or Brooklyn while a Manhattan man could get a show-up card in Manhattan. He noted that show-up cards in 1967 never fell below 13,429 monthly and reached as high as 26,093 in July. He was asked how it was that there might be shortages in one area and show-up cards given in the same area. He explained that men were required only to accept work in their classifications; also that there was a difference in employment levels from Monday through Friday, that is, that numerous show-up cards could be issued on Mondays and Tuesdays, but there could be weekly shortages of workers, because on Thursday or Friday employment needs were high. Hence, show-up cards did not necessarily measure surpluses available for shortage areas.[4]

One of the most interesting witnesses was a rank-and-file dockworker from Manhattan. He first observed that in order to shape in Port Newark he had to take the bus from Manhattan, adding, "Many longshoremen in New York hiring halls refuse to gamble in coming out to Port Newark as they are on the guaranteed annual wage, and if they shape . . . [and] they don't get hired, they lose a day's pay, as well as they are off the guarantee for that particular day"; they would also have the expense. "I would suggest that a longshoreman in the industry

[4] Waterfront Commission, "Public Hearing," pp. 43ff.

should be able to go to any hiring center to get a day's work. It's better than getting the guarantee." (But we have just noted that the employers were now prepared to permit it.) He noted that when they arrived they were confronted with the fact that "the only ones considered for the jobs . . . are Jersey men and the New York men are not recognized in the present setup." (This, of course, was criticism of the seniority system as it then functioned.) Frankly, he said, "We have many men that . . . would be willing to throw away the guarantee" if things were changed; and he pointed to employers who were present and said that they would vouch for his willingness to work. Then he went on, candidly saying, "The Waterfront Commission is responsible for it as well as the shippers and the union. Three of yous' are three years talking about these things, statistics. Why don't you find out the reason why this work isn't produced," adding, "I am not knocking anybody in particular. I think the whole three of you are to blame. I don't want to lose my pass [registration]. I've got 25 years or better in. [Yet] You can have the pass. I ain't doing nothing with it," meaning he was not able to get work. Commissioner Steven J. Bercik asked him if he really meant to blame the commission. He answered, "Certainly, I blame the Commission. You fellows are supervising these things. I can't be blamed for it. I want to work. You are stopping me from working. If I had the open shape, Tommy Maher [an employer] would hire me. You stopped him from hiring me. I can't shape outside in the streets like I used to. He can't hire me. He's got to hire somebody from this section so I can't go to work. Whose fault is it? There is no public loaders permitted on the pier. You've done away with my job. I can't load trucks no more like I used to. You got honesty, but no public loading. You got the -66 and -68 [meaning the previous entrants and the expected newcomers]. You've got everything you want and you have the politicians [the local ones favoring opening of the register] coming over here and want to give you more headaches, more new men who don't want to work [referring to men with "1966" seniority who were then creating a problem by rejecting work in the hold], just to take them off the relief rolls. All right, go ahead. I just wish that there's some money left for my pension. When you guys get finished with it, there may not be any." He insisted that men were willing to transfer from New York, that is, from Manhattan to Port Newark, "but job vacancies are not being posted in the hiring halls [that is, vacancies in gangs or on pier lists] like they were two years previously." He insisted that men would transfer "instead of getting the guarantee, which is worse than relief because the guys have to wait three months for it." He concluded, "I wish you fellows would get started and give us a chance to go to work steady. I don't want to travel. I want to move out here [Newark area]. I want to be a part of the whole setup."[5]

Chopin and Gleason each testified at length. Their testimony is significant and revealing when placed in juxtaposition with the total scene. The LPC had met, and the position of the NYSA was that opening of the register would have catastrophic consequences, in spite of manpower shortages in Port Newark, because the real issue was whether a portwide need existed. Chopin asked, "Can there be such a need . . . [with] fewer jobs in the port than there are men to fill them?" The task was to make the experienced men available on a reasonable and economical basis, not to add more men. To show how a current opening of the register would be in conflict with the purpose of the law, he recited standards in the Bi-State Compact which provided for regularization of work, balancing of supply and demand portwide, mobility, and full utilization of technological change. Insisting that the Waterfront Commission was required by law to consider all these things and to protect the existing work force and the needs of all the employers, he claimed that it was not proper to consider sectional interests without regard to the whole. He pointed out that there was simply a transfer of jobs to Port Newark. It was not new work.

[5] *Ibid.*, pp. 190–195.

He knew that it was the sectional priority system under seniority that was a major factor restricting mobility and full utilization of the work force and implied that this cause would be removed inasmuch as the NYSA and the ILA were then negotiating on "the establishment of portwide seniority, which would permit the industry to institute an effective . . . prior-day ordering system, unfettered by the present restrictive seniority hiring practices"; but he said he greatly feared that reopening of the register at that particular time would adversely affect the negotiations. His primary concern, of course, was the impact on the industry's liability for payment of the GAI. He warned, "You are only going to put more men in receipt of guarantees if you flood the port with additional men at this time."

Chopin took the opportunity to complain that the commission had prohibited use of a "gang carrier" system and dual licensing of longshoremen as checkers to ease that shortage. Each of these, although addressed to the total port, he implied, would help the situation in Port Newark. What Chopin drove at was that a reopened register without changes in regulations and without a negotiated agreement between the NYSA and the ILA would not only offer little relief but also create additional problems. He wanted the commission to defer to the negotiations because, until sectional restrictions were removed, they would continue to be plagued with shortages in one area in the face of surplus in others. He insisted that means other than reopening of the register had to be developed and he urgently requested that tripartite meetings be convened to work out changes in the hiring regulations. In parting, he challenged Tobin's quotation that steamship lines favored the opening of the register; "Please, believe me, gentlemen, these companies do not favor opening the register."[6]

Gleason, saying, "I am not dedicated to sell any jobs down the river for the men," contended that to reopen the register was

[6] Ibid., pp. 199–238; cf. Journal of Commerce, Feb. 23, 1968, p. 1.

not only unnecessary, but would be "destructive of the rights of ILA members throughout the port [and] of the benefits and working conditions which are established in our collective bargaining agreements." He insisted, supporting Chopin, that the basic economic fact was an oversupply of labor, saying that work opportunities portwide were shrinking, not expanding. He did not deny that Port Newark was experiencing shortages, but he was pointed in saying this was due to the fact that several companies had recently moved their operations there, "without adequate cooperation or notice to the working force." He insisted that the port was a single port, not a series of ports, and that it had been so recognized by the NLRB, by the Bi-State Compact, which itself treated the port as an entity, and by the collective bargaining agreements. The pressure to reopen the register, he insisted, was only an attempt by "a few employers to make a fast buck at the expense of the veteran longshoremen who need work . . . an attempt to deprive working men, who have devoted their lives to this industry, of the benefits which their collective bargaining agreements provide . . . a maneuver . . . unworthy of serious consideration." Employers were free to hire from one part of the port for work in another part, he said, but they had to pay travel time. Only after conforming with the requirements of the collective agreement was it proper to come before the commission with a proposal for reopening of the register. He criticized Tobin for "going around and soliciting all the business into one particular area and creating an imbalance." He was vitriolic in his criticism of Tobin's "concern over a newly consolidated shipping company," saying, "They had a consolidation of six lines that left 150 men behind them and moved in here without saying hello, goodbye, or the hell with you, and moved over here to put three gangs of men to work and the men that worked for them for 25 or 30 years were left behind." He also took a slap at the local politicians in Newark and people active in community affairs for becoming involved, but then he asked, "Where the hell is our fun mayor at? Why isn't he here to tell what happened to the payrolls that existed in the Port of New York?"

In talking about the forthcoming negotiations, he said, "I will give you a rassle and a hassle that you've never seen before, if we are going to be stymied into this just before contract time and because some of the operators don't want to pay the difference in the travel time to get the gangs." He expressed confidence—but he should have had tongue in cheek—that they would get portwide seniority in contract negotiations. If he had a real mandate to establish portwide seniority, it could have been done already because the employers had come to want it. When pressed about lifting the travel-pay requirement, Gleason said, "Are you asking me, Mr. Sirignano [executive director of the commission], to tear up my contract? Are you asking me to throw the union out the window?" Sirignano tried to insist that the travel time had been developed years before only for an emergency situation, whereas they then had a situation that was running on day in, day out.

But Gleason was not about to give it up for nothing. With reference to gangs left in Manhattan when companies moved out, Sirignano asked, "Is there any possibility of getting those . . . gangs transferred to Port Newark?" Gleason, "What did I say to you? You're trying to break down my contract. You got no business asking me this type of question." Sirignano kept pressing the point and Gleason angrily charged, "You are trying to break the contract now. You are asking me . . . to evade my contract. . . . You are butting into collective bargaining. . . . First, you want to break the contract, now you want to break the local. Is that what you are trying to do now? You want to break the locals." Gleason's final soft word was, "I said I will supply all the men needed for you and for the industry out here if the contract is lived up to 100 percent. That is what I am telling you."[7]

Partly to preserve Brooklyn for Brooklyn men, Scotto sought

[7] *Ibid.*, pp. 256–293; cf. *Journal of Commerce*, Feb. 23, 1968, p. 1.

an expression from all his members on the idea of portwide seniority, which would eliminate sectional seniority in Brooklyn. With the card ballot was sent an explanation that portwide seniority was "being promoted in those areas of the port that are losing tonnage" and that it would let Manhattan longshoremen with greater seniority take work in Brooklyn ahead of junior men from the borough.[8] It could hardly be considered less than a contrived ballot, but the fact that it was undertaken revealed the underlying problem of area self-interest and the fact that negotiating a portwide seniority system would not be easy.

The Commission Opens the Register

In mid-March the commission, in spite of the opposition, announced that because additional men were needed in Port Newark the register would be opened for six hundred new longshoremen and checkers in that area. It simply explained that while the collective bargaining agreement provided for movement of men from one section to another, little had been done "by the ILA or the NYSA, either by enforcing the contract provisions to accomplish such mobility or by changing the contract to facilitate the utilization of men not employed in other areas." It also found that the employers need not fear increased cost of the GAI, because, as it said, "Under the collective bargaining agreement, new men would not be entitled to any guaranteed income." But "to protect the men already in the industry," the commission said that new men could not be employed until all men previously on the register who made themselves available for employment had been offered work.[9] It needs to be repeated, however, that it was not the cost of a guarantee to the new men that concerned the NYSA. It was the cost of the guarantee owing to unemployed longshoremen in Manhattan or elsewhere,

[8] New York Times, Feb. 26, 1968, p. 74C.
[9] Waterfront Commission, Annual Report, 1967–68, pp. 10–11; cf. New York Times, March 13, 1968, p. 77M, March 18, 1969, p. 89C.

whose work had been transferred and would be done by new men.

The NYSA and the ILA held a joint meeting, looking toward an appeal to the courts. But one problem at a time is hardly enough in this industry. As they met at the designated time, Gleason arrived accompanied by a crowd of men who were protesting that they were being double debited under the GAI. Their complaint grew out of the fact that men were debited for not accepting work but were also debited by the amount of unemployment insurance payments collected. The matter had been referred to a joint review panel but the men were impatient. Seeing the crowd, Chopin, with annoyance, remonstrated, "We're getting tired of these daily mob scenes." The LPC refused to meet in such an atmosphere. Gleason insisted that they had not agreed to deduct both "hours and money," but the LPC held that the debiting was proper. The fact is that Gleason could not keep the problem at the level of the review panel nor could he control the men—the matter being symptomatic of Gleason's frustrations in leadership. One employer remarked, "It seems we are dealing with a completely irresponsible man, unable to settle any issue."

The NYSA and the ILA, in spite of sharpness in this interlude, argeed to institute jointly an action in court to overturn the commission's decision to open the register. Admiral John M. Will, the new president of the NYSA, said that the appeal was necessary because of the commission's "insensitivity to the complexities of labor-management relations." But before the court had time to act, a strike broke out—apparently a protest by longshoremen.[10]

The NYSA, of course, condemned the strike, and called for an emergency meeting of the LRC. The ILA asked for a postponement, but the employers refused. Anticipating a boycott of the LRC—a tactic the ILA had resorted to before when sticky issues were scheduled—the employers insisted that the meeting

[10] *New York Times*, March 19, 1968, pp. 1, 25, 44.

be held regardless and that Turkus issue a directive to end the strike. This Turkus was willing to do. The NYSA, even though it was a partner with the ILA against reopening of the register, went to court and got an injunction against the strike. When asked if he expected the men to return to work, Gleason said, "We are all law-abiding citizens, and we expect to live up to the rules and regulations of our courts. I don't want to sleep in the same bed that Mike Quill and John DeLury slept in," referring to two local labor leaders who went to jail for violating injunctions against strikes. When the men defied the order, the employers warned certain locals, only to hear, "No work today." Thereupon they served notices on Gleason and a number of local officers, but Scotto told some employers, privately, that Gleason could not possibly put the port back to work again. Meanwhile, the ILA appealed to Judge Frederick van Pelt Bryan, Federal District Court, who held that federal courts had no power to enjoin a labor-management dispute.[11] This, in a way, was ironic, indeed, because the strike was not a dispute between the ILA and the NYSA but between some ILA longshoremen and the commission. The strike continued.

The employers asked for a meeting with the commissioners, stating that the industry was at "wits ends," that the "situation was catastrophic," and that the employers thought "the Waterfront Commission acted precipitately on a matter that belonged in collective bargaining." The commissioners denied such interference, insisting that they acted solely under the Bi-State Compact, where it appeared that the employers were acting hand in hand with the ILA. The employers objected to any inference that they were not completely independent. One of the commissioners pointed out that the ILA had refused to wait for the courts. Yet the NYSA felt that the commission should have respected the fact that "not one company testified in favor of an open register" and that one of the Port Newark employers stated, "I protested bitterly on shortages of labor but I did not

[11] *New York Times*, March 21, 1968, p. 93C, March 22, p. 93C, March 25, p. 82C, March 26, p. 89C, March 28, pp. 1, 49.

favor opening the register unless no other means were available."

The employers wanted the commissioners to call in mediators from the two states, but they would not consent. Some of the employers felt that the commissioners were just being stubborn and wanted to fight the commission to a finish. Others, with less emotion, sharply stressed that the commission had precipitated the strike by the untimeliness of its action. They noted that their warning that there would be a strike had come true. One said, "You are not under bargaining pressure, we are. It costs you nothing. It costs us a fortune. . . . We want your help to get a return to work." A commissioner responded, "The trouble is that we will do anything except abdicate our responsibility under the statute. We have enough courage to make our own decision" without asking for mediators. Reminding the employers that they and the union gave the power to open the register by the legislation they jointly sponsored, the commissioners objected to being made the villains; yet the employers, in turn, objected to being placed in collusion with the ILA. When the employers persisted in having the commission call in mediators, the commissioners said, "You are asking us to give in to the union—we won't prostitute ourselves to this extent . . . [but asked] where is the union?" The simple answer was, "Out in the street; they won't even talk with us." When the commissioners said they were under tremendous pressure, an employer rejoined, "I know you have tremendous presures but I have a $650,000 bill to pay for nothing." One finally added, "Let us be practical. The ILA won't meet. You are in this, too. We need changes in your regulations. Right now it looks like a crusade of the ILA versus the Waterfront Commission." One from the commission agreed, "That is what it is." Another employer observed, "It is strange, the system we ask [the gang carrier system] is working successfully in other ports."

The employers were over the proverbial barrel. They could not prevail upon the commission. As they studied the legal aspects of the situation, they were confronted with a quandary; as one put it, "If we lose, the ILA will be more difficult than ever and, if we win, the ILA will put all kinds of impossible demands on flexibility."

Their "out" turned on the LRC. Turkus did a good bit of maneuvering to keep from holding a meeting because he knew that Gleason did not want one, fearing he could not control his own men and hold them to a decision to return to work, which was the most likely prospect. But the employers insisted that the meeting be held. Once in session they agreed—because both shared the feeling, but not necessarily for the same reasons that the commission was interfering with collective bargaining—to work out a supplemental agreement with Turkus' help, issued in the form of an arbitration award.

Ironically, most of the employers had approached the meeting with misgivings about their ability to achieve any agreement. As one put it, "You cannot cope with any labor situation in this port with the present attitude of the ILA toward the Waterfront Commission. . . . No plan to alleviate labor shortages will ever work when the union does not have full control of hiring, and this is not possible with a governmental agency intent on preserving its own identity." Some employers, expressing a viewpoint we have previously noted, wondered if they could get out from under the controls of the commission. "Maybe this is the time," one said, "but instinctively, I just don't feel we are big enough, or powerful enough, to bring the proper influences into action." Another, with some skepticism, asked, "Would member companies, or even principal customers, support a battle?" and asked, "Do they have any conception of the problem involved in trying to resolve labor disputes with a third party always imposing restrictions?" A realist said, "Although I am sure the Waterfront Commission will be even more expensive in the future, we would need a lot of salesmanship to put it over. In the meantime, we have to make a deal with the ILA and get the port back to work." Another—a true realist or a wishful thinker?—"I am convinced that our best policy is to settle back, take a long strike, and stop jumping through every hoop the

ILA holds up." But the majority wanted to work on an agreement, which they did, with surprising results.

The Turkus Award and the
ILA-NYSA Supplemental Agreement

Turkus' arbitration—obviously he chose his words to fortify the parties and to impress any public made aware of the arbitration award—found that the decision to open the register "was abruptly made and disrupted sound and bona fide efforts . . . to find a mutually satisfactory solution to the problem of achieving mobility" and "resulted in exposing the industry to a tremendous and irreparable needless injury and damage . . . and critically affected, impaired and complicated the delicately balanced employer-employee relationship of the parties and the collective bargaining negotiations for a new contract." Turkus also stated, for the same publics, that no other port in the country had a comparable governmental agency imposed upon it which "might seek to invade, impinge upon or conceivably frustrate the sole and exclusive contractual right" of the parties, "to agree upon the seniority rights of the contractually covered employees and the method of determining hiring preferences." He noted that "both the NYSA and the ILA [were] in accord that the Waterfront Commission [was] without lawful right or authority to interfere with this basic right of the parties," but also noted that the right of the commission to open the register was then in court litigation. But he also found, no doubt for the edification of the employers who had moved to Port Newark, that "those who want the benefits of the contract must forgo the fatigue and (as here encountered) the seeming frustration of supporting it." Apart from the findings, the only decision made by Turkus, however, was that the supplemental agreement "negotiated by the parties," but obviously under his guidance, was affirmed and made a part of his "determination and award."

This agreement provided for the formation, by the NYSA-ILA Seniority Board Subcommittee in each area, of a number of gangs which could be "dispatched in the full number provided by the contract" and that fill-ins should be hired by "licensed hiring agents designated by the sponsor." In the event that terminal labor was not available upon the morning of the arrival of the gangs, the gangs could be broken up to work as individuals. The most important feature of the agreement, however, was the affirmation of the seniority agreement and the priority of sectional hiring over portwide hiring, both in hiring of gangs and fill-ins. A detailed table of hiring priorities, specifying the hiring sequences in each borough was included. The agreement also reaffirmed travel time, but provided for debiting members of gangs who failed to accept assignments or who failed to appear for work. Furthermore, it provided that a man who shaped at a center other than his own would not be debited if the area was one where "reasonable opportunity for employment" existed; the employers designed the later proviso to prevent men from evading work while preserving GAI credits by reporting at a center where there was slight prospect of being hired. It was also agreed that "1966" seniority holders, who had been reputedly rejecting work, would be required to accept assignments in the hold or face cancellation of their seniority. Significant, too, very significant in fact, was the agreement that no one who had "not been properly granted seniority status by the NYSA-ILA Seniority Board" could be employed or considered eligible for employment. This was designed to require conformance with the hiring under the collective bargaining agreement before new men added to the register were hired. Finally, the computer was to be programmed to include "union standing" under the union shop agreement.[12]

The Commission Objects

Of course the commission was critical of the settlement. Tobin, in letters to the governors of New Jersey and New York, condemned the Turkus award, contending that it was

[12] NYSA-ILA, "In the matter of arbitration between New York Shipping Association and the International Longshoremens Association, March 28, 1969"; *New York Times*, March 29, 1968, p. 1.

"contrived to subvert statutes, the courts, and the legal responsibilities of the Waterfront Commission." He insisted that the findings made by Turkus substantiated rather than rebutted those on which the commission had concluded there was a need to open the register. He insisted—no doubt correctly, but there was no intention to do otherwise—that the new agreement would penalize employers in Port Newark even more than the old one. He charged a number of defects: failing to provide portwide mobility; giving the ILA the role of determining how much terminal labor an employer could add to his regular lists; blocking the six hundred men to be added to the register from achieving seniority status and, hence, employment; and preserving travel-time premiums. A most serious aspect of it, he thought, was that "it dovetails with continuing efforts over the years to paralyze or to destroy the Waterfront Commission."[13]

A month later the commission was unanimously upheld by the five judges of the Apellate Division. Hence, the petition of the NYSA and ILA to annul the order to reopen the register was dismissed. The question remaining, however, was whether it was an empty victory. Gleason expressed the nub of it when he said, "It is a moot matter anyhow, since we have the Burton B. Turkus arbitration award, which bars the hiring of any new men."[14] The commission would not let the matter rest thus. It got an injunction to stop the NYSA and the ILA from preventing employment of new men. The NYSA and the ILA then made a joint appeal and the matter remained in court until during negotiations.[15]

All during the controversy Gleason was very angry about shifting of business to Port Newark. The fact that this development brought conflict with the commission only intensified the anger. Gleason reiterated, often in no uncertain terms, that employers who shifted their business without discussing the

[13] New York Times, April 2, 1968, p. 93C.
[14] New York Times, April 24, 1968, p. 93C; Waterfront Commission, Annual Report, 1967–68, p. 13.
[15] Waterfront Commission, Annual Report, 1967–68, p. 13.

problem with the union would receive no grace. He said that the union accepted containerization but "to go out and shop around, bring new men into the industry while regulars get short shrift" was something the union could not tolerate. He was angry also about the development of business of freight forwarders—ones who assemble cargo and load it in containers for shipment—who, he said, could cause a revolution in this port. "We don't want these groups," he said, "with no investment in ships, to become subcontractors with control over the business." He was highly critical of companies which had fled Manhattan, "leaving men of twenty-five years' seniority behind," and giving work to freight consolidators who would hire new men to load containers. "Nobody," he said, "is going to consolidate, and move location, without first consulting the International ILA." The NYSA assured him that it had taken full cognizance of the forwarders and consolidators and did not want them in the NYSA. Some of the consolidators and forwarders already had contracts with teamster locals; thus allowing them in the NYSA could only cause jurisdictional difficulty.

The Negotiations

As early as April, Admiral Will gave a foretaste of what was ahead, warning everyone of the need for a quick start to negotiations because delay could only aggravate "existing splits in the ranks of both union and management." Knowing full well the deep divisions in his own association and those between employers in the various ports, and that the ILA was less unified than usual, he thought an early start would be somehow salutary; but how, or why, he did not say, except that the need was grounded in the "economics, technology and human adjustments . . . too complex . . . for deadline bargaining in a countdown atmosphere."[16]

Internal unification, unfortunately, was not something which the bargaining table was apt to produce, even though the process of negotiations, when skillfully conducted, produces con-

[16] *Journal of Commerce*, April 26, 1968, p. 1.

sensus or, at least, an acceptance of the results by interest groups within each side. The deep-seated internal divisions would not be healed through the bargaining process and would cause downright failure to achieve settlement until, literally, there was no place to turn. Alongside the divisiveness in New York, there was the fact that the interests of workers and employers in some of the other ports up and down the coast were jeopardized by the container revolution. Not every port could become a container port, and the revolution accentuated competition among the ports, appearing to threaten the life of some. The old objective of "national bargaining" was less likely, now, although pushed vigorously by Gleason. His insistence on it may have been only a cover for the disunity that neither he, nor anyone else, could overcome easily. Nor was Admiral Will's call for "sound, dispassionate and skillful negotiations and cooperation" to "prevent another ruinous strike" enough. Both parties needed a program to accommodate the deep differences internal to themselves. Neither had achieved one. Effective centralized leadership was impossible on either side.

Little wonder, when the structural unity of the two bodies was in shambles, that the process of collective bargaining appeared inadequate and ineffectual. The process of negotiation was not at fault; it was only being asked, or expected, perhaps, to do what it could not manage very well. The effort to accommodate or resolve structural defects at the same time that a collective bargaining agreement was being negotiated—in an industry as complex as this one—was bound to be a rough experience. When no one on either side had the power to achieve internal consensus prior to coming to the bargaining table, a trying experience was ahead for almost everyone.

Both parties held planning meetings in mid-June. The LPC met in a three-day retreat at Skytop in the Pocono Mountains. It had been hoped that representatives from the other ports would be present. Philadelphia was unwilling, at the time, to allow the NYSA to be spokesman, as previously, on the master contract issues. The South Atlantic and Gulf ports were not officially represented, greatly reluctant to give up local control. The New York employers agreed upon national bargaining on the five master contract issues, plus containerization, provided that the ILA would abandon its policy of refusing to work until full settlement was reached on all issues in each port. They would avoid a long postnegotiation strike by working out coast-wide bargaining with representation from all ports. But the NYSA could not get full authority from all of the North Atlantic ports and could get none from the South Atlantic and Gulf ports. Emissaries sent to each port later were received courteously with promises of consideration, but meaningful coalition was not developed. Philadelphia did not want even to send observers to negotiating sessions in New York and was obstinate until after negotiations were well under way.

Because of internal controversy, and to guard against further division, the NYSA decided to employ a cost accounting firm to evaluate how the costs of its activities and the various benefit programs should be allocated among its members. The cents-per-hour-worked contribution was hardly any longer acceptable to the conventional operators, who, utilizing substantially more men to move the same tonnage, felt they were paying disproportionately as compared with the container operators. The former wanted a new formula before negotiations were completed. As one shipper at the time said, "If we are asked to be 'good fellows' until after the event, the answer is 'no.' We want to know our cost exposure ahead of time." Yet one thing the LPC did decide early—to offset public statements often made by Gleason that they were going to negotiate two agreements, one for break-bulk and another for container operators—was that there would be only one agreement, not two. It was recognized that to be divided would be to be weak and give greater power to the ILA.

The ILA's Atlantic Coast Wage Scale Committee met in New York, on June 20, and shortly afterward in a broader meeting with representatives of the South Atlantic and Gulf ports. Gleason wanted to lay out the program for all, but no unified program emerged. Meanwhile, Gleason dropped "signals" or "feelers," saying they would go only for a one-year contract and, repeating again, that there would be two agreements. Stressing an old ploy, Gleason also said all containers were going to be stripped and loaded at the piers.[17] Although the ILA, too, failed to achieve internal consensus on a coastwide approach, Gleason kept making pronouncements that the various ILA groups would hold together. The ILA met as a large group, as usual, and its proposals, as usual, were a conglomerate of all demands, hardly a program. Leaders in New York could checkmate each other and leaders in other ports had the power to resist and block settlement in New York. No mechanism existed to produce agreement among the different groups with their separate centers of power.

Because they wanted to make an early start, the parties met on July 10. The morning newspapers carried the story that Chopin was not to play the role of spokesman.[18] Admiral Will's explanation was that employers in the other ports felt that Chopin was associated too much with the employers in New York for them to accept his leadership. Alfred Giardino, counsel for the NYSA, was given the assignment, but it was not explained how he was any less of a New York representative or how he could speak better for the other ports. Chopin was not being shelved, because he continued as chairman of the LPC.

National bargaining came center stage at the outset. Gleason explained that the increasing use of containers made it imperative. Giardino responded to say they were trying to retain the principle but noted that some ports had sought to withdraw because of the lack of local bargaining, or because local bargaining came too late. But Gleason would not let the union be blamed, echoing a previous theme, "Why can't the principals [meaning steamship companies with operations in other ports] do something? The time has come to demand a meeting of the principals. They sit down with the Seafarers, why can't they

[17] *New York Times*, June 18, 1968, p. 64; *Journal of Commerce*, June 12, 1968, p. 1.
[18] *New York Times*, July 10, 1965, p. 62.

do it with us? Why do we have to strike the outports to convince the principals that we mean business?" The fact was that the steamship companies did not control local employers, many of whom were reluctant to accept negotiations in New York, believing their economic survival was at stake. This was particularly true of Philadelphia, at this time aloof; it had even attempted to get other outport groups to join in opposition. Gleason would not drop the matter, derisively charging, possibly to cover his own dilemma, "They accuse the ILA of having little kingdoms! My God, the shipping industry is much worse as to local autonomy." Containers, he said, made it compulsory to get identical protection in all ports; but what he did not say was that some longshoremen in other ports feared that if they had the New York terms it would cost them employment. He had no more control of his own members in Philadelphia, or elsewhere, than steamship companies in New York had over local employers not subject to them in the outports.

The principal demands of the ILA were an hourly rate of $6.00, overtime at $12.00 an hour and a six-hour work day, or $60.00 for an eight-hour day; complete union jurisdiction over containers, that is, all containers to be stripped and loaded by the ILA; an additional four paid holidays, above the current twelve, and six weeks of vacation pay; a retirement pension of $400 a month after twenty years in the industry regardless of age, with $10.00 additional per month for each year of service over twenty years and a 50-per-cent widow's pension; a change of the GAI to the GWW (guaranted weekly wage of forty hours' pay); a two-year agreement with a money reopener in one year; and a signing of agreements in all ports on the same day, "one port down, all down." The ILA, in New York, in the process of demand formulation, had voted against a proposal to establish portwide seniority. The ILA had compiled a hard position on container handling and manpower utilization.

The NYSA proposals were for complete freedom in manning, consistent with safe practices; free movement of containers of all types without restriction; prior-day ordering of men for all crafts and portwide mobility; improved arbitration procedure; elimination of "quickie" strikes; and elimination of travel time. It was realized that improved utilization and increased control of the work force would have to be bought by a substantial monetary package, inclusive of employee security, but no monetary figure would be offered until it could be determined what they would get from the ILA.[19]

Both Gleason and Giardino, implying that a cooperative attitude prevailed, expressed optimism that a settlement could be reached before the September 30 deadline. Seasoned observers, however, knew that positions relating to container handling and manpower utilization were extremely drawn and tightly held, while "national bargaining," including the South Atlantic and Gulf districts, would be irreparably divisive. It would not be easy, when bargaining was shaken down to realities, to mollify the discordant voices. For example, Boston employers feared that a huge wage would be offered in New York in exchange for flexibility in handling containers. The latter would be of no value to Boston and the former highly detrimental. Philadelphia held similar fears.[20]

Gleason, paradoxically, sought national bargaining and promised his members in the outports things he could not deliver, feeling this would bolster his position. Paradoxically, he harangued the employers to bargain nationally while trying to divide them in New York. As noted, he had hinted that there would be two contracts, one for break-bulk operators and another for container operators, but when employers demonstrated a united front on this point, he craftily announced that if no agreement was reached the union would strike only the container operators at the deadline. In his mind they were the parties causing the problem of change and insecurity besetting the workers. When he encountered difficulty in holding the outports to his objective in New York, he tried to pacify by promises. He talked emphatically about unity to detract attention from his weaknesses in

[19] *New York Times*, July 11, 1968, p. 62M, July 13, p. 42M.
[20] *Baltimore Sun*, Aug. 16, 1968, p. 1.

control and, in doing so, committed himself to a position from which he would have trouble extricating himself.

To mollify New York employers, Gleason informed them that locals were directed to start local negotiations immediately; but he was careful to add that all localities would stand together and that no one port could vote on a contract, or sign an agreement, unless all did so on the same day; his view was that they had to stay together to survive because of technological change. Almost in the same breath he complained that some employers in New York were negotiating with the locals without regard to the International—no doubt alluding to the fact that informal discussions often went on between employers and union leaders in various areas. But if the union ranks were not solid, neither were the employers. Not once, but several times, some employers complained of leakages from one of their number to the union, ostensibly to curry some favor.

While seeking broader-based negotiations, Gleason challenged the requirement that he and the union had to deal with the staff of the NYSA and with stevedores, contending that he was going to bargain only with steamship companies, who alone would have been weaker bargainers. It was said that he even wrote to certain presidents of steamship lines asking them to participate in the negotiations. The consensus in the LPC, however, was that these requests should not be dignified with an answer.

Among themselves, remembering past negotiations, the employers reminded each other that the last contract cost a lot of money; a lot was wasted. Their perennial problem had been how to get, or keep, what they had bargained to get for what had been given. They knew they gave a good contract the last time but did not get what they paid for. But Gleason insisted that what the union got four years previously was negotiated by the President's Panel; while emphasizing that it was the container operators who were responsible for the loss in jobs and that the union was going to be mindful of the conventional operators, he said the union was not against cutting gangs. Apparently an inadvertence on his part, it caused immediate objection as Bowers and others took exception. The employers stated they did not intend to reduce the work force. In chorus, union spokesmen said, "Put it in writing." But the response of the employers was that it did not have to be written when said in front of 150 witnesses, meaning the whole Wage Scale Committee. Scotto asked, "Then you mean everyone in the work force will be guaranteed a living wage?" but the answer was, "It is more complicated than that." The employers were not looking for reduction in size of gangs as much as flexibility in the use of gang members. From the floor, in a chorus, "Job protection is the most important item."

Early on, Gleason invited federal mediators, saying, "We thought instead of waiting until the last minute, we should have you here to watch the progress." The employers were disconcerted, telling the mediators it was much too soon. Among themselves the consensus was, "As soon as the mediators are here the speech making starts all over again."

The NYSA Counterproposal

The NYSA made a counterproposal on August 6, with Baltimore employers agreeing to bargaining jointly on nine items, the five traditional ones plus containerization, union dues check-off, number of holidays, and length of vacation. Boston, Hampton Roads, and Philadelphia agreed to NYSA bargaining only on the traditional five. The NYSA offer was a forty-eight-cent package increase over a four-year contract—10 per cent for each of four years. (The ILA demands added up to about 100 per cent over two years.)[21]

The NYSA, on August 23, made still another proposal, a one-year extension of the current labor agreement, to permit study of the complexities of their problems, offering a package

[21] *New York Times*, Aug. 7, 1968, p. 72, Aug. 9, p. 57; *Baltimore Sun*, Aug. 7, 1968, p. 1; *Journal of Commerce*, Aug. 8, 1968, p. 1.

of thirty-five cents per hour, with the money to be allocated by the ILA.[22] For any improvement in the guarantee the employers wanted "effective use of manpower and true flexibility," things which would "profit from study apart from crises." Gleason responded, "Let me say this. We are beginning to get some of our points over to you and we have received a good offer here. We appreciate it. We have never received such a good offer so soon. A little more effort and it could be perfect. . . . The thirty-five cents for all the master items is the largest original offer ever made to the ILA," but, characteristically, "We think you still are keeping something in your pocket." He was careful to emphasize, also, that the ILA would not bypass any ports: "We want you to know this definitely," he said. Yet he was willing to say, "We will give proper consideration to your request to eliminate all travel time but we don't know what we will do. On abuses of the GAI, we don't want the abuses." As an afterthought, whatever his purpose, although it was probably to assert an independence he did not have, he said, "We are glad Senator Morse is tied up on the West Coast. He can't negotiate our contract while he is running for election." A couple of days later he announced that the ILA was not satisfied. Considerable opposition to a one-year contract had developed, in spite of the fact that the ILA had originally talked of a one-year contract. Giardino said, "You almost leave me speechless," and like an echo from the past, said, "We can't give more unless we know what the rest of the contract is going to cost." But Gleason retorted, "We are paying you with productivity. . . . When investing companies are buying up steamship companies [referring to the development of conglomerates] there must be much money around here." Shortly thereafter, however, the ILA cut its demand; now asking for a daily wage of $36 consisting of six hours at $4.00 an hour plus two hours at $6.00 per hour—an increase from $28.96 per day, slightly less than 25 per cent. But it stressed the notion of a "selective strike" against container-

[22] *New York Times*, Aug. 24, 1968, p. 62.

ships come October 1, while continuing to work conventional cargo ships.[23]

A brief interlude followed when the Executive Committtee of the ILA met in Miami. Thereafter the parties entered into trying days of sparring through the whole month of September. Because of news which leaked back the employers thought the meeting of the ILA in Miami had been aimed primarily at splitting the conventional and container operators, not only in New York but coastwide, although some thought this tactic only a ploy designed to deter future imposition of an injunction under the Taft-Hartley Act, because a strike against container operators only would not be a complete one and, therefore, not a national emergency. Giardino quickly told Gleason that they could not make a contract by trying to break either side into small units. Gleason said he was happy that the employers did not want to break the union apart and emphasized that because the ILA did not operate in New York only he had to have a national agreement. To disconcert the employers, he reiterated the old slogans, "No contract, no work," and, "None back unless all are back."[24]

Gleason never lost an opportunity to criticize the container operators and to emphasize the plight of both the conventional operators and the union: "The container is digging our graves and we cannot live off containers," "I can read the ads in the papers and it says here all conventional ships will be taken out of service," and "Do you want us to sign our own death warrant?" He certainly intended to make the container operators pay the burden imposed upon the men; nor was he talking only of New York, for one employer said, "Gleason is clearly saying the container operator is syphoning off business from the other ports and, therefore, the container operator will have to guarantee the security of these other ports, too." Gleason had promised a guarantee in every port. He would say that money alone could

[23] *New York Times*, Aug. 27, 1968, p. 81C, Aug. 28, p. 77M, Sept. 2, p. 36.

[24] *New York Times*, Sept. 6, 1968, p. 73.

not buy a contract, because they wanted security. They wanted an improved guarantee. The employers in New York, generally, were not opposed to giving more security, provided they got a suitable quid pro quo in exchange. Yet, one said, "I thought when we gave 1,600 hours four years ago it was a protection for your people when no work was available, not to pay them for doing nothing when work is available." The ILA had relished the Kheel award and was not willing to force men to travel very far, if at all, to accept employment. Nevertheless, Gleason usually said they could correct the abuses. Once, when asked how, he said, "Give us 2,080 hours and if a man refuses to work in his category, he will be penalized." The employers, of course, wanted more than a verbal assurance. They wanted category hiring broadened and they wanted more flexibility to make assignments. Scotto said, "A lot of us were never satisfied with the GAI and we are willing to admit abuses on both sides. If you are willing to talk full employment, we will listen."

Among themselves the employers debated whether or not to offer a greater guarantee. Some recognized, "It could well be that our expense on the guarantee would be nothing if everybody worked," yet realized, "But if we do it like the GAI, we never could afford it." Their constant problem was how to get mobility in the port, flexibility in assignments, and the elimination of restrictive practices. If they could get these things, some were prepared to change to permanent employment. In early September they prepared a draft of a proposal providing for a permanent work force for each employer and a pool. Both regular and pool men would have to be available five days a week. Most employers thought this was going too far; it would have to be portwide to work, and this would not be easy to achieve or to administer, and the Kheel award would have to go. They remembered that Gleason, once when aroused, had said, "We want 2,080 hours and we won't give up the Kheel award to get it," and he had also said, in spite of his earlier pronouncement favoring it, "Forget portwide seniority." The employers, of course, had known all along that Gleason could not deliver portwide seniority and that the ILA had voted against making it a demand.

The GAI, because of payments to malingerers, had become a serious problem, with men refusing to work if it seemed distasteful. Yet some employers optimistically concluded that the ILA, in effect, had signaled, "If the price is right and security is right, you have no fight." The realists, however, said they were naive, "The ILA is continuing to play the game as in the past, 'Give us more,' without ever indicating any give on their part." A common pessimistic view was expressed by one employer when asked what he thought of a 2,080-hour guarantee. He said, "I think it is suicide. It is built-in inefficiency."

On one occasion when the employers said that the method of computing GAI was encouraging men not to work, Gleason agreed, but he said, "We are ready to show you how you can get the men you need, if you agree to 2,080 hours," and went on to talk about a union hiring hall. Telling the employers they were losing two million dollars a year in "dead time," he said it could be saved if the union had control of hiring. The ILA's constant theme, of course, was that the commission had to go.

They could not escape from the commission, nor was it inclined to mark time during negotiations. The Newark problem, as will be recalled, was in the courts as negotiations were pursued. When the commission won the decision against the joint appeal of the NYSA and the ILA regarding opening of the register, it called a meeting. Commissioner Bercik, from New Jersey, had great pressure to do something for Newark. Some employers still wanted surplus men on the North River utilized, whereas Bowers insisted on "category" hiring and travel time, claiming that employers never sought men and that they would go to Port Newark "if some regular employment is offered." The employers sought a two-week delay from the commission, to give Manhattan gangs an opportunity to accept work. But Commissioner Bercik thought the commission was being "hoodwinked" and proceeded to court for an injunction charging the NYSA and the ILA with unlawful conspiracy to block the hiring of the six hundred workers who had been added to the register in Port Newark.[25] The employers, perturbed, urged the court to give a full hearing in order to avoid a possible walkout from the piers. The consensus among them was, "We are heading for a strike if the Waterfront Commission tries to ram through the hiring of these additional men."

Early in September the commission obtained the injunction, and the ILA and the NYSA had to consider what they would do if the commission moved on the hiring.[26] The ILA said that any attempt to hire the new men in Port Newark would be a breach of the Turkus arbitration agreement and it would refuse to go on with negotiations. Waldman told the commission so. Both parties hoped the federal mediators would tell the commission it was interfering with peace in the port by upsetting negotiations. The employers had a problem: if they suspended negotiations to dramatize opposition to the commission's actions, they might touch off a portwide strike with the current ILA tempers.

The employers discussed the role of the commission among themselves and speculated whether they could handle a union-management hiring hall through utilizing a small committee and escape the bad effects of the existing system. Some even wanted a small committee to study elimination of the commission. One, who had often expressed himself before, even to the commission, stated the viewpoint of several others who complained of constant interference with labor relations when he said, "They know nothing about our industry and their interference probably costs us ten times the amount of the two-million-dollar assessment. If they want to be a licensing agency and police force, okay, but they should keep out of union-management relations. I would wholeheartedly support a union-management hiring hall without the Waterfront Commission and let them confine their activities to investigation and police matters." Others counseled differently, one pointing out that the commission had always been willing to tailor its regulations to their needs, adding, "I don't like to hear talk of wiping out the Water-

25 *New York Times*, Aug. 21, 1968, p. 74M.
26 *New York Times*, Sept. 9, 1968, p. 1.

front Commission." They considered making a proposal which would assure better control of the work force and which would promote better response to assignments and minimize absenteeism, compatible with the Bi-State Compact. Certainly a considerable sentiment had arisen for a joint employer-union program with hiring centers staffed by NYSA-ILA agents, with the commission present, perhaps, for supervision only, with the parties having full power to hire, dispatch, discipline, and apply the seniority provisions.

It was not likely that the commission would be content until it implemented its decision to register new men. The legal minds of the NYSA and the ILA had discussed the possibility of further court action should the commission be upheld, that is, of challenge in the federal courts on the ground of interference with collective bargaining. Waldman had long argued that actions of the commission invaded collective bargaining rights—many times before this one—none of which was ever tested. He had sometimes asked the NYSA to join with the ILA in making the test, but the employers had never acquiesced. On this occasion the employers seemed decided to do it themselves; but they were easily diverted by the more immediate prospects of a renewal of the strike, making it more expedient to prevail upon the commission not to take action, particularly precipitous action. While there were rumblings from the docks, informal talks with Gleason and other ILA leaders were holding the lid on, because the men were told that steps were being taken in negotiations to alleviate the necessity for reopening the register.

The employers also decided to meet with Tobin and convince him that they were making progress in resolving the problem of manpower shortages. If some of the employers "who steamed him up in the first place" could be on a committee to meet with him directly, it might have a salutary effect in giving him an orientation different from the viewpoint he had espoused. There was a calculated risk, as some saw it, because the ILA might become angry and go on strike because of the meeting with Tobin. As it turned out, they met with one of Tobin's chief

aides, Lyle King. Tobin was willing to meet, too, but thought
the employers should meet with the commission first. This they
did, asking for restraint because they were working to resolve
the difficulties. The commission, however, contended that men
were not accepting work and would not move from Manhattan
to Newark. It was said, "They won't even go from Center 2 to
Center 1. . . . There is a hard core in Center 2 who just won't
work." But it was pointed out that Grace Lines had laid off 700,
whereas the commission figures showed only 100 to 150 men
were idle, so, obviously, Center 2 men were moving around.
Most pertinent, the employers stressed that they were involved
in important negotiations and wanted freedom to negotiate without fear of further interruption. In turn, the commissioners did
not like being blamed for the earlier strike, saying, "It was the
union's fault, and illegal." But some of the employers charged
the commission with violation of the seniority agreement by the
registration of new men. A commissioner remonstrated, "We have
said there is no seniority for these men. They are only hired after
everyone in the port has refused work"; yet added, "If they are
sent to take physicals and you refuse to examine them, we will
have to go to court." One of the commissioners said, "After that
last action, I'll be damned if I'll be intimidated by that union."
Chopin responded, "But, you will hold our coats while we fight
them. We are looking for a contract with this union. And,
justifiably the men are worried about job security. How can we
talk to them in this atmosphere?" The commissioner, still adamant, said, "I will not be intimidated; I have a public responsibility. . . . Do you expect us to surrender?" Some employers
pled for an atmosphere of mutual cooperation to solve problems,
not a stubborn determination by the commission to have its own
way. One said, "Forcing an issue right now, when the figures
indicate a burgeoning surplus of men [for the future] is no
service to the public or the industry. . . . Let the men who
have millions of dollars invested in this port make the decisions.
They have the real interest. It does not cost you anything."

Another said, "It seems to me that we are concentrating on the development of New Jersey and the death of longshoring in Manhattan. There is an awful lot of weight behind the New Jersey development while not enough is thought about Manhattan. The Port Authority is concentrating on New Jersey, not the whole port as required by law to do." The upshot was that the commission delayed opening the register.

When consensus among them in negotiations was that the GAI had to be increased for peaceful settlement, the employers engaged in speculation as to the possible cost. When one employer said that the potential liability would be $12 million a year, another said, "That is like looking at the top of the ocean, and the $12 million figure is an underestimate." He said he could not arrive at less than $24 million. Others feared even greater liability, based on the ILA's determination to keep the Kheel award. Some said to go up from 1,600 hours was impossible because "it has been a monstrous cancer; 2,080 hours will just breed more life into this corruption." One tried to say that Gleason was willing to bury the Kheel award, but others wanted to know by what magic. Some talked about a weekly guarantee with "any day out, no pay," but others felt that they could not control it. One added, "It is not so much hours per man the union wants, but a guarantee of 40 million hours a year because of the fear of loss of work" and they wanted to protect income for pensions and welfare. This was a new dimension to the problem.

The employers hardly ever escaped their internal differences. When Gleason asked a steamship president to arrange a meeting of five or six presidents, the LPC "scotched" the notion, but a member of the LPC said Gleason had told him, "I am not going to get it from you but from the principals." One employer said he would not be surprised if one principal had not suggested an agreement to $4.00 an hour, a $300 pension, and the 2,080 hour guarantee; but he added, dolefully, that he was misguided and poorly intentioned. This was the time when Admiral Will bravely was telling the Rudder Club, regardless of Gleason's maneuvers, "We are one association, we will not be divided."[27] Offsetting reports indicated that other ILA officials said that if Gleason tried to strike container operators he would have trouble in his own ranks, because "longshoremen are not about to starve when others work." It was not beyond belief that some break-bulk operators were looking forward to continuing work during a strike against container operators. At least one container operator said, "If break-bulk works, containers will work, too." They had to remind each other that they were one association and that one policy applied; that either all would work or none would work at the expiration of the contract. They would not permit fragmentation, just as the ILA would endeavor to prevent local attrition.

A perennial problem of the employers, often raised, was that the ILA, somehow, always became privy to the employers' thinking. It seemed to be an industry with no secrets. In spite of efforts to prevent it, a common practice was for ILA leaders to visit presidents of companies for informal discussions. It was officially frowned upon but difficult to check. Although the employers were constantly critical of leakage of information from their own group, they at the same time sought to find out what was going on within the ILA. The informal communications worked in both directions.

Reflecting on their difficulties, the employers discussed "what is bona fide bargaining?" All concluded, "The ILA is not bargaining, it is bullying." They charged that Gleason was saying "just a continual No, No; No give, until the price is right." They thought Gleason wanted their package to use as a floor to bargain from. Such a trap they did not intend to get into.

The Revised Proposal

The employers, on September 9, agreeing among themselves, came forward with a third proposal after considerable difficulty.

[27] *New York Times*, Sept. 13, 1968, p. 84.

Some feared a quick rejection and called on the federal mediators to make major moves to "prevent the inching to death" that the ILA was subjecting them to and to press the ILA into some hard bargaining. They knew that the ILA had a habit of taking a brief look and then rejecting everything, because of one or two items. They hoped the mediator could do what they had not been able to do, but it was up to them to take a strong position and stand on it.

In their revised proposal the employers had withdrawn a number of their original demands, reducing them to ten in all, and proposed a two-year contract with a fifty-eight-cent package, but they wanted portwide seniority and elimination of travel time. But the ILA promptly turned it down.[28]

In mid-September they were still at the table going over proposals "claw by claw." Positions had seemed to harden as the deadline approached. The employers concluded that Gleason had gotten the impression from too many sources in the industry that he was going to get what the union was demanding and that their problem was how to make him know that he had been misinformed. Several were convinced that there was need for top-level mediation. They were divided, as usual, about the need or the type, whether private or governmental. They speculated about individuals like Sylvester Garrett, arbitrator in the steel industry, or Arthur Goldberg. But one, inaccurately, said Goldberg was the one who prepared the resolution to oust the ILA from the AFL. They did not want Kheel; and they concluded that any suggestion for private mediation would only solidify a desire in the ILA to have Kheel. They dropped the notion.

In mid-September the ILA held a meeting, with more fireworks and differences than usual. There were speeches to steam up a desire to get more from the employers, although some bent their efforts to cool it. It was reported that Scotto almost took the meeting away from Gleason. At this time the veteran mediator, Moore, actively entered the talks. The ILA was heavily pushing the guarantee, and the employers kept telling themselves

[28] *New York Times*, Sept. 10, 1968, p. 77M.

and Moore, "We will not submit to making a racket out of the guarantee. The men must work or else." But Moore was experienced enough to ascertain the major issues. When Moore tested the employers by saying the ILA definitely would not give up the Kheel award, one employer revealed the depth of their feelings when he remonstrated, "Well, any industry would have to be out of their god-damned minds to have an agreement whereby any man could make his own selection of when and where to work and how often, and still get paid." He added that "if there is going to be a strike the ILA's approach to this is a sure guarantee of one." The employers let him know that on the GAI the men had to be available and had to work if they continued with the guarantee. But it was not just the guarantee in New York. The employers were really committed to it provided safeguards could be worked out, and Gleason had given assurance that they could be. The terms might not have been so difficult to spell out had it not been for the promise to the outports that they, too, would have the same guarantee. It was not just New York they were bargaining for. A difficulty was that Gleason was committed to no private meetings. He could not afford to be charged with deals.

The Deadline—Agreement Almost Reached

It was quite obvious from mid-September on that a strike was "locked in" with no alternative because the parties were hopelessly deadlocked. President Johnson directed Reynolds to intervene and he held separate talks with the parties. The employers had little hope. Gleason did not want him. Reynolds soon said, "Nothing forms a basis for optimism," and, "If we don't get something put together in the next forty-eight hours we aren't going to put it together." The *New York Times*, editorially, could only lament that "in a world of change the one constant is the abysmal state of labor relations on the Atlantic and Gulf waterfronts." Making note of Reynolds' "noxious task" and the fact that he had "been through it often enough before to recognize how slim are the chances of success," it said, "Even by the bleak standards of the past, the outlook for a strikeless accord is gloomy," because "the container revolution . . . has rekindled all the ILA's atavistic fears of the impact of progress on jobs." Underlying its lament was that, in spite of the promise of the GAI four years earlier, nothing had happened since to justify optimism.[29]

If Gleason was unhappy about Reynolds' presence he was also unhappy when an attempt was made to have him meet with the LPC and steamship presidents. He refused to go. But the employers were upset over another matter. They had been working on a "private paper," reflecting things they might give if the exchange were right, and had made copies available informally to Gleason and other ILA leaders; they discovered that it had been reproduced and distributed and that the press had been told that it had been considered and rejected. The employers thought this was an act of very bad faith. Although Gleason claimed that he did not know how it got out, the employers believed that it was deliberate, designed to support a claim publicly that the employers had offered 2,080 hours and that it was only other conditions on which they could not agree.[30]

Reynolds quickly learned the realities. Gleason had hardened himself into a corner by promising the outports conditions similar to those to be negotiated in New York—things he could not deliver—and by maneuvering locally amid the factions in New York and being secretive with his own vice-presidents. He learned that a New York settlement could not be extended to the other ports and, if the other ports could not settle, even a settlement in New York would not forestall a strike; also, that employers—although not of one mind—were willing to make certain concessions but not without guarantees ensuring mobility and flexibility in use of men. Reynolds certainly learned that some employers would make no concession ahead of a strike, because it would not prevent one and would only add to the

[29] *New York Times*, Sept. 25, 1968, p. 73, Sept. 27, p. 57M, Sept. 28, p. 32C.
[30] *New York Times*, Sept. 27, 1968, p. 93, Sept. 28, p. 57M.

cost later. Other employers, however, felt that if they failed to put forth every effort to avoid a strike, it would cost more to get a settlement during a strike. Several would not be rushed "to another precipice" and urged caution. When one said, "It is against all principles of good bargaining to expose ourselves at this time," one rejoined, "When you are dealing with the ILA forget principles; they never had any." One, less bitingly, added, "So long as we are sitting here and the ILA is in the building willing to talk, there is a chance." But Reynolds concluded that a strike was probably necessary. The leaders of the ILA were completely without unity; not only were the vice-presidents and Gleason not pulling together, they were pulling separately.

As the deadline rushed upon them, the employers came forward on September 27 with a proposition providing for a union-management hiring hall within the framework of the Bi-State Compact. The employers had discussed the notion with the Waterfront Commission and were quite sure it could be sold. The proposal gave a spurt to negotiations, creating much discussion, even almost an "atmosphere of levity"—mystifying to some employers who could not decide whether the ILA spokesmen did not care what happened or whether they felt they finally had a proposal their whole committee would accept. The ILA had long looked forward to participation in hiring. During the session Gleason had to leave and Field took over and would not let the meeting fall apart. Upon taking the chair, he said, addressing himself to Scotto and Bowers, "Now I'll settle this between you two." The real problem was getting consent from men in Manhattan, in the Chelsea and upper North River areas, and at the army base in Brooklyn, to changes which, in effect, would take their sinecures away. Bowers, in particular, was not going to agree to anything that his followers might not like. They had enjoyed work of handling baggage on the luxury-liner piers, which had fallen off considerably owing to the decline of North Atlantic steamship travel, but they found the GAI a very handy sinecure from which they could obtain wages when they did not work; they had always been more or less averse to traveling for work and they wanted to keep their bene-fits under the GAI just as they had been enjoying them. Deep opposition in the ILA existed generally against modification of the Kheel award and the concept of "qualified." These were more than hurdles.

They met late into the night trying to work things out. They met again the next morning with Moore and Reynolds.[31] They talked about the creation of a "superboard" to administer the GAI and seniority. Bowers quickly saw implications that his men would lose employment, and said that he could not sell the con-tract with the employers' proposed contract language. Giardino said, "I will take it out of strong contract language if we get an exchange of letters with Gleason." He was immediately checked, however, by one of his own committee who said, "We have no confidence in ILA letters. We have had them before." The problem was succinctly stated by another employer: "We have a group who has to work to get paid. And we have another group who can get paid without work. We are building up even bigger internal troubles." They were reminded of terms in the last agreement that they could not implement because the ILA sloughed off on the necessary meetings. To the ILA proposal that no NYSA staff members sit on the "superboard," one em-ployer responded, "It would just give them the opportunity to pressure employer members. This would be ghastly. It would emasculate our whole program." About the pension and retire-ment system which would have provided for early retirement, one of the employers asked, "Has the thought occurred to you that the hooligan will stay and the good workers will leave in order to get both the pension and a good job elsewhere?" He added, "How can you get any assurance that the guys who accept early retirement are the guys we are gunning for? Those hooligans have a sanctuary, their classifications, and they will cheerfully punch a machine for the next twelve years at $8,000 a year or more." Another added, "I am staggered that we can sit around this table and try to find ways of paying up instead of

[31] *New York Times*, Sept. 28, p. 57M, editorial, p. 32C.

fighting. They will strike anyway and you still have to figure on the outports. Industry around the world will hold us up to contempt for abject surrender." One asked, "Isn't it time for Bowers to start being a leader? His members have screwed the employers to the extent that they had to leave the North River. Now the employers are the bastards. They have screwed up the GAI to where these guys with category sanctuary will not retire."

Employers bore into Reynolds. An employer explained, "The ILA barons won't be leaders and they won't talk to each other." Another said, "Our people are tired and the situation is hopeless." Yet the mediators kept pressing for an accord.[32] When some employers talked to some of the local ILA vice-presidents, Gleason became angry, because he got messages through some of his vice-presidents before he heard them himself. But some employers understood that Scotto had told the mediators that Gleason had kept close-mouthed to his vice-presidents too long.

The parties met separately on Sunday and stayed until after midnight, which was into the "deadline" date, Monday, September 30. Reynolds tried to get the LPC to meet with the ILA and to make a formal offer, based on the informal discussion, but they refused, nor did they want an extension of the agreement beyond the deadline in order to continue bargaining. They simply concluded that the internal differences in the ILA made it impossible to achieve a settlement, particularly that Gleason could not get consent from the West Side leaders. One employer suggested getting their September 14 proposal out to the whole ILA membership. Another, expressing a consensus of futility, said, "That won't come until the fifty-ninth day of Taft-Hartley [when they would be asked for their 'last offer'], any sooner than that would be disaster." When one asked about the possibility of Congress enacting compulsory arbitration legislation and would this be a way out, the general consensus was not unless a Republican Congress was elected. As they departed, they intended to go sit it out and not meet further.

[32] *New York Times*, Sept. 30, 1968, p. 21.

The ILA could hardly have held such a confab. The local vice-presidents and Gleason did not speak as candidly to each other. But Gleason's main problem was with the West Side locals. In retrospect it seems clear that an agreement could have been reached during the last week of September but that it could not be sold to all in the ranks of the union. Gleason had asked the employers if they wanted an extension beyond October 1, but they answered only on the basis of assurance that work would continue in New York and in all the ports while discussions continued. This Gleason could not promise. It is doubtful that as of October 1 Gleason could have swayed Bowers. On the other hand, Scotto was vituperative, met with his stewards as soon as the deadline was passed and appeared on a newscast on television. He said, "We could have reached an agreement in New York without striking. We had . . . the best offer that management has made . . . in 25 years." Referring to the guarantee of 2,080 hours at $4.00 an hour for the first year, amounting to $8,320 a year, he went on to say, "There are certain union officials that find it impossible to go back to their membership and recommend that they accept the contract without strike."[33] Scotto was scornful that Gleason had not allowed discussion of the employers' offer for fear of "wildcat" action by locals 791 and 824 in Manhattan. He insisted that if the employers' offer had been put to a vote by the Wage Scale Committee it would have been accepted.

[33] "Sixth Hour News," Station WNBC-TV, 6:00 P.M., Oct. 2, 1968; cf. *New York Times*. Oct. 30, 1968, p. 74.

16 | Would Settlement Never Come?

The old, old show was on again when President Johnson immediately appointed a Taft-Hartley board, the seventh in the industry in twenty-one years. The board was headed by David L. Cole, well-known arbitrator and mediator, experienced and adept at handling tough situations, who was assisted by Peter Seitz, another arbitrator, and Monsignor George Higgins of Washington. Gleason symbolically shrugged, "We'll come back at the end of eighty days and be in the same position. We don't cool off very fast." But the board lost no time, met with the parties and reported to the President the same day, saying the parties were so divided that "this dispute may persist indefinitely." It recognized that the dispute was complex and quite correctly stated, although simplistically, that one of the greatest impediments to settlement was that contractual guarantees offered in New York would not be binding on the whole industry. A temporary injunction was issued next day and the ILA ordered the men back to work.[1]

It is of significance for a future incident that when Gleason appeared before the board, ostensibly to head off a recommendation for the issuance of an injunction but also, of course, to put the ILA in the best light possible, he surprisingly stated that the "union was ready to offer millions of dollars from an existing joint labor-management royalty fund [the container fund] as subsidies to keep conventional cargo ships operating for the sake of national security and to ease displacement of workers by

[1] *New York Times*, Oct. 2, 1968, p. 27, Oct. 3, p. 93.

containership mechanization."[2] Later, this statement led the "Dockers News" to take umbrage. The widely distributed leaflet asked, "Where is the Container money?" and told longshoremen that "a big steal is in the making." A push to distribute the container royalties as a Christmas bonus had led Gleason to say there was not enough to go around. The leaflet expressed amazement that "Gleason wants to give the money back to the ship owners." If Gleason had made reference to governmental subsidies to aid conventional shippers, it would have been different, but it is not likely that a *New York Times* reporter misinterpreted or misreported. The "Docker News" was explicit about the use of ILA money:

We longshoremen, who bust our asses climbing all over those containers stacked two and three high on deck, and who take all the chances when they buckle, we want that money now! We have waited, we have listened to all the speeches, we are fed up!!!
NOW—MR. GLEASON, WE ARE TELLING YOU . . . WE WANT THAT CONTAINER MONEY NOW!!! WE WANT IT AS A CHRISTMAS BONUS!!!
And, as a step to show we mean business, we are calling on all Rank and File Longshoremen to STAY HOME, THURSDAY, OCTOBER 31, 1968. . . . It's time we went on a strike for ourselves.[3]

Most observers, however, did not take the strike call seriously.

The employers had met by themselves on October 1, primarily perhaps, to prepare for appearance before the board—which they thought was a good one—but they also made a significant decision, voting to discontinue allocating expenses of the NYSA and the costs of the things provided in the labor agreement solely on the basis of manhours worked, although no new system had been devised. They set up a committee of conventional and container operators to work on it. Above all, the employers, to establish the appearance of complete unity, gave the LPC a vote of confidence.

The entire ILA Wage Scale Committee had met to ridicule

[2] *New York Times*, Oct. 2, 1968, p. 27.
[3] "Dockers News," Oct. 24, 1968 (mimeographed).

and oppose the temporary injunction. Gleason opposed making the injunction permanent, contending that governmental officials who supported it ought to be called for cross-examination on their statements about a national emergency. "All they are doing," he said, "is dragging out the affidavits from the other [previous] cases, changing the names on them and submitting them. . . . In 1965, we went back on strike for 33 days in most ports, and 56 days in the rest, and this country survived. Certainly if the country's economy, health and safety had been endangered, they would have taken some action like special legislation. But because they couldn't prove it then, they didn't try."[4]

Cole Mediates

Immediately President Johnson asked Cole to accept an assignment to serve as "special mediator," a new role for one serving on a Taft-Hartley board.[5] Shortly afterward, for the first time in the history of the Taft-Hartley Act, the ILA appealed to the courts to vacate the injunction on the grounds that there was no emergency. Waldman said, "The ILA and its officials are aroused by the injustice of this injunction." He ridiculed the government's reference to an adverse effect upon the balance of payments, contending that the government had swallowed much more in the copper industry strike and insisting that the ILA was being discriminated against.[6] But the ILA did not prevail and was no doubt glad of it. The injunction had been protested but the union was saved from the strike.

In his role as special mediator, Cole was a little frightening to the employers, because, as they put it, "He wants *a* settlement," whereas they wanted an "acceptable" settlement. They felt that they would have to make sure that Cole got the proper messages and they would have to guard against being led into a detri-

[4] *Baltimore Sun*, Oct. 5, 1968, p. 1, Oct. 9, p. 1.
[5] *Baltimore Sun*, Oct. 11, 1968, p. 1; *New York Times*, Oct. 17, 1968, p. 85.
[6] *Baltimore Sun*, Oct. 22, 1968, p. 1.

mental agreement. On the other hand, they thought Cole could be useful in convincing the ILA about the realities of a legitimate settlement. Some even suggested that Cole could be useful in connection with the continuing manpower problem in Port Newark, as one put it, by "pointing out to Tobin that his continued insistence on getting his way is nothing more than pure unadulterated meddling, fouling negotiations." Cole met with the parties jointly at the outset in an all-day session, but quickly decided to hold separate meetings; he could not deal with the parties en masse because the inducement to speech-making was too great. Possibly to impress Cole as well as his own Wage Scale Committee, Gleason had taken a tough stand and enlarged the issues. He did not "cool off," although this was the rationale of Taft-Hartley injunctions. The employers, in turn, tried to impress upon Cole that agreement had been close in New York and that they had failed to achieve it only because of the differences in the ILA in New York on top of the promises Gleason had made to the outports.

The employers told Cole that, while they desperately needed manpower in some areas, they were paying hundreds of men for not working because the Kheel award had given a license and an opportunity to malinger, which many men had exploited, and they were spending millions of dollars for which they were getting nothing. They frankly conceded that they expected to make provision for employment security, but in exchange for mobility and flexibility. They carefully explained the baronial ILA leadership and why Gleason could not lead to a settlement.

Cole, like any other mediator, sought to find ways to break the barriers to settlement, how to get behind the incessant talking and to identify the real issues and how to stay with them. He knew he would have trouble getting an agreement in such a big body as the Wage Scale Committee—a big procedural problem confronted him. He was told by the employers that that was their problem, too, but that Gleason was afraid not to face the total group, or that he used the whole-group approach to avoid criticism he could not manage. Cole told the employers that there was a current trend in the labor movement for the rank and file to dictate to union leaders. They told him, in turn, that they were dealing with a union where no one could lead, that no one could control all the vice-presidents, who always had to respond to their local constituencies. They pointed out that Bowers simply had to call for a rank-and-file rejection when he was not satisfied, that Bowers, like others, could not go counter to the position of men in his local who wanted to retain all the advantages they enjoyed. The employers tried to tell Cole that Gleason could not square with the Wage Scale Committee until he was sure they all got what they were looking for or were convinced they could not get it. They hoped he could do what they were not able to do.

The employers' predicament was that their taking a really firm stand would result in everything being broken off, and they could not afford to do it. And, of course, no mediator wants to provoke a breakoff, unless it is necessary to effectuate an ultimate settlement; a mediator normally wants to keep the parties together, or at least wants to keep them dealing with each other even when the most he can do is to serve as a go-between.

Cole's job was to find a way to help Gleason out of the box he had got into by promising so much to the outports. On this, one employer said that he could not see anything to get Gleason out of his position unless they were willing to commit economic suicide.

Wanting forty days to close out bargaining in the other ports, Cole, during the latter part of October, set November 10 as the target date for an agreement in New York. Gleason promptly moved it up to November 8 to coincide with his birthday. Cole voiced optimism and the employers worked to revise their demands. But Gleason, attending the Second International Container Services and Equipment Exposition at the Baltimore Civic Center, where he was one of the speakers, gave assurance that the ILA was not against modernization. Nevertheless, he found "ammunition" in speeches of others. He said, "This morning, all I've been hearing . . . is the millions and more millions being made, going to be made, being spent and so forth, by or on, containers." He veritably shouted, upon hearing estimates of increased use of containers, "That's what I've been telling the operators. Wait until we get into those negotiations tomorrow."[7] He rode his theme of dire consequences, and Cole's voiced optimism was not enough to turn the parties closer together.

The next day, the one-day rank-and-file stoppage to protest refusal to divide the royalty fund actually took place, to the surprise of many, and bargaining stopped. Gleason nonchalantly remarked, "They'll be back to work tomorrow."[8] But it took five days. Walkouts in some parts of the port, however, may have been directed to the decision of the Waterfront Commission to press for employment of the newly registered men. Chopin felt that the attorney general should be doing something about the strike because of the Taft-Hartley injunction, whereas the latter seemed to sidestep on the ground that his concern was only with health and safety nationally, not with one locality. Nevertheless, investigators from his office asked which ILA leaders were responsible. They went to Newark where the strike was widespread, but found racial overtones which added to the complexities. Mostly, however, they seemed reluctant to move until after the pending national elections. Some employers urged them to go after Gleason with the hope of forcing him to assume proper leadership. Gleason, however, wasn't too much concerned with the stoppage in Port Newark because it was hitting at the container operators. Many employers refused to meet with the ILA: "I don't see any good purpose being served by negotiating with a union which can't control its men." Other employers were critical of the Waterfront Commission, claiming that its investigators "watched violence by the '1966' men and took no action, whereas a regular ILA man would have lost his pass." Some employers were critical of both Gleason and Cole for not doing something.

[7] *New York Times,* Oct. 30, 1968, p. 73, Oct. 31, p. 85M; *Baltimore Sun,* Oct. 30, 1968, p. 1.
[8] *New York Times,* Nov. 1, 1968, p. 85M.

The New Offer Rejected

By November 6 the stoppages petered out and bargaining resumed. The employers came forward with their new offer, a three-year contract carrying wages up to $4.25 per hour and a $300 pension at age sixty-two. But there were many detailed matters contained in a nine-page attachment to the five-page offer. Within a few days it was rejected, Gleason saying, "We'd be crazy to accept. This amount will be wiped out by inflation." In turn, the employers said they were "flabbergasted."[9] They were adamant about going no further. When Cole pointed out to them that to stand fast on their position would only lead to a strike on December 20, they generally agreed but remonstrated that their predicament was only because no one in the ILA could settle without a strike. One employer expressed his view: "We never get down to brass tacks until the ILA is convinced, through important government intermediaries, that this is our very top offer, that there is nothing more." When some employers told Cole he would have to make the deal on their current offer, he is said to have replied, "With the guarantees given I do not understand what Gleason has to fear." But employers felt he had their message, that they were at the end of the road.

Some employers at this time thought it was time to start looking to Scotto and other vice-presidents "to take it away from Gleason." Some employers reported that some of the vice-presidents had told them, "It is about time you employers took a hard line to prove to the outport representatives that they can't get everything they have been promised."

Gleason's birthday was not observed with a settlement. Instead, his present turned out to be a strong message from the employers that they had reached the end of the line. The employers urged Cole not to call more meetings "until the ILA is ready to bargain." Yet, off to themselves, one employer said, of

[9] *New York Times*, Nov. 2, 1968, p. 73, Nov. 7, p. 93.

the last meeting with the ILA, "It was a healthy session, if only for the fact that they listened and got some messages they may not have gotten before." He noted that Bowers had attempted to break up the meeting, "Because he feared it was getting some-where," not to his liking.

The day for the employers' "last offer" under the Taft-Hartley Act was approaching, yet Cole saw no hope in calling the parties together. Gleason began to complain—he needed help, as usual—"It sure doesn't seem like anyone wants to make the effort to bring the parties together and get an agreement before it is too late. And the deadline is getting closer and closer. . . . Then they'll blame me and the union for a strike. Why don't they do something productive for a change."[10] It is ironical that Gleason could rail against government involvement and bravely assert his independence, but yet be almost utterly dependent on the help of governmental intermediaries. It was symptomatic of his position. Of course, it was not just New York; the other ports could not get off dead center either.[11]

Giardino told the members of the LPC that they had a right to tell the NLRB that a "last offer" would be futile, that they withdrew their proposal and had nothing to offer. But after due consideration they decided they would submit their last proposal as their "last offer," even though they expected rejection, but asked the NLRB to mail their offer to all longshoremen. The NLRB was willing, if the NYSA paid the bill; it was willing. Cole, in his role as chairman of the board, reported to President Johnson. Cole expected the "last offer" would be rejected but he found "little real strike sentiment" and, although none of the issues were resolved, stated that the two sides were "awfully close in a lot of respects";[12] but this had been true also late in September and the same difficulties persisted. Gleason immedi-

[10] *Baltimore Sun*, Nov. 26, 1968, p. 1.

[11] *New Orleans Times-Picayune*, Nov. 21, 1968, p. 1.

[12] U.S. Board of Inquiry into the Stevedoring Industry Dispute on the Atlantic and Gulf Coasts, Nov. 30, 1965; Bureau of National Affairs, *Daily Labor Report*, no. 236, Dec. 4, 1968, pp. D–1, D–3.

ately called for a rejection. Expecting rejection, one employer said, "The ILA leaders know this is a good offer, but none of them are willing to take on the outport locals. They are waiting for Gleason to fall on his face there. Then they will step up and stomp on him in New York."

With the balloting just ahead, Cole felt that it was time to get the parties back to negotiations, and they met briefly. The executive committee of the AFL-CIO was meeting in Miami and the executive committee of the ILA decided to have a meeting there, too.[13] Some employers were told by some of the vice-presidents that there was a three-hour confrontation between Gleason and various vice-presidents, who expressed dissatisfaction with the conduct of negotiations. Gleason retained control, however, but it was not obvious that he could continue to do so. He returned from Miami, "not as arrogant," so the employers thought, but only relatively humbled. They concluded that he feared a long strike, which he had no power to prevent.

On December 10, the men voted. In New York, the rejection was 8,796 to 871, but almost 8,000 did not bother to vote. In the other ports the rejection was even more decisive, 15 to 1.[14] That same day, Cole went to Washington and met with the President, cabinet officers, and Meany. They would have the secretary of commerce twist the employers' arms and Meany those of the ILA. When Cole met with the parties afterward and informed them of this visit and said that everybody was worried about a strike, Gleason was peeved, apparently because he felt slighted when no one in Washington had bothered to speak to him; he, naturally wanted to be in on everything and, certainly, he did not want to be undercut in anyway. Gratuitously he added that he had "begged for an offer prior to September 15 so they could make an agreement, something that both sides could have lived with, but nothing happened." Later, with some scorn, he noted

[13] *New York Times*, Dec. 3, 1968, p. 88, Dec. 4, p. 92C; *Baltimore Sun*, Dec. 5, 1968, p. 1, Dec. 6, p. 1.
[14] *New York Times*, Dec. 9, 1968, p. 92, Dec. 11, p. 94C, Dec. 12, p. 94C.

that "Reynolds came in two or three days . . . a nice guy but he did not care . . . he was only here to get back to Washington quickly, to put the injunction on us." Cole, troubled by Gleason's reaction, asked the employers if Gleason was more likely to listen to Meany than to the President. One replied, "Only if he is free to do so." Cole was seriously considering moving the meetings to Washington.

Gleason, the Vice-Presidents, and the Outports

Gleason did not calm down quickly. He no doubt felt that Cole's visit to Washington had put him on the spot. He vented his feelings by lashing out against the employers, "I have begged, but I am through begging. I don't want a strike, but I am going to let it happen. Fear is there. I can't stop it. My men in the outports are fearful of the future," although he shortly said, "It is the least of my intentions to walk away from negotiations." He continued to vent his feelings, heaping vituperation on the container operators. In Cole's presence he incited the Wage Scale Committee and let the hotheads from the floor do likewise. Cole realized that when Gleason was in the presence of the Wage Scale Committee it was impossible to reason with him. Hectic days followed—maneuvering, conjecturing, philosophizing, considering strategy—there was no end. Cole, the true mediator that he was, kept seeking alternative approaches. But how could a mediator, even as experienced and able as Cole, bring the matter to a settlement?

The major procedural problem was how to get away from meeting with the whole of the Wage Scale Committee. Some employers thought it might be a good thing if Cole called only the leaders to Washington, as one expressed it, "to get away from the mob scene." More important, perhaps, was that Gleason had little maneuverability within his own organization, was desperately looking for a way off the hook, but was in no position to make choices. Because of this, other employers felt that to move the meetings to Washington would simply supply a new forum for speechmaking. Still other employers, contending that Gleason was not able to deliver a settlement, said that the only possible way to avoid a strike was to bypass him and go to the key vice-presidents. They told Cole so. But this would be ticklish. They would certainly risk Gleason's antagonism. Of course, they did not intend to do it openly, they would tell the key vice-presidents that without their help there would be no contract. They would put their cards on the table and say they were willing to get Gleason out of the fire, with their help. Yet, could they count on the vice-presidents to help Gleason? A realist among them put their predicament sharply, "We will only postpone the inevitable. There is not enough money in this industry to meet Gleason's demands." The fact is that some of them were considering sweetening their offer, but those opposed said, "If we put more money into a package, he will want it applied to the whole coast. Our alternative is to stand up to him now. We may end in a strike, but it will be short-lived and we may save a lot more money than trying to rewrite the rules at this late stage." Another one added, "We say we can't trust Gleason. He says he can't trust us. We are both right." He was followed, "We have tried all the honorable ways to get a contract. If we try to change this package, it seems to me we are just talking more money. And, I don't think that is the way out. The way we have been playing this has not gotten anything done." Unless they were prepared to take the strike outright, they seemed to have no alternative but to work behind the scenes. The majority felt they should try it.

Cole, in mid-December, arranged a small meeting with a few vice-presidents, but included Gleason, and a few members of the LPC. The surprising thing was that Gleason did not try to torpedo it in front of his big committee, because bad feelings had increased between Gleason and some of the vice-presidents. The latter thought he was trying to play "a one-man game" or, more correctly put, "a two-man game." He had brought his son Tommy, an attorney for the ILA, in as his closest confidante, and the vice-presidents resented the father-and-son team, "trying to run away with the ILA," as some put it. Cole had decided that a behind-the-scenes meeting was worth a try, expecting that if it failed they would have to move the meetings to Washington. Everyone involved was to swear that the meeting never took place.

It appears that the vice-presidents wanted more money, which they would allocate. A question in the minds of some of the employers was whether they could get rid of the onerous conditions if they put up the money. Some doubted that if their proposal were rejected, even when sweetened, they would thereafter be able to buy anything with it, feeling that once out it could never be withdrawn.

Instead of more money at this juncture, the employers put forward a proposal on joint hiring. The vice-presidents were not completely satisfied, saying, "You got a deal on the hiring. All we need is another dime and it is wrapped up." The immediate reaction was, "No, and say it fast." The vice-presidents reacted in complete silence when they were told it was unfair to try to sneak another dime on top of their offer of joint hiring. Gleason is reported to have jumped in, to beg or cajole, "Go see if your committee will give up the dime?" But the reported answer was that he was told by one, "I won't even ask. I can't face them. Why don't you give up the dime?" His reported answer was, "Oh, that's no trouble, they [his vice-presidents] all want me to give it up."

Later Cole expressed surprise to some employers that they had waited until such a late hour to come up with their offer on hiring and wanted to know why it had not come sooner. But the employers felt it was too bad that he still did not understand the ILA. They pointed out that it did no good to make offers when the ILA was unable to agree internally, because they could not buy anything by doing so. Cole suggested that it would be a shame to fail to get an agreement over a dime, but the employers said, "Make sure it is their dime, not ours." Cole kept trying to hold them together. There was danger that there might be leakage about the secret meetings but they kept talking. Finally, if the employers gave the dime, they were assured that upon achieving settlement New York would return to work regardless of the state of local negotiations in other ports.

Optimism pervaded the port as word spread that Cole had achieved an oral agreement on the basis of a revised employer offer. Without revealing details, Cole said, "If the union goes for the management offer, it'll be a deal." It blew up completely. A news bulletin, out of Chicago, stated that the employers were preparing a $1.60 package.[15] Giardino said dolefully, "It could wreck the whole thing." How did the news get out? Was it the ILA? Was it employers? The employers in the outports wound up in staring unbelief that the New York employers would sell them out with ten cents in order to get the ILA to abandon the "one down, all down" principle, that is, that New York would return to work before the outports completed their negotiations. But southern ILA leaders also felt that they were being abandoned.

Uncertainty overshadowed developments, largely a product of differences in the ranks on both sides as between the views held by management and union leaders in the outports as compared with those of their counterparts in New York. The reactions of employers in the outports led one employer in New York to say, "The problem we face is not of our making, but of the employers in the South who refuse to come to the twentieth century. When this bargaining is completed, I intend to press for final agreement by management to completely coordinated bargaining." On the other side, the curious thing was that Gleason had begged for the dime to help him assert his political strength in the outports, but almost immediately rumors circulated that if Philadelphia employers did not agree to the $1.60 figure, the ILA would strike the whole coast until they did, exactly the opposite of what the ILA leaders had promised. Some New York employers began to fear that they were going to be victims of a milking process and said, "Our public state-

[15] *New York Times*, Dec. 17, 1968, p. 93.

ment must be, 'There is no proposal. The mediators sounded out both sides and certain compromise solutions are still under discussion.' " But, most likely, it was too late.

The informal agreement, in any event, had to be presented to the full Wage Scale Committee. Cole attended the meetings, and in spite of his congratulatory statement that they had won a generous settlement, it was shouted down and angrily ridiculed, largely as a result of fears from the outports that New York would go back to work leaving the outport leaders with terms they could not persuade their employers to accept, and they would be left to go it alone.[16]

The outport leaders in the union railed against scuttling the principle of "one down, all down," but Gleason told them he had not abandoned it. When the employers heard this, one said, "Remember when he came down begging for the extra dime; he would sell the agreement, and he would sign it right then?" New York employers were full of recriminations, having offered the extra dime solely on the promise of no stoppage in New York.

Gleason was in deep trouble with the outports. He was aware that the Philadelphia and Boston locals wanted to split off and bargain separately. He wanted Cole to put the pressure on, even to getting the White House to go after Philadelphia and Boston. Of course, the employers in these ports did not want the settlement, as one from Boston put it, "Boston is playing for its very existence." It was quite obvious that Boston and Philadelphia would take a strike rather than submit. With a day to go to the deadline, Baltimore balked, too. Reynolds arrived to assist in mediation, suggesting to Cole that in other ports there was a desire by the ILA to consider an extension; he suggested that the government would be willing to supply any gimmick needed to accomplish it. The employers in New York, however, had no interest in an extension unless meaningful discussions could take place in the outports.

The ILA was warned that if there was a strike there would

16 New York Times, Dec. 18, 1968, p. 93C.

most likely be restrictive legislation—particularly once the new Republican administration was in office. The employers in New York wondered if Meany was aware of this possibility and if he would put pressure on Gleason and the ILA to avoid a strike. But there was a limit to what Meany could do, in any event. The employers were told that Gleason was scared. He was reported to have said, "If I postpone my strike, I will lose my union." If he said this, it was no doubt based on the question of his ability to hold the outports.

A last-ditch effort by Cole on the afternoon of December 20 was made when he suggested that three or four employers sort of drift to the floor when he was talking to ILA vice-presidents, so as to have a meeting without the attention of the big Wage Scale Committee. The key vice-presidents from New York were there, and a few from the outports. The question was where to go from there, and there was no place to go. The deadline was reached, the injunction was lifted, and a strike was under way. But it was Christmas week and, while they met on the twenty-third, they did nothing but rehash details. The big news was that Chopin was ill, later revealed to be a heart attack.[17]

As the days passed, resentment in the ranks of the ILA over the role Tommy Gleason was playing increased. Most leaders in New York felt he was putting himself forward too far. This was disconcerting to the employers, too, because whom they spoke to and dealt with was always a delicate matter. They could easily be victims of a crossfire. Of course, they wanted to know who was running things, "Tommy or Teddy, or who?" One employer suggested they line up the vice-presidents and "let them straighten up Gleason junior." They knew, of course, that unless Teddy agreed, there would be no contract, because even if he could not produce a contract he could block one. They approached some of the vice-presidents, to see if they could lead to an agreement, but one of them said, "Forget it, the two Gleasons are on a rampage."

[17] New York Times, Dec. 20, 1968, p. 94C, Dec. 21, p. 73C, Dec. 23, p. 78C.

The consensus at the New Year was that Teddy Gleason was feeling that maybe Congress would have to bail him out because he had oversold and was helpless. Washington, in fact, was becoming increasingly concerned, and word spread that a strong presidential statement was being prepared. It was understood that Meany had agreed with President Johnson that legislation was necessary, but told the President he would publicly condemn it. The President then would make no move. Wirtz raised the possibility of another eighty-day injunction but was told that this would be more harmful than helpful, although the employers suggested appointment of a commission to investigate and report back to the President.

The employers were getting restive and adamantly insisted on no concessions, although some thought it was essential to find a way to persuade the outports to go along with the $1.60 package. Nevertheless, the consensus was to let Congress, Meany, the President, or others, put the pressure on. When it was suggested that they take "a hard line, but do it intelligently," by letting Gleason know privately what they intended, one said, "I get the feeling Gleason does not want a contract in New York. He is just waiting for the coast to warm up." This caused another to get angry, "They are trying to force us to bargain on top of bargaining." Another added, "We have got to stop talking to them so they understand we are at the end of the road, because now they are just trying to erode their concessions to us."

But Cole kept them meeting, although there was much discordant talk. Category hiring and the GAI were discussed at length, yet one doubted that they were achieving any consensus. The break-bulk employers held a meeting to discuss a separate contract but convinced themselves that a separate one was not practical. Giardino asked the LPC to withdraw all offers and appeal to the President for compulsory arbitration. The feeling was, however, that the lame duck administration would push it aside. Nevertheless, they appealed directly to the President, pledging compliance with any settlement made by any "responsible tribunal provided by statute." Once he heard of the appeal,

Gleason quickly rejoined, saying the ILA was opposed to compulsory arbitration, "We are not in Russia," he said.[18] Employers asked themselves, "Why didn't Meany act?" The answer was, "Meany has spoken to Gleason repeatedly, but Gleason blames it all on the outports." To bolster himself, Gleason complained to the employers about the news stories and efforts, as he described them, to fragment the union, asking the shippers to reassess their position and strive for a master contract. He is reported to have warned the employers that nobody would be able to handle the union if it got in the wrong hands and that there was evidence that people were trying.

An Oral Agreement for New York—$1.60

January 9 turned out to be a big day, perhaps "the longest bargaining meeting in the long and turbulent history of the port."[19] While Gleason at the outset criticized the telegrams the employers had sent to Washington, the fact was that he and others in the ILA were getting concerned about the possibility of legislation ten days hence when the new federal administration would take office under President Richard M. Nixon. The vice-presidents had forced a meeting because Giardino had told them that if the conditions needed to control administration of the GAI were not agreed to completely, then the question whether the GAI would continue would remain open and would go to arbitration, including portwide seniority. At this meeting they discussed all the issues, category hiring, clinics and welfare, GAI and payments under Social Security, discipline, use of dispatchers in employment centers as provided in the proposal on hiring, debiting, and travel time. By nighttime they were down to three items, with no assurance that they would continue. Scotto is reported to have blurted out, "Teddy, I am fed up with all this back and forth nonsense. I will be honest. The language they came back with is what we have been feeding them. Let's once and for all say what we want. Stop this

[18] *New York Times,* Jan. 8, 1969, p. 94C, Jan. 9, p. 94C.
[19] *New York Times,* Jan. 11, 1969, p. 65C.

playing games. I admit I am getting confused and fed up. Say what you mean." Gleason is reported to have responded in anger, but they pressed on. One employer put it differently, "They want to keep hammering now that we are on our knees." At 6:00 A.M. they were still going, with containerization and category hiring only remaining. Then they came to agreement on containers. Gleason is reported to have said, "I am going to tell my Wage Scale Committee this applies to all North Atlantic ports." But the New York employers repeated their oft-stated position, "We can only commit New York, it is up to you to get it elsewhere."

Category hiring remained, and Gleason said they were standing on their position and could not see why the employers felt it so important; asking why would they agree to dispatchers to see that everybody works if they did not mean it? But when asked, "Suppose we know a guy is a faker, what can we do about it?" the ILA response was, "We will do it. It is easy. If the hiring agent complains about 'John Doe' and tells it to the dispatcher, then you got no trouble when it comes to the joint committee." Cole asked if there was anything that could give the employers more assurance that the ILA would cooperate against malingering. Scotto answered, "Some of us said that we would never let it get to arbitration, that we would settle it in the committee." Giardino then suggested, "Let us say that the NYSA-ILA contract board shall have power to do this." Scotto said, "This board is to be a shield, not the sword," and others then began belittling the employers' fears. Giardino surmised that perhaps the board could take appropriate action in cases of malingering, wherewith Cole said, "That means your position on categories is dropped and you will rely on the good faith of the board." Giardino said, "Yes, we will look at some language that says this." Thereafter they made arrangements to go to the Waterfront Commission to discuss the role of the dispatcher. It wasn't long until a clarifying question came up about the disciplinary clauses and Giardino read some language that provided that after the filing of a grievance and arbitration an employee could be discharged. Gleason reacted immediately, "I never agreed to life sentences," and another union spokesman said they were willing "to accept expulsion from the industry for a limited time only, not forever." But they appeared to have reached a settlement on the longshoremen's contract.

They met on the weekend to start negotiations on the various "craft" agreements. At the same time there was the problem of the outport settlements. The New York employers wanted a meeting where Cole would have Gleason say the New York longshore agreement was settled. Sunday evening such a meeting was convened. Cole apologized for the long meeting all day Friday and through the night into Saturday but said he was pleased that they had achieved a New York agreement. Gleason promptly said that unless the outports got the $1.60 they would be supported and that they had to get it before they took a vote in New York. But Cole went with him to a meeting of the New York District Council and the agreement was accepted unanimously. Gleason returned to tell the employers, "Well, I want you to know it was not easy, but I sold it. I told you I would." While it appeared that they had a settlement, some details were still open, and the craft agreements had to be settled. A completely new question was raised when Willy Carr, prominent in Local 791, asked if the men were going to be debited for the days of the strike. The unanimous response of the employers was, "Is he nuts?" but Carr said that his local would hold up the vote unless the employers agreed not to debit. Gleason said, "We don't expect to get paid for the strike but we don't want to be debited for those days, too." Caught by surprise, Giardino said, "This is the first I have heard of it," and, ignoring the earlier spontaneous reaction of his colleagues, added, "We are not taking any stand on it either way. We will look at it when it comes up." Giardino and Gleason shook hands and it appeared that New York really had an agreement. But only a few minutes later Gleason was still saying the agreement in New York depended on what happened in the outports. It was painfully obvious to some employers that nothing was signed. It was obvious, too, that at least two weeks would be needed to settle in the outports. Also, they had some work to do with the commission to assure the acceptability of the new hiring provisions,[20] discussed in the next chapter.

In mid-January, while awaiting developments in the outports, employers in New York had second thoughts. "What did they get for their money except the strike?" "Wasn't the package really more than $1.60, when administrative costs were included?" "Were they going to guarantee 40 million man hours regardless of the strike?" "Why do we have to wait on settlements in the outports, when all they are doing is trying to make better terms than New York?" "Why not seek legal means to force a return to work?"

Gleason "pooh-poohed" the latter notion, but it seems quite clear that a major reason why the settlement in New York was not "reduced to writing" and the "oral agreement" was not submitted to the membership for ratification was that Gleason and the ILA remembered the "unfair labor practice" charge levied during the previous negotiations, when the employers had to resort to the NLRB to get the strike terminated. Gleason had simply shifted the onus on the employers in New York by insisting they had to prevail upon their counterparts in the other ports to accept the settlement. "Now it's up to the other ports to fall in line," he said, "It's up to the industry to get the ships working again."[21]

Pressures were being exerted on Washington and on the governors of New York and New Jersey. Governor Rockefeller and the two senators from New York appealed to President Nixon and Secretary of Labor George Shultz to give the strike their attention. Many employer groups in New York made similar appeals. Senator Jacob Javits spoke in the Senate and suggested that they might have to consider the question of compulsory legislation.[22] The employers were not particularly pleased about Shultz's insistence that the parties work out their own deal.

[20] *New York Times*, Jan. 13, 1969, p. 1, Jan. 14, p. 89C, Jan. 15, p. 93C.
[21] *New York Times*, Jan. 21, 1969, p. 78M.
[22] *New York Times*, Jan. 22, 1969, p. 93C, Jan. 23, p. 93C; *Journal of Commerce*, Jan. 22, 1969, p. 1.

The Outports Object

New York employers thought that mediators were not exerting enough leadership in the outports and considered putting pressure on the employers and getting Gleason to do likewise on his members, but one employer said, "The ILA in the outports are telling Gleason where to go." An employer complained, "I resent the idea that New Orleans can keep New York on strike while they negotiate a more favorable contract." He was challenged by another who said, "It is none of our business. Let's put our own house in order," and argued against any connivance in New York to offset any possible advantage the employers could gain in the other ports.

Gleason, for his part, blamed the employers in New York for not putting pressure on the employers in the outports. Of course, he also blamed the employers in the outports, saying, "They are trying to prolong the dispute to get help from Washington to make a better deal." But some of the New York vice-presidents still rankled because the strike had not ended. Scotto urged that, because the agreement was not ratified, the offer be changed and that they be given the $1.60 in wages and they would vote on ratification immediately. Bowers supported the idea: "We made a mistake. We should have taken the $1.60 as a package to divide later." Another said, "Gleason hoped to use the South Atlantic to bust the North Atlantic but it won't work that way." The employer response was, "We told you long ago that we did not have the power to consolidate bargaining and so long as the ILA says, 'No port works until all ports work,' then these people can sit there doing nothing." But Gleason's rejoinder was, "We cannot do what you are intimating without tearing this union apart."

At the end of January they were still wrangling over who ought to be doing what and who had the power, or lacked the power, to do anything. Neither the union nor management spokesmen in New York knew the key. Was it Philadelphia or was it the Gulf? The employers discussed the prospects if they went to the NLRB. Would the NLRB consider forcing ratification in only one port, in view of North Atlantic ratification in the past? Some argued that the NLRB had always held that New York was the proper bargaining unit. The employers got desperate, called Gleason and told him he better get over and give them some answers. Gleason and Field appeared, as requested. Giardino said, "We have been over every phase of this situation. Our people say, 'When do we get to work in New York?' We can't control the outports and you can't control your people in the outports, so let us get back in New York. We want an honest reappraisal." Gleason said, "We, too, are much disappointed by the way things have gone. Let us forget the outports." But the employers felt that the locals in Philadelphia and New Orleans were able to ignore Gleason. One said sharply, "You are fooling around with dynamite and I tell you, if we don't go to work this week, it doesn't make any difference when we do." Gleason simply repeated the old refrain, "It is funny that in spite of New York being the headquarters for all these lines, they can't use any pressure in the outports." The response was, "There is not a steamship company in New York that has any financial interest in any other port." Another one added, "We are powerless to tell anyone in Philadelphia what to do." One added, "We are being held hostage in a situation not in our control and you know it, because if we had the influence it would have been straightened out long ago." Gleason admitted that the ILA in Philadelphia was too independent for him to handle. Complicating his problem was the fact that the Blacks in Philadelphia were asserting themselves more forcefully than before and they had the support of the southern locals. Furthermore, Gleason feared that he would not be representing the whole ILA if he fragmented the North Atlantic. One employer told him, "The quickest pressure you can apply in Philadelphia is to put New York back to work. You owe it to your own membership in New York." Gleason responded, "I am holding a meeting. . . . We may very well do that. Yet I tell you, to withdraw your offer now could wreck my control." One of the employers asked him, "If Philadelphia remains a holdout, would the one port down, all ports down be changed?" Gleason answered, "I, for one, can change very fast, if other things are right. I would be the last one to hurt the industry that always fed me." Giardino and the employer emphasized that if New York did not return to work immediately they would have to take drastic action.

Some employers were still working on Shultz, but when they suggested a meeting in Washington he said, "Don't come down here." The pressure continued to build up to go to the NLRB. One said, "We have been too complaisant. It is time to get tough, regardless of what happens." It was suggested that pressure be put on Gleason privately, not in a large meeting. At this time Gleason had refused to accept terms negotiated in New Orleans because they did not include the fifty-mile clause on containers stating that all work on cargoes loaded into containers within fifty miles of the port, or cargoes discharged from containers destined to locations within fifty miles of the port, had to be done by ILA members, even if it meant unstuffing and re-stuffing.[23] The local ILA leaders there defied him, however, contending that they were satisfied.

Cole, who had been appointed by President Johnson and had dropped out with the change in administrations, was reappointed by Shultz early in February to resume efforts at mediation.[24] Because no progress was being made, the NYSA decided to withdraw the agreement unless the men returned to work immediately. A press conference was set to announce the decision, but high officials of the government persuaded them not to make the announcement.

The ILA executive committee met in Houston on February 6 to head off legal action through the NLRB. Gleason warned the NYSA against forcing a ratification vote, saying, "The only thing we can do if forced is to advise the men to vote against it."[25] But Gleason would be forced by an ultimatum from Scotto that if something did not happen by February 10, he would start

[23] New York Times, Feb. 3, 1969, p. 53M; Baltimore Sun, Feb. 3, 1969, p. 1, Feb. 4, p. 1.
[24] New York Times, Feb. 4, 1969, p. 61M.
[25] New York Times, Feb. 7, 1969, p. 61M, Feb. 9, p. 94.

a back-to-work movement. Gleason convened his executive council. Pressures continued to mount. When an employer again urged going to the NLRB, another said he had been berated that very morning by Scotto for not having done so already. But Giardino said, "If we go that route, the ILA leadership will urge rejection," and he tried to explain the limited powers the courts might have in the situation. But Scotto, joined by Bowers—who felt assured that conditions favorable to his membership had been preserved in the GAI—approached some of the employers and suggested that they approach Gleason and get him to be the originator of the idea of going to the NLRB. With three days to Sunday, after some more equivocation, the employers decided to file charges with the NLRB, telling Gleason what they were doing. Giardino had lunch with him the next day, designed to gauge his reaction in the event of an election and try to get his cooperation. He was pleased to learn that Gleason seemed to think it was a way out. Such a conclusion was reinforced when Judge John McGohey directed the ILA to conduct a ratification vote by the fourteenth.[26]

At the time the agreement was negotiated in mid-January, Gleason had written to the membership saying, "Your Wage-Scale Committee and I recommend you to accept the final offer when the vote takes place." Even though he had just spoken against being forced to conduct a vote, he quickly changed and now favored ratification. In fact he fell back on what he said in the letter, saying, "How can I change the letter?" It was easy now to let the letter speak for him. The vice-presidents had already threatened to buck him if he urged a "no" vote. The ILA Executive Council met and agreed to a vote on the fourteenth. Gleason then appeared at a joint meeting with the employers and said he had made his views clear over the wire services: "I favor the ratification of this as a good contract," ending by making reference to difficulties with dissidents, saying, "The underground is working hard to sabotage us." The ILA wanted

[26] *New York Times*, Feb. 12, 1969, p. 1.

the NRLB to conduct the vote but upon refusal made its own arrangements. The men voted to accept the agreement, with 9,377 in favor and 3,448 opposed—the heaviest vote against acceptance occurred in those areas of the port where there was least work.[27] The men quickly responded to the call to get cargo moving. The strike was over in New York. The men knew the monetary settlement was good and the guarantee of 2,080 hours a year could hardly be rejected. A closer look at the major terms of settlement, however, will provide the introduction to the next negotiations.

[27] *New York Times*, Feb. 13, 1969, p. 90, Feb. 16, p. 1, Feb. 18, p. 65M.

17 | The 1969 Settlement and Negotiations in 1971

The most sticky issue in negotiations in 1969 had been containers, difficult because of the differing—and sometimes conflicting—interests between the break-bulk and container operators, plus the determination of the ILA to protect work for its members. The union achieved its objective of making sure that cargoes in container shipments, other than full loads directly from or to the beneficial owner of the cargo, were handled only by ILA members. They set specific rules "to protect and preserve the work jurisdiction of longshoremen." All stuffing—placing of cargo in containers—and all stripping—removing cargo from containers—of all cargo coming from within a fifty-mile circle from the center of each port, had to be done on a waterfront facility by longshoremen. Rules to prevent evasion were specified in some detail, subject to renegotiation at the request of either party—with refusals to work on containers during periods of renegotiation being permitted—and unsettled disputes not being subject to arbitration; all interpretations not settled in negotiations were to be determined only by a court of competent jurisdiction.

The Settlement of 1969

Along with the container clauses, the master-contract "package" provided for the following increases, in cents per hour:

	Oct. 1, 1968	Oct. 1, 1969	Oct. 1, 1970
Wages	.38	.25	.35
Pensions	.10	.13	.05
Welfare	.05	.07	.02
Vacation & holiday	.07	.07	.02

The length of vacation was increased by an additional week in the first contract year and another in the second, with qualifications left to local bargaining. An additional holiday was provided for in the third contract year, again, eligibility being left to local bargaining.

For the Port of New York, pensions were liberalized in amount and included a disability pension, an early retirement pension, and widows' benefits as well. To assure the necessary funds the employers agreed to pay for pensions and welfare on not less than 40 million manhours, although it was known that hours to be worked would be considerably less. The grievance machinery was changed to provide for five arbitrators instead of one, but included Turkus, each to be available in alphabetic rotation upon twenty-four hours' telegraphic notice. Arbitration hearings were separated completely from the LRC meetings, and awards were due in not more than thirty days. Discharged employees were to be suspended from all work in the industry, but one could grieve under the grievance machinery and, failing to win, could apply to the LRC for reinstatement after six months to work for other employers. Travel time was continued, but only for employees in the industry before October 1, 1968.

The controversial GAI was continued, but on the expanded basis of 2,080 hours, eligibility being limited to those who originally qualified and with currently active seniority. A Contract Control Board to administer all contract provisions relating to hiring, seniority, and guarantee matters was provided for, with an equal number of representatives from top level ILA officials and members of the LPC. It was to develop standards and policy and be responsible for dispatchers, employed and directed by the Contract Control Board, in each of five hiring centers—the centers were to be reduced to one each for Manhattan, Brooklyn, Staten Island, Hudson County, and Port Newark—but it was made clear that hiring was to remain the exclusive function of each employer's hiring agents. The dispatcher, however, was designed to give the ILA and the NYSA a role in the centers short of circumventing the law with respect to the hiring function; that is, the dispatcher was to stand between the hiring agent and the agents of the Waterfront Commission and was given responsibility for "dispatching workable gangs with full complement of employees (in order to avoid breakup of gangs and loss of time while gang members are supplemented) in accordance with the current contractual hiring and seniority provisions."

It was intended that abuses under the GAI would be eliminated and looseness in administration tightened. To this end detailed procedures regulating hiring and the income guarantee were spelled out. All seniority employees had to be included in some employer's list—membership in gangs being so considered—with prior-day-ordering of all list men within their center area, and, subsequently, when it could be introduced, prior-day ordering of all others. Both of these would entail programming the computer—not easy, particularly with respect to the latter. Hiring was to follow categories "in accordance with existing seniority principles." It was agreed that "men at the centers [had to] accept assignments and work." The Contract Control Board was given authority to institute retraining and to utilize discipline to assure that men would be available for work regularly. It was agreed that abuses were burdensome and should be avoided and that employees in problem areas, from which shipping companies had moved, were to be given opportunities to accept permanent list jobs in other areas. Debiting was continued, with progressive penalties for successive refusals. Although inverse debiting was not eliminated, an effort was made to limit its extent. The Kheel award was, thus, not eliminated and only modified slightly. The register was to be opened permanently, with new men brought into zones as needed, but a program had to be worked out with the Waterfront Commission to have all applicants referred to the Contract Control Board for screening, physical and mental examinations, and zone assignments.[1]

Administration of the GAI went from bad to worse. After the long strike everyone naturally turned to private business matters, trying to get cargoes moving again. The ILA leaders, too, were preoccupied with outport negotiations. The setting up of the Contract Control Board required considerable doing, and the outport negotiations, which were not settled until early April, kept some of the principals busy.[2] Part of the problem in administration of the GAI, however, was the perennial tendency of the ILA to make agreements to which it had little expectation, perhaps intention, of being held. Pressure could be put on the local employer not to effectuate changes—perhaps the knowledge that pressure might be applied deterred an employer who wanted to evade trouble—and if the changes agreed to were not implemented and the terms of the agreement were ignored, the intended quid pro quo was eroded. Also, individually the employers were not as anxious to achieve full utilization of manpower, if the effort might invite trouble, as the industry claimed it was. Collectively, employers, through the NYSA, seemed to lack the power to realize their due. Inertia, the inability to push forward promptly to take the gains or protections in the agreement, was the malaise. The employers gave much to get an agreement; it did not need to be all loss. They made gains on paper; if they had claimed them they would have achieved greater flexibility in use of the work force and much-improved control over hiring as well as relief from evasions and abuse. Eventually, the cost of the GAI exceeded even the direst forebodings. Men would "badge in" and run to employment outside the industry, getting their guarantee and earning other wages.[3] The increase in

---

[1] NYSA-ILA Settlement Terms, Jan. 12, 1969.

[2] *Baltimore Sun*, March 26, 1969, p. 1, March 28, p. 1; *New York Times*, March 30, 1969, p. 86, April 4, p. 73; *Journal of Commerce*, April 10, 1969, p. 26.

[3] *New York Times*, April 2, 1971, p. 65, April 3, p. 48; NYSA, Report No. 2787, Feb. 6, 1970.

cost for the GAI is shown in the following figures, beginning with the last year under the previous contract:

Contract year	Total costs in dollars	Costs in cents per manhour
1967–68	3,070,219	7.7
1968–69	5,986,030	17.6
1969–70	24,340,472	74.1
1970–71	29,034,892	93.1

The estimated cost for 1969–1970 and 1970–1971 had been about $15 million yearly. The increase in costs threatened to destroy the NYSA, particularly because the question of how it was to be paid for took so long to settle, and would not stay settled.

Along with the GAI, the major problem confronting the employers was working out a new assessment formula for paying the costs of all the contractual benefits: pensions, welfare, and clinics; the "shortfall" in hours (the difference between the actual hours and the 40 million manhours agreed to as a base for the payments, which was simply a way of saying that not less than so many dollars would be available for pensions and welfare); holidays and vacations; GAI; and the expenses of the NYSA. The ILA was not directly involved but was more than an interested observer, because it wanted to make sure there was enough money for benefits. It will be recalled that the employers, on October 1, 1968, the day the strike began, had approved a resolution to discontinue the manhour type of assessment. In the following April they agreed to a statement of principles, but difficult intergroup bargaining was still ahead between the break-bulk and container operators.

It was not easy to work out a new formula on which everyone could agree. It could hardly have been done while negotiations with the ILA were still going on, because the settlement terms bore on the matter. Many of the ILA demands had been directed against the container operators, and would they prevail? What they would have to give, or what the ILA would give up in exchange for what, was of critical concern to both groups, although their interests were far from alike and the terms of settlement would affect the size of assessment needed.

After negotiations the employers found it difficult to work out a solution, for the formula meant dollars and cents and their internal negotiations were strained. The formula had to be a compromise between a manhour basis of assessment and one based on tonnage. The old formula overcharged break-bulk operators, whose manhour requirements on tonnage handled was high relative to those of container operators. With a straight tonnage formula, container operators would have been overcharged and would have been taxed on innovation and efficiency.

The Assessment Committee finally came up with a proposal in February 1970. The manhour contributions in effect at the close of the last contract, in the amount of 93.1 cents per manhour, were to continue.[4] In addition, each would pay $1.23 per ton of cargo handled, this to cover the increased costs of the latest contractual improvements, the increased cost of GAI, plus the "shortfall" liability.[5] The employers could not agree on the proposal. Whether the formula would have been more favorable to one group than to the other may be moot, but certainly the terms of the 1969 contract with the ILA did not affect all alike. Break-bulk operators had gained little or nothing when the ILA dropped certain of its demands, such as their right to stuff and strip *all* containers and increased royalty payments.[6] Obviously, the ILA had not given these up without getting consideration in wage increases, improved pensions, and the like, as well as the "shortfall" agreement. The terms of settlement had imposed additional costs on both, but not necessarily uniformly, although the container operators probably gained the most and held a

[4] They were comprised of the following items: pensions 47 cents, welfare and clinics 31.5 cents, GAI 12 cents, and NYSA administration 2.6 cents.

[5] NYSA, Report No. 2787, Feb. 6, 1970.

[6] U.S. Federal Maritime Commission, *Agreement No. T-2336—New York Shipping Association Cooperative Working Agreement*, Sept. 22, 1971; cf. NYSA, Report No. 2967, Sept. 24, 1971.

prior advantage besides. In deciding upon the assessment, each group wanted to protect its own interests.

A factor, not present before, had arisen from a decision of the U.S. Supreme Court in the Volkswagen case,[7] which established the requirement that assessment formulas, because they had an effect on charges levied on different types of cargoes, had to be approved by the Federal Maritime Commission. This requirement may have caused some additional delay, although it may have been helpful because the FMC played a mediatory role as well as a judicial one. Conditional approval of a modified manhour and tonnage formula was given on March 11, 1970, and this led to a formal recommendation in August; it, too, was a combined formula. It pacified the container operators somewhat, who had threatened to bolt the NYSA, and carried through to oral arguments before the FMC in October. But three container operators still balked and, having failed to make payments because they contended that any charge other than a manhour charge was a violation of the collective agreement and was illegal, caused the NYSA to bring suit against them in November to collect $3 million. But, on November 23, the FMC approved the formula, settling the matter, at least, temporarily.[8]

At this time the negotiated rates on pensions and welfare and clinics were 75 cents and 49.5 cents per manhour, respectively, but it must be noted that these figures were set with regard to the "shortfall" agreement and actually set the monetary obligation of the NYSA for these items. The NYSA, in the usual manner, had set the following additional rates of contribution: vacations and holidays 71.9 cents per manhour; GAI 55.5 cents per manhour, and NYSA administration 4.0 cents per manhour. Altogether the items totaled $2.549 per manhour. To defray these costs, the assessment formula continued the .931 cents per

[7] Volkswagenwerk Aktiengesellschaft *vs.* Federal Maritime Commission, 390 U.S. 261 (1968).

[8] *Journal of Commerce*, Feb. 20, 1970, p. 26, Aug. 14, p. 24, Oct. 8, p. 1, Nov. 23, p. 1, Nov. 25, p. 23.

manhour, payable by all employers, and the remainder was to be covered by the tonnage rate, which, having started at $1.23 per ton, was raised to $2.23 per ton. The increases were required by the mounting cost of the GAI, primarily, but it was known that the "shortfall" liability was increasing, too, because of the decline in manhours worked. Employment in the industry was down about 10 per cent.

A matter which might have kept down the costs of the GAI was the contractual provision for prior-day ordering, but the employers were slow in implementing it. This was not just because the computer had to be programmed. Because the provision was designed to lower the costs associated with the delays in getting men to the piers after hiring, one might think that implementation would have been pushed much harder than it was. Again, some employers were not particularly interested; a launching was not attempted for two years, and it faltered. The hiring agents, especially, disliked prior-day ordering of fill-ins because it would take away their opportunity to reward good workers by giving them the better jobs in the shape-up at the centers. Prior-day ordering would be like hiring blind. Also, their bosses "gave them hell" if they overhired by even two or three, because the cost of each unnecessary man ran upward from fifty dollars a day. The numbers actually needed could be more closely ascertained in the morning than on the previous afternoon.

In December 1970 there was a one-day wildcat strike when introduction of prior-day ordering was set, although it was mainly over a problem with checkers. They claimed they had never accepted it and refused to do so, because it deprived them of the opportunity to choose their employment in the morning, when they could see what work was available. They did not want to be hired "blind" through central hiring. The Contract Control Board held a meeting to discuss the complaint.[9] Most employers simply got along with the old hiring procedure.

[9] *Journal of Commerce*, Dec. 14, 1970, p. 1.

All was not well in the industry, and the future was a concern of both employers and the union. The ILA leaders knew that the GAI was being abused unjustifiably but, what is more, they were troubled by the fact that employment on the docks was in a steady decline. Manhours of work, averaging slightly better than 40 million annually in the years of the prior agreement, had fallen to 33.9, 32.8, and 30.8 million, respectively, for the years of the current agreement. The number of men employed in each of the last three years had been 22,531, 19,692, and 17,568 respectively.[10]

ILA and ILWU Rapprochement

Bridges, on the West Coast, was similarly concerned, and had some special problems of his own. During the autumn of 1970, meetings for mutual commiseration were convened to consider strategy for the negotiations each would face by the middle of the next year. This new rapprochement between the ILA and the ILWU was singular in view of the state of belligerency that had always prevailed between them, and the few surreptitious contacts that had been made by interested persons usually had only served to accentuate conflict between them, once revealed. Now they began to seek common ground upon which to deal with the employers. Gleason, by invitation, attended the ILWU convention in Hawaii in April, and Bridges reciprocated by accepting an invitation to appear at the ILA convention in Miami in July.[11]

By the time of the ILA convention, the negotiations on the West Coast had come to an end and a strike was under way. Bridges, noting that the last time he had attended an ILA convention was in 1935—when his local was a part of the ILA— dwelt on their "common problems" and said, "A lot could be done with alliance." He told the delegates he saw no reason why there could not be cooperation between the two unions leading

[10] "Statement on Behalf of the Council of North Atlantic Shipping Associations (CONASA) to the Pay Board," May 2, 1972.

[11] *Journal of Commerce*, Sept. 9, 1970, p. 1.

up to possible merger, "We've got to bargain with one committee, even if we are not one union." But he warned the ILA, too, obviously referring to the GAI, "If you take the profits out of it, the company is going to go broke. . . . I am facing certain economic facts. . . . Getting paid for not working, it might sound good but I am afraid that we can't win the battle over the long haul." He was as worried, however, as they were that "with dwindling man-hours, more tons moving with fewer men . . . people outside don't savvy what is going on." About his strike, then in its third week, he said, "I expect that strike out there to go on for two or three months, but we know what a longshoreman's strike is. It takes about two months to get tightened up, and then you say, 'Well, you are really on strike,' and that is about where we are."[12] What he did not explain was why his strike would take so long, what the internal difficulties were that could not be managed without taking a long strike, that the younger men in his union were out of sympathy with his leadership and negotiations of the past. He would have to go through a long strike to have the rebellious ones in his ranks chastened. In spite of the strike, military cargoes were being loaded, and this averaged a couple of days' work a week and took some of the sting out of the strike; it probably helped prolong it, too. Bridges, also, did not elaborate on the trouble he was having with the Teamsters over stuffing and stripping containers.

The ILA got a candid lecturing at the convention from the perspicacious maritime reporter from the *Baltimore Sun* who had become chairman of the Federal Maritime Commission, Mrs. Helen Delitch Bentley. Known widely in the industry already for her accurate and candid reporting and generally well received in the ILA—one reason, no doubt, why they had invited her—she asked, "Is it not proper for the convention to reexamine old tactics and old policies in the light of new conditions and

[12] ILA, *Proceedings of the Forty-Second Convention, July 19–22, 1971*, pp. 119–126; cf. "ILWU Convention," *Monthly Labor Review*, Aug. 1971, pp. 60–61; *New York Times*, July 21, 1971, p. 36; *Baltimore Sun*, July 21, 1971, p. 1.

new needs?" With candor she added, "The bargaining process . . . has been a record of failure . . . in this industry . . . [but] its implications will have meaning this year only if the mistakes of the past are repeated. . . . Neither court injunctions nor personal appeals from the White House or from friends in Government or the Congress have been able to alter the pattern . . . [yet] the methods and tactics of the past will not work in the new era of containerization." Gleason did not respond to many of the points she made but addressed himself only to the possibility of a strike, saying, "Many operators are looking for a wipe-out of the guarantee on September 30. . . . I am not going to be a fool and call a strike and take those men off the guaranteed wage."[13]

But more important governmental personages had spoken. Shultz, while secretary of labor, had had the Department of Labor make an anaylsis and prepare a report on the costs of the previous longshore strike.[14] The conclusion was reached, and widely publicized, that the stoppage had not cost very much. Even though the findings were bitterly challenged in the industry, Shultz used them to fortify his philosophy that the government should not get involved in labor and management negotiations in the longshore industry, nor get excited if negotiations led to a work stoppage. He is reported to have warned the parties publicly not to count on intervention by the government.[15] Shultz, however, was warned that he should not make statements that the government would not become involved unless people in Washington really meant it, for the government had never been able to stand aloof before. Nevertheless, the official and publicized stance in Washington was that intervention would be shunned. Principals from both sides were called to meetings in Washington where they were put on

[13] ILA, *Proceedings of the Forty-Second Convention, July 19–22, 1971*, pp. 46–52.

[14] U.S. Department of Labor, *Impact of Longshore Strikes on the National Economy*, Jan. 1970, pp. 4–9; *New York Times*, Aug. 18, 1971, p. 33.

[15] *Business Week*, Aug. 14, 1971, p. 28.

notice not to expect governmental help and that the Taft-Hartley procedures would not be invoked. Of course, no one had ever frightened the ILA leaders into a settlement before, and it was not likely that they could be frightened into a settlement this time. Yet, Gleason was worried and, no doubt to hide his own predicament, repeated often that *he* had a promise from the government that it would not step in. He had earlier said, "Let's stop being adversaries. . . . Let's put the cards on the table face up. . . . Let's trust each other. I haven't got a formula that I've got to stand by, that's final."[16]

Preparations in CONASA, Gleason, and the Reorganization of the NYSA

While the ILA and the ILWU had been arranging meetings, East Coast employers, for reasons entirely of their own, were meeting, too. With the lack of unity among the ports in the previous negotiations and with the difficulties associated with local negotiations still in mind, a new negotiating organization was created by them in October 1970. Called the Council of North Atlantic Steamship Associations (CONASA), it was designed to deal coastwide with coastwide issues. The intention was that local negotiations would be undertaken separately by each association in each port simultaneously with CONASA's coastwide negotiations. Once coastwide agreement was made and local negotiations in a port were completed, the objective was that both agreements would be put into effect in the particular port immediately. As of April 1971, however, when public pronouncements of the parties called attention to the commencement of negotiations, it was not clear whether the ILA would bargain with CONASA, even though for years it had pushed for coastwide negotiations; at least, the ILA had not expressed itself one way or the other. Nor, by the eve of negotiations, had all port management groups committed themselves formally to be represented by CONASA, which cast some uncertainty

[16] *Baltimore Sun*, June 4, 1971, p. 1.

on whether meaningful coalition could be achieved and maintained.[17]

In approaching the previous negotiations, the ILA had used the ploy that separate agreements would be sought, but now it sometimes looked as if such separate agreements might be forced by division in the employers' ranks. ILA leaders knew that the GAI had accentuated the internal struggle among the employers and they knew that the GAI would have to be corrected, but they did not want to give it up. They heard both groups of employers say that it had to be scuttled. At the same time, their own internal controversies appeared to continue, and there was little evidence that there could be a different approach to the bargaining table. The apparent internal calm at the placid ILA convention belied the truth. Gleason had gained a new four-year term as president without opposition, but hardly any of the younger leaders were not looking ahead to 1975, biding time. No one had wanted to make a challenge. Some were not beyond thinking Gleason might have serious trouble in negotiations, and some would not have been unhappy to see him lose control of the organization. Gleason knew that he faced tougher problems than ever before. But he was not alone. Bowers, even, was quite worried, as well he might have been, for work in his area of the port was dwindling fast, and the attack on abuses of the GAI were aimed at his members more than on those of any others.[18]

Gleason's immediate security rested on the conduct and outcome of the negotiations. He did not want a strike and feared that he would be forced into one. Yet, he permitted flamboyant demands, like extension of the New York GAI to all Atlantic and Gulf ports even when he knew that the NYSA was determined to get rid of it in order to survive. He knew that a strike might bankrupt enough shipping companies—ironically, a way of escape for them—that major changes would have to take

[17] *Journal of Commerce*, Oct. 15, 1970, p. 26, April 20, 1971, p. 30, July 26, p. 1.

[18] *Local 824 Bulletin*, July 1971, editorial.

place. He knew that his insecurity increased directly with the determination of the employers to escape from the costs of the GAI. Could he allow it and survive? It was a good question whether others in the ILA would let him do what was needed, whether he could pull off a settlement and maintain control. It would not be conscience that would keep him from making compromises to avoid a strike to save his own position. He could change quickly; he had said so himself, when the conditions were right.[19] There should be little doubt that he was aware of a new temper among the employers. It may seem strange that they gained bargaining strength as they, themselves, became harder pressed to survive; but, then, this may be one of the factors in the power quotient in bargaining.

But a serious matter suddenly plunged the industry into confusion, and the outcome was a major development in the industry. When the NYSA announced, late in June, that the assessment for the last three months of the agreement would be increased from $2.23 to $3.23, seven large container companies promptly resigned from the association, intending to negotiate a separate agreement.[20] The prospects for bargaining, scheduled to begin on August 18, were clouded, although it could be expected that Gleason would not look kindly on a group of container operators. How might negotiations be carried on, by whom and for what group?—obviously a major problem with negotiations just ahead.

Reorganization of the NYSA and reassignment of the bargaining function was immediately undertaken, aimed to bring the container companies back into the fold. Accordingly, responsibility for negotiations was placed in the hands of the stevedores, some of whom worked with container cargoes as well as with conventional ones. Stevedores had long wanted a greater role. Traditionally, they had held only second-class status at the bargaining table under the rules of the NYSA, notwith-

[19] *New York Times,* July 20, 1971, p. 20.
[20] *Journal of Commerce,* June 30, 1971, p. 1.

standing that they, the practical men, were the ones most intimately acquainted with the problems of the industry. But their business relationships had changed rapidly in recent years: the small companies had dropped out and only a few large ones remained, and, more important, their relationship to shipping companies had changed. They now rented the piers and terminals and had large investments in equipment in their own names. No longer were they in a position to simply pass on increased costs to steamship companies, which had been more concerned with ships and their costs than with cargo handling. They had to make their businesses pay in handling cargo or they would be out.

In restructuring the association, the NYSA amended its bylaws to effectuate the change and elected new officers. James J. Dickman of Universal Terminal and Stevedoring Company, president of CONASA, was elected president of the NYSA, and Michael Maher of Maher Stevedoring Company was elected vice-president, supported by a board of five other prominent stevedores, plus a representative from each of three steamship companies, one of which was a break-bulk operator, another a container operator, and the third a foreign-flag operator. The new executive would take over negotiations—with a committee of five stevedores assuming responsibility—administration of the fringe benefits, and the activities of the association itself. Chopin retained the title of chairman but he was to play no role in the negotiations.[21] The restructured NYSA got off to a shaky start, with little time to prepare—although CONASA had been at work for some time on the most important issues—but it, together with CONASA, had a potential for engaging in more effective bargaining. The stevedores were more unified, could not be bluffed about the industry because they understood it as no others did, and they were not apt to be as soft as many steamship companies had been. The financial predicament of the

[21] George Panitz, "NYSA Shifts Bargaining Authority," *Journal of Commerce*, July 12, 1971, p. 1; see also July 26, p. 1; *New York Times*, Aug. 12, 1971, p. 58.

industry no doubt added backbone to the demand to eliminate costly abuses. The stevedores turned out to be a determined group who could tell ILA leaders the real score. They would be tough and courageous, yet practical—they did not want to destroy the ILA. Whether they will continue to be effective remains to be seen.

Nixon's "Phase 1" and Early Negotiations

On August 15, just three days before negotiations were to begin, President Nixon, in an effort to curb inflation, startled the nation by imposing a ninety-day freeze on prices and wages. The period of the freeze came to be known as Phase 1 and was set to run until November 12, at which time Phase 2 would begin, but under terms which no one at the time knew. The negotiations that followed were colored by these developments.[22]

At this time the West Coast had been on strike for a month and a half, and events on the two coasts would affect each other in a way that had never been true before. Note has already been made that Bridges faced considerable opposition from his rank and file, who felt that he had neglected local issues, and that in a very real sense he had "thrown the ball" to the insurgents. He had probably underestimated the determination of this opposition, without it, he could have easily reached a settlement with the employers, the Pacific Maritime Association, but realizing that the insurgents would reject any settlement made, he had to let the strike run its course. When the negotiations in New York were about to get under way, Bridges' strategy seemed to be to let his strike drag on for another six weeks until the expiration of the East Coast agreements, on September 30, and a shutdown of all ILA ports on the Atlantic and Gulf coasts. A national dock tie-up, the first one in history, would give him more leverage, he thought, to assert his leadership and effectuate a settlement. J. Curtis Counts, director of the FMCS, intervened in an effort to break the deadlock by summoning top management and union leaders to meet with the governors of seven

[22] *Wall Street Journal*, Aug. 25, 1971, p. 28.

western states, who had been placed under considerable pressure from the public. The meeting had to be canceled because Bridges refused to attend. What could he gain but embarrassment by attending such a session when his problem was primarily internal? A West Coast employer then pled with President Nixon to call a "summit conference" at San Clemente, saying, "The only way we can get it [the big money package] on the table is to have the President to get everybody out of the present deep freeze." Abe Raskin, the perspicacious labor reporter, poked a little fun by wondering, "Now that Nixon has arranged to meet with Chou En-lai, can he be induced to sit down with that other prominent Marxist, Harry Bridges?"[23]

The ILA and CONASA met on August 18, the latest start since the end of World War II, amid confusion about the scope of the bargaining. Representatives of CONASA could not consider all the demands the ILA put forward because many of them fell outside of acceptable coastwide negotiations, such as size of gangs, gangs working only as a unit, safety, training, time off for bereavement, and increase of royalties on containers.[24] Furthermore, the ILA stated that all ports would vote the same day on local settlements as well as on coastwide ones. But the employers insisted that the ILA should no longer enforce its policy of "one port down, all ports down," feeling that once CONASA and the ILA reached an agreement it should be ratified, and as local negotiations were concluded in a port the agreement should be voted upon and, if accepted, put into effect immediately. The ILA viewed this as an effort to create a "break ranks" policy and would not agree to it. Scotto said, "Management knows we're not going to break ranks. They are making an impossible demand." On the other hand, Dickman said they were merely seeking to ensure a measure of stability under the agreements and insisted that local conditions in the ports were not interrelated. The talks really collapsed quickly because of

[23] *New York Times*, Aug. 16, 1971, p. 27.
[24] The ILA demands had been out since June; see ILA, "Proposals for a National Agreement," May 27, 1971.

the atmosphere of uncertainty created by the wage and price freeze. After Gleason broke off the first meeting, he remarked to the press, "It's a pathetic group. They're trying to back me into a strike when I don't want one. I don't think they know what they are doing." But, owing to the wage freeze, one employer reflected the truth when he said, "I don't think anyone really knows what to do, what the effects of the wage policy will be." In a cynical vein, a union official remarked, "The management people came in and said they were in full accord with the President. I expected them to play the 'Star Spangled Banner.' I guess they figure there is no use negotiating themselves if they can get the White House to do it for them."[25]

The truth is that the ILA leaders were almost as uncertain as the employers. They, too, had to wait and see what Phase 2 would bring regarding policy on wage increases. Gleason quickly said that there was nothing to be gained by a strike on October 1, that they would wait until the end of the freeze. Contributing to the formulation of this stance, however, was the employers' insistence that the GAI would end with termination of the contract at midnight, September 30. Unless improvement in its terms were achieved, they wanted their liability terminated. The ILA did not intend, however, to give the employers an opportunity to terminate the GAI. They would keep working and the onus of acting would fall on the employers. The ILA leaders no doubt felt they were in a better position than the employers, for if the GAI, or the seniority system to which it was related, were altered or discontinued it was almost certain that enough men would walk out to close the port. Furthermore, the men had always been inclined to walk out if no agreement were reached, following their old adage of "no contract, no work." Probably there would be a strike no matter what. If a strike occurred, followed by a probable Taft-Hartley injunction, the status quo would be maintained for eighty days, meaning that the employers would have to carry

[25] *Journal of Commerce,* Aug. 10, 1971, p. 1, Aug. 12, p. 1; *New York Times,* Aug. 18, 1971, p. 33; *Baltimore Sun,* Aug. 19, 1971, p. 1.

the costs of the GAI for almost three additional months. This they did not want.

Secretary of Labor James Hodgson and Counts, in mid-September, began meetings with the parties, and the employers offered a minimum-pay plan in place of the GAI. It was continuously kept alive and presented again formally on September 29 after the NYSA rejected an ILA counterproposal on the ground that it was insufficient to cure the abuses admitted by the ILA. Dickman said, "We have rejected their proposal. Our side is just not going to buy his [Gleason's] saying he'll take care of the abuses." He stated categorically that the shippers did not want a strike, saying he did not think the ILA wanted one either, but added, "It's a question of going bankrupt." Under the minimum-pay plan the employers offered to pay every GAI eligible a minimum of 2,080 hours per year, inclusive of vacation and holiday pay, and thereby end the casual nature of employment. Every eligible longshoreman, checker, clerk, maintenance man, or other craft waterfront worker would be placed on the regular payroll of a direct employer or carrier, that is, in a list position. Dickman, explaining that this was a huge financial undertaking, said that nevertheless the industry was willing to shoulder it to get rid of the GAI, which under the three years of the current agreement had cost over $60 million, the major portion of which "was paid out with absolutely no return in productivity when, at many times, shortages of manpower existed."[26] The number of men who worked not at all or very little was placed in excess of two thousand. Actually, there were 1,185 men who worked not a day but collected the full guarantee.[27]

The West Coast Strike—Taft-Hartley

As negotiations on the East Coast approached the deadline, the dispute on the West Coast had dragged on to the point where

[26] NYSA, Report No. 2969, Sept. 30, 1971; *New York Times*, Sept. 29, 1971, p. 1.

[27] NYSA Press Conference, "The Basic Position of the New York Shipping Association," Oct. 7, 1971.

President Nixon felt he could no longer stand aloof. While on a trip to the West Coast he called on the parties to settle. He warned that if a strike on the East Coast were to occur he would be obliged automatically to invoke the Taft-Hartley Act, which he had studiously avoided doing. He had thought a one-coast tie-up did not constitute a national emergency. Concurrently, W. J. Usery, Jr., under secretary of labor and Andrew Gibson, maritime administrator, met in New York with the parties in a last-ditch effort to get a settlement. The President expressed optimism that the West Coast dispute would be settled over the weekend, the issue being simply—but stickily—whether ILWU or Teamsters would have jurisdiction over loading and unloading containers at terminals near the docks.[28]

The East Coast negotiations produced no agreement and the men walked out at the deadline. Once this happened and it was clear that a settlement was not going to be reached on the West Coast, President Nixon invoked the emergency provisions of the Taft-Hartley Act and appointed a five-man board. It split itself in two and held one hearing in San Francisco and the other in New York; it found a need for an injunction on the West Coast but did not recommend one for the East Coast. The fact is that after President Nixon had said an injunction would be automatic if the East Coast struck, strong reaction from employers in New York flooded in to plead the unwisdom of enjoining the strike. They objected to the GAI payments which would have to continue during the period of a Taft-Hartley injunction. Further, on the record was the Department of Labor study, heralded by Schultz while he was Secretary of Labor, which had concluded that previous stoppages were not very damaging. Ironically, the NYSA and shippers individually had challenged the findings that a strike on the longshore was not prohibitively costly. Whether politics influenced the two board members who

[28] *New York Times,* Sept. 27, 1971, p. 68, Sept. 28, p. 66, Sept. 30, p. 1, Oct. 2, editorial, Oct. 4, p. 77; cf. P. Ross, "Waterfront Labor Response to Technological Change: A Tale of Two Unions," *Labor Law Journal,* vol. 21, July 1970, pp. 397–419.

whisked through the hearing in New York—the brief hearing was given little publicity or fanfare—or whether they were convinced by the arguments, they recommended that the strike on the East Coast not be enjoined at the time. Actually the whole coast was not tied up. Philadelphia was working under a local joint agreement not to cease work during the period of the wage freeze, and some Gulf Coast ports refused to strike on the ground that the GAI, which had caused the failure in New York negotiations, was of no concern to them. They continued at work, much to the chagrin and annoyance of Gleason, who ordered them to comply with the decision of the union to strike.[29]

ILA pressure forced some locals, like Philadelphia, to join the strike, but West Gulf locals refused. Philadelphia employers appealed to the NLRB, contending that the men had unfairly violated their agreement. A court order forced the men back, as did another in Baltimore, where it was held that the strike was a secondary boycott and illegal. And the same was true in New Orleans and Mobile, where the courts found that the strikes were solely for the purpose of helping the New York local and were not the result of impasse in local bargaining.[30] The upshot was that the ILA changed its tactics and engaged in local bargaining in all ports simultaneously in order to eliminate the basis of charges of secondary boycott.

The Pay Board and East and West Coast Settlements

The wage freeze was set to expire on November 12, but the President had created a tripartite, fifteen-man Pay Board to administer Phase 2 of his program. It set the guideline of 5.5 per cent for approvable wage increases. This naturally became a factor in negotiations. Again, Counts became involved. He made public announcement of hopefulness, saying that any settlement

---

[29] *Journal of Commerce*, Aug. 23, 1971, p. 1; *New York Times*, Oct. 4, 1971, p. 77; Oct. 5, pp. 1, 81, Oct. 6, p. 65, Oct. 7, pp. 1, 33.

[30] *Wall Street Journal*, Oct. 19, 1971, p. 1, Oct. 26, p. 1, Nov. 8, p. 7; *New York Times*, Oct. 19, 1971, p. 56, Oct. 26, p. 65, Oct. 27, p. 94, Nov. 4, p. 86.

before the end of the "freeze" would be treated as an existing contract under Phase 2, and would be allowed to take effect unless challenged by one of the parties or five members of the Pay Board, warning that stricter application of the 5.5-per-cent limitation on wage increases would apply to a later settlement.[31] This announcement did not rush them, but negotiations picked up as they were shifted to Miami, where the leaders of the ILA were to attend the AFL-CIO convention; the negotiations were shifted, too, to coastwide issues rather than local ones. It was the first meeting of CONASA and the ILA since their abortive meeting on August 18. The employers made a proposal, and for a time it appeared that real progress was being made. But the ILA rejected it, and Counts advised the administration in Washington that there was no possibility of a settlement. Scotto dolefully remarked that the ILA decision not to accept the employers' proposal "has to be one of the biggest mistakes we've ever made."[32] The GAI was still the big stumbling block, together with a difference over contributions for pensions and welfare. The ILA was holding to a guarantee of hours and employers wanted a specific dollar commitment.

A Taft-Hartley injunction was sought and obtained by the government late in November, running to February 12, 1972. Neither party appeared to oppose it at first, but the NYSA tried to block making it permanent, arguing that resumption of the GAI was too burdensome.[33] Strangely, perhaps, the parties soon began making progress in negotiations, agreeing to put prior-day ordering into effect on December 13.[34]

While New York seemed to move toward settlement, the West Coast dispute was intractable. Secretary Hodgson urged Congress to act swiftly on new legislation to control disputes

[31] *Wall Street Journal*, Nov. 12, 1971.

[32] *New York Times*, Nov. 17, 1971, p. 93; *Wall Street Journal*, Nov. 18, 1971, p. 5; *Baltimore Sun*, Nov. 24, 1971, p. 1.

[33] *New York Times*, Nov. 25, 1971, pp. 1, 30, Nov. 29, p. 70; *Baltimore Sun*, Nov. 29, 1971, p. 1.

[34] *New York Times*, Dec. 4, 1971, p. 62.

in the maritime industry. The members of the ILWU over-whelmingly rejected the "last offer" of the employers just before the Taft-Hartley injunction was to expire on Christmas Day. The strike did not resume immediately, however, for Bridges apparently did not want to go it alone and began talking more openly about merger of the two unions. But it was the consensus that Gleason, although he had met with Bridges and had some kind of understanding about holding together if settlements achieved were undermined by the Pay Board, did not want to get tied in with the West Coast.

On January 6, CONASA and the ILA reached an agreement, although local negotiations in each port still had to be con-cluded. New York reached an agreement in only two weeks, on January 21, on local conditions. Yet some uncertainty hovered, because the other ports still had to settle and the Pay Board would be a hurdle. It had just knocked down a settlement in the aerospace industry from 12 per cent to 8.3 per cent, con-sidered to be boldly higher than the 5.5-per-cent guideline. The settlement for New York was calculated at 41 per cent over three years.[35] A provision in the settlement provided for can-cellation by either party on thirty days' notice if the Pay Board did not approve the settlement.

While local negotiations in the other East Coast ports were going on, the strike resumed on the West Coast in mid-January, primarily in failure to agree to a $1.00 royalty per ton on con-tainer cargoes not loaded by ILWU members. As a result, President Nixon requested special legislation to stop the strike. The oddity in this was that if compulsory arbitration were im-posed, what would it do to the Pay Board? An arbitration award would no doubt be far in excess of the Pay Board guidelines, and could the Pay Board live with such a possibility? The board seemed on rickety ground to start with.[36] Meanwhile, the ILA and East Coast employers agreed to a month's extension beyond

[35] *New York Times,* Jan. 14, 1972, p. 29c; *Wall Street Journal,* Jan. 10, 1972, p. 1.

[36] *New York Times,* Jan. 23, 1972, p. 1, sec. 4.

the expiration of the Taft-Hartley deadline, that is, to March 14, to allow for completion of local negotiations. This had the effect of postponing submission of the wage settlement to the Pay Board.

Early in February, Congress passed contingency legislation calling for arbitration of the West Coast dispute. President Nixon then said that he would not sign the bill pending further efforts at settlement, but that if no settlement was reached soon he would sign it. Rather than have governmental arbitration imposed upon them, the parties got together with Sam Kagel, the port arbitrator, who led them to a settlement. Of course the wage portion of the agreement had long since been set, calling for a 34.3-per-cent increase in wages and fringes, the wages in two steps; a 75-cent increase to $5.00 retroactive to December 25, and a 40-cent increase on July 1, 1972.[37]

The Pay Board thus got the West Coast settlement first, for it was not until mid-March that East and Gulf Coast settlements were completed and votes taken. Labor mounted a drive to keep the board from trimming the settlement. But the board, in mid-March, rejected the full increase and permitted only an increase of 14.9 per cent—a 10-per-cent rise in pay and fringes, plus 4.9 in fringes not covered by the rules. The labor members walked off the board in protest, but Bridges was silent about resuming the strike. He would wait and see what happened to the East Coast application.

The Pay Board staff concluded that the East Coast increase in wages was not justifiable. Both the ILA and the NYSA took exception to the findings at a public hearing early in May, insisting that the full increase should be approved because of the great improvement in productivity and savings in costs effectuated by the other terms of settlement providing for greater flexibility in use of manpower. The Pay Board staff recognized the number of tons moved per manhour had increased but noted, also, the labor cost per ton had not declined but had generally

---

[37] *Wall Street Journal*, Feb. 22, 1972, p. 1.

risen. Further, it claimed that it could not verify CONASA's projection of productivity increases and would not give weight to it. Projected savings might not be realized and were hardly a basis for justifying the whole of the negotiated increase. It may seem strange that at the very same time the shippers were seeking, with ILA support, increases in rates from the Price Commission. On May 8, the Pay Board trimmed the increase from 70 cents per hour to 55 cents. Instead of permitting a 15.2-percent increase, it thus permitted a 9.8-per-cent increase. When the ILA asked the board to reconsider, it denied the plea. Late in June both sides accepted the ruling of the board. The Pay Board seemed to have won a victory; but the settlement was liberal, too, and the ILA knew it, and so did the men.

The wage issue before the Pay Board obscured the really important changes in the agreement in New York. The changes heralded a new day on the docks, with the stevedores in control on the management side and with ILA leaders knowing there was going to be a new day or there would be no industry. The terms of the agreement reflect the intention to make important changes. Administration of the agreement was placed in a joint committee known as the NYSA-ILA Contract Board, composed of not less than five or more than nine International or Atlantic Coast District vice-presidents and a like number of employer members of equal stature in their companies and who were directors of the NYSA, each side having a total of five votes. This board was to develop and administer policy and all necessary standards with respect to contractual provisions and benefit plans. It appointed co-counsel to be executive assistants to the board. It was given full responsibility for labor relations, grievances, and arbitration; for guaranteed annual income; for hiring procedures, seniority, and prior-day hiring; containerization and lash ships (ships on which loaded barges were hoisted and lashed); assessment and collection of hourly and tonnage contributions; welfare and clinics; pensions; and vacations and holidays. All joint bodies provided for in the agreement were subject to its control, for example, the LRC, the seniority boards, and the GAI Review Panel. The board became the trustee of all the jointly administered benefit funds, and a new trust fund was set up, known as the NYSA-ILA Fringe Benefits Escrow Fund, into which all assessments collected were to be deposited, that is, all monies for pensions, welfare and clinics, GAI, vacation and holidays, and a newly agreed-upon amount, $2 million, to be disbursed as an end-of-the-year bonus in lieu of travel time, which was being abolished. If the needs of the GAI fund exceeded the amount provided for in the agreement, $10 million, the trustees may borrow from the escrow fund. The tonnage assessment was reduced from $3.23 to $1.50 per ton. This of itself is some measure of the contractual savings expected by the changes in the GAI. The total liability for all funds was limited to $60 million a year.

The hiring centers were to be used primarily for dispatching, not for hiring, which was retained, as it had to be by law, as the function of hiring agents. Their assignment continued to be the "responsibility of dispatching workable gangs with full complement of employees (in order to avoid breakup of gangs and loss of time while gang members are supplemented) in accordance with the current contractual hiring and seniority provisions as well as standards for selectivity created by the Board on a non-discriminatory and objective basis." This provision was designed to eliminate the cost of obtaining fill-ins for absentees, but, in practice, they served mostly in a shop-steward function.

The income guarantee was extended to all employees in the bargaining unit who worked at least seven hundred hours for employer members during the contract year, October 1, 1970, to September 30, 1971, who currently held seniority status. Individuals who held another daytime job were disqualified. Men were also disqualified if they were offered list positions by the area subcommittee and refused to accept them, if they left a list position for any reason other than to accept immediate reassignment to another list position, or if they continuously failed to make themselves available for employment. Employers were required to submit schedules of list vacancies to area subcommittees, who would fill them from GAI eligibles, first from the area, then from the zone, and finally from anywhere in the port. All men on lists were to be available on a prior-day order basis and had to accept work in their list jobs for their employer within their zones. If not hired from the list, men were to be available under the prior-day-ordering plan, which went into effect in the previous December, and they had to report. Hiring at the center on the same morning was limited only to filling vacant positions for that particular day caused by absentees. Prior-day ordering and the basis for hiring on the same morning had to conform to existing seniority principles.

Longshore labor categories were reduced to three: hold, other parts of the ship, and pier or terminal. A holdman was required to accept any work offered. Men in the other two categories were required to accept any work offered except holdwork. Debits for refusal were progressive, rising to four for each offense, cumulated annually. "Debits shall be imposed on a portwide basis by inverse seniority, without restriction on the number of men debited and without regard to the number of jobs offered. . . . Employees entitled to the income guarantee shall be debited without any restriction on the number of men debited on a port-wide basis even if the job offered to such employee has been filled by an employee who is not entitled to the guarantee, the principle of inverse debiting being limited only to the extent that jobs are filled by employees entitled to the income guarantee."

This settlement provides a basis for improved conditions, although its effectiveness has not yet been tested sufficiently. Both parties will have to work to make it a constructive tool. Apparently the stevedores are determined to make it work as negotiated; the ILA, if it is wise, will seize the opportunity to place itself in a better role. It appears to have been much more responsible in these negotiations than in any other.

18 | Denouement

The shifting nature of labor and management relations and of events in the longshore industry in the Port of New York make assessments of the past and predictions for the future difficult. In this state of flux, bargaining has seemed to slip from bad to worse. Opportunities for improvement have often been lost by default or ineptitude. The malaise inherent in the structure of the industry and within the organizations of both the ILA and the NYSA has precluded reform even when there were good intentions in some quarters. Divisiveness has persisted in both parties.

The developments in the 1971–1972 negotiations may point to—and may help to produce—a somewhat different picture in the future. Certainly a summary drafted before these negotiations could have held little hope for anything but more of the same, for events before that time added up to a failure of the practice of collective bargaining. Perhaps the parties have simply been overtaken by events and only appear to be different. On the other hand, perhaps the technological revolution, caused by rapid introduction of the container, is forcing changes in management (certainly in the NYSA) and in the thinking of the union, making it impossible to continue along old lines. Technological change in other industries has often created problems where few existed before, but in this industry it may not only change the industry's functions—it may force significant changes in approaches to labor and management relations, without which the industry cannot survive. Although most of the leaders on both sides are still there, power has a way of shifting, and perhaps enough people in the right positions are sufficiently aware of the need for survival to make constructive relationships a reality.

An evaluation of the past quarter century of hectic labor and management controversy on the docks—particularly with reference to the practice of collective bargaining—carries a significant message, albeit mostly a negative one. Hopefully, it may not be the final word, after time has tested the settlement of 1972. Although President Nixon's price and wage control program may have influenced the course of the last negotiations as much as the new pressures in the industry, it would appear that the new provisions have a more climactic and more genuine character than those in earlier settlements. The issue of wages was not the central one, although it provided some drama before the Pay Board. What is more, the temper of the relationship may have undergone more than a sea change. Altogether, it is a happier task to write a denouement after the 1972 settlement. Hopefully, it points to a new era, in which the lessons of the past should contribute to a better future.

The Bargaining Process as Followed by the ILA and the NYSA

Tested against the model of collective bargaining presented at the outset—a private, two-party rule-making process—bargaining as practiced in the longshore industry in the Port of New York has been distorted, if not emasculated, time and again. So poorly has it been practiced that once-staunch defenders of bargaining in the ranks of the employers swung around in desperation and became advocates of compulsory arbitration, which of course does not preserve private two-party decision making. Repeated failures, amid almost insoluble difficulties, caused this transformation, although the change was not universal. Concurrently, on the other side of the table, ILA leaders who had eschewed government generally as an unfriendly institution, often vigorously excoriating governmental interference, took help gladly—often prayed or begged secretly for governmental help even while denying the fact, the settlement of 1962–1963 being the most extreme example—whenever effectuation of terms through the collective bargaining process was not possible by their own power. Frequently, the lack of power was due to the inability of the top leader to control the local leaders, not to any overriding power in the employer group. Frequently, however, this absence of an effective central force in the ILA—due to the extreme autonomy of the parts—made it impossible to do the obvious, for example, in negotiations over elimination of the abuses under the GAI. The ILA would sometimes make compromise with employers, but often the union then took its due without giving the agreed *quid pro quo*, as in the settlement in 1969, because employers did not want to court trouble and allowed things to drift.

Often the employers girded themselves for battle, laid plans collectively, expressed determination vigorously, as they did for the first time in the negotiations in 1955–1956, but whenever the going got tough, as it commonly did through the intransigence of the ILA leadership, the ranks weakened. What the employers needed—what employers in other industries where collective bargaining was practicd effectively always had—was a determined stand, even at times an assault; but the ILA leaders were good at bluffing, and, often following a pattern of delay or even obstruction, after an agreement was reached, they avoided delivery on their promises. The ILA was often able to thwart the strategies of the employers by diffusion, making a noise here and a noise there, placing pressure at the weak spots in the employer ranks.

The postulates of collective bargaining, as identified in the opening chapter, have all been present, but they have not all served effectively, at least not all the time. Both *mutuality and conflict of pecuniary interest* (within the context of the mutual acceptance of the societal system) are not always neatly balanced. It does not seem that the parties see the need to preserve the industry in their self-interest equally, but probably shortsightedness or selfishness rather than willfulness often led the ILA to minimize the long-run welfare of the industry. So ingrained has been deal-making psychology and its constant shadow—the notion of taking while leaving the devil to take the hindmost—that the welfare of the industry has been ignored. The ILA probably wished to stop short of undermining existing business, although parts of the organization have been reckless —the most conspicuous example again being the GAI. In a sense the ILA has not always sustained the mutuality of interest, for it often failed to see the business that never came, the jobs that were not there because of burdens to the industry to the point where business was precluded, that is, business went elsewhere or was not even generated. The ILA, it appears, has felt that sustaining the volume of business was solely the employers' problem. But even if this was primarily the employers' responsibility, the ILA in it own self-interest should have been more concerned with the welfare of the industry than it appears to have been. This lack of effective concern was largely the result of the parts taking what they considered their due, even though the whole suffered, and the organization collectively not being in a position to check or discipline local unions or groups of individuals—the perennial problem of structure and government within the union. The interests of the leaders differed from those of the members, and the interests of the members differed among themselves and from sector to sector, to a more pronounced degree in this industry than in most others.

The *internal restraints*, as already indicated, were only partly operative. The formal ones in the ILA and the NYSA were not always functioning and could not restrain conduct inimical to the whole. On the other hand, some informal ones were so powerful that top leaders could not bargain effectively—the local centers of power often created situations bordering on anarchy, observable in the infighting within the ranks on both sides in almost every major negotiation.

External restraints, of course, are another matter. Neither party has been able to ignore these, although not all external restraints have been as controlling as might be supposed. Some have been manipulatable, within limits, such as certain governmental restraints which could be influenced politically. When actions reached the illicit, however, or the normal restraints were not effective, the state government sometimes imposed regulations. The Waterfront Commission is the most notable example.

Economic restraints have not seemed to limit the activity of the ILA or of its parts. They have influenced employer behavior, but when higher costs were applied uniformly, all suffered together and, perhaps, could shift the burden to the users of the port services. Sometimes government subsidies to some shippers has lessened the economic burden.

Perhaps the industry has been weakest in meeting the requirement for a rough *balance of power*. Normally, negotiating structures or activities are modeled to effectuate balance in power. Both parties recognized this and made various attempts to improve their positions. The employers made several: insistence on bargaining for the Port of New York only; resort to the tactic of "Boulwarism" and the use of Fred Rudge Associates as consultant; rejection of coastwide bargaining—first explicitly in 1951 and again in the negotiations in 1955–1956 when they utilized the NLRB to check the ILA, although they inadvertently gave their position away subsequently—but later positively moving toward coastwide bargaining; and in the creation of CONASA in 1971. The ILA, too, made several attempts to improve its negotiating position, in its persistent efforts to achieve broader-based negotiations; in its attempts to get back into the AFL following expulsion from the federation in 1953, culminating in the return in 1959; even in flirting with the Teamsters and with Bridges. Of course, the ILA never achieved a unitary position internally on any one of them. As has been pointed up repeatedly, leaders have lacked sufficient control over individuals and groups as well as locals to hold the reins securely. Yet, the ILA, in spite of internal weakness—but actually because of it—has had more power to hold its position and to exploit employer weakness, than the employers have had to hold their stance. The employers have generally given more than they expected, a chronic predicament particularly noticeable in the settlements of 1957, 1963, and 1969.

As a *finding-out process,* collective bargaining in the industry has been somewhat ridiculous. Because of the many voices and centers of power, settlement positions often had not been formulated precisely, or were not known to the nominal spokesman, and positions shifted even while the other party was trying to discover what they were. Although the mediators as well as the employers faced the same problem with the union, the employers were also ambiguous and erratic about their position. They, too, have had multiple voices, in fact their meetings at times were a veritable babble. With pressure, they eventually produced proposals, but their bargaining has not been as effective as that in other industries where at some point it is clear what the settlement positions are. In fairness, the finding out of the settlement position of the ILA was less a problem than the fact that settlements could not be sold internally. It was probably this latter condition more than the former which caused the employers, at one stage, to shift to favor compulsory arbitration, which would force a precise statement of demands for the arbitrator, and a final result would emerge in the arbitrator's award. By thus avoiding uncertainty, perhaps they would have fallen into other snares.

More subject to criticism, as just suggested, is the other aspect of the process of collective bargaining, the *achievement of consent* of the constituents to the terms of the settlement. Long before people began to complain, as they have done recently, about rank-and-file rejection of agreements negotiated by officials elected to do so, longshoremen in New York often rejected settlements. ILA officials seldom seem to have thought, while an agreement was being negotiated, that the rank-and-file longshoremen needed to be informed and convinced that the terms were the best that could be gained. Often the men hardly knew the terms they were voting on. Some officials were probably genuinely surprised by rejection when they thought they had liberal settlements; others seem to have expected, if not invited, rejection, harboring the notion that they could go back and get more. But the employers sometimes contributed to this problem by granting more to get the men to work, thus creating an expectation that rejection would always produce more. At other times the employers held their ground and second ballots produced consent not present in the first. In either event, the leaders of the ILA had not assumed their responsibility to achieve consent to their efforts, either because of neglect or because they recognized the impossibility of satisfying all the parts. Suspicion of leaders, too, led to rejection of agreements the first time around, beginning with the rejection in 1945 and repeated often thereafter. But leaders, not able or not willing to face their members, allowed the consent process to run the gamut of repeat balloting, a phenomenon bitterly underscored by Scotto in negotiations in 1968. If not the most artful way of achieving consent, it at least fulfilled the need, eventually.

The surface characteristics of the process of negotiations, of course, have conformed to the normal pattern in industry generally, albeit with some unnecessary exaggerations. No union can outdo the ILA in starting with *exhorbitant demands*. These demands were not only the necessary overstatement to assure bargaining maneuverability in the finding-out process, they were the result of functional defect of not being able to do more than assemble all demands whatsoever. *Numerous meetings* have indeed been another fact of life, drawn out by endless harangue, and serving to meet internal political needs rather than to play the usual feeling-out role while simultaneously revealing settlement positions. Both parties went through the motions of bargaining but not artfully as in other industries. *Deadlines* were always present but frequently were changed—or lost force— through Taft-Hartley procedures, which were habitually invoked. Deadlines were also often postponed by agreed-upon extensions, because settlement positions were usually not revealed by the time of the formal deadline. The deadline often was not allowed to play its role of infliction of cost upon each party separately, and somewhat equally, for refusal to settle. The *corridors* were utilized almost as much as the table. The informal conversations in this industry are legend, but, again, neither side had a spokesman with the power and knowledge about the terms of settlement who could consummate an agreement with his counterpart on the other side. It is symptomatic of the relationship that it usually took an outsider—from the top level of government—to sift out and consummate the settlement.

On the emotional level *launching of the new agreement* was usually easy. The problem was not to dissipate the aggressions built up during the process of negotiations. Usually settlement was such a relief that everyone was pleased to hear the news and get back to work. The technical launching, however, was often difficult. Many times the "memorandum of settlement" left loose ends or provided for subsequent working out of details, and the parties never moved through these periods efficiently or gracefully. Here is where the employers frequently lost what they thought they had gained in exchange for what they had given. Usually everyone was so fatigued by the interminable negotiating and beset by the pressures to get on with daily duties that they procrastinated. Neither side trained lesser functionaires in the ranks about the terms of the agreement. Administration is replete with examples of the neglect, notably in grievance handling, administration of seniority, and administration of the GAI.

Bargaining Structure

The inadequacies of the bargaining structure have been one of the industry's largest and most chronic problems, veritably a pathological one. It has been an issue in practically all negotiations since the stoppage of 1951. Never disentangled from other problems, and even when not raised as a direct issue, it has upset the bargaining table time and again. The individualism in the industry, or the self-centeredness of the parts—in both ranks—and the autonomy cherished by the parts on each side, could never be overcome for a program of improvement.

If business competition is the life of trade, and if it gave special color to developments in the longshore industry, it hardly has been a positive influence on union and management relations. Inside the Port of New York unity never existed, unless it has come with reorganization of the NYSA in 1971. The development of CONASA should help in the broader industry, too, but competition between ports may interfere with overall programming, for the welfare of each port is a prime consideration for those who make their living in it. These interests, on both the labor and employer sides, are not easily subordinated to an overall interest. Although no sufficient overall interest may exist, the establishment of more interrelationships should be constructive.

The Role of Government

The federal, state, and local governments have played a varied and multisided role in negotiations, depending upon the occasion. Government has never been able to escape the role of peacemaker, and it has had to go beyond mediation to the providing of a settlement—by cajoling or by force. Vocally abhoring governmental intervention, the parties generally welcomed, certainly expected, and sometimes pled for it. The strike was hardly ever allowed to run its traditional course, so that bargaining was obfuscated and sometimes ridiculous. The union never learned the humiliations and searing effects of a strike, from which it had to extricate itself by its own efforts, and the employers never took this kind of strike. Some were not willing to do so, for they predicted ruin to themselves before capitulation by the union. Some were not able to outlast the union; or, if they were able, were not allowed by the government to take the kind of strike needed. There were strikes—some of fairly long duration after the expiration of Taft-Hartley injunctions—but these were not the type needed and the union could count on governmental pressures eventually to bring a favorable "compromise." The ambivalence of government, never knowing when to go in or when to stay out, has minimized the role of the traditional strike. More than one skilled mediator has been baffled by the bargaining situation, with never enough experience or time to understand it. Governmental mediators, it is well known, seek settlements, and in principle, this aim is good. In this industry, however, the mediation usually led to the seeking or forcing of concessions from employers. It was easier to seduce, some might say rape, the employers. While the employers did not always seem to enjoy it, they always came back to the same old bed, probably because they had no other choice.

The federal government's role was not limited to mediating disputes or to settling them by whatever devices seemed necessary—that is, to its traditional role. It was rarely reluctant at the critical moment to invoke the emergency procedures under the Taft-Hartley Act, but its record in doing so falls short of constructive achievement and hardly merits more than a commendation for promptness or predictability in action. The record is maudlin indeed. The federal government also played a regulatory role, as it did on occasion when the NLRB was called into action. But here, unless its controversial behavior in hurrying the election for bargaining agent in 1954 is held against it, the record of government meets the standards of administrative agencies. The role of the NLRB in this industry is not different from its role in other industries.

The Waterfront Commission

More controversial has been the role of state governments, that is, of the states of New York and New Jersey in creating the Waterfront Commission, the bistate agency designed to curb criminal activities and to regulate the process of hiring. Growing as it did out of the investigations of crime and corruption on the waterfront, the commission has been a major factor in the industry as a crime-detecting and law-enforcing agency. But also pertinent to the labor relations story is the other basic function of the commission, regulation and improvement of the labor market situation and the operation of hiring centers. It naturally ran into opposition, at times, from employers as well as from the ILA. But its primary, and continuous, opposition came from the ILA because the commission was assigned to perform functions which respected unions do as a matter of integrity and service to their members. Without judging all of the commission's actions, it must be concluded that this governmental agency has exerted a salutary influence for nigh on to two decades.

It is not strange that the ILA wanted to regain some control over hiring, for this is a legitimate aim of labor unions. But there is little doubt that the ILA had forfeited its right to control in the longshore labor market by callous disregard of the interests of much of the rank and file, even by its abuse of many men in many respects. There also seems little doubt that the ILA has never proved that it can be trusted to regulate the labor market without allowing old evils to return. It had a golden opportunity with the establishment of seniority. Its lack of administration of this program served mostly to prove that the commission was still needed. Likewise, its behavior with respect to the GAI continued the doubt about the ability or willingness to behave responsibly, although certainly the employers were also guilty of allowing the shameful conditions to spread. They were never willing to demand their due and defaulted abjectly. They should have insisted in 1968 on undoing the damage inflicted in the matter of debiting by the Kheel award, but they did not force the ILA to give up the advantage that men had from it in being able to shun work and get paid anyway. They should have seen to it that the ILA helped them administer the GAI with integrity.

Whether the functions of the Waterfront Commission should have been placed in two separate agencies may be debatable, that is, whether the policing functions should have been in one agency and the functions of regulating the labor market and hiring in another. But even if the functions had been so separated, and if the ILA had been no more constructive in its approach to the hiring function, and if the employers had remained too preoccupied with other matters to exercise management prerogatives, the commission would have continued to be a necessity with respect to surveillance of the hiring function. It will no doubt continue to be needed into the future.

The Waterfront Commission has been a major factor in labor relations on the waterfront in the Port of New York because the hiring of longshoremen is a central fact of life and significant parts of the collective agreement deal with it. The law and the collective agreement overlap, but while the former respects the practice of collective bargaining the latter cannot supersede or displace the requirements of the law. The commission, therefore, accommodates the terms of the collective agreement in its administration of the law only to the extent that it does not conflict. Actually the commission has helped implement some parts of the collective agreement, cooperating with employers and/or employers and union, as the case might be; but sometimes conflict, not cooperation, has been the more common thing because the union, and sometimes the employers, chafed over the restraints or requirements of the law. The ILA continually sought to eliminate the law or circumvent it. It has never lost an opportunity to challenge or excoriate the commission.

The commission was born with the blessing of some employers but with the antagonism of others. Almost to a man, officialdom of the ILA was antagonistic to it, and publicly remains so. But the longshoremen's reactions were mixed, depending upon how they saw the law and the agency administering it. Many longshoremen came to look upon the commission as the source of good on the waterfront, more perhaps than the number who looked to the ILA for protection. Many have seen the agents of the commission as friends and protectors. But some workers have never done so because their interests lay elsewhere, and at times large numbers, aroused about particular developments associated with the commission, have made protests and even gone on strike against the commission.

Although the commission has often been charged with interference with collective bargaining or with obstructing administration of argeements—inevitable no doubt in view of the role

assigned it—the conclusion must be that the commission has interfered relatively little, apart from not letting the parties have their
own way. It has blocked agreements that would have interfered
with administration of the law, but this is hardly interference
with collective bargaining. Collective bargaining in all industries
operates within the constraints of law—the difference in the longshore industry being that a special law governs the parties and
places special restraints upon them, but only in the matter of
hiring and related matters, that is, exclusion of certain undesirable persons from the waterfront. One of the most extreme
actions, no doubt questionable to some, was the writing of the
provisions of the seniority agreement into its regulations in order
to make them enforceable by the commission. This, of course,
would not have been done had seniority been administered
with integrity by the union. Also, but in relation to seniority
and the manpower problem created by the geographical shifts
in work opportunities in the port, the commission, prodded by
others, endeavored to solve a problem by going contrary to the
wishes of the two parties and around the requirements of the
agreement, even to pressing the parties to modify their agreement. This action did verge on interference and was bound to
create antagonism to the agency. Some employers have expressed
themselves forcefully in opposition to the commission in the
matter of regulation of the supply of longshoremen and insistence upon the rigid hiring regulations.

The Labor Market

The healthfulness of the labor supply and the organization
of the labor market are interrelated and of great consequence to
all the parties, but interests in the matter are not harmonious.
The union should be the watchdog for the men, but historically
it has failed in its responsibility, at least to the whole, and sometimes grossly neglected the men's interests.

Certainly, improvements have been made in the organization
of the labor market, commencing with the elimination of the
open shape-up, and eventually involving the hiring centers, the

regulations of the commission, the seniority system, and the GAI, which are complexly interrelated. The commission instituted the first controls on the number of men, by creating registration and by setting minimum employment standards as a test of retention of registration. It decasualized the labor market to a considerable extent. The seniority system carried decasualization further, although the commission had to take a hand. But manpower problems, aggravated by the technological changes revolution-izing cargo handling, have never been solved, and the labor market has continued to be chaotic as geographical centers of employment have shifted. In fact, the industry, on both sides, has become divided over manpower issues, and self-centeredness has prevented the industry-wide approach necessary for a ra-tional solution. Controversies over seniority classifications and district priorities and over travel-time payments reflected the divisions. The GAI, a rational innovation, designed to improve the labor market and the welfare of the men on the one hand and the employers on the other by providing flexibility in assign-ment and mobility in hiring, was not rationally implemented and administered. Even the second time, the extension of the guar-antee was not accompanied by improvement in administration, with the result that more serious problems confronted the parties than ever before. The most recent agreement should undo the damage if administered with integrity.

The Longshoremen in the Port of New York

Often appearing secondary in the negotiations and in the internal struggles of the union, the condition of the individual longshoreman, nevertheless, has improved during the past quarter century, but this has been due, in some part, to factors outside the union, even when the ILA became involved in programs of betterment—for example, in changes in hiring which led to the system of seniority. The ILA took action in introducing sen-iority agreements chiefly because of the appearance of the Waterfront Commission and the administration of its regulations, from which many of the leaders of the union tried to escape, and because of the assault by the AFL and the appearance of the IBL, with which the union had to do battle. Because the seniority program was sometimes observed in the breach, the Waterfront Commission was led to write the terms of the agreement into its regulations in order to enforce recognition of the tenure of longshoremen. When seniority was established, however, the union, or rather its parts, did not wish to support portwide seniority, which would have been beneficial to long-service longshoremen—and to the industry, as the employers belatedly discovered—and it entrenched borough and sectional barriers to the possibility of a portwide system. Yet, in spite of the entrenchment of provincialism, the seniority system was one factor which made possible the introduction of the GAI, which further improved the lot of longshoremen—paradoxically helping some in the union who, at the inception of seniority, had selfishly insisted upon a narrow base for it. The difficulties surrounding these improvements for labor were compounded by technological changes in the industry leading to containerization.

However, although technological forces within the industry in most major ports led to adjustments in the labor market and pointed the way to greater regularity in employment,[1] much credit is due the ILA, particularly to the sagacity of Gleason, that it held singlemindedly to the objective of protecting the interests of longshoremen. Unfortunately the union could not manage its own house sufficiently to control abuse of the GAI or to avoid interminable negotiations as a result of infighting. Even if the individual longshoreman has sometimes seemed to be lost sight of, obviously he is now better off. His earnings have improved, a product of both increased hourly rates of pay and more regularity in employment. Although current changes in the industry are having an adverse impact upon some workers—as well as a highly beneficial one upon others—the typical longshoreman enjoys a better life.

In 1945, the straight-time hourly wage rate of longshoremen

[1] Jensen, *Hiring of Dock Workers*, and Jensen, *Decasualization and Modernization of Dock Work in London*.

was $1.50. In 1970–1971, before the increase approved by the Pay Board, it was $4.60; afterward it was $5.15. By reaching back to the mid-fifties, from the time the ILA had rebuffed the challenges to it as bargaining agent, a comparison of average weekly earnings for the year 1955–1956 with those in 1970–1971 reveals an increase from $105.77 to $201.92, during which time the average straight-time hourly rate increased from $2.42 to $4.60. Average weekly earnings of nonagricultural workers, during the same period, increased from $70.74 to $126.91, based on average straight-time hourly rates of $1.80 and $3.43, respectively.[2] The increase in the earnings of the nonagricultural employees is 79 per cent, whereas the increase in the earnings of longshoremen is 91 per cent. In this same period the Consumers' Price Index increased by 49 per cent, hence, the real increase in earnings of longshoremen was only 42 per cent, but this is a respectable improvement. It is also revealing to compare earnings and wage rates of longshoremen with those in building construction, which are generally considered to be as substantial as any. The average weekly earnings of construction workers in 1956 were $101.92 and in 1971 they were $194.04, based on average hourly rates of $2.80 and $5.42, respectively. The hourly rates of construction workers were slightly higher than those of longshoremen, but the earnings of longshoremen are slightly higher than those of construction workers, due, no doubt, to the fact that longshoremen enjoy more hours of work at premium rates—roughly 30 per cent of the hours worked by longshoremen are at overtime rates.

In the year 1970–1971, approximtaely 900 longshoremen—not considering the craft groups—received earnings in excess of $15,000; and some, no doubt surprisingly, running to double this

[2] For statistical data on wages and earnings in the longshore industry, see Jensen, "Hiring Practices and Employment Experience of Longshoremen in the Port of New York," *International Labor Review*, vol. 77, April 1958, p. 24, and Jensen, "Decasualization of Employment on the New York Waterfront," *Industrial and Labor Relations Review*, vol. 11, July 1958, pp. 543–544. For statistical data on wages and earnings in other industries, see statistical tables in *Monthly Labor Review*.

figure and more. Modal earnings were $10,500, although the arithmetic mean was $8,740. The lower mean arises from the fact that approximately 1,000 men received less than $1,000, and another 2,000 less than $5,000. These low-income longshoremen were obviously "moonlighters" from other employments or newcomers who had not qualified for the GAI. Overall, it is modal earnings which is the best measure of well-being of long-shoremen.

Earnings, of course, do not tell the whole story. A larger percentage of the men have steadier employment than in the past, and a more regular flow of income is no doubt an improvement. But employment is undergoing change, and the longshoreman of the future will be more of a machine operator than a mauler of cargo. Because of the changes, the number of longshoremen will decline. The changes in the labor market and the transformation in longshore work will not come about without difficulty —the problems have beset recent negotiations—but it can be hoped that there will be a better employment situation in the future, produced by better labor and management relations.

The Key to the Future

The structure of bargaining and improved negotiations have paved the way to recent progress, although both these factors were more apparent in the internal relations of each party rather than in relations between the parties. The latter, however, have necessarily improved, too. If either side could have done more about its own internal government, it might have forced the other to do more. The employers have needed a more unified organization with enough authority over the membership to administer an overall program. Local deals and individual actions without regard to the whole have been the bane of the existence of the NYSA, both in negotiations and in the intervals between. The more authority a coastwide organization may need—and much can be said favoring some centralization—the more difficult it will be to create the necessary coalitions, for real coalition even in the Port of New York has been impossible in the past. The current question is whether CONASA will succeed. The answer looks favorable.

The ILA has needed overhauling, for a union should be, in fact, a union. Yet the many local unions with private and local interests—some have called them "baronies," and this has not been a just caricature—have obstructed efficiency. Port geography has made it difficult to deal with the longshoremen as a single body, which should have been the primary concern. Autonomous protection of local interests intensified the geographical separations. When this understandable parochialism began to serve to undercut the longtime longshoremen in favor of local newcomers, it became less and less defensible. The situation did not originate in perverseness; the nature of the industry produced a labor market situation which led to this characteristic structuring. Pervasive waterfront psychology has also augmented the fracturing, as has the desire of leaders to perpetuate themselves in office.

Leadership is commonly forged in crisis situations. No crisis in the ILA has brought forward a leader who could mount the opposition and carry the organization to a unity of the whole. Seniority could have been used to knit the organization together in the Port of New York, but the selfish, localized interests, prevailed. What emerged only exacerbated the problem the employers faced in trying to move together to a portwide program. They did not have the power, under the priorities that they had helped to create, tolerate, and sanctify, to produce a more rational administration of the labor supply. Neither did they utilize seniority or the GAI to this end. They gave the GAI and never collected what was needed for the welfare of the bona fide longshoremen as well as for their own. The union, for its part, could not mount a reform in the long-run interests of longshoremen either. It allowed the local interests to maximize their private ends even while to do so undermined the security of the whole.

A union mindful of the long-run interests of longshoremen in company with forward-looking managements concerned with the welfare of the whole industry as well as with their individual interests is needed. The protection of the bona fide longshoreman can be accomplished only when the industry settles into more productive arrangements.

Selected Bibliography

Books, Monographs, and Special Occasional Papers

Background

Barnes, C. B. *The Longshoremen.* New York: Survey Association, 1915. 287 pp.

Commons, J. R. *Labor and Administration.* New York: Macmillan, 1913. 431 pp.

International Longshoremen's Association. *Proceedings of the Convention,* 1902, 1903, 1910, 1911, 1912, 1915, 1919, 1921, 1931, 1935, 1939.

Ogg, E. *Longshoremen and Their Homes.* New York: Greenwich House, 1939. 58 pp.

Stern, B. *Cargo Handling and Longshore Labor Conditions.* U.S. Department of Labor, Bureau of Labor Statistics, Bulletin 550, 1932. 539 pp.

———. "Longshore Labor Conditions in the United States and Port Decasualization," Report to William H. Davis, Administrator of the Shipping Code, November 10, 1933. Typewritten.

Swanstrom, E. E. *The Waterfront Labor Problem.* New York: Fordham University Press, 1938. 186 pp.

U.S. Commission on Industrial Relations. *Final Report and Testimony,* vol. 3. Washington, D.C., 1915.

U.S. Shipping Board. *Marine and Dock Labor-Work, Wages, and Industrial Relations during the Period of the War,* Report of the Director of the Marine and Dock Industrial Relations Division. Washington, D.C., 1919.

Concurrent with the Period of the Study

Bernstein, I. *Turbulent Years: A History of the American Worker, 1933–1941.* Boston: Houghton Mifflin, 1970. 873 pp.

Bird, F. L. *A Study of the Port of New York Authority.* New York: Dun & Bradstreet, 1949. 220 pp.

The Citizens' Waterfront Committee. *The New York Waterfront.* New York, 1946. 146 pp.

Galenson, W. *The CIO Challenge to the AFL.* Cambridge, Mass.: Harvard University Press, 1960. 732 pp.

Goldblatt, L. *Men and Machines: A Story about Longshoring on the Westcoast Waterfront.* San Francisco: International Longshoremen's and Warehousing Union and Pacific Maritime Association, 1963. 161 pp.

Gorter, W., and G. H. Hildebrand. *The Pacific Coast Maritime Shipping Industry, 1930–1948,* vol. 2, *An Analysis of Performance.* Berkeley: University of California Press, 1952. 113 pp.

Griffin, J. L. *The Port of New York.* New York: City College Press, 1959. 154 pp.

Hartman, P. T. *Collective Bargaining and Productivity—The Longshore Mechanization Agreement.* Berkeley: University of California Press, 1969. 307 pp.

Jensen, V. H. *Hiring of Dock Workers and Employment Practices in the Ports of New York, Liverpool, London, Rotterdam and Marseilles.* Cambridge: Harvard University Press, 1964. 317 pp.

Johnson, M. M. *Crime on the Labor Front.* New York: McGraw-Hill, 1950. 243 pp.

Kennedy, T. *Automation Funds and Displaced Workers.* Cambridge: Harvard University Graduate School of Business Administration, 1962. 374 pp.

Larrowe, C. P. *Shape-up and Hiring Hall.* Berkeley: University of California Press, 1955. 250 pp.

Port of New York Authority. *Container Shipping: Full Ahead.* New York, 1967. 143 pp.

——. *Metropolitan Transportation 1980.* New York, 1963. 380 pp.

——. *The Next Twenty Years: A Forecast of Population and Jobs in the New York–New Jersey–Connecticut Metropolitan Region, 1965–85.* New York, 1966. 32 pp.

——. *A Selected Bibliography, 1921–1962.* New York, 1962. 110 pp.

Raymond, A. *Waterfront Priest.* New York: Henry Holt, 1960. 269 pp.

Rosenbaum, E. "The Expulsion of the International Longshoremen's Association from the American Federation of Labor." Ph.D. dissertation, University of Wisconsin, 1954. 731 pp.

Russell, M. *Men along the Shore.* New York: Brussel & Brussel, 1966. 310 pp.

Schneider, B. V. H., and A. J. Seigel. *Industrial Relations in the Pacific Coast Longshore Industry.* Berkeley: University of California Institute of Industrial Relations, 1955. 89 pp.

Schulberg, B. *On the Waterfront.* New York: Random House, 1955. 320 pp.

Tobin, A. J. *Crime on the Waterfront: Port Authority Plan for Relief,* address before New York University Law School, March 5, 1953. New York, 1953. 33 pp.

Articles in Periodicals

Bell, D. "Last of the Business Rackets," *Fortune*, vol. 43, June 1951, pp. 89–91ff.

——. "Some Aspects of the New York Longshore Situation," *Proceedings of the Seventh Annual Meeting of the Industrial Relations Research Association*, Dec. 28–30, 1954, pp. 298–304.

Carey, P. A. "Jesuit School Helped Clear up New York City Waterfront," *Industrial Bulletin*, vol. 39, June 1960, pp. 2–24.

Corridan, Father J. M. "Longshoremen's Case," *America*, Nov. 20, 1948, pp. 65–66. "Waterfront," *America*, Oct. 8, 1955, pp. 38–41.

Cullman, H. S. "Challenge on Our Waterfront," *Brooklyn Eagle*, Sept. 1952 (series of articles).

Fairley, L. "The ILWU-PMA Mechanization and Modernization Agreement: The Union Viewpoint," *Proceedings of the Sixteenth Annual Meeting of the Industrial Relations Research Association*, Dec. 27–28, 1963, pp. 34–47.

Goldberg, J. P. "Containerization as a Force for Change on the Waterfront," *Monthly Labor Review*, vol. 91, Jan. 1968, pp. 8–13.

Gottlieb, J. "The Man Who Shut Down the Port of New York," *The Reporter*, April 27, 1954, pp. 28–31.

Groom, P. "Hiring Practices for Longshoremen," *Monthly Labor Review*, Nov. 1965, pp. 1289–1296.

Grossman, A. "Labor Regimentation on the New York Docks," *Trade Union Courier*, Sept. 2, 1955, pp. 12–13.

"Harry Bridges and Joe Ryan," *Fortune*, vol. 39, Jan. 1949, pp. 152–154.

Horne, G. "Kingless Jungle: New York's Waterfront," *Nation*, Feb. 21, 1953, pp. 163–165.

Horvitz, W. L. "The ILWU-PMA Mechanization and Modernization Agreement: An Experiment in Industrial Relations," *Proceedings of the Sixteenth Annual Meeting of the Industrial Relations Research Association*, Dec. 27–28, 1963, pp. 22–33.

Hutchinson, J. "Corruption in American Labor Union," *Political Quarterly*, vol. 72, July–Sept. 1957.

"International Longshoremen's Association: Dock Union Is Pariah to Labor Movement Itself," *Business Week*, April 19, 1952, pp. 64–66.

Jensen, V. H. "Computer Hiring of Dock Workers in the Port of New York," *Industrial and Labor Relations Review*, vol. 20, April 1967, pp. 425–427.

——. "Decasualization of Employment on the New York Waterfront," *Industrial and Labor Relations Review*, vol. 11, July 1958, pp. 534–550.

——. "Decasualizing a Labor Market: The Longshore Experience," in A. Siegel, ed., *The Impact of Computers on Collective Bargaining*. Cambridge: MIT Press, 1969. Pp. 226–259.

——. "Dispute Settlement in the New York Longshore Industry," *Industrial and Labor Relations Review*, vol. 10, July 1957, pp. 588–608.

——. "Hiring Practices and Employment Experience of Longshoremen in the Port of New York," *International Labour Review*, vol. 77, April 1958, pp. 342–369.

"Labor Movement: Dirt on the Waterfront," *Commonweal*, Nov. 23, 1951, pp. 172–173, Dec. 21, pp. 274–276.

Lens, S. "Labor Rackets, Inc.," *Nation*, March 2, 1957, pp. 179–183.

Meyers, H. B. " 'Wrangdoodle' Time on the Docks," *Fortune*, vol. 77, Sept. 1968, pp. 84–89.

Morse, Senator W. "Longshore Dispute Settlement," *Congressional Record*, Jan. 22, 1963, pp. 700–703, 1043–1045.

——. "Longshore Negotiations," *Congressional Record*, Jan. 12, 1965, pp. 580–583.

Murphy, M. J. "Water-front Labor," University of Illinois *Law Forum*, Spring 1959, pp. 65–80.

"New Concepts in Labor Relations on New York's Waterfront," *Business Week*, Feb. 2, 1952, p. 30.

"New York Waterfront," *Fortune*, vol. 40, Dec. 1, 1949, p. 210.

Nossiter, B. D. "Waterfront War, Round Two in New York," *Nation*, Oct. 8, 1955, pp. 298–302.

"Profile, The ILA's 'Teddy' Gleason," *American Labor*, vol. 2, Sept. 1969, pp. 21–29.

Raskin, A. H., "How the Docks Shape Up Now," *New York Times Magazine*, June 12, 1955, pp. 13, 42.

——. "The New Labor Leaders—a Dual Portrait," *New York Times Magazine*, Jan. 1959, pp. 30ff.

——. "Union Leader and Big Business Man," *New York Times Magazine*, Nov. 15, 1953, pp. 13ff.

Rosenblatt, M. "Joe Ryan and His Kingdom," *Nation*, Nov. 24, 1945, pp. 548–550.

——. "The Scandal of the Waterfront," *Nation*, Nov. 17, 1945, pp. 516–519.

Ross, P. "Distribution of Power within the ILWU and the ILA," *Monthly Labor Review*, vol. 91, Jan. 1968, pp. 1–7.

——. "Waterfront Labor Response to Technological Change: A Tale of Two Unions," *Labor Law Journal*, vol. 21, July 1970, pp. 397–419.

Schulberg, B. "How One Pier Got Rid of the Mob," *New York Times Magazine*, Sept. 27, 1953, pp. 17ff.

——. "The Waterfront Revisited," *Saturday Evening Post*, Sept. 7, 1963, pp. 28, 44.

Todd, C. "Jungle on the Waterfront," *New Republic*, May 4, 1942, pp. 596–597.

Tyler, G. "The Waterfront: Loot, Blood and Politics," *New Republic*, Jan. 5, 1953, pp. 6–7.

Velie, L. "Big Boss of the Big Port," *Collier's*, Feb. 9, 1952, pp. 18–19, Feb. 16, 1952, pp. 56–58, 60.
Vorse, M. H. "The Pirates' Nest of New York," *Harper's*, April 1952, pp. 27–37.
Whalen, R. G. "Two Generals Patrol the Docks," *New York Times Magazine*, Nov. 29, 1953, pp. 20ff.

Newspapers and Periodicals

Principal Sources

New York Herald Tribune, 1945–1965.
New York Times, 1945–1972.
Todd Daily Maritime (daily composite of news items), 1967–1972.

Others

Baltimore Sun.
Brooklyn Longshoremen (ILA Local 1814).
Daily Labor Reports (Bureau of National Affairs).
"Dockers News" (anonymous, mimeographed).
Fact Sheet (ILA).
The Journal of Commerce (New York City).
Local 824 Bulletin (ILA Local 824).
The Longshore News (ILA).
New Orleans Times-Picayune.
New York Post.
The Pilot (NMU).
Seafarers Log (SIU).
Voice of 856 (ILA Local 856).
Wall Street Journal.
Waterfront News (IBL).

Government Publications and Materials

Local and State Government Publications

New York, City of, Mayor's Joint Committee on Port Industry. *Labor Conditions Affecting Waterfront Commerce, Report of Subcommittee, No. 5*, Hugh Sheridan, Chairman. Aug. 1951.
New York, City Planning Commission. *The Port of New York: Proposals for Development* (New York, 1964).
New York State. *Record of the Public Hearings Held by Governor Thomas E. Dewey on the Recommendations of the New York State Crime Commission for Remedying Conditions on the Waterfront of the Port of New York*, 1953.
——, Crime Commission. *Fourth Report of the New York State Crime Commission* (Port of New York Waterfront), Leg. Doc. No. 70, 1953.

——, Crime Commission, *Public Hearings* (Port of New York Waterfront) 5 vols., 1953.

——, Department of Labor. "Board of Inquiry on Longshore Industry Work Stoppage, Report of Proceedings," 3 vols. 1951. Typewritten.

——, Department of Labor. *Final Report to the Industrial Commissioner from Board of Inquiry on Longshore Industry Work Stoppage, October–November 1951, Port of New York*, Jan. 22, 1952.

——, Legislature, Joint Legislative Committee on Docks in the City of New York. *Report,* Leg. Doc., No. 34, March 22, 1961, and *Final Report,* Leg. Doc., No. 37, Feb. 20, 1962.

——, Legislature. *Report of the New York State Joint Legislative Committee on Industrial and Labor Conditions.* Albany, N.Y., 1943.

——, Supreme Court, County of New York. Referee's *Interlocutory Report,* Index No. 11232/1955, NYSA *et al* (plaintiffs) and ILA *et al* (defendants), Simon H. Rifkind, Referee, Jan. 10, 1956.

Waterfront Commission. *Annual Report,* 1953–54 to 1971–72.

——. "Conference on the Seniority Arbitration Award," transcripts, Nov. 26, 1958, Jan. 7, 1959, and Jan. 27, 1959.

——. "Conferences," March 2, 8, 16 and 17, 1955. (Each day numbered separately.) Typewritten.

——. "Hiring Regulations for Registrants," effective May 6, 1963.

——. *Interim Report on Current Work Stoppage,* March 25, 1954.

——. Memoranda in Opposition to Bills (1964–1965).

——. "Memorandum in Opposition to Senate Bill, No. 3067, Print No. 3253 and to Assembly Bill, No. 4922, Print No. 5083." April 3, 1965.

——. "Proposed Revised Hiring Regulations," Feb. 1, 1963. Mimeographed.

——. "Public Hearing, IV, Oct. 15, 1954." Mimeographed.

——. "Public Hearing to Determine Whether Applications for Inclusion in the Longshoremen's Register Should Be Accepted," Feb. 20, 21, 1968.

——. "Regulations," 1953. Periodically supplemented or revised.

——. "Revised Regulations," May 6, 1963. See also NYSA Report 2142, May 3, 1963, and NYSA Report 2166, Aug. 13, 1963.

——. "Seniority Hiring of Longshoremen in the Port of New York," Report by Percy A. Miller, Director, Information Centers and Licensing, July 19, 1960.

——. *Special Report to the Governors and Legislatures of the States of New York and New Jersey,* Dec. 1960.

——. *Special Report to the Governors and Legislatures of the States of New York and New Jersey,* July 1970.

United States Government Publications

Boards of Inquiry. (Listed by dates.)
Report and Final Report to the President in the Labor Dispute in the Maritime Industry, June 3, 1948 (Wallen Board).

Boards of Inquiry (*cont.*)

Report to the President on the Labor Dispute Involving Longshoremen and Associated Occupations in the Maritime Industry on the Atlantic Coast, Dec. 4, 1953. Includes also a Report to the President on Oct. 5, 1953 (Cole Board).

"Proceedings before the Board of Inquiry on the Labor Dispute Involving Longshoremen and Associated Occupations in the Maritime Industry on the Atlantic and Gulf Coast, Nov. 22–23, 1956" (Holland Board).

Report to the President on the Labor Dispute Involving Longshoremen and Associated Occupations in the Maritime Industry on the Atlantic and Gulf Coast, Nov. 24, 1956 (Holland Board).

Final Report to the President on the Labor Dispute Involving Longshoremen and Associated Occupations in the Maritime Industry on the Atlantic and Gulf Coast, Jan. 23, 1957 (Holland Board).

Report to the President on the Labor Dispute Involving Longshoremen and Associated Occupations in the Maritime Industry on the Atlantic and Gulf Coast, Dec. 7, 1959 (Farmer Board).

Report to the President on the Labor Dispute Involving the International Longshoremen's Association and the Maritime Industry on the Atlantic and Gulf Coasts, Oct. 4, 1962 (Fleming Board).

"Transcript of Proceedings of the Board of Inquiry in the Matter of a Dispute between the Shipping and Stevedoring Companies, Atlantic and Gulf Coasts, and the International Longshoremen's Association," Oct. 2, 1962 (Fleming Board).

"Statement of Board of Inquiry," Oct. 30, 1962 (Fleming Board). Typewritten.

Second Report to the President on the Labor Dispute Involving the International Longshoremen's Association and the Maritime Industry on Atlantic and Gulf Coasts, Dec. 3, 1962 (Fleming Board).

First Report of the Board of Inquiry into the Longshoring Dispute on the Atlantic and Gulf Coasts, Oct. 1, 1964 (Schmertz Board). The official text is also contained in *Daily Labor Report*, Oct. 2, 1964.

Second Report of the Board of Inquiry into the Longshoring Dispute on the Atlantic and Gulf Coasts, Nov. 30, 1964 (Schmertz Board).

First Report to the President in the Stevedoring Industry Dispute on the Atlantic and Gulf Coasts, Oct. 1, 1968 (Cole Board).

Second Report to the President in the Stevedoring Industry Dispute on the Atlantic and Gulf Coasts, Nov. 30, 1968 (Cole Board).

Congress, House, Committee on the Judiciary. *New Jersey–New York Waterfront Commission Compact, Hearing on H.R. 6286, H.R. 6343, and S. 2383*, 83d Cong., 1st Sess., July 22, 1953.

——, House, Committee on Merchant Marine and Fisheries. *Labor Problems of the American Merchant Marine, Hearings on H.R. 5734*, 84th Cong., 1st Sess., 1955.

———, House, Committee on Merchant Marine and Fisheries. *Maritime Labor Legislation, Part 2, Hearings on H.R. 2004 and H.R. 2331,* 88th Cong., 1st Sess., 1963.

———, Senate, Committee on Interstate and Foreign Commerce. *New York–New Jersey Waterfront, Subcommittee Hearings pursuant to S. Res. 41 on Waterfront and Port Security, Part 1,* 83d Cong., 1st Sess., March–June, 1953.

———, Senate, Committee on Labor and Public Welfare. *To Clarify the Overtime Compensation Provisions of the Fair Labor Standards Act of 1938, as Amended, Hearings before the Subcommittee,* 81st Cong., 1st Sess., 1949.

———, Senate, Committee on Labor and Public Welfare. *Hiring Halls and the Maritime Industry, Hearings before the Subcommittee on Labor and Management Relations,* 81st Cong., 2d Sess., 1950.

———, Senate, Committee on Military Affairs. *Report from the Subcommittee on War Mobilization, Subcommittee Report No. 3, pursuant to S. Res. 107,* 78th Cong., 1st Sess., Oct. 7, 1943.

Department of Labor, Bureau of Labor Statistics. *National Emergency Disputes, Labor and Management Relations (Taft-Hartley) Act, 1947–68,* (Bulletin No. 1633) Sept. 1969.

———, Bureau of Labor Statistics. *Impact of Longshore Strikes on the National Economy,* Jan. 1970.

———, Bureau of Labor Statistics. *Manpower Utilization—Job Security in the Longshore Industry—Ports of New York, July 1, 1964.* Issued subsequently were reports on the ports of Boston, Philadelphia, Baltimore, Jacksonville-Charleston, Mobile, New Orleans, and Houston-Galveston.

Federal Maritime Commission. *Agreement No. T-2336—New York Shipping Association Cooperative Working Agreement,* Sept. 22, 1971.

Federal Mediation and Conciliation Service. "Recommendations to the New York Shipping Association and the International Longshoremen's Association," Sept. 24, 1962. Mimeographed.

Maritime Administration, Office of Maritime Manpower, Division of Labor Studies. *Summary of Longshore Strike, 1964–65,* July 15, 1966.

National Labor Relations Board. *Decisions and Orders. (Listed by volumes.)*

Vol. 107, Bargaining Unit, 1953, pp. 364ff.

Vol. 108, Bargaining Unit, 1954, pp. 137–158.

Vol. 109, Challenged Ballots, 1954, pp. 310ff. Certification, pp. 791ff.

Vol. 116, Bargaining Unit, 1956, pp. 1183ff.

Vol. 118, National Bargaining, 1957, pp. 1481ff.

Vol. 134, National Bargaining, pp. 1279ff.

———. *Nineteenth Annual Report,* 1954.

———. "Regional Director's Report on Challenges and Obligations, in the Representation Dispute between the International Longshoremen's Association and the International Brotherhood of Longshoremen" (1954).

Pay Board. Staff Submission Papers—*PMA-ILWU Case,* Washington, D.C., March 14, 1972.

——. *East and Gulf Coast Longshore Submissions of the Parties.* Washington, D.C., n.d. [March 1972].

——. *Summary and Analysis—East and Gulf Coast Longshore,* Washington, D.C., n.d. [April 1972].

"Presidential Commission," Reynolds, J. J. (Chairman), T. W. Kheel, and J. J. Healy. "Recommendations on Manpower Utilization, Job Security and Other Disputes Issues for the Port of New York," Sept. 25, 1964. Mimeographed.

Secretary of Labor and Director of the Federal Mediation and Conciliation Service, W. W. Wirtz and W. E. Simkin. "Recommendations for Settlement of the Dispute Between the New York Shipping Association and the Atlantic Coast District, International Longshoremen's Association, AFL-CIO," Dec. 19, 1962.

Private Reports and Documents

American Federation of Labor. *Report of the Proceedings of the Seventy-second Convention of the American Federation of Labor,* St. Louis, Sept. 1953. Pp. 53ff. On expulsion of the ILA.

——. *Report of the Proceedings of the Seventy-third Convention of the American Federation of Labor,* Los Angeles, Sept. 1954. Pp. 50ff. On support of the IBL.

——, Executive Council. "Reply of George Meany to the ILA on Recommendations Made by the Executive Council," 1953.

——, Executive Council. "Report by the Committee of Five to Inquire into and Evaluate the Report of the New York State Board of Inquiry in Connection with the Claimed Difficulties Involving the Longshoremen in New York." New York: AFL, 1952. 32 pp. Mimeographed.

——, Executive Council. *Report to the Seventy-third Convention of the American Federation of Labor,* Sept. 1954, pp. 27–31. On expulsion of the ILA.

——, Maritime Trades Department. *Program for Greater New York Harbor Port Council,* 1951, p. 5.

——, Maritime Trades Department. *Program for the Greater New York Harbor Port Council,* Jan. 13, 1952.

American Federation of Labor–Congress of Industrial Organizations. "Memorandum—S.I. 3067—Mackell Bill," 1965.

——. *Proceedings of the Third Constitutional Convention of the AFL-CIO,* San Francisco, Calif., Sept. 17–23, 1959. Vol. 1, pp. 419–431, vol. 2, pp. 373–375. On readmission of the ILA.

——. *Proceedings of the Fourth Constitutional Convention of the AFL-CIO,* Miami, Fla., Sept. 1961. Pp. 557–558. Resolution on Waterfront Commission.

Bureau of National Affairs. *Wage Hour Cases,* vol. 6, 1947, pp. 527ff, vol. 8, 1949, pp. 20–39.

Citizens' Waterfront Committee (Godfrey Schmidt *et al.*). "Code of Fair Dealing Proposed to the International Longshoremen's Association for Its Appraisal and Implementation" (1956). New York, 1956. Mimeographed.

Council of North Atlantic Shipping Associations (CONASA). "Statement on Behalf of . . . to the Pay Board," May 2, 1972. Mimeographed.

International Longshoremen's Association. "Answer of the International Longshoremen's Association, AFL, to the Report of the New York State Crime Commission Dealing with the Waterfront of the Port of New York," in House of Representatives, Committee on the Judiciary, *New Jersey–New York Waterfront Commission Compact,* as listed above.

——. "Answer . . . to the Report of the New York Crime Commission Dealing with the Waterfront of the Port of New York, Submitted to the Governor and Members of the Legislature of the State of New York," June 1953. New York: Wilgian Press, 1953. Mimeographed.

——. "Changes to be Made in General Cargo Agreement, as amended September 18, 1959 at 80 Broad Street." Processed.

——. *Constitution and Rules of Order,* as Amended at the 35th Convention held in New York City, July 23–27, 1951. Pp. 58ff.

——. *Directory of the ILA,* March, 1951. 190 pp. April, 1963, 157 pp.

——. "Memorandum of ILA in Support of Bill to Close the Longshoremen's Register and to transfer the Waterfront Commission's Hiring Centers to Joint Labor-Management Operation," April 27, 1965. Mimeographed.

——. "Memorandum in Support of the Bill to Close the Longshoremen's Register and to transfer the Waterfront Commission's Hiring Centers to Joint Labor and Management Operation," April 27, 1968. Mimeographed.

——. Memorandum, Walter L. Eisenberg to Thomas W. Gleason, "Recent Developments in Cargo Handling Methods in the Port of New York and How They May Affect the Coming Negotiations with the Shipping Industry," April 16, 1962. Mimeographed.

——. "Petition of Grievances of the International Longshoremen's Association and the Longshoremen of the Port of New York and Their Program for Relief and Improvements for a Better Port," presented to the Citizens' Waterfront Committee, Oct. 28–Nov. 28, 1955. Mimeographed.

——. "The Problem Arising out of Changes in Methods of Cargo Handling," Jan. 7, 1959.

——. *Proceedings of the Convention of the International Longshoremen's Association,* 1947.

———. *Proceedings of the Thirty-seventh Convention, July 11–15, 1955.*

———. *Proceedings of the Thirty-eighth Convention, July 15–18, 1957.*

———. *Proceedings of the Thirty-ninth Convention, July 13–16, 1959.*

———. *Proceedings of the Fortieth Convention, July 15–18, 1963.*

———. *Proceedings of the Forty-first Convention, July 13–17, 1967.*

———. *Proceedings of the Forty-second Convention, July 19–22, 1971.*

———. "Proposal for Abolition of the Shape-Up and the Establishment of a New System of Hiring in the Port of New York and Vicinity," July 15, 1953.

———. "Proposal of International Longshoremen's Association Containerization Agreement with the New York Shipping Association," Oct. 29, 1959. Mimeographed.

———. *Proposals for a New National Agreement,* June 4, 1971. Mimeographed.

———. "Proposal to the NYSA and All Steamship Companies and Stevedoring Companies Covering Loading and Unloading of Tall Cargoes from Portland, Maine to Brownsville, Texas," Aug. 1956. Mimeographed.

———. *Report of International President Joseph P. Ryan Tendered to the 35th Convention, International Longshoremen's Association,* July 23, 1951.

———. *Report of Thomas W. Gleason, 35th Convention, ILA,* July 13, 1959. Processed.

———. *Report on Recommendations Made by AFL Executive Council, February 3, 1953.* Washington, D.C., 1953. 17 pp.

———. "Statement in Behalf of the ILA, AFL-CIO, October 2, 1962," (Fleming Board). Mimeographed.

———. "Statement of the International Longshoremen's Association, AFL, on the Report, dated Jan. 22, 1952 of Industrial Commissioner's Board of Inquiry." 114 pp. Mimeographed.

———. "Statement of Thomas W. Gleason to the Federal Pay Board," May 2, 1972.

———, Atlantic Coast District. *Proceedings of the Twenty-third Quadrennial Convention,* July 1967.

———, Atlantic Coast District. *Proceedings of the Twenty-fourth Quadrennial Convention,* July 1971.

———, Executive Council and Entire Negotiating Committee. *To All ILA Members in the Port of New York.* New York, Jan. 13, 1965.

———, Executive Council and Entire Negotiating Committee. *To All ILA Members in the Port of New York.* New York, Feb. 24, 1972. Included with the message was the CONASA "Memorandum of Agreement," the "Settlement for the Port of Greater New York Conditions," and the "Procedures for Regulating Hiring, Income Guarantee, Fringe Benefits, and Contract Administration."

——. New York District Council. "Earnings of Longshoremen and Checkers in New York in 1956 and 1957," May 1957. Mimeographed.

——, New York District Council. "Effect of Deregistering Longshoremen Who Do Not Earn a Vacation," Jan. 1, 1958. Processed.

——, Wage Scale Conference Committee. "Changes to be Made in General Cargo Agreement," Aug. 3, 1959.

——, Waldman, L., and Waldman, S. "Before the Board of Inquiry, Statement on Behalf of the International Longshoremen's Association," Jan. 21, 1957.

——, ——. "Final Report of Survey of International Longshoremen's Association Locals," July 28, 1952.

——, ——. "Statement of the International Longshoremen's Association, AFL, on the Report, dated Jan. 22, 1952 of Industrial Commissioner Corsi's Board of Inquiry," 1952. Mimeographed.

New York Shipping Association. "Arbitration Reports," 1955–1971.

——. "Address of Alexander P. Chopin before the International Convention of the International Longshoremen's Association," Miami Beach, Florida, July 14, 1959.

——. *Brief of New York Shipping Association, Preliminary Statement before the National Labor Relations Board* (1954).

——. *Brief of New York Shipping Association, Inc., and Its Member Employers before the National Labor Relations Board,* Case No. 2-R-C-8388 in the Matter of the New York Shipping Association and International Longshoremen's Association, AFL-CIO, petitioner, and International Longshoremen's Association, Independent (intervenor), 1955.

——. "Comments of the NYSA on proposed Revised Regulations of the Waterfront Commission," March 8, 1963.

——. "Counter Proposal on Hiring Procedures on and after December 1, 1953," Aug. 28, 1953.

——. *Exceptions and Brief of the Charging Party, New York Shipping Association, Inc. and Its Employer Members before the National Labor Relations Board,* Case No. 2-CB-1841 (1956).

——. "Labor Relations Committee Reports," 1955–1971.

——. "Memorandum of New York Shipping Administration to Committee on Labor and Public Welfare of the U.S. Senate," May 1950.

——. *A Proposal for Three Years of Industrial Peace,* 1956.

——. Reports. (Selected reports numbered seriatim by dates and listed chronologically.)

"Recommendations Relating to Waterfront Labor Employed on Piers and Wharves," Report No. 769, Jan. 29, 1953.

"Memorandum of the New York Shipping Association to the Committee on Labor and Public Welfare of the U.S. Senate" (Senate Bill S838), Report No. 814, May 13, 1953.

"Statement by John V. Lyon, Chairman, New York Shipping Associa-

———. Reports (*cont.*)

tion, at Public Hearings Before Governor Thomas E. Dewey on the Fourth Report of the New York State Crime Commission," Report 825, June 9, 1953.

Joseph Mayper, Counsel, "Before the Board of Inquiry, Memorandum on Behalf of Employers, Oct. 3, 1953," Report No. 863, Oct. 20, 1953.

"Statement of Last Offer of Settlement on Behalf of Employer Members," Report No. 886, Dec. 8, 1953.

"Memorandum of Settlement, General Cargo Agreement," Report No. 1373, Feb. 20, 1957.

"Master Contract with the International Longshoremen's Association, Independent," Report No. 1471, Dec. 18, 1957.

"Seniority Arbitration Award," Report No. 1551, Nov. 10, 1958.

"Management's Proposal for New NYSA-ILA Contract," Report No. 1654, Aug. 17, 1959.

"Statement Submitted to the Board of Inquiry," Report No. 1680, Oct. 7, 1959.

"Containerization Arbitration Award," Report No. 1839, Nov. 21, 1960.

"In the matter of arbitration between New York Shipping Association and International Longshoremen's Association, AFL-CIO, Containerization Arbitration Award," Report No. 1840, Nov. 23, 1960.

"Dissenting Opinion of ILA Arbitration Board Member," Report No. 1844, Nov. 30, 1960.

Alexander P. Chopin, Chairman, NYSA, Address at the Foreign Commerce Club Dinner, Grand Ballroom, Commodore Hotel, New York City, April 18, 1962, Report No. 2017, April 30, 1962.

"Management Proposals for New NYSA-ILA Contract," Report No. 2048, Aug. 1, 1962.

"Review of Association's Position," Report No. 2070, Oct. 2, 1962.

Statement by Alexander P. Chopin, Chairman, NYSA, before the House Merchant Marine and Fisheries Committee at Hearing to Consider HR 1897, Report No. 2133, April 2, 1963.

"Longshore Seniority Amendment, April 11, 1963," Report No. 2137, April 15, 1963.

"Management's Proposals for New NYSA-ILA Contract," Report No. 2258, July 14, 1964.

"Last Offer," Report No. 2285, Nov. 27, 1964.

"In the matter of arbitration between ILA and NYSA," Report No. 2434, March 10, 1966.

"In the matter of arbitration between ILA and NYSA, Award," Report No. 2565, Oct. 9, 1967.

"Favorable Initial Decision of Presiding Examiner in Federal Maritime Commission Case," Report No. 2967, Sept. 24, 1971.

"NYSA Offer to the ILA for the Port of New York, September 29, 1971," Report No. 2969, Sept. 30, 1971.

New York Shipping Association–International Longshoremen's Association. *Agreement negotiated by the New York Shipping Association with the International Longshoremen's Association for the Port of Greater New York and Vicinity*, Effective Aug. 21, 1947.

——. *Agreements negotiated by the New York Shipping Association with the International Longshoremen's Association for the Port of Greater New York and Vicinity*, Effective Oct. 1, 1951.

——. *Agreement between the International Longshoremen's Association and the New York Shipping Association of the Port of Greater New York and Vicinity, General Cargo*, Effective Oct. 1, 1954.

——. *Agreement between the International Longshoremen's Association and New York Shipping Association, Deepwater Steamship Lines, and Contracting Stevedores of the Port of Greater New York and Vicinity, October 1, 1954 to September 30, 1956.*

——. *General Cargo Agreement Negotiated by the New York Shipping Association with the International Longshoremen's Union for the Port of Greater New York and Vicinity*, Oct. 1, 1956–Sept. 30, 1959.

——. "In the matter of arbitration between the New York Shipping Association and the International Longshoremen's Association . . . in the Port of Greater New York and Vicinity," Dec. 31, 1945. See also Bureau of National Affairs, *Labor Arbitration Reports*, vol. 1, pp. 80–87 (Davis award).

——. "In the matter of arbitration between the International Longshoremen's Association and the New York Shipping Association," Nov. 5, 1958 (Jensen award).

——. "In the matter of arbitration between New York Shipping Association and the International Longshoremen's Association, Memorandum on Behalf of the New York Shipping Association," Aug. 19, 1960 (Stein award).

——. "In the matter of arbitration between New York Shipping Association and the International Longshoremen's Association," LRC Report No. 156, July 11, 1966 (Kheel award).

——. "In the matter of arbitration between New York Shipping Association and the International Longshoremen's Association," Oct. 6, 1967 (Kheel award).

——. "In the matter of arbitration between New York Shipping Association and the International Longshoremen's Association," March 29, 1968 (Turkus award).

——. "Labor Relations Committee Reports." Periodically, 1955–1972.

——. *Memorandum of Settlement*, dated Feb. 18, 1957.

——. "Memorandum of Settlement," dated Dec. 2, 1959, NYSA Report No. 1697, Dec. 3, 1959.

——. "Memorandum of Settlement," dated Jan. 20, 1963.

——. "Memorandum of Settlement," 1964.

——. "Memorandum of Settlement between the New York Shipping Association and the International Longshoremen's Association," Jan. 22, 1965.

——. NYSA-ILA Settlement Terms, Jan. 12, 1969 (including) Attachment "A," "Procedures Regulating Hiring and Income Guarantee."

——. "Seniority Board Minutes," 1955–1968.

Port of New York Authority. *Annual Reports,* 1945–1971.

——. Letter, PNYA to Senate and Assembly Committees, March 30, 1965.

——. *Statutory Plan Recommended by the Port of New York Authority to Improve Waterfront Labor Conditions, Presented to the New York State Crime Commission,* Jan. 29, 1953.

Urban League of Greater New York, Industrial Relations Department, Waterfront Committee. "An Indictment of the 'shape up' hiring system in the Port of New York which fosters racial and individual discrimination," June 1959.

Index

Strife on the Waterfront

Designed by R. E. Rosenbaum.
Composed by York Composition Co., Inc.,
in 11 point linotype Janson, 3 points leaded,
with display lines in monotype Bulmer.
Printed letterpress from type by York Composition Co.
on Perkins and Squire Special Book, 50 pound basis.
Bound by Vail-Ballou Press
in Columbia book cloth
and stamped in All Purpose foil.